French Theatre Today

STUDIES IN

THEATRE HISTORY

AND CULTURE

Edited by

Thomas Postlewait

French Theatre Today

THE VIEW FROM NEW YORK, PARIS AND AVIGNON

EDWARD BARON TURK

UNIVERSITY OF IOWA PRESS, IOWA CITY

University of Iowa Press, Iowa City 52242
Copyright © 2011 by the University of Iowa Press
Printed in the United States of America

Design by Richard Hendel

www.uiowapress.org

The University of Iowa Press is a member of Green Press Initiative
and is committed to preserving natural resources.

Printed on acid-free paper

Library of Congress Cataloging-in-Publication Data
Turk, Edward Baron.
French theatre today: the view from New York, Paris,
and Avignon / by Edward Baron Turk.
    p. cm.—(Studies in theatre history and culture)
Includes bibliographical references and index.
ISBN-13: 978-1-58729-992-6 (pbk.)
ISBN-10: 1-58729-992-5 (pbk.)
ISBN-13: 978-1-58729-993-3 (e-book)
ISBN-10: 1-58729-993-3 (e-book)
1. Theater—France—21st century. I. Title.
PN2635.2.T88 2011
792.0944′0905—dc22
                        2010050569

To Isabelle de Courtivron

Contents

Preface

Beyond Beckett and Genet

Which contemporary French stage works have you seen?

If you are a casual Francophile, you are likely to mention Yasmina Reza's *"Art,"* a smart comedy that was a box-office hit when it played in English translation on Broadway in 1998. Or her amusing *God of Carnage*, a darling of the New York critics in 2009 and the winner of three Tony Awards, including Best Play. Or perhaps Alain Boublil and Claude-Michel Schönberg's megamusical *Les Misérables*, which ran in midtown Manhattan through most of the 1990s and continues to be produced around the globe—although most of its more than 50 million viewers are possibly unaware of its French stage origins.

Others might point to productions at regional or university theatres of a title or two by Samuel Beckett (d. 1989)—who was of course Irish but lived in Paris and wrote in French as well as in English—or maybe an out-of-the-way revival of a work by Jean Genet (d. 1986) or Eugène Ionesco (d. 1994). Yet—like the so-called theatre of the absurd with which Beckett and Ionesco have often been linked—these playwrights and their brand of innovative stagecraft are now part of a somewhat distant past.

More adventurous seekers of contemporary French culture in the United States might plausibly name the director Ariane Mnouchkine, who has presented a handful of her astonishing works in Los Angeles and New York. Or they might name the playwright Bernard-Marie Koltès, whose premature death in 1989 deprived French theatre of one of its younger luminaries but whose legacy has sparked recent festivals in such cities as New York and Atlanta. I live in Boston, Massachusetts, where I have been a professor of French literature and film history for many years. I confess that until recently I had not seen *any* of these artists' works except for the occasional Beckett or Ionesco at local campus theatres.

Revelation in Provence

Imagine my surprise when upon a friend's prodding I spent part of July 2004 in the charming French city of Avignon, deep within Provence. This is where the famed Avignon Festival and the huge fringe program that runs parallel to it take place each summer. French theatre today, I quickly discovered, is not just alive and well. It is extremely vibrant.

Each day I encountered superb French actors, gifted directors, and such major contemporary playwrights as Joël Pommerat, Koffi Kwahulé, Olivier Py, and Philippe Minyana—writers whose names were new to me. I discovered powerful stage works for which traditional concepts of action, dialogue, and character had little bearing but in which video, acoustic design, and dancelike moves were central to each piece's fabric and meaning. It was also a thrill to reconnect with some of the classic authors I had studied in school and even taught on occasion, not just Beckett, Ionesco, and Genet—which was where my knowledge of modern French theatre stopped—but earlier giants like Corneille, Molière, Hugo, and Feydeau, whose plays also enjoyed inventive stagings.

Having written on French and American movies during much of my career, I am familiar with the pumped-up and fairly exclusive atmosphere of international film festivals. How refreshing it was to discover that Avignon's theatre jamborees emit a more congenial and less bombastic strain of energy. Commercial concerns are by no means absent. Yet since no prizes are awarded, audiences are free to choose and judge stage works with little advance media hype. On sidewalks and at café terraces the buzz deals more with a work's artistic success than its box-office potential.

The heady effect of my first whiff of Avignon was also due to the basic fact that its attractions—unlike those of Cannes and Sundance—are live, not canned. Notions of liveness are of course always in flux: the conceit of a wholly pristine, unmediated "live" performance is largely wishful thinking. Still, in our present cultural environment, where video screens are unavoidable and point-and-click digital amusements seem to have won the lion's share of our leisure time, it is easy to forget the subtler and more urbane pleasures associated with watching a theatrical production as it unfolds within the intimacy of (mainly) real space and time. After years of devotion to the undeviating, unidirectional flow of movie images, I found it wonderful to feel the kick of human immediacy and spontaneity intrinsic to most live performance. To be immersed among actors and audiences collectively generating the energy of a shared physical and imaginative experience was truly refreshing.

A triple frame of reference

My brief stay in Avignon was a personal and professional turning point. It prompted me to plan a full year's sabbatical in France, from July 2005 through August 2006, in order to explore current French theatre in greater depth. As luck would have it, I soon learned that a good number of France's most interesting theatre artists were going to land on New York City stages during the first half of my projected leave as part of an elaborate, lengthy festival called ACT FRENCH.[1] This news kept me happily stateside for six theatre-drenched months in the Big Apple. It also brought an unanticipated cross-cultural dimension to my budding endeavor.

ACT FRENCH: A Season of New Theatre from France was a bold effort to enhance American contact with the contemporary French stage. It was the brainchild of the Cultural Services of the French Embassy in New York and the Association française d'action artistique (AFAA, or French Association for Artistic Development), a division within France's Ministry of Foreign Affairs that since its founding in 1922 has promoted the French arts worldwide. (AFAA has since changed its name: in 2006, to CulturesFrance, and then again in 2011, to Institut français.) ACT FRENCH came on the heels of two New York projects that AFAA and the Cultural Services had also spawned: French Moves, a showcase for contemporary dance, in 2001, and Sounds French, a platform for new music, in 2003. In the planning stage of ACT FRENCH, these governmental agencies offered advice to potential presenters. They also funded junkets to France to show off what they considered to be exciting new theatre pieces. The final choice of works, however, fell entirely to the New York–based programmers and producers who, it was rightly claimed, best knew the tastes and interests of their audiences. The festival was thus as much a reflection of the sentiments of a certain slice of the New York theatre establishment regarding contemporary French theatre as it was of what is actually taking place in France.[2]

• • •

Between July and mid-December 2005 nearly thirty performance events took place in venues ranging from mainstream locales like Lincoln Center and the Brooklyn Academy of Music to such downtown sites as Performance Space 122, The Kitchen, and the Ohio Theatre. The variety of offerings was impressive. The roster included writers, directors, and actors already familiar to American connoisseurs of French theatre as well as talented artists who had never before played to U.S. audiences. There were both traditional plot- and dialogue-driven plays and edgier hybrids that combined poetic speech with choreography, state-of-the-art sound design, and new visual technologies. Some events were performed in English; others, in French with English supertitles. In addition to these thirty shows, ACT FRENCH cosponsored frequent roundtables with French artists and their U.S. peers, readings by prominent French and American playwrights, and scholarly lectures and panels.[3]

For me, ACT FRENCH was a superlative if sometimes dizzying crash course on numerous aspects of the current French theatre scene. It handily paved the way for the other phases of my immersion into the field: a six-month stay in Paris and a month's sojourn in Avignon for the July 2006 edition of the festival. As a result, this book's organization is a triptych. In part 1, New York, I offer close-ups of French theatre works singled out for their presumed attractiveness to certain American audiences and critics. In part 2, Paris, I depict a more expansive range of French theatre pieces as they play out on their own soil. In part 3, Avignon, I try to capture the subject within a more fluid context that is, intriguingly, both eminently French and resolutely international.

With the voice—almost—of an amateur

French Theatre Today: The View from New York, Paris, and Avignon recounts my yearlong involvement with this topic. It also reflects research pursued since that year of intense activity. One of my goals in these pages is to situate many of the nearly 150 stage pieces I attended within contexts and time frames that stretch over a number of years both prior to and following the particular performances I saw. In other words, this book can serve as an introduction to diverse tendencies of French theatre during the first decade of the twenty-first century. I make no claim to exhaustiveness, and I hope that my findings will spark readers to explore still other aspects of this rich field.

I mainly aim *French Theatre Today* at theatre enthusiasts and Francophiles who are curious about an aspect of French culture that is inadequately known in the United States. While it is not specifically written for academic specialists, I hope that the book's openness to the varieties of French stage performance, along with its account of my personal experiences, will make it fresh and rewarding for veteran scholars as well as for students of contemporary world theatre. Additionally, I would be pleased if the book acts as a useful reference for American theatre professionals—especially producers, directors, dramaturgs, and repertory programmers—who have the ultimate authority and good fortune to determine which new French works will reach audiences on these shores.

In researching and drafting *French Theatre Today*, I often told friends and colleagues that I saw myself as an *amateur éclairé*, an enlightened amateur, since I started out having little knowledge about this area of French culture while at the same time being quite familiar with a few adjacent fields. Even as I became more and more *éclairé* about current French theatre, it was the *amateur* in me—from the Latin *amare*, 'to love'—that often kept the upper hand. My overall intent is thus twofold: to supply the reader with pertinent aesthetic and intellectual perspectives on aspects of contemporary French theatre, and to convey—and possibly arouse a like response in others—my sustained affection for the topic.

Acknowledgments

For making time to speak with me about their work, I express warm gratitude to Jean-Marie Besset, Anne Delbée, Koffi Kwahulé, Arthur Nauzyciel, Valère Novarina, José Pliya, Philippe Quesne, Pascal Rambert, Fabrice Rozié, Marion Schoevaert, members of Superamas, Ivan Talijancic, Gisèle Vienne, and Michel Vinaver. I also profited from conversations with stage professionals on both sides of the Atlantic and heartily thank Faye Allen, Lucien and Micheline Attoun, Astrid Bas, Jonathan Cristaldi, Antonio Díaz-Florián, Kevin Doyle, Paul-Emile Fourny, Del Hamilton, Darina al-Joundi, Guila-Clara Kessous, Mirabelle Ordinaire, Henry Pillsbury, Travis Preston, Mark Russell, Hilario Saavedra, Bastien Thelliez, Paul Verdier, Eric Vigner, Guy Walter, and Barbara Watson.

I received both moral and practical support for this project from the Cultural Services of the French Embassy in New York, and I especially wish to thank Nicole Birmann-Bloom and Emmanuelle de Montgazon for their sustained interest. In Boston, the advice and assistance I obtained from Brigitte Bouvier, Eric Jausseran, Frédéric Martel, and Anne Miller of the French Cultural Services were precious. I also salute, for their encouragement, Elisabeth Hayes, executive director of the French American Cultural Exchange (FACE), based in New York, and Jean-Marc Granet Bouffartigue and Marie Raymond of the performing arts department of the Association française d'action artistique (now Institut français), based in Paris. Denise Luccioni, who served as artistic liaison for New York's ACT FRENCH, proved also to be a remarkable facilitator for much of my work in Paris and Avignon: her generosity of spirit is awesome. I am grateful, too, to the administration of the Avignon Festival, especially its codirectors Hortense Archambault and Vincent Baudriller, for their interest and assistance.

Several specialists in theatre and/or French and Francophone culture kindly read early drafts of selected chapters, and in some cases the entire manuscript. For their insights and suggestions I thank Brigitte Bouvier, Odile Cazenave, Roger Célestin, Jean Decock, Gideon Lester, Judith G. Miller, Tom Sellar, Emmanuel Wallon, Philippa Wehle, and Liesl Yamaguchi. I am also beholden, for conversations and exchanges, to Sylviane Bernard-Gresh, Chantal Boiron, Sabine Bossan, Caroline Eades, Joëlle Gayot, Emilie Lacombe, Joyce Maio, Cécile Peyronnet, Jonathan Rabinowitz, Brigitte Salino, Geneviève Sellier, and Jerry Weinstein.

Among my colleagues at the Massachusetts Institute of Technology, I tip my hat to those who helped me sustain the ardor, energy, and time required to bring this volume to fruition: Patsy Baudoin, Alan Brody, Cathy Culot, Gilberte Furstenberg, Elizabeth Garrels, Sabine Levet, Shigeru Miyagawa, Johann Sadock, Irving Singer, William Uricchio, and Jing Wang. Particular thanks go to Jeffrey Pearlin for technical assistance regarding the book's illustrations. I also appreciate the generous financial support granted to me by the Dean's Office of the MIT School of Humanities, Arts, and Social Sciences and by MIT's French Initiatives Endowment Fund. I dedicate this book to my longtime friend and MIT colleague Isabelle de Courtivron. Isabelle awakened me to the joys of Avignon at festival time and to the pressing need for a book such as this one; over the years, she has been an able advocate of all my book projects, and I am deeply grateful.

Part of the pleasure of pursuing primary research in three separate cities came from those whose friendship and hospitality are unflagging: in New York, Karen and Greg Dimit; in Paris, Alain Hardel; in Avignon, Francine and Christian Ménard. At home in Boston, Philip Cobb and David Lapin are, as always, never-failing allies.

Finally, I wish to thank Tom Postlewait, editor of the Studies in Theatre History and Culture series, in which this book appears, and Holly Carver, who has just stepped down from the directorship of the University of Iowa Press. Working with the two of them has been a delight.

Introduction

French culture in decline?

In late November 2007 *Time* magazine's European edition ran a cover story titled "The Death of French Culture." The reporter, Donald Morrison, lamented that "France today is a wilting power in the global cultural marketplace," and he cited a recent poll in *Le Figaro Magazine* showing that only 20 percent of Americans considered culture to be "a domain in which France excels."[1] Trotted out were the names of mid-twentieth-century Gallic luminaries who once enjoyed international fame: Albert Camus and André Malraux, François Truffaut and Jean-Luc Godard, Charles Trenet and Edith Piaf.

In response, the French philosopher Bernard-Henri Lévy—who had recently made a splash on these shores with *American Vertigo*, a book on U.S. culture and politics—pointed out the dubious logic of measuring the health of a nation's culture "by the degree of curiosity that it excites at the heart of the dominant culture (today, that of the United States)."[2] The British journalist John Lichfield, in *The Independent*, likewise rebuked *Time* for being "rooted in a cartoon transatlantic definition of French culture." Lichfield argued that the worldwide profiles of such contemporary figures as architect Jean Nouvel, fiction writer Michel Houellebecq, and pop musicians Daft Punk and Etienne de Crécy signal not a decline but a "revival of French artistic creativity."[3]

The sociologist Frédéric Martel, an expert in French and American arts policy, conceded that France "is no longer a great cultural power." But rather than give in to "masochism" and "mourning," Martel urged his fellow citizens to "rediscover our energy, our vivacity, and openness to the world."[4] One of Sweden's Nobel Prize committees was perhaps ahead of Martel's programmatic curve when it chose the French novelist Jean-Marie Gustave Le Clézio (b. 1940) as its 2008 laureate in literature. Not surprisingly, the globe-trotting author of *Désert* (*Desert*,

1980)—who spends part of each year at his home in Albuquerque, New Mexico, and whose books regularly explore non-Western cultures—was virtually unknown to most Americans. Only a handful of his more than forty volumes of fiction and essays were then currently available in translation from U.S. publishers.

What about French theatre?

It is telling, I think, that neither the *Time* reporter nor his respondents evoked French theatre. Such neglect possibly reflects the tired premise that the French language automatically prevents France's stage works from traveling far. Part 1 of this book will refute this notion. Yet in choosing for its cover illustration a look-alike of the late great mime Marcel Marceau (d. 2007), *Time*'s editors also implied that the only French stage actor who can hope for global fame must be one who dares not speak. As we will see throughout this volume, a good part of the truly exciting theatre taking place in France today is in fact no longer wedded to the exquisite *belle langue* (beautiful language) that was a central feature of most French theatre from Jean Racine (d. 1699) to Jean Giraudoux (d. 1944). Emphasis may now fall more on choreography, visuals (film and video), and digitized sonic environments than on ultrapolished dialogue or even on casually uttered exchanges. Moreover, for the younger generation of stage artists in France, American culture is not something to fear, snub, or compete with. It is simply one more rich source to draw upon in fashioning new works. Hollywood blockbusters and TV sitcoms, ethnic comedians and online gaming, Toni Morrison and Dennis Cooper, Tony Kushner and Julie Taymor—these are just a few of the influences from the United States that are invigorating the contemporary French stage.

Influence in the opposite direction tends to be less common. Still, an awareness of things French among U.S. theatre practitioners and playgoers is growing—thanks in good measure to festivals like Under the Radar, the yearly international event run by Mark Russell at New York's Public Theater; and Crossing the Line, the fall array of transdisciplinary artists produced by New York's French Institute/Alliance Française in partnership with numerous New York cultural institutions. Also notable are increasingly adventuresome programming at various regional theatres and university campuses; aggressive public and private efforts to ensure that French literature in translation—theatrical and otherwise—will occupy a larger place within the catalogs of American publishing houses; and, despite budget cuts, the tireless work of the French Cultural Services and of the Alliance Française network nationwide to host transatlantic visits and tours by French theatre personalities and companies.

A high-profile brouhaha

Just as I began my plunge into the world of French theatre, the subject became front-page news. Many of France's top dailies and weeklies were slamming the 2005 edition of the Avignon Festival for being "elitist" (*Les Echos*)[5] and for adopting "a radicalism that is forcing the public to run away" (*Le Point*).[6] Reporters stigmatized the offerings as "the self-satisfied work of cheeky cliques" (*Le Figaro*)[7] and as "assaults on truth, intelligence, modesty, humility, and dignity" (*L'Humanité*).[8] In print and on TV were accounts—often erroneous—of boos, walkouts, and flare-ups bringing performances to a standstill. "Has the Avignon Festival gone insane?" shrieked *Le Nouvel Observateur*.[9] Some members of the critical establishment even wanted the festival's youthful codirectors, Vincent Baudriller (b. 1968) and Hortense Archambault (b. 1970), to be fired on the spot.

What had happened?

At first, much of the controversy swirled around Jan Fabre (b. 1958), the Flemish pluridisciplinarian who was that year's *artiste associé* (artist-in-residence)—a recent festival innovation conceived by Baudriller and Archambault to confer greater coherence upon each year's programming. Two of Fabre's own works—*Je suis sang: conte de fées médiéval* (*I Am Blood: A Medieval Fairy Tale*, 2001) and *L'histoire des larmes* (*History of Tears*, 2005)—played in the Honor Court of the Popes' Palace, the festival's most prestigious venue. For some, Fabre's displays of full nudity, real bodily fluids, and barely simulated violence were an insult to the setting's grand aura. Others decried the fact that Fabre's pieces, along with those of many of the artists he helped program that July—such as Pascal Rambert, Gisèle Vienne, Mathilde Monnier, Romeo Castellucci, and Jean Lambert-wild—gave greater weight to mixtures of dance, music, body art, and multimedia stage design than to written texts and conventional acting. In French, the shorthand phrase for these opposing slants is *théâtre d'image* versus *théâtre de texte*; a slightly more precise formulation might set *a theatre of the actor's body* against *a theatre of dramatic literature*.

France suddenly found itself in a noisy culture war much like the famous Querelle des Anciens et des Modernes (Quarrel of the Ancients and the Moderns) that had shaken the Académie Française in the late seventeenth century. With the festival still in progress, Renaud Donnedieu de Vabres, then France's minister of culture, raced from Paris to Avignon and convoked an emergency caucus with theatre journalists. After the meeting he reaffirmed his support for Baudriller and Archambault, guaranteeing both their "artistic independence" and the state's continued financial support for their efforts.[10]

Still, the controversy raged on. Within weeks of the festival's close there was an outpouring of hurriedly put-together books on the subject. The cultural and political savant Régis Debray took a conservative and polemical stance in *Sur le pont d'Avignon* (On Avignon Bridge). Viewing Avignon 2005 as a perversion of the ideals of Jean Vilar, who founded the festival in 1947 (and who in fact had brought cinema and dance into the mix as of the 1960s), Debray groaned that "cultural democracy now means the right of anyone to express his [so-called] talents regardless of prior artistic training."[11] Georges Banu and Bruno Tackels, in a collection of essays and responses titled *Le cas Avignon 2005* (The Avignon Affair, 2005), interpreted the midsummer uproar as a "rich and stimulating" sign of "a true transformation in the performing arts."[12] They reminded readers of Vilar's celebrated dictum: "As long as the theatre is in crisis, it is in fine health."[13]

With greater detachment and time for reflection, Antoine de Baecque—in his 2008 book *Crises dans la culture française* (Crises in French Culture)—depicted the turbulence as a disquieting but ultimately salutary wake-up call for reconsidering the relationship between "culture" and "society," by which he meant the disconnect that still prevails between many of today's risk-taking artists and a general citizenry whose tax money supports creative innovation and experimentation but whose tastes increasingly lean toward mass-market entertainment.[14] From an American viewpoint, the way de Baecque formulates the issue is revealing. As in the United States, theatre in France increasingly occupies a smaller space within the overall cultural landscape; likewise for both countries, national and local print, radio, and TV coverage of the theatre arts has undergone severe reduction. Still, a recent in-depth study of cultural practices in France shows that between 1997 and 2008 the percentage of French people aged fifteen and older who attended at least one professional play in the course of a year rose from 16 to 19 percent.[15] (In the same period, and for the same group, attendance at classical music concerts dipped from 9 to 7 percent, whereas the percentage who attended at least one amateur theatrical event rose from 20 to 21 percent, and the percentage who frequented street theatre shot up from 29 to 34 percent.) Irrespective of such qualitative fluctuations—and more important for cross-cultural understanding—is an observation by the French sociologist Emmanuel Wallon, who notes that theatre in France has consistently held "a substantial spot in the symbolic sphere of things" and therefore remains central to current "debates and controversies over cultural policies": "Even if [theatre's] record in democratization is found wanting, [the French people's] consciousness of theatre's Athenian roots keeps it linked to an ideal of democracy and allows people to passionately conceive of it as a mainspring of citizenship."[16]

France's rhetorical tradition

For readers of this book, the Avignon brouhaha can help place a good deal of contemporary French theatre activity in broad historical perspective. When educated Americans ask where the new Sartres, Ionescos, and Genets are, they are making a reasonable assumption about cultural continuity and the great line of literary dramatists that France has spawned since the Renaissance. From Racine to Anouilh, from Voltaire to Camus, from Beaumarchais to Genet, French theatre has excelled at *rhetorical* playwriting. Such theatre dramatizes Big Themes—like heroism and destiny, social injustice and individual responsibility, the nature of consciousness and the deficiencies of language—through the conceptual lenses of Big Thought Systems: Roman Catholicism, secular humanism, Romanticism, Surrealism, existentialism, and so on. Rhetorical theatre makes arguments, fabricates illusory worlds, and moves audiences with the beauty or cleverness of its polished, declamatory language. This tradition has guaranteed that plays by Molière, Feydeau, Pagnol, and Ionesco are regularly produced outside of France and are studied in French classes worldwide.

In 1960, when the American scholar Wallace Fowlie published his influential *Dionysus in Paris: A Guide to Contemporary French Theatre*—a volume whose introductory chapter bears the same title as this book, "French Theatre Today"—he informed readers that his "principal concern" was "the evolution of the serious play" as it approaches "a form of tragedy in our day."[17] Accordingly Fowlie organized his study by themes: the first three parts dealt with "approaches to tragedy" (Jean Giraudoux, Jean Cocteau, Henry de Montherlant, Jean Anouilh), "religious theatre" (Paul Claudel, Georges Bernanos, François Mauriac), and "theatre of ideas" (André Gide, Jean-Paul Sartre, Albert Camus, Julien Green); his final part, on "experimental theatre" (Antonin Artaud, Samuel Beckett, Jean Genet, Arthur Adamov, Eugène Ionesco, Georges Schehadé), interpreted the bulk of these authors' works as "philosophical in intention" and bringing into prominence "a new [brand of] *literary* play" (my emphasis).[18] Fifty years later we are acutely aware that much new writing for the stage, in France or elsewhere, is not necessarily playwriting. We also recognize that the basic fabric of much theatrical performance can no longer be represented and memorialized by an array of published volumes designated as "plays" or "dramas." And like most other arts, today's theatre—and our critical response to it—is subject to the more general dynamic of a creative tension between an evolving print culture and an emergent digital culture.[19]

Text-based playwrights still occupy an important part of the French theatre scene. But as the "scandal" of the 2005 Avignon Festival showed, the rhetorical norm has lost considerable ground to a form of spectacle that relegates writerly, literary texts—what we usually think of as an author's *play scripts*—to the periphery of its concerns. In this newer theatre, now sometimes loosely referred to as "postdramatic,"[20] attention falls more centrally on the fluid, interdependent relations among such elements as visual imagery, bodily movements, a self-conscious recourse to media other than theatre, and in-the-moment transactions between performers and spectators. If stage works like these—which have in truth been around for decades—can throw into a tizzy a segment of the seasoned theatregoers who regularly attend the Avignon Festival, it is little wonder that, no matter their quality, they have not yet been widely perceived as obvious candidates for productions in the United States and for serious study in our language and literature classrooms.

Change . . .

As an outsider with few preconceptions, I found it exhilarating that my initiation into a precious slice of France's cultural life coincided with a lively debate on its health. I quickly saw that the existence of the enormous state-subsidized sector of French theatre was not in jeopardy but that the expansive spread of the forms it might take was very much in question.

France's text-based theatre may well be the orchid that refuses to wilt. Yet in the first decade of the new century, much of it no longer corresponds to the rhetorical strain that had thrived up to and including the theatre of the absurd. The absurdists, in their dislocations of conventional technique and rational thought, often pointed to life's putative meaninglessness. But that theme itself was deeply *meaningful* and hence much in line with the rhetorical tradition. In a lot of current theatre, by contrast, artists who create texts for the stage do not aim to transmit, even implicitly, fixed meaning from the playing space to the spectator. Instead, they invite spectators to shape or carve out meaning(s) for themselves, placing the bulk of the sense-making process on the shoulders of the audience.

As we shall see, many recent developments in both the text-based tradition and the more exploratory hybrids are due in large measure to revised notions of what comprises theatricality within an overall cultural landscape that is increasingly dominated by mass-mediated and digitized entertainments with global reach. (Between 1997 and 2008, the number of home-computer users in France soared from below 1 percent of the population to 83 percent.)[21] Contemporary trends are further molded by the increased crossover of elements belonging to what used to be considered the fairly distinct performance ranges of "high" and "low" art. They also result from stage artists' increased engagement with practices and currents that are not specifically or even primarily French. Indeed, an underlying dynamic giving impetus to many of the individuals and works dealt with in this book might best be referred to as a renewed cosmopolitanism—a tendency that confounds any critical effort to approach French theatre as a cultural phenomenon that is "naturally," "essentially," or "uncomplicatedly" French.

Theatre in France is being transformed in part by such diversely ecumenical figures as Ariane Mnouchkine, Valère Novarina, and Philippe Quesne, who are, respectively, reconfiguring the place that world politics, vibrant poetry, and new technologies can occupy on today's live stage. Equally influential is the increased presence of ethnic minority and bicultural voices, from the experimental theatre of Koffi Kwahulé to the enigmatic dramaturgy of Marie NDiaye to the in-your-face sketch and standup comedy of Souria Adèle. Experimentalists such as Pascal Rambert and Gildas Milin are pursuing stage visions that owe much to the historical avant-gardes but are very much in sync with contemporary global concerns; and James Thiérrée and the Collectif AOC, in different ways, are transmuting European circus traditions into powerful new expressions of human freedom and vulnerability. Also exerting substantial impact are impassioned French writers like Olivier Cadiot and Olivier Py, who strive to safeguard theatrical lyricism from the homogenized, formulaic verbiage churned out by the transnational pop-entertainment and mass-culture industries. At the same time, authors like Joël Pommerat and Philippe Minyana signal through their idiosyncratic practices a certain "return" of the literary, text-based dramatist—but with new twists that enable them to break loose from timeworn Gallocentric conventions. Moreover, France's dean of alternative text-based theatre, the octogenarian Michel Vinaver, continues to renew himself and to enthrall audiences through his ingenious polyphonic verbal style, even as his political and economic insights—conditioned in large part by his experience with Americans and with the United States—tend to unsettle them.

... and continuity

Yet today's French theatre is not solely about radical change. One of the joys of exploring contemporary theatre in France is observing the care, respect, and inventiveness with which its practitioners work to keep classic plays and authors alive. I therefore devote a chapter to major revivals of works by Molière, Paul Claudel, and Edmond Rostand. I also pay attention to current theatrical fare that appeals to spectators who are most comfortable with familiar forms and genres. In this regard I consider recent comedies and dramas of the "boulevard" (non-state-subsidized) variety, as exemplified in works by Josiane Balasko and Samuel Benchetrit; and those of a more sophisticated kind found in pieces by such commercially popular, dialogue-driven playwrights as Jean-Marie Besset, Yasmina Reza, and Eric-Emmanuel Schmitt.

In the spirit of inclusiveness that characterizes so much new French theatre, and to give a representative account of my own experience as a spectator, I round out the survey with observations on two related areas: Paris's lively opera scene—including bold new productions of Mozart and a Peter Sellars–directed world premiere of a French-language opera with libretto by Amin Maalouf; and France's wealth of circus entertainments, both the traditional and the newly envisioned.

Theatre and the real world

"Theatre," wrote the Czech playwright Václav Havel, "is always a sensitive seismograph of an era, perhaps the most sensitive one there is."[22] When they are useful, I will suggest links between works discussed in *French Theatre Today* and the social and political climate in which they unfolded.

The next-to-last year of Jacques Chirac's presidency was laden with unresolved national problems and growing anxieties among the French. Sometimes these troubles impinged directly on the theatre world, as in the murky future of special unemployment benefits for the entertainment industry's 120,000 freelance workers, known as *intermittents*—a situation that led to the protest cancellation of the 2003 Avignon Festival; pinpointed, for many, the generalized "crumbling . . . of a certain [French] conception of culture as a public service";[23] and still has not reached a satisfactory resolution. Sometimes playwrights—such as José Pliya, Philippe Minyana, and Maïmouna Gueye—addressed social issues and topical themes openly in their works. More often I encountered hazier but no less telling instances of the dynamic Havel hints at in imagining theatre as "a sponge that quickly soaks up important ingredients in the atmosphere around it."[24]

The period I focus on in this book very possibly holds no more privileged cultural and political significance than any other recent moment I might have chosen. Still, 2005–2006 was in some ways crucial for a process that is profoundly affecting France in these first years of the new millennium: reassessment of the very notion of a "French national identity" and a rethinking of France's relations with other European and transatlantic powers and cultures.

The bumps and thuds that are inevitable parts of such a process were particularly strong and audible that year. They occurred in the sociopolitical arena, most notably, the French electorate's repudiation in May 2005 of the proposed European Union constitution; the November riots by underprivileged and ethnically diverse youths living in suburban housing projects; mass demonstrations throughout the winter and spring by middle-class students and workers protesting job insecurity; and a general crisis of confidence in France's leadership, exacerbated by the so-called Clearstream scandal. This last incident pitted the Gaullist party's Jacques Chirac–Dominique de Villepin faction against that of the aggressively ambitious Nicolas Sarkozy, then minister of the interior, who claimed that Villepin was part of a conspiracy that had tried, two years earlier, to smear his reputation and soil his presidential ambitions. A high court acquitted Villepin of all charges in January 2010.

In the yearlong aftermath of the July 2005 Avignon tempest, perturbations in the theatrical arena were similarly jolting. Doubts were rising about the legitimacy of many of the institutional mind-sets and practices central to much state-supported French theatre activity since World War II. President Nicolas Sarkozy has seemed bent on altering these very mind-sets and practices—more from economic and pseudopopulist motives than from artistic, inspirational, or humane concerns. As theatre historian Robert Abirached noted in 2010, the profession's current "profound disarray" results in good measure from "a lack of joint serious discussions . . . between the Ministry of Culture and artists" and from a programmatic "withering of the very notion of government-supported theatre in favor of an endorsement of art as a commodity subject to the law of supply and demand." Although the ministry still fortunately houses, per Abirached, a number of "competent and valuable public servants who were witnesses to past practices," he fears that the younger cadre of officials are "ignorant of the [ministry's] vibrant traditions."[25]

France's identity issue

In October 2009 President Sarkozy called for a national debate on what it means to be French today. He delegated oversight of this yearlong enterprise to Eric Besson, his minister of immigration, integration, national identity, and cooperative development. The creation of this new ministry in 2007 had already sparked controversy since critics viewed the official coupling of immigration policy to matters of so-called national identity as a blatant bid by Sarkozy's center-right party (the Union for a Popular Movement, or UMP) to win over voters in regional elections who normally support the Front national (FN), Jean-Marie Le Pen's ultranationalist political party that celebrates a mythic pristine Frenchness from which outsiders are by definition excluded. (Despite this UMP tactic, the FN still won some 20 percent of the 2010 regional elections in southeastern France, a traditional stronghold for Le Pen.)

Moreover, Sarkozy and Besson's national identity conversation—which took place partly on Internet chat lines and mostly at town-hall meetings organized by prefects and subprefects throughout France—was, for some political observers, yet again "a flimsy cover for political exploitation of anti-immigrant sentiment—and a blatant ploy to deflect economic anxiety onto minority targets."[26] Indeed, perhaps the greatest challenge facing France in the coming decades is to reconcile two contradictory aspects of its social and political character: on one hand, its republican ideals of universal liberty, equality, and fraternity along with its frequently noble historical record of providing asylum to immigrants and political refugees; on the other hand, the substantial discrimination encountered by many of its growing non-white and non-Christian populations, especially those whose ethnic origins lie in the Maghreb or sub-Saharan Africa.

To its credit, France remains one of the more generous European countries with respect to immigrants: in 2009 alone, 180,000 became naturalized citizens. Statistics show that France's Muslim population—at about five to six million, the largest of any Western European country—is "generally speaking the most secularized [*laïcisé*] and the best integrated in Europe thanks to its higher percentage of mixed marriages."[27] And according to a 2008 Conseils-Sondages-Analyses poll, only 39 percent of the French (as compared with 60 percent in 2000) believe that there are "too many immigrants" in France, with

73 percent (as opposed to 39 percent in 2000) asserting that they consider immigrants to be "a source of cultural enrichment." Among "fears concerning French society," "the decline [*la perte*] of a national identity" ranks only eleventh, with various economic issues topping the list.[28]

Minister Besson, however, was convinced that the national conversation would allow the French, first, to reflect carefully on what he dubbed with obvious ardor an "inherited model"—one that comprises a long-cherished language, specific values, and a sanctioned lifestyle—and, second, to interrogate "our capacity to preserve all that marks France as unique: its public services, its culture, its language, its influence."[29] Yet Didier Fassin, a political anthropologist who has battled to have Besson's ministry shut down, asserts that this exercise actually aggravated "what had been brewing for several years [in pockets of France and elsewhere in Europe], namely resentment and hatred of others, pettiness, and withdrawal." Fassin notes that the national discussion quickly devolved into a tainted forum that promoted a political climate (embracing both the left and the right) of increased hate-mongering, stigmatization, and an unhealthy "obsession with Islam."[30]

A humane alternative: the place of theatre

The purported conversation of 2009–2010 was often just foolish and at other times seriously menacing. It was perhaps most misguided in its implicit assumption that French identity could be conceptualized as a unitary, self-evident entity—this in the wake of a decade during which various French racial and religious minority groups had been increasingly arguing for their full rights as citizens and had been asserting more demonstratively than ever the validity of their ethnic cultures.

It would be reckless, and far too idealistic, to propose that contemporary French theatre offers a sure antidote to the propagation of slogans, stereotypes, and misinformation that are part and parcel of the politicized public discourse surrounding this bungled debate—which despite the awkwardness of its recent format will in all likelihood soon give way to more nuanced and less politically polarizing projects for understanding what it means to be French. To speak of contemporary French theatre as a unified entity is in truth no less reductionist than to posit a singular, homogenous French identity. Yet as we shall see, a good part of current French theatre self-consciously situates itself as an alternative to the simplistic and manipulative discourse inherent in today's politics and mass media. Much of this part is concerned with a view of human identity and subjectivity that stresses multiplicity and fluidity. Much of it demonstrates people's precious ability to evade fixed or prescribed behavioral scenarios. And much of it celebrates the thrilling potential for reinventing the self that arises out of the spirit of community that can take hold between performers and spectators and out of the ensuing recalibration of how we relate to language, to our bodies, and to others.

• • •

My primary emphasis in this book falls on the cultural and aesthetic dimensions of contemporary French theatre, not on the sociopolitical. Despite all the jabbering about France's cultural decline and, more specifically, the alleged decay and irrelevance of its theatre, I find the latter to be, on balance, remarkably vital, inclined toward both innovation and concern for its audience, and as open to international influence as it is respectful of national tradition.

Robert Lepage, the Quebec-born playwright and stage director, has remarked that even though people have constantly proclaimed theatre to be dead over the past five decades, it is more useful and germane to recognize that Western theatre is currently at the start of a powerful process of resurrection. "Cinema killed theatre; television killed cinema; and the Internet has killed television," Lepage asserts. "But so much the better! [Competing media] don't kill, they liberate. I think theatre has finally been freed up to become [in its own way, as did painting in the wake of photography] Cubist and Dadaist, expressing things that have yet to be expressed."[31] In much of what follows, we will bear witness to this newer and often freer sense of identity and expression that distinguishes a large part of current French theatre.

Part 1
New York

I write differently . . . in New York
than in Paris. . . . It is as if I rediscover
the French language there, connect
with it differently.
— French playwright
Bernard-Marie Koltès, 1987

Border-crossings

An astounding discovery

Ariane Mnouchkine's *Le dernier caravansérail: odyssées* (The Last Caravan-Stop: Odysseys) is a gripping saga of the plight of political refugees from Afghanistan, Iraq, Iran, Russia, Chechnya, Bosnia, and parts of Africa. It was both the centerpiece of the annual Lincoln Center Festival in July 2005 and the kickoff event for ACT FRENCH — which would not resume programming in New York City until late September. Performed in two three-hour parts, this sprawling piece marked the first New York appearance of Mnouchkine's legendary company, Théâtre du Soleil, since October 1992, when her cycle of four Greek tragedies, *Les Atrides*, ran at the Park Slope Armory under the auspices of the Brooklyn Academy of Music. Its success prompted Lincoln Center to host Mnouchkine's next major work, *Les éphémères* (Ephemera), in summer 2009.

Festivals, with their deep roots in ancient and medieval sacred ritual, have the potential to lift us out of our everyday lives. At their best, international performance festivals extend our imagination and boost our capacity for empathy. As Nigel Redden, director of the Lincoln Center Festival, noted in *Playbill Arts*: "It's a question of there being other wonderful things in the world than the ones we know."[1] From its inception in the summer of 1996, the Lincoln Center Festival has showcased outstanding, challenging events from around the globe. For me, Mnouchkine's epic work was an astounding discovery.

Theatre, travel, and the creative imagination

To accommodate the enormous scale of *Le dernier caravansérail*, Mnouchkine (b. 1939) had a large tent specially built in Damrosch Park—the open expanse immediately south of the Metropolitan Opera House that in winters hosts the Big Apple Circus. As she does in France at the Vincennes Cartoucherie (a collection of former munitions warehouses on the eastern margins of Paris that has been her company's permanent venue since 1970), Mnouchkine made sure that before reaching their seats, ticket holders would already begin to shift from the world of the mundane to the rarefied, ritualized realm of her theatre. Thus, near the entry to Damrosch Park stood push-carts with Middle Eastern foods for sale. In the courtyard, where arriving spectators gathered amid the rows of young maple trees, soft strains of Eastern European–sounding music floated from unobtrusive speakers.

In order to gain access to the tent, which sat six hundred, ticket holders first had to move along one of two inclined pathways, each trimmed with roped balustrades and a white, scalloped canopy. Resembling gangplanks, these parallel lanes subtly alerted viewers that a significant voyage was in store for *us* no less than for the play's refugees. The spectacle of police officers checking bags and totes for weapons was by then commonplace at many New York theatres. But because *Le dernier caravansérail* opened just ten days after the July 7 London bus and subway bombings, the police presence, combined with the vaguely seafaring setting, may well have worked to strengthen in us some subliminal psychic link between travel, the creative imagination, and potential bodily harm.

Once inside the great tent, theatregoers encountered Mnouchkine's actors quietly applying their makeup while seated at wooden dressing tables. These tables were set within metal scaffolding that, bleacher style, supported the tiered rows of padded public benches. Such calculated preperformance confrontation of actor and spectator is a standard feature of Théâtre du Soleil productions. Its effect is at once fascinating and troubling. Here we were, being treated to an insider's glimpse of the usually hidden mechanics of stagecraft; yet having intruded into a normally private space, I was also a bit embarrassed at ogling these self-possessed performers as if they were caged curios. At first I tried looking away. Then I felt an urge to engage in more dignified interaction—which I eventually did at the first intermission by striking up a conversation with Sébastien Brottet-Michel, a French-born actor who plays Fawad, the young Afghan whose fiancée is murdered by the Taliban for having been intimate with him. As the play proceeded, I came to realize that my initial unease was actually in keeping with *Le dernier caravansérail*'s overall intent. Mnouchkine compels us to take a long, hard look at the heart-wrenching state of the world's refugees—these new incarnations of Ulysses who are prevented from finding secure homes—and she dares us to remain indifferent.

I can tell your stories

At an afternoon Lincoln Center symposium held in her honor, "Does Art Matter?," Mnouchkine, speaking in polished English, maintained that she never pursues stage projects that do not seem, at least to her and her actors, "absolutely indispensable."[2] The germ for *Le dernier caravansérail*, she explained, took hold in spring 2001, after her first visit to Sangatte, the little seaside town on France's northern coast where the Jacques Chirac government and the French Red Cross had, in 1999, set up a camp to provide urgent care for a few hundred refugees from the war in Kosovo. Soon this camp began tending, with much difficulty, to the thousands of asylum-seeking Afghans, Kurds, and Iraqis who despite legal obstacles hoped to find permanent sanctuary in the United Kingdom.

Sangatte is just a half mile from the entrance to the Channel Tunnel, and Mnouchkine realized that many hopeful refugees viewed this spot as their last, or final, "caravan-stop" before the sea. With traffickers and hoodlums abetting and exploiting these stateless people, France's then minister of the interior, Nicolas Sarkozy, and his English counterpart, David Blunkett, ordered Franco-British immigration squads and French riot police to tighten surveillance and control. These constraints simply prodded many of the displaced to continue risking their lives by smuggling themselves into trucks and ships or fearlessly cascading onto the Eurostar or a passing freight train. Under political and diplomatic pressure from Great Britain, where many likened this new wave of immigrants to "an invading army,"[3] Sarkozy closed down the Sangatte camp on December 30, 2002. (Ever since, illegal migrants fleeing strife in Afghanistan, Eritrea, Pakistan, and elsewhere have continued to camp out among the brambles and beaches near the port of Calais; another high-profile crackdown, ordered by immigration minister Eric Besson, took place in September 2009.)

"I started interviewing [these refugees] well before the [2002] shutdown," Mnouchkine noted. "I stressed to them that I wasn't a journalist and that they wouldn't have to worry about being identified if they spoke freely to me. I said, 'There's really only one thing I can do for you. I can tell your stories.' So even though most were only slightly familiar with TV and movies, and many knew nothing at all about theatre, a number of them were eager to talk to me. From then on I felt I'd made a solemn promise to bring their tales to others."[4]

In early 2002, while on tour in Asia, Mnouchkine and Shaghayegh Beheshti, one of her many polyglot actors, visited other refugee camps in Australia, New Zealand, and Lombock Island (Indonesia) and amassed recorded interviews and written testimonials. The Algerian-born French dramatist and philosopher Hélène Cixous—Mnouchkine's longtime personal and creative partner, whose most recent work for the company had been the Noh-inspired eco-morality play *Tambours sur la digue* (*The Flood Drummers/Drums on the Dam*, 1999)—tried to mold these into a cohesive theatrical text. But *Le dernier caravansérail* resulted instead from six months of videotaped improvisational work based on the acquired documents and carried out by Mnouchkine's corps of thirty-six actors, some of whom are themselves refugees.

Kinesthetic identifications

Théâtre du Soleil has always been run as a cooperative: every member of the troupe, including the artistic director, earns the same modest wages, and each contributes to multiple aspects of a production. Although Mnouchkine has the final word in artistic decision making, she emphasizes the collective authorship and execution of *Le dernier caravansérail*, bestowing prime creative credit, even for the mise-en-scène, on her actors: "I gave them a basic structural principle and they ran with it, brilliantly. . . . All I did was let the cream rise to the top."[5] Mnouchkine's method of *création collective*, based on group research and subsequent improvisation, was first on display in her 1970 production of *1789*, a retelling of the early moments of the French Revolution. In having a director's or even an entire company's vision largely displace that of an individual playwright or of an established dramatic text, Mnouchkine was building on a collective concept of spectacle making that had been explored by such equally socially committed pioneers as Erwin Piscator (1893–1966) in Germany during the late 1920s and Bertolt Brecht (1898–1956), whose Berliner Ensemble's visit to Paris in 1954 was especially influential. (Brecht had been almost unknown in France before then.)[6]

One early stroke of group inspiration led to *Le dernier caravansérail*'s most arresting stage device. All of its characters, as well as the minimalist props and sets for each of its forty-two scenes, are on wheels. Players and objects enter, exit, and move about on low dollies of various size that are pushed and pulled, often at top speed, mainly by other actors serving as stagehands. Visible to the audience, the latter remain crouched on stage throughout each episode and thereby function as additional silent witnesses to the action. Thus we see — on an otherwise deep, empty stage — trees, utility poles, dwellings, clinics, sweatshops, and sundry parcels of urban and rural land that trace sweeping ellipses and parabolas before coming to temporary rest for each plot vignette. Throughout the piece the performers' feet never touch the floor.

In some measure the company's use of this mobile device is a gesture of tribute to theatrical continuity: in ancient Greek tragedy, a platform known as an eccyclema would frequently be wheeled out at a play's end to disclose the slaughtered bodies of characters. The insistent use of dollies in *Le dernier caravansérail*, however, is primarily in service of a grave modern-day crisis, for it allows the spectator, in profound kinesthetic identification with the dramatis personae, to experience the dizzying rhythms of open-ended diaspora in a frightful world where individuals do not steer their own destiny and where the privilege of security and fixedness is always deferred. Kinesis, it has been said of much contemporary theatre and dance performance, has largely replaced mimesis: rather than *imitate* action, kinesis *embodies* it. In this regard *Le dernier caravansérail* arguably succeeds in sparking in the viewer what the theatre scholar Joseph Loach has referred to as "a newly experienced affective cognition and corporeal empathy."[7]

Sequences cinematic

The stunning initial images of part 1, "Le fleuve cruel" ("The Cruel River"), hurl viewers into the vortex of precarious escape. A simple wicker basket, hoisted by a crude rope-and-pulley device, is a smuggler's vehicle for getting a wretched group of women, children, and men across a roiling river separating the central Asian republics of Kyrgyzstan and Kazakhstan. Deafening gales (simulated by the bass chords of the company's principal music composer and performer, Jean-Jacques Lemêtre) and treacherous waves (rendered, with a nod to Asian theatre tradition, by a half dozen actors and technical crew who, on either side of the wide stage, fiercely shake huge bolts of silky gray fabric) threaten to wreck the bobbing basket and drown the refugees.

With dialogue muffled and gesture paramount, Mnouchkine evokes a silent-movie aesthetic.[8] This opening scene especially brings to mind the famous climax of D. W. Griffith's *Way Down East* (1920), where ice floes carry the abandoned and delirious Lillian Gish downstream toward a precipitous waterfall. But unlike Griffith melodramas, which guarantee last-minute rescues and happy endings, Mnouchkine is preparing us for six hours of nearly incessant peril and uncertainty. Hence this river scene ends with a volley of gunshots and insults between the smugglers and those for whom they have just risked their lives. "Kyrgyz bastards! You race of dogs!" shouts one refugee, having reached momentary safety on land. "Kazakh bastard! . . . Stop moving across my country!" bellows one of the smugglers in return. Throughout *Le dernier caravansérail* the lines between heroism, egoism, and exploitation of others often blur, with all characters navigating a moral terrain as slippery as the wheeled platforms on which they physically move.

The start of part 2, "Origines et destins" ("Origins and Destinies"), is equally spectacular, though here Mnouchkine's eye-popping staging is redolent of recent Hollywood action movies (see fig. 1). We are now on the high seas, with a dozen refugees in the hold of a rickety Indonesian boat that nearly capsizes from breaking whitecaps (nicely limned by a huge stretch of white fabric rolling downstage to envelop the gray); calm soon returns, but a broken fuel pump leads to a fire below deck and hopes for survival fade once more. Suddenly, however, the sound of advancing helicopters and the sight of military men being cranked down from above on sturdy, high-tech cables restore the migrants' spirits—only to be dashed seconds later when, amid the pandemonium of whirling rotors, crashing waves, and their own anguished screams for help and pity, they stare, defenseless, as

1. *Anguished refugees on the high seas at the start of part 2 of Théâtre du Soleil's* Le dernier caravansérail: odyssées. *Photo © Martine Franck/Magnum Photos.*

the coast-guard officers blare over loudspeakers: "Australia does not accept you!" The scene ends in near total quiet, with the surviving boat people left adrift.

Against conventional realism

Watching *Le dernier caravansérail* requires intense attention. Many stories overlap and intertwine, but not always. Most of the plotlines go unresolved. Still, Mnouchkine imposes formal unity through sustained pacing—a kind of *adagio maestoso* that infuses the work with neoclassical grace and beauty and that counterbalances its horrific content. Similarly, Mnouchkine frequently alternates staged episodes with textual projections, in elegant white English script on a gray backcloth, of the actual testimony, letters, and poems of her interviewees. In simultaneous recorded voice-over, her actors or the informants themselves recite the words in their original language while the stage remains bare. A framing device for the entire work is a friendly letter sent (and read aloud) by Mnouchkine to a female refugee she met in Indonesia, informing this woman that the company is now ready to perform their version of her personal story.

In an otherwise laudatory review, Charles Isherwood of the *New York Times* found these intervening verbalized moments to be "untheatrical" and too suggestive of "PBS documentaries."[9] For me, these interludes brought welcome relief from the unceasing nightmarish quality of what was being enacted on stage. By stressing the whimsical, familial, amorous, and sacred aspects of the refugees' everyday lives, these words attested to the full humanity and idealism of a class of people who, as we observe them in their frenzied flight, often have to squash their finer instincts. Michael Feingold, writing in the *Village Voice*, likewise suggested that Mnouchkine seems "to abdicate the work of the theatre" while trying instead "to do the work of a U.N. report." Feingold judged the opening scenes of the work's two parts to be "among the most thrilling theatre moments made in our times," yet he noted that the rest of the work did not equal them in "full power."[10] In some sense Feingold is correct. But I think the real strength and challenge of *Le dernier caravansérail* lie precisely in its string of quieter, more modest scenes. No less visually absorbing and stylized than the opening of parts 1 and 2, these episodes trade popular cinematic thrills—high suspense, staggering scenic design, quick flamboyant action—for the less predictable and less easily processed representations of real people's experiences played out in what feels, both viscerally and mentally, like *real* places and *real* time.

Mnouchkine has always considered conventional realism to be her artistic "enemy" since "by definition, the theatre, like all art, is transposition or transfiguration." But "to reject realism," she says apropos of *Le dernier caravansérail*, "in no way means that I reject reality."[11] She maintains that the slapdash images of refugees found in the news media, in mass-audience movies, and on the Internet are those that gravely falsify reality: "The media always show these people as if they were simply a horde of unshaven men with large glazed eyes. . . . What if we actually tried putting ourselves in their place? That's something which the theatre can help us do."[12] Indeed, Mnouchkine here, as elsewhere in her oeuvre, denies us the easy illusion of psychological "depth" and "back story." She compels us to work arduously with her players as they slowly, intimately convey the weight of lives lived and decisions taken.

Stolen moments of joy

Nowhere is the feeling of abiding menace more palpable than in the work's otherwise uplifting final scene. This idyllic tableau vivant brings together the light-skinned and the dark; adults and children; the privileged and the poor; Britons, Central Europeans, and Middle Easterners—all enjoying, in silence, a picnic atop the white cliffs of Dover. Up to this point in *Le dernier caravansérail*, fragile moments of human warmth and tenderness pop up only to vanish in a flash: a gruff Bulgarian smuggler-pimp sings a sweet folk song by cell phone to his faraway child, but he is soon murdered; on the road in Bosnia-Herzegovina a big-hearted fugitive shares his precious meal of a tiny egg, swiped from a bird's nest, with his companion, but he will fail to reach his destination. By contrast this final episode amplifies and sustains themes of human decency and solidarity. Mnouchkine's décor—until now mostly austere, ugly, claustrophobic, and pallid—suddenly brims with life, beauty, expanse, and color: bread and wine are abundant and freely shared; trees are in lustrous bloom; a spirited seagull (made of paper and attached to a long, flexible pole manipulated by a nimble stagehand/actor) soars flamboyantly, its robust and ear-splitting squawks a kind of acoustic homage to achieved freedom. And yet, just as the cliff setting implies the risk of a fall, so the shadowy presence of a group of Islamist thugs and clerics hatching some secret scheme at the picnic's start reminds us that this new-found happiness is in no way absolute.

Nonetheless, in the best tradition of theatrical finales, Mnouchkine gives rich embodiment here to the Persian proverb that a character cites earlier in the production and that seems to serve as the work's ultimate statement: "Life passes, like a mysterious caravan. Let us steal its minute of joy."

Theatre and politics

Mnouchkine has long perceived herself as an engaged witness of history. Her 1995 production of Molière's *Tartuffe* transposed the action to contemporary Algeria, the better to expose the undying duplicities of religious fundamentalism. Her collaborations with Hélène Cixous have often dealt with the disruptive legacies of colonialism, including the torture of the Khmer people in *L'Histoire terrible mais inachevée de Norodom Sihanouk, roi du Cambodge* (The Terrible But Unfinished Story of Norodom Sihanouk, King of Cambodia, 1985) and the traumatic partitioning of India in *L'Indiade, ou l'Inde de leurs rêves* (The Indiad, or India of Their Dreams, 1987). In *La ville parjure, ou le réveil des Erinyes* (The Perjured City, or The Awakening of the Furies, 1996), Cixous and Mnouchkine assailed France's HIV-tainted blood transfusion scandal and gave voice to victims of other corrupt medical, political, and social institutions.

To protest the inaction of Europe and the United States toward Serbian barbarity in Bosnia, Mnouchkine, in the late summer of 1995, joined François Tanguy, Olivier Py, Maguy Marin, Emmanuel de Véricourt, and other high-profile French performing-arts figures in a thirty-day hunger strike. When the Vincennes Cartoucherie itself became an asylum for many *sans-papiers*, or illegal immigrants, the company created *Et soudain des nuits d'éveil* (And Suddenly Wakeful Nights, 1997), a four-hour stage work about the complicated interactions between a group of French actors and a cohort of Tibetan refugees.

• • •

Around the time that *Le dernier caravansérail* was having its run at Lincoln Center, real-world events confirmed the urgency of the issues the play addresses. On July 11, 2005, Nicolas Sarkozy, newly re-installed as France's minister of the interior and positioning himself for a presidential run, announced in Marseilles that because "[the French] do not want to see their borders with the rest of the world collapse," he was establishing a multiministerial task force to re-assess French immigration, refugee, and residency policies. Sarkozy, himself the son of a Hungarian refugee, made clear that he sought stricter financial and housing requirements for immigrant workers who hoped to bring their families to France; the denial of visas for those "suspected of polygamy or mistreatment of women"; and a massive increase in the use of biometric databases by French consul-ates worldwide—already in effect in such cities as Minsk (Belarus), Lubumbashi (Congo), and Annaba (Algeria).[13]

The minister's wish to bring "greater balance" to immigrant flows won only mixed support that week from *Le Monde*'s editors, who re-minded readers of France's "tradition as a land of refuge and human rights protection."[14] (In Paris alone, the government was then feed-ing, housing, and providing clothes and medical care for nearly 10,000 undocumented immigrants.) A few days later, on an official visit to Madrid, Sarkozy called for "the systematic expulsion . . . of all Mus-lim religious leaders who advocate killings" and the deportation of "illegal immigrants who are being exploited by terrorist rings or who have entered Europe clandestinely."[15] Despite protests from left-wing and human rights associations, Sarkozy, on July 26 and with the aid of British officials, sent forty Afghans illegally residing in France and the United Kingdom on a one-way trip from Roissy to Kabul aboard a chartered jet.

How ironic, I thought, to read about these events online and in the daily newspapers, with a cup of warm coffee at my side, and then recall that one of the more chilling scenes in *Le dernier caravansé-rail* depicts deportation officers who brutally manhandle a black Afri-can refugee as they drug him and drag him onto a plane at Roissy's Charles de Gaulle Airport. Mnouchkine concedes that there is no easy political answer as European nations balance the needs of refugees against national security: "I myself do not advocate a total opening of our borders. I don't want tyrants and executioners [entering France]. But if we defended more ardently and without hesitation our own democratic principles of secularism, equality of men and women, equal access to education, health, housing, and justice . . . we'd be less concerned, I think, with defending our borders."[16]

• • •

At the symposium "Does Art Matter?" Mnouchkine noted that the power of art and especially of live theatre certainly "matters for the enemies" — by which she meant ideologues, censors, and bigots. "Think of Kabul," she stated, "where the first thing to be destroyed when war broke out was the building that housed a theatre." She admits that a work like *Le dernier caravansérail* will not change such people. But it can, she insists, "strengthen the will for good, for peace, and for progress" among those already inclined to support a struggle that, she feels deeply, is part of the collective responsibility of first-world nations.

Does this mean, one audience member asked, that Mnouchkine is simply preaching to the converted? Robert Brustein, reviewing *Le dernier caravansérail* in the *New Republic*, similarly wondered whether such "exercises of conscience" lead simply to "theatre as a form of therapy."[17] "No," Mnouchkine responded emphatically, "because people who think of themselves as converts are often in fact not fully so. Many viewers of *Le dernier caravansérail* tell me that the play transformed their grasp of the refugee problem from journalistic knowledge to a kind of knowledge that can only be conferred by the theatre, one that is much more painful and complex and destabilizing."[18]

The cost of making and marketing alternative theatre

In France, Mnouchkine's troupe has for decades been supported by handsome annual government subventions: its stipend for 2005 totaled nearly 1.5 million euros.[19] The desire of Lincoln Center's Nigel Redden to include *Le dernier caravansérail* in the Lincoln Center Festival stemmed largely from his personal conviction that America's recent and current wars were aggravating, as a kind of "collateral damage," the worldwide refugee problem; American audiences, he felt, urgently needed to view refugees as "individuals" rather than "statistics or stereotypes."[20] But Redden conceded that a vital determinant in acquiring Mnouchkine's play was also the fact that Lincoln Center's president, Reynold Levy, who had previously headed the International Rescue Committee, was willing to go to bat in the search for private financial support.

Le dernier caravansérail did smash business in New York. For many East Coast culture vultures, Ariane Mnouchkine is a brand name: the news of a forthcoming visit guarantees advance sales. But it was not a foregone conclusion that Théâtre du Soleil would expand the ranks of its U.S. public without extra prodding. The week before the start of the Lincoln Center Festival, David Kornhaber, writing in the *New York Sun*, in fact took to task "the French avant-garde" as "an insular dramatic universe fiercely committed to its own legacy even at the expense of being ignored by the rest of the world." Rightly associating Mnouchkine's "commitment to experimentation and internationalism" with that of Peter Brook and Robert Wilson, Kornhaber nonetheless lamented that "since the 1950s, France has produced little in the way of easily transferable commercial theatre."[21] What plays he had in mind went unstated; one recalls that the absurdists, even in translation, were rarely big box-office hits in the United States. Perhaps Kornhaber was waxing nostalgic for a time when Jean Anouilh's sex farce *La valse des toréadors* (*The Waltz of the Toreadors*, 1952) was an international hit or when Alfred Lunt's 1954 Broadway production of Jean Giraudoux's *Ondine* (1938), starring Mel Ferrer and Audrey Hepburn, won the Best Foreign Play award from the New York Drama Critics' Circle. ACT FRENCH would demonstrate to New Yorkers that French theatre had long moved beyond such quaint fare.

The *New York Times* featured several prefestival pieces aimed to cushion the impact of some of the more demanding offerings at Lincoln Center, especially those bucking the conventional two-hour format. In the Sunday arts section, Jonathan Kalb made a compelling case for "marathon theater," suggesting to readers that *Le dernier caravansérail* might well join the ranks of such other successful New York "group endurance experiences" as the Royal Shakespeare Company's eight-and-a-half-hour *Nicolas Nickleby* (1981 and 1986), Tony Kushner's seven-hour *Angels in America* (1993), and Chen Shi-Zheng's twenty-hour *Peony Pavilion* (1999). In "our impatient consumerist age," Kalb wrote, the prize for "those who soldier through masterly marathon dramas by someone like Ms. Mnouchkine" can be "extraordinary," that is to say, "an odyssey through uncharted physical and spiritual territory where the theater loses its trick-box aspect and becomes a site of unexpected communion and awful reckoning."[22]

Two days earlier the *Times* culture critic Margo Jefferson usefully offered "An Avant-Gardist's Guide to the Lincoln Center Festival" and a miniprimer on the "experimental theater" of a Mnouchkine or a Wilson (whose Indonesian epic, *I La Galigo*, was also on the summer roster).[23] Jefferson's article covered such basic points as narrative nonlinearity, media hybridity, and the artists' expectation that audiences will exert critical faculties as they watch and listen. It is hard to imagine a similarly didactic piece appearing in a French newspaper that, like the *Times*, speaks mainly to college-educated readers. Still, Jefferson understood that a work like *Le dernier caravansérail* would make uncommon demands on many viewers.

A global theatre for our times

In 2003, a fresh subject appeared on the list from which humanities students in French high schools could choose as they prepared for their final-year *baccalauréat* exams: "The Works of Théâtre du Soleil, from Eastern Traditions to Western Modernity." Implicit in this measure, designed for students concentrating in theatre arts, was the Ministry of National Education's view that Ariane Mnouchkine's creative achievements are as worthy an object of secondary-school study as those of Victor Hugo, Anton Chekhov, or Michel Vinaver—canonical (male) playwrights who have also been recent objects of instruction and examination. More explicit was an acknowledgment that for all its prestige as a French institution, Théâtre du Soleil is—in its inter-, trans-, and supranational dimensions—an exemplary hybrid, belonging as much to "world" or "planetary" culture as to that of France.

Indeed, viewers of *Le dernier caravansérail* in New York—and in other cities where the production toured, such as Berlin and Melbourne—heard very little of the language of Racine and Molière, Giraudoux and Sartre. At least 80 percent of the play's dialogue was spoken in the native languages of its non-Francophone characters—with the Persian, Kurdish, Russian, and Pashto translated into English via supertitles projected onto surfaces of the various sets. The company itself included at that time people of thirty-five different nationalities who, collectively, spoke twenty-two different languages. Mnouchkine insists that Théâtre du Soleil is, in practice, "French," and she demands that its members conduct their activities entirely in French. But at the same time she recognizes that her troupe's multiethnic and multinational composition "reflects what the world today is, and what France is, and will continue to be, I hope."[24]

Le dernier caravansérail is arguably Mnouchkine's most ambitious attempt to create a global theatre for our times. In this regard it is the culmination of her career-long efforts at cultural crossbreeding. Antonin Artaud, dazzled and thrilled by the body-centered ritual forms of the Balinese Theatre in Paris in 1931, had been among the first to trumpet the need to dismantle the classic French dramatic tradition with infusions of non-Western theatre practice. Mnouchkine has followed that call, and she has recurrently turned for inspiration to traditional forms from Japan, China, and India in order to create something entirely new. Even when rehearsing *Tartuffe*, as shown in the documentary film *Au Soleil, même la nuit* (Even at Night the Soleil Shines, 1997), she rejects a player's delivery, shouting "Don't act French!" (*Ne jouez pas à la française!*) — by which she means that the actor needs to strip himself of personal ego and Conservatory rhetorical style, and must strive to offer his lines in free and simple response to the blaze of energy being generated by his acting partner and the human situation they find themselves in.

At one of the several Lincoln Center performances of *Le dernier caravansérail* I attended — while the house lights were on and people were still scrambling for their seats — I watched as Mnouchkine's actors, having left their dressing tables *en groupe*, quietly filed past their guru, each exchanging with her the Hindu *namaste*, the slight bow with hands clasped to the chest, palms joined, and fingertips pointing upward. "For some it's religious, for others superstitious, for others just a habit," Mnouchkine told one American reporter about these shared gambits. "Our actors never step on the stage without realizing that it relates to spirit and the progress of the mind."[25]

Mnouchkine in French perspective

One cannot underestimate the import of Mnouchkine's sustained dialogue with Asian theatrical traditions. But she and her company's towering place in contemporary staged spectacle must also be appreciated as the outgrowth of a long tradition of twentieth-century *French* theatrical visionaries, of which Artaud was simply its most flamboyant exponent. Mnouchkine in fact points to Jacques Copeau (1879–1949) as a prime source of her view of the theatre as a "temple."[26] One of France's first great modern apostles of reform and renewal, Copeau had thorough contempt for the narcissism of most actors, the undisguised greed of the typical theatre manager, the vulgar staging of boulevard farces, and the cozy bourgeois themes of naturalistic theatre—all of which dominated the French stage as of the Belle Epoque. In founding his Théâtre du Vieux-Colombier (1913), Copeau dreamed of a company that, like some ascetic knightly order, would commit to a quasi-monastic vocation from which "stardom" and box-office "triumphs" would be banished. While Copeau never reached this goal, Théâtre du Soleil is perhaps its closest approximation. Mnouchkine's return to Shakespeare and Molière for primal inspiration, her revitalization of commedia dell'arte masks in such plays as L'Age d'or (1975) and Les Atrides (1992), her employment of a resident dramatist (Cixous), and her rejection of Italianate theatre design in favor of an open, Elizabethan-like stage and hall—this was all part of Jacques Copeau's ideal vision.

André Gide (who with Copeau founded La Nouvelle Revue Française in 1909) described in his diaries a serious flaw in what he called Copeau's "elitist" view of theatre and actors: the search for "stylistic purity" in "an art form that is essentially impure."[27] Mnouchkine's far more pragmatic stance toward both the realities of money and the unique personalities of her actors draws on the successful praxis of Copeau's more flexible student Louis Jouvet (1887–1951), the beloved actor-director who ran the Théâtre de l'Athénée from 1934 until his death. "Jouvet knew how to connect art with life," notes Mnouchkine admiringly.[28]

Mnouchkine's own legendary rapport with young actors is on vivid display in the film by Eric Darmon and Catherine Vilpoux, Au Soleil, même la nuit, a three-hour documentary on the company's rehearsals of Tartuffe. Screened at the Bruno Walter Auditorium as part of the ACT FRENCH and Lincoln Center festivals, it shows us the director—with her trademark shock of bushy white hair, loose-fitting clothes, and eyeglasses hanging from a string around her neck—tirelessly at work. Mnouchkine's uncompromising insistence that her actors discover the right physical vocabulary to convey both character and situation is seen to reflect the lasting influence of her own teacher in the 1960s, Jacques Lecoq (1921–1999), a renowned master of mime and improvisational technique. Sometimes Mnouchkine appears on screen as a caustic and fearsome matriarch. At other times she radiates an earth-mother aura of serenity and wisdom. She can be playful and even flirtatious. But above all she is respectful of her players' humanity. Just as we watch her painstakingly help her actors work through doubts and uncertainties, we also see them help their leader sort out and transcend certain demons of her own. One actor aptly describes working with this company as "a school for life."

Another Copeau disciple, Charles Dullin (1885–1949), was perhaps the most influential historic role model for Mnouchkine's overall artistic mission. Dullin's description of the Atelier, the innovative theatre space he created in the early 1920s, applies equally to Mnouchkine's Théâtre du Soleil: "The Atelier is not a theatrical business; it is a laboratory for dramatic experimentation. We chose this word [*atelier*] because it seems to express our notion of an ideal corporative organization, one in which the strongest of individual personalities submits to the greater requirements of collaboration."[29] Mnouchkine, speaking of both her company and its audience, likewise asserts: "My theatre is neither a shop, nor a business office, nor a factory. It is a workspace [*un atelier*] for meeting and sharing; it is a temple devoted to reflection, knowledge, and sensibility. It is a home where people can feel comfortable, with cool water if they are thirsty and something to eat if they are hungry."[30] Théâtre du Soleil's leader also aligns herself with the outlook of Jean Vilar (1912–1971)— the Dullin protégé who founded the Avignon Festival in 1947 and took over the direction of the Théâtre National Populaire at the Palais de Chaillot in 1951. For Vilar, theatre was above all a public service. Viewing his project as one of democratization and decentralization, Vilar sought to make France's theatrical heritage and its attendant political potential as readily available to the broad base of the French nation as were water and electricity.

Mnouchkine seems to concur as well with the famous turn of phrase by the stage director Antoine Vitez (1930–1990), who, recycling a tenet of the German classical playwright Friedrich Schiller (d. 1805), construed popular theatre as "elitism for everyone" ("*un théâtre élitaire pour tous*"). To bolster her view that one must always listen to the public but not necessarily submit to it, Mnouchkine again references Vilar, who famously said: "It is a question of having the courage and the stubbornness to bestow upon the public what it only vaguely knows that it needs." "That," Mnouchkine adds, "was Vilar's gamble. . . . [T]o raise the level, to heighten the bar. Always trying to capture what is more truthful, more difficult. Attempting to decipher the world, and then trying to make it understood, felt, lived."[31]

• • •

Le dernier caravansérail showed New Yorkers that Mnouchkine is not afraid to make political waves. Yet for all her anger and impatience over the frightful real-world events that made this production "inevitable," Mnouchkine reveals herself in this staggering piece to be more an idealist than an ideologue. She aims less to proselytize and to scapegoat than to make us feel, imagine, and empathize. In this sense—its postnational cosmopolitanism and multiethnic makeup notwithstanding—Théâtre du Soleil is very much part and parcel of a twentieth-century French messianic tradition that Mnouchkine has boldly extended into this new century. Mnouchkine's work also stands in clear contrast to the so-called postdramatic theatre of the late twentieth and early twenty-first centuries.[32] *Le dernier caravansérail*—as well as Mnouchkine's subsequent works *Les éphémères* (2006) and *Les naufragés du Fol Espoir (aurores)* (Shipwrecked of the Wild Hope [Dawnings], 2010)—emphatically does *not* discard, retreat from, or aim to transcend the basic features generally associated with the term 'dramatic.' For all their fragmentation and stylization, the narrative actions and emotion-filled situational crises in *Le dernier caravansérail* constitute the bulk of the work's content and much of its theatrical interest. While they are often more sketched than fully developed, the creation of individualized and identifiable characters and the depiction of their interpersonal tensions are fundamental to Mnouchkine's goal of heightening spectator empathy. And the revelry she takes in exposing the mechanics of spectacle making in no way compromises her goal of engaging, in a quasi-documentary representational fashion, with the genuine world that exists beyond that of the stage.

Mnouchkine's oeuvre also stands apart from that of the expanding number of contemporary French theatre artists who explore the entanglements of performance and new media technologies. Ours is an age when audiences in most first-world countries "watch" world dramas—be they of war, crime, natural disaster, famine, or epidemic—as they unfold for us on TV and computer screens. Mnouchkine prefers that we connect with real flesh-and-blood bodies, not pixels on a video screen. Indeed, one of the most callous vignettes in *Le dernier caravansérail* depicts an Australian refugee review tribunal that is conducted via video conferencing: the actors playing a white Australian judge and her assistants are shown on stage as they move about freely in their comfortable Melbourne office; the harassed and confined Iraqi asylum seeker is seen only via a televised medium-close head shot, the better to treat him and his drama with heartless detachment.

• • •

The contemporary French playwright Enzo Cormann (b. 1953) has thought deeply about the time-honored relationship between Western theatre and the themes of war, persecution, exile, terrorism, and diaspora: "Far from engaging in a banal fascination with the suffering and blood of others . . . and beyond mere service as catharsis, the theatre's incessant return to matters of war demonstrates an indispensable need to reposition the reality of war within [an alternative] political space."[33] Cormann names that space *"un espace de pensée"* ("a space for reflection"). It is the *artistic* space in which ordinary politics become poeticized. It is the *privileged* space — at once physical, mental, and spiritual — that engages and embraces, on equal footing, the actors and the audience in a shared experience of suspended judgment, reexamination of values, and, ultimately, deepened understanding. It is the *ethical* space that serves as an antidote to, as Cormann puts it, "the reification of social relations, the oppression wielded by the mass media, and the infantilizing consensus mentality that are the bases of the globalized market economy."[34]

Such a salutary space will perhaps never change the world absolutely. But it indelibly alters our view of that world and of our relation to it. It is the space, at once fragile and potent, that Ariane Mnouchkine generously brought to Lincoln Center in July 2005.

Star Power, Gallic Style

The actor as auteur

In France, major actors typically travel between the worlds of the theatre and the cinema with more ease and regularity than their American counterparts. ACT FRENCH enabled New York audiences to bask in the live presence of three glamorous performers whose work is known on this side of the Atlantic mainly via film and video technology: Marie-France Pisier, Patrice Chéreau, and Isabelle Huppert. In varying ways these celebrated figures make an intriguing case for the notion of the stage actor as *auteur*, or a major creative force. Through their compelling deployments of voice and body in real time and space, each conferred a strong personal imprint upon unusual theatrical material.

An idol from our youth

For U.S. cinephiles of a certain age, Marie-France Pisier (b. 1944) will perhaps forever be linked to the memory of Colette, the sweet object of Antoine Doinel's first unrequited love affair in François Truffaut's semiautobiographical short from 1962, *Antoine et Colette*, the film that marked her screen debut. Of her eighty-plus subsequent movies, Pisier is probably best recalled in this country for her roles in such classics as Jacques Rivette's *Céline et Julie vont en bateau* (*Céline and Julie Go Boating*, 1974), Jean-Charles Tacchella's *Cousin, cousine* (1975), and Truffaut's *L'amour en fuite* (*Love on the Run*, 1979), which Pisier cowrote with the director and in which she again appears as Colette—now a lawyer and still able to ruffle the heartstrings of the emotionally confused Antoine (Jean-Pierre Léaud). Those of us who saw her on stage in Fabrice Rozié's *Liaison transatlantique* at Florence

Gould Hall, on East Fifty-ninth Street, may have felt a bit like Truf-faut's protagonist: here was a female idol from our youth who, now in her early sixties and making her American theatre debut, was as captivating as ever.

In the play's final moments Pisier walks off stage in exalted amor-ous triumph, having just recited an exit line worthy of a heroine of medieval romance: "There will be no death between you and me." Pisier is not, however, playing some mystical Yseult who pledges eter-nal love to her absent Tristan. She is portraying Simone de Beauvoir (1908–1986)—the world-renowned proponent of Jean-Paul Sartre's very unsentimental brand of existentialism and the cerebral femi-nist who exposed and analyzed the unequal status of contemporary women in her pathbreaking book *The Second Sex* (1949–1950). In the preceding hour, we in the audience were privy to the vulnerable, romantic, passionate—some might even say reactionary—facets of an intellectual whose public persona, an inspiration for generations of women worldwide, was usually one of emotional control and per-sonal autonomy. Here, however, we watch and listen as this mighty icon of open, honest, and equal relationships (her lifelong partner-ship with Sartre having served as a textbook model) informs her American lover, the Chicago-based writer Nelson Algren (1909–1981), soon after their second U.S. tryst, in 1947: "You have not to be faith-ful in the conventional way if you don't feel like it. But for myself, I just know I could not sleep with any man now until I meet you again. I just could not bear to feel another man's hands or lips when I long so bitterly for your beloved hands and lips. I'll be faithful as a dutiful and conventional wife just because I could not help it—that's the way it is."

This stunning alliance of Beauvoir and convention creates much of the fascination of this one-woman show—a reduced, English-language adaptation of Rozié's three-act play, which premiered to critical acclaim in Paris at the Petit Théâtre Marigny in fall 2002 and went on to enjoy a full New York staging at the Harold Clurman The-atre in spring 2006. In the complete version, Algren engages with Beauvoir in dialogue that comes directly from her autobiographical novel *Les Mandarins* (1954). The stripped-down edition at Florence Gould Hall, directed by Sandrine Dumas and adapted by her and

Pisier, gave us only Beauvoir—and was thus more in line, formally, with the play's main source, Beauvoir's posthumously published love letters to Algren, whose epistolary replies have yet to be made public.[1]

Dumas's mise-en-scène was artfully casual. On a wide, nearly empty stage, two spotlights beamed steadily: one illuminated Pisier as Beauvoir, who read selected letters while seated at a café table, stage left; the other shined on a slightly shabby, grass-green easy chair, stage right—an apt metaphor for the hard-living, unpretentious absent midwesterner.

Existential empathy

Readers who have sampled Beauvoir's prolific seventeen-year correspondence addressed to Algren know that it is a cornucopia of literary and theatre-world gossip. The letters detail lunches with Jean Genet and the actress Arletty; dress rehearsals for Sartre's numerous stage works; the schadenfreude that greeted Albert Camus's failed theatrical adaptation of his novel *La Peste*; Boris Vian's sluggish efforts to render Algren's Pulitzer Prize–winning novel, *The Man with the Golden Arm*, into a decent French translation; and charged encounters with the likes of Richard Wright, Violette Leduc, and Jacqueline Kennedy.

Liaison transatlantique offers a few of these piquant, contextualizing anecdotes. But in step with Rozié's original concept, Dumas and Pisier focus almost exclusively on Beauvoir's inner feelings and on the unusual relationship of two lovers who—not unlike Tristan and Yseult—attempt to fabricate via their letters and an occasional out-of-the-way trip an emotional universe solely unto themselves. As Rozié (b. 1965) told me: "In selecting letters for the play, my major criterion was that they be phantasmatic scenarios in which Beauvoir is no longer Simone de Beauvoir, Sartre's companion, but a different woman, a happier and more fulfilled woman."[2]

The odds against the lovers' success were enormous, and that is where this stage work's dramatic tension lies. Algren was apparently the first man to bring Beauvoir full sexual satisfaction. Her love for him was more intense and complete than any she had known. But in no way could she seriously envision pulling up stakes to live permanently as his wife in the States—a domestic arrangement he, however, was all too willing to contemplate. Perhaps the most moving moments in *Liaison transatlantique* are those in which Pisier as Beauvoir contrasts her devotion and commitment to her lifelong companion Sartre, "who does not care much for sexual life. . . . we dropped it after about eight or ten years rather unsuccessful in this way," with her carnal passion for Algren. Contemplating a summer together in a remote cottage on Lake Michigan, Beauvoir exults: "Oh, Nelson! I'll be so nice and good, you'll see. I'll wash the floor, I'll cook the whole meals, I'll write your book as well as mine, I'll make love to you ten times a night and as much in the day." When Algren finally rejects Beauvoir to remarry his first wife, the feminist philosopher concedes, with surgical precision: "I did not give my whole life to you; I gave my heart and all that I could but not my life. . . . I could not desert Sartre and writing and France." Still, following their first breakup in 1951, Beauvoir—with Pisier putting to fine use the higher register of her normally husky voice—wails: "I'll be buried with your ring on my finger; and as long as I live, I'll never be utterly lost for you; you'll be evicted from my heart never."

• • •

In a panel discussion that followed her final performance at Florence Gould Hall, Pisier explained her attraction to this particular role: "I liked the fact that Beauvoir was writing *The Second Sex* at the same time that she was having this love affair."[3] Pisier, whom *People* magazine in the 1970s dubbed "The Gallic Jane Fonda,"[4] confided that she had first met Beauvoir in real life via the street demonstrations they both took part in when she was a young law and political science student at the University of Paris. Active in the Mouvement de libération des femmes (Women's Liberation Movement), Pisier, along with Beauvoir, was one of the 343 women in the public eye who signed a manifesto, published by *Le Nouvel Observateur* on April 5, 1971, in which they admitted to having had illegal abortions, thus running the risk of imprisonment. The still svelte and petite Pisier added: "I remember Beauvoir looking very much like a stiff professor. . . . I was eager, with this play, to show that she was also a warm and deeply involved lady in love."[5]

Pisier was not trying to impersonate Simone de Beauvoir. In the Paris production Pisier's costumes and hairstyle did actually mimic well-known photos of Beauvoir. For this American version Pisier aimed, she said, only to capture the "rapid speech and the up-and-down quality of Beauvoir's intonation."[6] Yet she coupled the quickness with a softness of inflection and a lilting, often sultry intonation that was unexpected but quite appropriate to Beauvoir's epistolary effusions of sentiment, dreamy longing, and inevitable letdown. This was the private, intimate, seductive Beauvoir that Pisier, with subtlety and intelligence, constructed for this theatrical occasion. Moreover, Pisier chose to set off the verbal flow of Beauvoir's unbridled passion with very guarded body language. Clearly and wisely, she wanted us to grant total attention to Simone de Beauvoir's words. In a large hall and without electronic amplification, she delivered them not just with reverence but with profound empathy.

Unexpected bravado

As I took my twelfth-row seat at Symphony Space on Manhattan's Upper West Side, the look of the stage added to my daylong fear that we were in for a tedious evening. The layout was bare except for a spindly black music stand downstage, left of center, and two plain straight-back chairs, one right of center, the other at the extreme right. In the rear some weatherworn ladders leaned against the large theatre's exposed brick inner wall. This grim décor seemed, alas, the perfect setting for Dostoyevsky's wretched Underground Man to spout his case on behalf of misery and despair as a way of life.

Yet something marvelous happened seconds after Patrice Chéreau (b. 1944) ambled on stage. His appearance was unimposing: wearing sensible eyeglasses, he held a hefty script in his left hand; beneath the unbuttoned jacket of his loose black suit was an untucked black button-down shirt. Short and a bit squat, he projected absolute blandness. From the moment he opened his mouth, however, Chéreau annihilated my high-school memories of the insufferable Russian who holds forth endlessly on such uninviting topics as his overdeveloped consciousness, the oppressive grip of the laws of nature, and the queer pleasures that can result from a severe toothache. For in this one-night-only reading, based on a recent French translation from the Russian (with English supertitles flashed on a shallow rectangular screen, stage rear), Chéreau cagily dispensed with the arid part 1 of Dostoyevsky's text, which begins with the famous "I'm a sick man . . . a mean man" and ends with the narrator telling us how "bored" he is with "constantly doing nothing"—a sentiment many of us in senior English class shared as we struggled to get through those first thirty pages of dense, abstract prose. Instead, Chéreau zeroed in on the Underground Man's vividly detailed reminiscences of part 2 (which, if memory serves, we students were instructed *not* to read, probably due to their raciness). These included the hotel dinner party with old schoolmates, to which the narrator shamelessly invites himself and at which, drunk and nasty, he is treated with total contempt; and his botched encounters with the young prostitute Liza, whom he patronizingly lectures on conventional morality and whose signs of real love he cruelly rejects.

The happy result was an evening's encounter not with the paralyzed, self-loathing antihero burrowed in a mousehole but with his earlier incarnation at a time when the Underground Man was still intrigued (with ambivalence, to be sure) by the possibilities of power, passion, and worldly success. Indeed, this was an Underground Man in urgent need of Ritalin: restless, impulsive, hyperkinetic. Only at the start of this performance did Chéreau stand placidly near the music stand that nominally served as a lectern. For the rest of the show he fabricated a being in furious motion—crouching, stretching, pacing, even running across the stage—and only occasionally looking down at his handheld script.

Chéreau's vocal delivery, conforming to a nineteenth-century style of grand theatre, was effusive, expressive, and emphatic. Possessing a deep, often throaty baritone, he made no effort to mask his frequent wheezes, sniffs, and snorts. Throughout, he made us feel the text's syntactic rhythms, pauses, and punctuation. Short phrases like *"Ah bon?"* ("Oh, really?") and *"D'accord"* ("OK") were never throwaways: he milked them for maximum dramatic impact—and laughs. Indeed, his reading highlighted the farcical overtones of the tight spots the masochistic Underground Man repeatedly creates for himself. From someone largely associated with pioneering stage experimentation, we were given an entertaining, almost nostalgia-soaked slice of *le bon vieux théâtre*.

• • •

The show ended with the same matter-of-factness with which it had begun. Chéreau—faithful to Dostoyevsky's text—impassively informed the audience, "I no longer want to speak," and simply walked offstage. The ovation was noisy and led to three curtain calls. The cheers, I now realize, were not just for this delectably delivered curio. Some of us had come to the show mainly to catch a glimpse of the man who had gained legendary status with his iconoclastic staging of Wagner's *Ring of the Nibelung* in 1976 and who had won worldwide commercial success with his film adaptation of Alexandre Dumas's novel *La Reine Margot* (*Queen Margot*) in 1994. Yet many in the audience had latched on to the subtler sense of occasion that this single evening in Manhattan carried. They were grateful that Patrice Chéreau, who in recent years has repeatedly vowed to direct only operas and movies, was once again drawn to his first love, the dramatic stage.

For here was the man who, as of the 1970s, had given French theatre several of its most potent shots in the arm. His intensely sensual 1973 staging of Marivaux's *La dispute* (*The Dispute*, 1744), for example, exerted as much mold-breaking impact on how future generations of directors would reinterpret classic texts as had, in previous years, Bertolt Brecht's *Threepenny Opera* (1928) and Peter Brook's Royal Shakespeare Company mounting of *King Lear* (1962). His 1983 revival of Jean Genet's *Les paravents* (*The Screens*, 1961) at the Théâtre Nanterre-Amandiers, which Chéreau then ran, was the last Genet production for which the genius writer himself (d. 1986) took part in rehearsals, had heated arguments with the director, and attended opening night festivities; apparently pleased, Genet granted Chéreau exclusive rights to the play through 1999.[7] Chéreau's most lasting impact on the course of French theatre may well turn out to be his series of collaborations, begun in 1983, with the then little-known playwright Bernard-Marie Koltès (1948–1989); those works arguably marked the most fruitful creative union of a stellar director and a heavyweight writer since Roger Blin's production of the 1953 premiere of Samuel Beckett's *En attendant Godot* (*Waiting for Godot*).

Far more modest, the event at Symphony Space was a further instance of what Chéreau identifies as a force that has driven virtually all of his professional activities: "I have always lived in fear of repeating what I've already done." It also divulged an artistic aim that Chéreau holds dear and that he regrets not always achieving: "to tell serious stories . . . with a light touch."[8]

A question of language

Surely the most controversial event of ACT FRENCH was Isabelle Huppert's superstar turn in *4.48 psychose*—a program that was also part of the 2005 Next Wave Festival of the Brooklyn Academy of Music (BAM).[9] To begin with, this was a French-language production of a British play, not a French one. For many European theatre companies, the work's author, Sarah Kane (1971–1999), holds near-cult status. Her plays have been mounted more often in France and Germany than even in her native England. But Kane, who took her own life at age twenty-eight, was barely known to many American theatregoers—although a Royal Court production of *4.48 Psychosis* (in English) played in New York and Los Angeles in October 2004 to fine critical response, and Manhattan's Soho Rep mounted her astonishing debut play, *Blasted* (1995), four years later.

Sarah Kane is a difficult playwright. Her writings are acutely poetic and antinaturalist. In the 1990s critics sometimes lumped her with the "in-yer-face" British dramatists—a taboo-breaking group that included Mark Ravenhill, Judy Upton, and Joe Penhall. Because of her black humor and seemingly detached fascination with the grotesque, she has also been compared with Samuel Beckett and Edward Bond. *4.48 Psychosis*, Kane's final effort, is possibly the most experimental of her ventures: she wrote it using the typographical conventions of modernist, collage-like poetry, and there are no indications even of how many actors might be required for a staged production. (The play premiered with three actors at London's Royal Court Jerwood Theatre Upstairs in June 2000, sixteen months after Kane's death.) Hans-Thies Lehmann has judged *4.48 Psychosis* to be *the* outstanding example of sustained tension between the dramatic and the postdramatic and, as such, to perpetrate a powerful "'attack' on the spectator."[10]

Marketing such a work in the United States, even to New Yorkers likely to attend Next Wave Festival programs, posed special challenges. Print ads spoke of it as the "searing portrayal of a mind *on the verge* of psychological collapse" (my emphasis).[11] This blurb, however, was a touch misleading since *4.48 Psychosis* is a play that *from its outset* exposes the mental recesses of a psychotic writer, already in the throes of a breakdown, just hours before he or she (the text does not specify the protagonist's sex) intends to commit suicide. Other advance media coverage in New York and southern California, where this French production had its U.S. premiere as part of the UCLA Live Fourth International Theatre Festival, was more candid. "It's not the Folies Bergère," warned *Vogue*.[12] "*Spamalot* it ain't," echoed a *New York Times* reporter in a preview feature.[13]

Joseph Melillo, BAM's executive producer, went so far as to send a signed letter to each advance ticket holder two weeks prior to opening night. In it he explained that we would be seeing a "nontraditional play" for which "there are no characters, plotline, time, location, or staging notes indicated in the script." He also disclosed that "Ms. Huppert" (b. 1953) will stand "mostly in place throughout the performance." This was a slight bending of truth: she in fact stands *totally* in place for the play's 105 minutes. Then came the real bombshell, a quoted message from the production's prime mover, Claude Régy (b. 1923), aptly referred to by Melillo as "one of France's most acclaimed contemporary directors." "It would be destroying Isabelle Huppert's work," Régy asserted, "if one had to look up too often in order to read the supertitles. Therefore the supertitles will be relatively rare, but sufficient enough to communicate the essential themes . . . and to show chiseled samples of Sarah Kane's laconic and modern writing style."[14] The message was clear. We were not to expect easy entertainment, and if we had very little French, we might want to do some homework before heading to BAM's Harvey Theater on Fulton Street. To smooth the way, enclosed with each letter was a discount coupon good for any Sarah Kane play purchase at Shakespeare & Co. bookstores.

• • •

Some theatregoers heeded Melillo's advice. Twenty minutes before my first visit to the show, as I exited the Nevins Street subway station, I noticed a middle-aged man a few feet ahead of me. Not only was he climbing the stairs with his head buried in the Methuen (London) edition of Sarah Kane's text; he valiantly kept reading as he negotiated both the vehicle-congested walk across Flatbush Avenue and the army of pedestrians, hot-dog stands, and trinket stalls that pepper the route to the Harvey Theater. At each of the performances I attended, I saw several young people in the front rows who, text in hand, strained to read along whenever the stage lights cooperated. Yet were not these conscientious spectators doing precisely what the play's director felt unnecessary and distracting? Gauging by the group laughter elicited by some of the untranslated lines, I would guess that about one-fifth of each day's audience was French-speaking. I imagine that most other viewers paid some attention to the sporadic supertitles, though these were flashed on a screen so near the theatre's unusually high ceiling that only people in the upper balcony were able to view them with ease. Perhaps there were also daring souls who, while understanding no French, disregarded the translation altogether and focused—as Régy had urged—solely on the performance.

Two things, however, were certain.

First, about a half hour into the show (it happened each night I was there), a handful of frustrated viewers got up from their seats and exited the large auditorium; from then on, a dribble of early departures took place with each brief pause in the stage proceedings. Although they tried to be unobtrusive, these defectors stirred up enough distraction to make complete concentration by the rest of us all the harder to sustain. Second, virtually all who did stay to the very end—around 95 percent of a house that holds about 850 patrons—showed strong enthusiasm for the work with exuberant final applause and multiple shouts of "Bravo!" We were, I think, deeply aware that the French actress whom Susan Sontag once extolled as "a total artist" and "an actor of unlimited ability"[15] had just given us—in her New York stage debut—an unparalleled, indeed, a historic performance.

A flawless mating of actor and role

The house lights dim to black. When the glaring stage lighting comes on, Huppert, immobile, has her feet planted floor center. (There is no raised stage at the Harvey.) She rivets her demonic gaze, half glazed, half ferociously alert, on the space directly opposite her (audience center). Behind her is a sparkling charcoal-gray scrim through which we hazily glimpse, stage right, a male figure dressed in an orange T-shirt and red pants. Huppert, her ash-blond hair tautly drawn into a short ponytail, wears a skintight royal blue T-shirt and black leather pants. With her arms stiffly hanging at her sides and her hands clenched, she maintains a slight forward bend in her shoulders (see fig. 2). This awkward stance accentuates the table-top flatness of her abdomen and the thinness of her entire body. Her

words will soon suggest that one of the conditions her character suffers from is anorexia nervosa: "I can't eat. . . . I am fat. . . . My hips are too big. . . . I dislike my genitals."[16]

Several times in the course of the evening she pivots her neck, just briefly, in order to gaze left or right. Every few minutes she extends a finger or two; at two moments of wild, angry emotion she splays both palms. Otherwise Huppert keeps to a state of near paralysis for the whole performance. Such a bravura feat of constrained athleticism gives savage expression to her character's unyielding intent to make her body implode. At the end of each New York performance (there were eleven) Huppert literally limped off stage, apparently having lost some circulation in her legs.

The spectral male figure, we soon infer, is sometimes the mouthpiece for an imagined psychiatric profession, sometimes the voice of a probable lover. Delivering less than 5 percent of Kane's text, he provides this production's only moments of live movement through space: several times he walks off to the wings only to return later to his usual spot, stage right. Both he and the fuzzy space he occupies seem to work mostly as externalizations of parts of the protagonist's troubled mindscape. This hyperminimalist staging deployed only two other visually arresting devices. Variously angled quadrilateral pools of yellow light surrounded Huppert's feet to mark many of the scene shifts, which were also punctuated by blackouts and recorded acoustic effects. More flashy were the repeated projections onto the huge scrim of seemingly random numerals, configured in depth and ranging from 2 through 100. These corresponded loosely to the flood of numbers that the female figure twice recites and whose meaning remains elusive; they may also relate to the passing of minutes toward the apocalyptic hour of 4:48 A.M. signaled by the play's title— a time of day which the speaker calls "the happy hour": the moment when "sanity," along with "desperation," "visits," and when "I shall hang myself / to the sound of my lover's breathing."[17]

. . .

True to his word, Claude Régy thus gave us little to focus on other than Huppert's face and speaking voice. And in some sense

(opposite) 2. *Isabelle Huppert's constrained athleticism in Claude Régy's production of Sarah Kane's 4.48 Psychosis. Photo © Pascal Victor/ArtComArt.*

the director was quite right. For regardless of whether or not you knew French, Huppert's unmiked vocal apparatus fashioned a sound sculpture that was as aurally affecting and emotionally unsettling as a Schoenberg song cycle or monodrama. You ignored it at your peril: it was basically the whole show. At first Huppert's slow monotone and ultraprecise articulation of discrete syllables suggested a digitally simulated voice. Soon the voice exhibited mounting anger against the ogling, diagnosing shrinks who forever claim to have "secret knowledge of my aching shame." Later in the piece—which juxtaposes poetic imagery, seemingly random snatches of conversations, and repeated clusters of verbs or nouns that defy logical understanding—Huppert accelerated to an astounding velocity as her character detailed, fiendishly and caustically, the drugs she receives or administers to herself on the sly: "Melleril, 50mg. . . . Lofepramine, 70mg, increased to 140mg, then 210mg. . . . Fluoxetine hydrochloride, trade name Prozac, 20mg, increased to 40mg. . . . Thorazine, 100mg. . . . 100 aspirin and one bottle of Bulgarian Cabernet Sauvignon, 1986."[18] All the while, our eyes stayed fixed on Isabelle Huppert's mesmerizing face: the pale skin, the high cheekbones, the impossibly wide mouth, the upper lip that curls lazily beyond the lower to result in the famous Huppert pout.

It was a familiar face. Most of us knew it well from three decades of movies, in many of which she also plays women who go insane— such as Claude Goretta's *La dentellière* (*The Lacemaker*, 1977), the film that brought Huppert to international attention; Claude Chabrol's *Madame Bovary* (1991) and *Merci pour le chocolat* (*Nightcap*, 2000); and Michael Haneke's *La pianiste* (*The Piano Teacher*, 2001). But at the same time we were watching a cryptic face, one that seemed to be as absent as it was present, as coolly distant as it was burningly intimate. Indeed, what we saw and heard at the Harvey Theater was perhaps the quintessential Huppert, a near-flawless mating of actress and role. For just as Sarah Kane refuses to let us know the events that led to her protagonist's psychosis, so Huppert, as she so often does in her films, stimulated our curiosity about this woman whose agony she was embodying while simultaneously deepening the mystery that surrounds the character—and the performer.

Too elitist for Brooklyn?

Huppert was fully in sync with Régy, who first directed her in a 1991 Opéra Bastille production of Paul Claudel and Arthur Honegger's stage oratorio *Jeanne d'Arc au bûcher* (*Joan of Arc at the Stake*). At a preperformance dialogue with *4.48 psychose* ticket holders at BAM, Régy (using a translator) noted: "I always say that if an actor is incapable of being and not being at the same time, he won't do anything interesting."[19] In this regard the Régy-Huppert-Kane combination made perfect artistic sense. But it did frustrate many reviewers. A *New York Times* critic, skeptical about whether Kane's extraordinary text can ever be adequately transposed to the stage, chided Régy for the inherent contradiction between, on one hand, his professed aim of "intimacy" between actor and audience and, on the other, the limits on genuine "communication" that his decision about partial English supertitles imposed.[20] *Time Out New York*'s Adam Feldman decried Régy's "arrogant textual chop job" that left the production, for non-French speakers, "infuriatingly opaque."[21] While acknowledging Huppert as "mesmerizing," Frank Scheck in the *New York Post* compared the audience "desperately casting glances at the overhead screen" to "commuters at Penn Station awaiting train information."[22]

Régy defended his dramaturgic vision with eloquence and conviction. "I focus on writing [*écriture*] and language," he said at the pre-show event. "This isn't the only way to conceive of theatre. But it's mine." Moreover, he asserted, "the living matter of writing is not written." With references to the poet Rainer Maria Rilke, the painter Paul Cézanne, the playwright-novelist Marguerite Duras, and others, Régy argued that the heart of language resides in what is inexpressible and immaterial, in a kind of "mysterious black matter" that lies between words and does not depend on words. "That's why I took the risk of furnishing few supertitles in *4.48 psychose*. . . . To limit yourself to words is to skirt the essential."[23] As he puts it in the French TV documentary *Claude Régy, le passeur* (Claude Régy: The Enabler, 1997) that was screened in Manhattan as part of ACT FRENCH, "It's a question of searching out the writer's state of mind before he or she even writes a word; only when you listen to the silences, to the pre-text [*le pré-écrit*] can you start to discover how to actually speak the words."[24]

Claude Régy's decades-long contribution to expanding the bounds of theatre in France has been enormous. The many dramatists whose "silences" have spoken to Régy, and whose works he has almost single-handedly introduced to French audiences through his state-supported company Ateliers Contemporains, include Duras, Nathalie Sarraute, Harold Pinter, Tom Stoppard, David Storey, Peter Handke, Botho Strauss, Edward Bond, and David Harrower. Yet his perceived arrogance in New York City surely added fuel to those on this side of the Atlantic who too hastily choose to view the French, both in the arts and in politics, as puffed-up elitists.

But one can just as easily argue that Régy's stubbornness is a mark of artistic integrity. As he once put it: "Theatre is useless unless it incorporates an inscrutable explosive—something incomprehensible. Theatre must be the vehicle for an act of concentrated resistance, both more violent and more tranquil than common rational discourse."[25] In other words Régy, at BAM, was conducting business as usual. Indeed, he belongs to an extraordinary group of established senior stage directors in France—Roger Planchon (d. 2009), Peter Brook, Ariane Mnouchkine, Georges Lavaudant, Bernard Sobel, André Engel—who came of age in the 1960s and 1970s and conceived of themselves, in varying ways, as "complete" theatre artists, as high-concept director-*auteurs*. Their revitalization of the French stage was sweeping. But it often came, as numerous theatre historians have noted, "at the expense of every other participant in the theatrical enterprise: writers, actors, designers, technicians, and audiences."[26]

The palpable stamp of great performers

Taken together, Ariane Mnouchkine's and Claude Régy's programs brought to ACT FRENCH exemplary instances of the director as *auteur*, the director as star. Nevertheless, the three internationally famous performers who lent so much glamour to ACT FRENCH also imposed themselves above and beyond directorial constraints. Marie-France Pisier drew on a deep personal identification with her subject to vivify little-known facets of Simone de Beauvoir's life and personality. We could sit in the hall and listen to Beauvoir's words with our eyes closed and still feel the subtle power of the actress's performance. It was, in effect, Beauvoir's voice *through* Pisier. Patrice Chéreau's broadly physical reading of Dostoyevsky may have struck purists as self-indulgent. Yet the actor-director gave us a delightfully fresh, highly visual portrayal of the Underground Man. We had to listen with our eyes as well as with our ears. It was, so to speak, Dostoyevsky *plus* the showman Chéreau.

In the case of Isabelle Huppert, it was almost as if she succeeded—both with and in spite of Claude Régy's help—at channeling Sarah Kane's creative psyche. Kane's protagonist was at once identical to and bursting out of Huppert-the-actress. We needed our ears. We needed our eyes. But we also needed to feel within our gut the agony, terror, and despair of one woman's pain. Here was contemporary French theatre at its most visceral and perhaps its most darkly beautiful.

 **Three
Fresh
Voices**

Playwrights and ethnicity

It is frequently said that the promise of contemporary American theatre lies in the creative hands and minds of our nation's minorities. The contributions of African American, Asian American, Latino, gay, and feminist playwrights have, indeed, over the past several decades transformed and revitalized the American theatrical landscape, be it within local communities, nonprofit regional centers, or the commercial mainstream, including Broadway. The same cannot be said regarding the impact on the overall French theatre scene of France's major ethnic minorities: its blacks (mostly of sub-Saharan and Caribbean family background), its *beurs* (of North African family origin), its Asians, and its Portuguese (the latter is the nation's largest recent immigrant group).

If France does not have obvious equivalents for an August Wilson, a Suzan-Lori Parks, or a David Henry Hwang, it is partly because French society has traditionally kept a lid on American-style identity politics and on the radical questioning and constant revisions of what it might mean to be a French citizen within a multiethnic society. This reticence is now changing. Frédéric Martel—who has studied the ways in which American cultural practices can provide useful new models for the French—notes with respect to government-supported French theatre: "The defenders of [artistic, noncommercial] French theatre must set off again to connect with ordinary people and make cultural diversity a reality. . . . It is no longer possible to ignore this public, to be deprived of its talents, and to refuse its stories."[1]

ACT FRENCH included three notable French-language playwrights whom some Americans—and French—would be inclined, perhaps a bit too swiftly, to classify as "black authors": Koffi Kwahulé, Marie

NDiaye, and José Pliya. The French until recently consigned writers such as these to the somewhat condescending category of '*francophone* literature.' Yet what is especially intriguing about this trio of dramatists is their shared ambivalence with respect to the very concept of black identity and to the supposed impact of one's ethnicity on one's art—a guardedness that marks them in today's changing social climate as very French and very contemporary.

In part 2 of this book we will examine other aspects of the growing minority presence, including that of *beurs*, within today's French theatrescape. By highlighting in this chapter some of the paradoxes surrounding these three major midcareer playwrights, we will see that the realization of Martel's call for a culturally diverse French theatre *à l'américaine* is not so straightforward as might be hoped for.

Koffi Kwahulé

Five young brunettes in blue jeans, sneakers, and white T-shirts position themselves behind a horizontal row of black metal music stands. They are inmates of a prison for the criminally insane. To their left is another woman, a blonde in a tailored black suit. She is the instructor-therapist who comes each week to help them put on a play. To their right, supposedly in Room 119, sits a cellist who repeatedly plunks and bows a haunting eight-note motif from *Misterioso*, the 1958 Thelonious Monk composition described by the inmates as "a chant luring death to our door."

The published French-language text of Koffi Kwahulé's *Misterioso-119* gives neither the number nor the names of the characters and is devoid of stage directions.[2] But distinct personalities rapidly insinuate themselves through the recurrent shotgun articulation of obsessive thoughts: breasts that are too large; a wish to emigrate to America; a violent, bloody loss of virginity; a delusional desire to care for children in a nursery school. The choral effect of these quick, brief exclamations is reinforced visually by the actors who repeatedly raise and lower, in unison, their music stands; it is counterbalanced by lengthier, more lyrical monologues/solos and two-voiced scenes/duets. Little by little we come to understand that each of these women was a victim of extreme trauma and each went on to commit heinous crimes, including infanticide. We also discover—and this provides the play's dramatic arc—that the most vocal and aggressively charismatic of the inmates has developed a crush on the instructor; that the instructor has reciprocal feelings, tinged with dark masochism; and that the teacher virtually facilitates her own murder/self-sacrifice by the young woman who, in a communal shower scene at the play's end, joins her fellow inmates in disposing of the corpse, partly through a rhapsodic, cannibalistic feasting on select parts.

• • •

ACT FRENCH's sponsorship of a plan to bring about the first English-language version of this powerful new play by Koffi Kwahulé (b. 1956, in Abengourou, Ivory Coast) was international in the fullest sense of the term. Kwahulé's more than twenty-five French-language theatre pieces include such prizewinners as *La dame du café d'en face* (1994) and *P'tite-souillure* (2002). His works have been produced in places as diverse as India, Denmark, Canada, Poland, and Hungary. Monologues from his plays are reportedly among "the most performed audition pieces for entrance into Paris's National Theatre Conservatory."[3] Yet until recently Kwahulé was barely known in the United States. In 2005, *Misterioso-119*—commissioned by the Théâtre National de Bretagne—had yet to have a full production in any language.

Auspiciously, in the spring of that year the New York–based Lark Play Development Center lent its assistance to the Montreal-born playwright Chantal Bilodeau to begin work on a first-draft translation of *Misterioso-119*. Then, in late August, Kwahulé, who mainly resides in France, joined Bilodeau, as well as the stage director Liesl Tommy (originally from South Africa) and a group of six ethnically varied U.S. actors, at the Berkshire (Massachusetts) Theatre Festival for two weeks of intense collaboration and several public readings under ACT FRENCH's auspices. Finally, in late October the New York Theatre Workshop (in the East Village) and the Lark Center (on Eighth Avenue and Fifty-fifth Street) staged, in their rehearsal studios, public readings of Bilodeau's polished translation, with Kwahulé in attendance. These New York readings were riveting. They hatched a more ambitious Lark project, now completed, to have Bilodeau translate and publish seven of Kwahulé's plays.[4] In conjunction with that undertaking, a staged reading of *That Old Black Magic* (*Cette vieille magique noire*, 1993) took place at the Lark in May 2010 and a month later the

Harlem School of the Arts presented *Bintou* (1999), Kwahulé's most frequently performed piece.

Beyond "otherness"

As an African writing in French and living in metropolitan France, Koffi Kwahulé has given much thought to issues of personal identity and assimilation/integration and how they affect him as an artist. "The posture I've adopted," he explained in New York, "is to keep myself somewhat removed from specific cultural pigeonholing. . . . The truth is that, for me, the French language is simply an instrument, like a piano, which I bring to new life through my own theatrical language, a language that is always 'elsewhere.'"[5] When I asked him about the implications of the inmates' being played in this production by New York actresses of Asian, African, and Hispanic descent, and the sole figure of authority's being clearly marked in appearance as European American, Kwahulé responded that this was accidental and irrelevant: "If all the actors are white, black, or yellow, it wouldn't make a difference. My play can be done by any ethnicity and it will, I hope, always be the same story."[6]

A year later Kwahulé joined such literary lights as Edouard Glissant, Nancy Huston, Dany Laferrière, Wajdi Mouawad, and Dai Sijie in publicly repudiating the terms *'francophone'* and *'francophonie'* as patronizing vestiges of a defunct French colonizing mentality. Instead, these multinational authors advocated the notion of a transnational "world literature written in French" (*"une littérature-monde en langue française"*).[7] The urgency for this change in nomenclature was vividly demonstrated, they noted, by the fact that in fall 2005 non-Hexagon-born authors won five of France's seven major book prizes.

In this context Kwahulé is representative of a trend that links numerous contemporary playwrights from Africa and the Caribbean who write in French. In the 1980s many black *"francophone"* dramatists consciously sought to break with European theatrical models, which they viewed as a constraining legacy of colonization, in order to develop an aesthetic of specifically African "otherness." Such writers as Niangoran Porquet (Ivory Coast), Werewere Liking (Cameroon), and Sony Labou Tansi (Congo) preferred to take inspiration from the communal traditions of African storytelling or local ethnic folklore or sacred ritual; they would frequently violate the rules of "standard" French vocabulary and syntax, as well as conventional Western dramatic forms, in their efforts to assert specific collective identities.

As of the mid-1990s, however, a new generation of playwrights—Kwahulé, Kossi Efoui (Togo), Gerty Dambury (Guadeloupe), Moussa Konaté (Mali), and others—has chosen to emphasize individual destinies and ordinary lives while continuing to experiment formally. In their search for personal artistic voice and vision they have un-self-consciously drawn on a multiplicity of widely known national heritages ranging from ancient Greek mythology to Noh theatre to the French Symbolist poets to Hollywood cinema. The result has been what one scholar has playfully called "the Frankenstein syndrome"—a hybrid theatre in which dream, myth, and invention are deployed without explicit reference to a tangible patrimony or, for European audiences, to a reassuring "Africanness."[8] As Kwahulé told the Lark Center audience: "Even though I don't speak English, my plays have a rhythm and phrasing that's akin to American English. It comes, I think, from my lifelong exposure to Hollywood movies."[9]

Still, an African-inflected dimension inheres in all of Kwahulé's work. "My ideal writer," he says, "is [Thelonious] Monk."[10] In fact, the form and feel, the syncopated sounds and repeated rhythms of *Misterioso-119* are perhaps best appreciated as a tribute to African American blues and bebop. This is why many who attended the New York readings, myself included, felt that a more elaborate mise-en-scène of this chamber work might needlessly distract from its central attraction—the pulsating musicality of the text as delivered by the performers and heard and felt by its audience. Like most of Kwahulé's oeuvre, the piece is a fine specimen of theatre of *la parole*, or theatre of the word—a mode of writing and performance that we will explore in greater depth in chapters 4 and 8.

France glorious, France wrongful

Many themes in *Misterioso-119*—marginalization, immigration, exile, incarceration—are similar to those that were treated with more geopolitical grounding by previous generations of so-called black *francophone* playwrights. This politically engagé theatre tradition embraces the Martinique-born Aimé Césaire (*Une saison au*

Congo [*A Season in the Congo*], 1966), the Congolese Maxime N'Debeka (*Le président* [The President], 1970), and the Ivorians Bernard Dadié (*Monsieur Thôgô-Gnini*, 1970) and Bernard Zadi Zaourou (*L'oeil* [*The Eye*], 1983)—to name just a few. By contrast Kwahulé chooses to develop his social and political themes in what one commentator aptly calls "a fantasy space, a space of metaphor."[11] Bolstering his turn toward "a theatre made of hybrid constructs and collages,"[12] however, is a thorough mindfulness of the African diaspora "with its history of surviving kidnapping, rape, and violent resettling."[13] Indeed, Kwahulé's capacity to engage in a "transnational" theatre—whereby the time-honored nexus of a particular language and a particular nation and its culture no longer obtains—would probably not be possible without the efforts of earlier dramatists and other "*francophone*" artists, activists, and scholars who succeeded at raising Europeans' (and of course French people's) consciousness of their countries' central and not at all metaphoric role in the history of modern slavery and colonization.

Several real-world events occurring near the time of the ACT FRENCH festival reflect this overall climate of increased enlightenment in France. In late January 2006, for example, President Jacques Chirac invited to the Elysée Palace the Comité pour la mémoire de l'esclavage (Committee for the Commemoration of Slavery), headed by the Guadeloupe-born novelist-activist Maryse Condé (b. 1937). The head of state seized this moment to announce that May 10—the date on which France's parliament had voted, in 2001, to treat slavery and slave trading as "crimes against humanity"—would henceforth be a day of national observance for what he called the "indelible stain" of slavery on France's history.[14] Chirac had already been the first French president to acknowledge, in 1995, France's responsibility in the deportation of Jews during World War II, and he was the first to pay official homage, in 2004, to the contributions of African-born soldiers during the Liberation period. This remarkable creation of a commemorative day for slavery put an end to a controversy that had erupted when a law passed by Chirac's own majority party on February 23, 2005, called for history syllabi in the schools to give special attention to "the positive role" of France's overseas presence—an embarrassing clause Chirac eventually managed to get annulled. As the president made clear in proclaiming the new May 10 observance: "A great nation must assume responsibility for its entire history. The glorious moments, but also the wrongful."[15]

The 2005 suburban riots

At the very time that ACT FRENCH was moving into high gear—with over twenty different events scheduled for November—a gripping drama of a less than glorious nature was being enacted on the suburban streets of France's major cities. In the longest stretch of civil unrest since the student protests of 1968, young people from multiethnic urban outskirts (*les banlieues*) and government housing projects (*les cités*) torched cars and buses (1,408 on the night of November 6 alone); vandalized local schools, town halls, and businesses; and ambushed police officers and firefighters. The Théâtre de Louvrais, a popular theatre in the northern suburb of Pontoise, suffered serious damage when a car smashed through its front door. This largely uncoordinated outpouring of violence was triggered by the accidental deaths from electrocution of two teenage boys—one of Mauritanian and the other of Tunisian origin—who were allegedly fleeing random police checks in the Paris suburb of Clichy-sous-Bois (Seine-Saint-Denis).

For many observers, especially among the foreign press, the spontaneous turmoil that spread throughout the nation was the result of long-simmering anger and frustration on the part of French Arabs and French Africans "who have found themselves caught for three generations in a trap of ethnic and religious discrimination."[16] The parents and grandparents of these youngsters had been led to believe that the route to a fulfilling life was to embrace the republican ideal of French citizenship—a lofty abstraction that refuses to concede ethnic, religious, and cultural differences in the public domain. Yet the long-standing realities of de facto ghettoization, job discrimination, severe unemployment, and chronic police harassment have made many young French citizens feel scorned and cut off from traditional French society, with little hope for inclusion and a better future.

Unlike the U.S. race riots of the 1960s, this season of unrest was not being propelled by subcultural agendas according to which categories like "black" or "brown" or "Muslim" were being exalted as "better" or "beautiful." The message instead was that the sound of one's name, the color of one's skin, the place where one does or does not worship, must *in practice as well as in theory* become irrelevant to being treated as fully French.[17]

The riots and Kwahulé's Jaz

On the second evening after the riots began, some of us on this side of the Atlantic were vicariously immersed in the gritty feel and rancid smells of life in a French suburban housing project. As a windup to New York University's ACT FRENCH–related Symposium on Francophone Theatre, the Caribbean-born dramatist-director Gerty Dambury (b. 1957) gave a reading in French of Kwahulé's *Jaz* (1998). In this dramatic verse monologue, a young woman, Jaz, describes being raped at knifepoint by a thirtysomething married neighbor in a public toilet that she and others regularly use because of the broken plumbing in her apartment building. Referring to herself mainly in the third person, Jaz vividly evokes both the assault and her plan to murder the aggressor; or perhaps, we are led to think, she has already done so. Kwahulé's imagery, as in *Misterioso-119*, is graphic. The delicate, beautiful Jaz is described as "emerging like a lotus" from "a place where everyone wades in his own shit."[18] But also like *Misterioso-119*, any trait that might point to a specific race or ethnicity is absent. The *cité* itself goes unnamed, and its topography is fanciful: Yolk of the Egg Street, Incense Boulevard, the Hide Your Joy district.

Dambury chose to have her audience at the Maison Française sit in total darkness as she, unseen and apart, read Kwahulé's forty-page script into a microphone from an alcove adjacent to the conference hall. This inspired *mise en lecture* caused us to focus on the transcendence that the dramatist (in clear homage to Toni Morrison's 1992 novel, *Jazz*) grants his protagonist through the very act of her efforts to speak and to give personal, jazzlike voice to her horrific experience. Jaz's body may be forever ravaged, but the music of her speech—moving in and out of past, present, and future—guarantees her lasting humanity. Dambury's antistaging was thus, almost to an ironic extreme, in full accord with what Kwahulé refers to as his color-blind project of "de-racialization": "If I speak forcefully about humanity, I am necessarily speaking forcefully about Blacks."[19]

Context, however, has a way of trumping intentions. Those of us who shared in this commanding performance could not factor out our knowledge of the skin color and geographic origin of the actress on the other side of the wall; or of those of the author seated with us in the shadows; or of the specifically ethnic, as well as social and economic, factors that were giving rise to the scattershot violence in France's *cités* that very night. Nor should we have. As the scholar Sylvie Chalaye noted in a lecture delivered earlier that day, the poetics of Kwahulé and his contemporaries "feeds on difference and alterity"; it "assumes the hybrid nature of colonial history" even as it "switches it around in strong new inventive ways"; and it "forces [people] to be responsible when confronted with history's mass graves."[20]

At the end of a published essay on the symbolic weight of the black female body in much contemporary French African and French Caribbean theatre, Chalaye puts the matter more bluntly: "In these plays bodies incarnate power struggles that go back to the dawn of time. Sexual aggression becomes emblematic of ontological aggression, the aggression that involves possession of the other, appropriation of their bodies, an occupation, a colonization." The rape in *Jaz*, she specifies with perhaps a touch of overstatement, "dramatizes the historical rape of all peoples who have endured genocide and [colonial/diasporic] acculturation."[21]

Marie NDiaye and the inhumane possession of the Other

It is tempting to apply some of Chalaye's ideas to Marie NDiaye's *Hilda*—an ACT FRENCH event in American translation (by Erika Rundle) that began its month-long run at the 59E59 Theaters a few days later that November. Originally mounted at the Théâtre de l'Atelier in 2002, *Hilda* tells the story of an unhappy, well-off housewife, Madame Lemarchand, who hires a local woman sight unseen to be her domestic maid and nanny largely because she is enchanted by the sound of her name, "Hilda." For ninety minutes we observe the Machiavellian Lemarchand as she wields her economic superiority over Hilda's working-class husband, Franck Meyer, sadistically and lewdly alienates Hilda from her spouse and children, and seemingly demolishes Hilda's sense of identity as well as her own, succumbing in the end to a near-psychotic state in which she can barely differentiate herself from her servant. Perhaps the best evidence for what Chalaye calls "ontological aggression" lies in the striking fact that the title character has no lines and never appears on stage. Hilda is the play's all-pervading referent, but she is voiceless and disembodied from the start.

Hilda is clearly a play about bodily appropriation, symbolic rape, and inhumane "possession of the Other" (Chalaye's term). Yet is it a play about race? Marie NDiaye (b. 1967) is not from Africa or the Caribbean. She was born in Pithiviers, central France, to a white mother and a black Senegalese father, and she grew up in a middle-class neighborhood outside Paris. NDiaye sometimes identifies as a "*métisse*," a woman of mixed race. Although the term '*métis(se)*' is not widely used in France, she has asserted that this identity contributes to her overall sense of "*étrangeté*," or otherness. It is a difference she embraces, she says, "not in a sorrowful way, but simply as an objective reality"—likening it to that of being a writer "in a society where most people are not."[22]

With respect to *Hilda*, NDiaye acknowledges that "I wanted first to write about slavery, but I didn't want to write a historical play. So I thought about relationships based on power: the power of one human being over another human being."[23] Still, Frédéric Ferney, who reviewed *Hilda*'s Paris premiere for the daily newspaper *Le Figaro*, could not resist labeling the dramatist as racially "other." He opined, rather presumptuously: "Marie NDiaye is black: the ancestral memory of slavery, the Black Code [Louis XIV's notorious edict on blacks in French America], the slave trade. All this scars her, hurts her, and leaves a knife in her heart."[24]

In point of fact *Hilda* is explicitly about class, not race. As written, Franck and Hilda are, like Madame Lemarchand, in no way marked as persons of color.[25] The play directly assails the *gauche caviar*, or "limousine liberals" who advertise their leftist credentials while exploiting and belittling the underprivileged from whom they extort respect. Lemarchand tells Franck early on, with patronizing politeness: "I don't whip or injure Hilda. . . . And I try to like her, and even to speak to her. She gets ten dollars an hour."[26] Yet later, when she informs a dumbfounded Franck that she plans to loan Hilda and her services to some friends, Madame spouts vitriol: "Your kind of people are filled with this atrocious sense of entitlement [*cet affreux esprit d'assistés*] and you're constantly begging, without even being aware of it. . . . You have no sense of duty or indebtedness."[27]

To be sure, this is the kind of crypto-racist/xenophobic language some French people were cavalierly applying to the youngsters rioting in the *banlieues* that November. However, for all its sociopolitical resonance, *Hilda*, much like Kwahulé's *Jaz*, is not a naturalistic portrayal of everyday social relations. The work's dramatic power results more emphatically from the morbid psychosexual hold that Hilda and her employer exert on each other, conveyed by the mounting gothic, almost neo-expressionistic attention NDiaye allots to such intimate matters as clothing, hair, hygiene, and birth control. This unsettling mind-body dynamic may, to borrow Chalaye's words, "go back to the dawn of time." But it pertains less obviously to racial "genocide" and imposed mass "acculturation" than to an obsessive, archaic, and perhaps even universal human bent toward one-on-one vampirism—a thematic strain found in many of NDiaye's works.

• • •

Explicit evocations of race are by no means absent from Marie NDiaye's substantial body of theatre and prose fiction. In the author's presence, and as part of the Play Company's New Work/New World Series, ACT FRENCH coordinated a staged reading of several scenes from *Papa doit manger (Papa's Got to Eat)* in a translation-in-progress, again by Erika Rundle. Pigmentation and the clichés it provokes are a central matter in this story of a black African father's return to the Courbevoie (Hauts-de-Seine) apartment of his white French wife and two mixed-race daughters after a ten-year abandonment. "This absolute, imperious tint of my skin gives me the advantage over dull skin like yours," the father boasts to one of his daughters at the play's start.[28] Yet Papa's pridefulness is ambiguous: it may partly be a defense against admitting his failure to have integrated into a discriminatory French social system, and it may partly be a response to what we progressively discover to be the near-pathological racism of his in-laws; but it may also have less to do with matters of specific flesh tone than with a sense of disenfranchisement shared by virtually *all* of the play's cruel, soulless characters regardless of their color.

In 2003 *Papa doit manger* was incorporated into the repertory of the Comédie-Française, making NDiaye the youngest playwright and only the second female author (the other is Marguerite Duras) to have a work mounted on the Comédie-Française's main stage in the venerable Salle Richelieu. Famously, it prompted the company to appoint as a *pensionnaire*, or junior member, its first black actor, the Malian-born but French-trained Bakary Sangaré (b. 1964), who took on the title role. (Sangaré had performed throughout the 1990s with Peter Brook at his Paris-based International Center for Theatre Research.) Since then NDiaye—especially in such novels as *Trois femmes puissantes* (Three Strong Women, 2009) and in her debut screenplay *White Material* (2010, directed by Claire Denis and starring Isabelle Huppert)—has fashioned plots in which mixed-race relationships occur more frequently and more matter-of-factly. She has also reluctantly become more outspoken about French society and politics.

As a preface to *La condition noire: essai sur une minorité française* (The Black Condition: An Essay on a French Minority Group, 2008), the first major study of the status of blacks in France—written by Marie's brother, the historian Pap Ndiaye (*sic*)—NDiaye penned a story, "Les soeurs" ("The Sisters"), about two mixed-race siblings: one light-skinned, capable of "passing," yet full of self-loathing; the other dark-toned, subject to discrimination, but able to succeed socially and professionally.[29] The following year, in response to a cultural magazine interviewer's question concerning France under President Sarkozy, NDiaye asserted that she, her husband (the novelist Jean-Yves Cendrey), and their three (biracial) children had moved to Berlin two years earlier in part because she found France's current social climate "monstrous," with its right-wing politicians embodying "stupidity" and "a denial of difference."[30] When just weeks later she won the Prix Goncourt, France's highest literary award, for *Trois femmes puissantes*, a number of male politicians chided her for having transgressed the supposed professional obligation of "verbal restraint" ("*réserve*") that becomes a Goncourt laureate—even though the interview took place well before the granting of the award and even though this so-called *devoir de réserve*, while possibly applicable to certain government functionaries, has no bearing on the Republic's writers. The media tried to spin the subsequent noise into a clash about freedom of expression (which it was), but the matter came to a halt when NDiaye generously conceded in a radio interview on Europe 1 that her remarks may have been "excessive" and when Eric Raoult, the most vexed of the UMP parliamentarians, allowed in turn that all he really hoped for was "moderation," not "silence."[31] Still, NDiaye found it telling and troubling that Frédéric Mitterrand, then Sarkozy's recently appointed minister of culture, chose to remain neutral on the matter rather than rush to the artist's defense.[32]

The French literary critic Nelly Kaprièlian, who judges NDiaye to be "one of our greatest writers," defines the unusual place she occupies in contemporary culture in these terms: "NDiaye grapples with what most of today's French writers condescendingly refuse to admit: the biases of class and race, and the power imbalances that get played out within families. . . . In an ocean of tasteful, well-mannered, and sentimental literature, NDiaye's texts seem to be among the only ones that stay connected to life as it is."[33]

José Pliya

"I was born in Benin [West Africa]; I am a French citizen who was educated in the French language; I have an affinity for Spanish speakers; and I have spent a lot of time in Anglophone countries; so all these paths make up my history and enrich my world, my imagination, and my authorial voice. . . . I am not so much a writer who is 'in-between' ['*entre-deux*'] as one who is 'multiply in-between' ['*entre-multiple*']."[34] Thus asserts José Pliya (b. 1966), another leading black contemporary French-language playwright. He is the son of Jean Pliya (b. 1931), the West African statesman, dramatist, fiction writer, and evangelical preacher. Unlike his father—whose best-known plays, *Kondo, le requin* (Kondo, the Shark, 1966) and *La secrétaire particulière* (Private Secretary, 1973), deal with national history and local politics—José Pliya positions himself within broader, transnational contexts. He in fact holds a doctorate in modern literature from the University of Lille (France); he headed the Alliances Françaises of North Cameroon and of Dominica (Windward Islands, West Indies); he founded the Franco-Creole Theatre Festival of the Caribbean; and since July 2005 he has been the artistic director of L'artchipel, scène nationale de la Guadeloupe (Leeward Islands, West Indies).

Although his work has received accolades in Africa, Europe, and the Caribbean, José Pliya is little known in the United States. ACT FRENCH remedied this gap by sponsoring—in cooperation with the

SoHo Think Tank, the Ohio Theatre, and the project's mastermind, Professor Philippa Wehle of Purchase College of the State University of New York—a weeklong Pliya festival in early November. It included staged readings in American translation of *Une famille ordinaire* (*An Ordinary Family*, 2001), *Nous étions assis sur le rivage du monde . . .* (*We Were Sitting on the Shores of the World . . .*, 2003), and *Cannibales* (*Cannibals*, 2004), as well as a full French-language production imported from Paris's Théâtre du Lucernaire: *Le complexe de Thénardier* (*Trapped*, 2001).

Le complexe de Thénardier won the 2003 Prix du Jeune Théâtre de l'Académie Française (the French Academy Younger Playwright Prize). It was first mounted in Paris at the elegant Théâtre du Rond-Point in November 2002 as part of the inaugural season of that theatre's new artistic director, Jean-Michel Ribes. Ribes's mission was and remains to showcase living playwrights—a choice that was in part a response to a decadelong trend of producing perhaps to excess the works of a recently deceased troika of younger (white) French writers for the stage: Bernard-Marie Koltès (d. 1989), Jean-Luc Lagarce (d. 1995), and Didier-Georges Gabily (d. 1996). Ribes's selection of an African-born artist, plus his decision to direct the play himself, thus carried substantial symbolic weight. "What I find astonishing about José Pliya," Ribes told an interviewer at the time, "is that he is shaped by the traditions of Benin . . . but at the same time he is very Western."[35]

In public, Pliya—much like Koffi Kwahulé—underscores the universal character of his writings: "I make no claim to be able to speak for any one color, or for any one country, but, rather, I speak of the human being, of, quite simply, being human."[36] Yet—like Marie NDiaye—he often deploys themes in his works that either explicitly or implicitly, at times centrally and at other times peripherally, relate to ethnicity, diaspora, and postcolonialism.

Moral order in crisis

A one-act play for two characters, *Le complexe de Thénardier* takes place in a rat-infested middle-class home in a nameless country racked by years of civil war and genocide. It depicts the struggle of a young woman, Vido, to take physical and emotional leave of her demanding mistress, La Mère (The Mother), who long ago granted the girl political refuge and domestic work. Because La Mère's identity has become defined by her power over this individual, she refuses to give her blessing to Vido's wishes.

Pliya claims that his breakthrough in writing this piece did not occur until he was on the phone with his own mother, a real-life source for the fictional La Mère, and the two of them started speaking in Fon, an indigenous language of southern Benin: "I'd been writing the character in French, when she really should have been speaking Fon. I suddenly realized that what I needed to do was to translate the musicality of Fon into French."[37] The name 'Vido' is in fact an abbreviation of 'Vidomingon,' which in Fon means 'hired girl.'[38] Yet as Pliya told the audience after one New York performance, the play's content probably owes a lot to such European stage archetypes as Medea, Antigone, and Brecht's Mother Courage. While the names of La Mère's unseen children, 'Igor' and 'Snéjana,' may lead us to imagine that the action takes place in post-Soviet Eastern Europe, Pliya insists on his piece's "de-localization": "It doesn't matter which war is going on. What matters are the human truths beneath appearances and the dramatic forces that are at work."[39]

The production at the Ohio Theatre (on Wooster Street in SoHo) was directed by Vincent Colin. It featured Sylvie Chenus as La Mère and Hyam Zaytoun as Vido. Carole China's supertitle design—in its visual clarity, viewer-friendly placement, and quality of translation (by Philippa Wehle and Ellen Lampert-Gréaux)—was the best of any ACT FRENCH event. The staging was aptly abstract and minimalist. Except for the blanket Vido placed over La Mère's corpse at the play's start (the story unfolds in flashback), the only major props were four low wooden stools whose spatial rearrangement from sequence to sequence seemed to mirror the progressively changing emotional dynamic between the two women. The actresses' bodies never touched except once near the end: La Mère, threatening to destroy Vido's identity papers and denounce her to the police, gingerly laid her hands on the young woman's shoulders—a gesture as condescending as it was pathetic. "I didn't save you, I exploited you," La Mère ultimately admits before ingesting rat poison. "I'm using you to fill up the breach of my own youth. That's why I can't let you leave."

This summary may make the play sound like it could be titled "Cosette's Excellent Revenge on Madame Thénardier"—the wicked innkeeper in Victor Hugo's *Les misérables* to which the play's actual title alludes. But Pliya urges that we not make too much of the literary reference; what is important in his version, he says, is that La Mère—who presumably once saved Vido from a barbaric death—"now becomes, because of her emotional overdependence on the ward [her 'Thénardier complex,' so to speak], her own self-executioner."[40] Moreover, at the play's end we have no assurance that the hesitant and perhaps delusional Vido will find the emancipation she has so mulishly pleaded for.

Such existential murkiness and open-ended ambiguity are found in many of José Pliya's works. They signal intriguing affinities with playwrights as varied as Sartre, Beckett, Koltès, and NDiaye. But for Ribes—whose Rond-Point production, with its angular neo-expressionistic set, was only a shade less spare than Colin's[41]—the disturbing and violent breakdown of moral order that suffuses *Le complexe de Thénardier* is at once "reminiscent of Greek tragedy" and evocative of something non-European. "Perhaps African writing [*les écritures africaines*]," Ribes suggests with well-intended idealism, "enables us to get to the heart of the question—with more courage, freshness, and clarity—of what human moral relations are all about."[42]

The universal horrors of evil

José Pliya's scope is certainly expansive. In *Une famille ordinaire* he treats the links between so-called "ordinary" family relations and the German genocide of European Jews during World War II. Pliya recalls initial reactions to his choice of subject: "Some people said that an African doesn't have the right to speak about this, because it doesn't concern him, it's not his story. Others said, 'You can't understand such suffering; had you written about Rwanda, well, that would have made more sense; but even then. . . .'"[43] Pliya did in fact consider treating the Rwandan tragedy but he found it "still too personally raw."[44] Moreover, he emphasizes, "no one has a monopoly on suffering and horror."[45]

Though I did not attend the New York reading-in-translation of *Une famille ordinaire*, I saw a full production a few months later in Paris at the Théâtre de la Tempête, which is part of the complex of theatres that, along with Théâtre du Soleil, inhabit the Vincennes Cartoucherie. The play's director, Isabelle Ronayette, and its designer,

Annabel Vergne, juxtaposed a horizontally elongated, ultranaturalistic set of the rambling Hamburg apartment the family occupies from 1939 to 1945 with, extreme stage left, a constantly running, vertically framed video projection that included street scenes of Hamburg today and shots of an elderly woman who represents the script's retrospective narrative voice, Vera—the little granddaughter we never see on stage. In its sustained multiplicity of time and space frames, this media mix resembled, on a magnified scale, the kind of hypertext experience we typically encounter on personal computer screens. It was a clever strategy for underscoring both the contemporary relevance of the play's subject (genocide) and the questionable reliability of certain efforts to research and report on it (the skepticism and vigilance that the use of web-based information calls for).

Indeed, the chill of Pliya's dramaturgy results from both the believability and the uncertainties that surround the play's account of unseen horrific events: the son's alleged slaughter of five hundred Jews from the Polish ghetto in Majdanek, done ostensibly to prove his manhood to his peevish father; the father's sexual acts with the son's frustrated wife, who initiates the encounter; the old man's decision to kill Vera's best friend, the Jewish girl from next door who has taken refuge in the family's apartment. This is theatre, of course, not documentary history. Pliya's aim (with a clear intellectual debt to Hannah Arendt's concept of the banality of evil and to the historian Daniel Goldhagen's *Hitler's Willing Executioners*)[46] is to show the potential for evil in us all—including himself: "I belong to the generation of the Rwandan genocide . . . a frightful reality that constantly forces me to reflect on the nature of evil, its mysteries, and its dark logic."[47] "*Une famille ordinaire*," Pliya candidly wrote in program notes for this production, "is *my* story; the story of *my* family viewed as if in a photo negative, in order to exorcise my grief, my evil."[48]

Skin tone on the world's shores

Personal circumstances also triggered a second Pliya play that enjoyed a reading during ACT FRENCH and a major production in Paris during my midwinter 2006 stay: *Nous étions assis sur le rivage du monde* . . . . When, in 2002, Pliya was an artist-in-residence at a cultural center in Fort-de-France, Martinique, one of his children—who is of mixed race—informed her parents that a classmate, Mélissa, had advised her not to play with black students since Pliya's daughter was obviously "above" them. Mélissa, it turned out, was herself a dark-skinned black. This self-hatred and the self-imposed apartheid it promotes were, Pliya realized, rampant among contemporary Martinicans and in fact had a centuries-long history. He decided to inject these themes into his work in progress.

"My plays," Pliya claims, "are neither white nor black. They are neutral [*incolores*]." [49] Yet skin *tone* is at the very heart of *Nous étions assis sur le rivage du monde* . . . . It depicts a fierce tug of war between The Woman, a cosmopolitan who has returned to the unidentified island of her youth, and The Man, who basks in the sun and informs The Woman that the familiar beach where she has come to swim—the Rivage du Monde (literally, the World's Shore)—is now a private space that is forbidden to her (see fig. 3). Why? Because, The Man eventually says, "You don't have the right skin color" (*"Vous n'avez pas la bonne couleur de peau"*). [50]

The play's Paris production took place at the Théâtre de la Cité Internationale after having had a run at Montreal's Festival du Théâtre des Amériques in May 2005. It was "world theatre written in French" in perhaps the best sense of the notion: authored by a Beninese; directed by a Québécois, Denis Marleau; and performed in Paris's fourteenth arrondissement by a quartet of actors hailing from Haiti, Martinique, and Guadeloupe. As The Man, the brawny, bald, and very dark-skinned Ruddy Sylaire dominated the stage, lolling and crawling about in swim trunks with the allure of a hungry bulldog ready to pounce. As The Woman, Nicole Dogué moved flowingly: her toasted-almond linen tank top and skirt draped her slender torso and limbs and blended with her café-au-lait complexion. Intensifying the actors' physical contrast was a raked stage that separated, along a razor-sharp horizontal midstage line, a spotless, bedazzling white beach and a perfect blue sky.

After the final dramatic climax, in which The Woman successfully fends off The Man's attempted rape, The Man, suddenly repentant, wonders: "Perhaps there's another solution . . . for colors and men . . . something other than separation." The Woman, however, refuses his invitation to remain and talk things through. As she takes her leave,

3. *Irreconcilable difference embodied by Ruddy Sylaire (The Man) and Nicole Dogué (The Woman) in José Pliya's* Nous étions assis sur le rivage du monde . . . , *directed by Denis Marleau. Photo © Victor Ponelli/ArtComArt.*

she asserts grimly: "There's no way out, no solution, no hope that the two of us will be able to sit down calmly, some day on the shores of the world. That's the way it is."[51] End of play.

Like many of Pliya's works, *Nous étions assis sur le rivage du monde . . .* depicts social injustice and the darkness of the human heart that seems to sustain it. But it offers no program for change. The night I saw it at the Théâtre de la Cité Internationale, a large number of *lycée* students, including many visibly belonging to ethnic minorities, were in attendance—a sure sign that the theatre's staff, then under the direction of Nicole Gauthier, had been actively engaged in school outreach. Still, in the light of the November 2005 suburban youth riots, the pessimism of The Woman's final words in Pliya's play is sobering.

Social theatre and minority youth

The spring 2006 issue of *Cassandre*, a quarterly that focuses on artistic activism, dealt exclusively with the crisis of the *banlieues*. In an interview with José Pliya, and with specific reference to *Nous étions assis sur le rivage du monde . . .* , a journalist queried the author about the apparent parallel between, on one hand, his play's depiction of "anti-light-tint" prejudice and, on the other, the "anti-white racism" that is often perceived as emanating from the *cités*. "Both phenomena," Pliya said, "are linked, in the sense that when you fabricate a separate space and make it an island, a day will come when the people on the other side of the island, on the other side of the barrier, will show up at your door and demand an explanation. In their torching of cars, the kids in the *banlieues* have been asking questions of those who occupy France's middle and upper regions—people who are more than happy to ignore them and to imagine they live on separate islands. . . . The republican ideal, which I strongly believe in, has grown weak. If the Republic doesn't find the way to understand what is happening, it will all start up again—and much more violently."[52]

• • •

Can theatre itself connect directly with France's outer-city underprivileged and make a difference for the better? A natural link between artistic enrichment and social progress has been axiomatic in much official French thinking since the Enlightenment and Revolution eras. As the nineteenth-century historian Jules Michelet memorably put it: "Place the arts in the hands of the people, and tyrants will quake."[53] From Jean Vilar's revival of the notion of a National Popular Theatre in the years immediately following World War II; to the many policies on regional artistic dispersion in the 1960s spearheaded by André Malraux, France's first minister of culture, and leading to the creation of first-rate theatres in such working-class Paris outskirts as Aubervilliers, Gennevilliers, Ivry, Nanterre, and Sartrouville; and on to the profuse financial stimulus for both the "major" and the "minor" arts by Jack Lang's Ministry of Culture in the 1980s and early 1990s, modern French cultural policy has had a messianic inspiration. Its varying buzzwords have been 'decentralization,' 'democratization,' and 'popularization.' Its abiding goal has been to bring the best of French culture to those traditionally removed from it.

In recent years this approach to the arts—like so much else in French society—has come under heavy criticism. In his provocative book, *La culture, pour qui? essai sur les limites de la démocratisation culturelle* (Culture, for Whom? An Essay on the Limits of Cultural Democratization, 2006), Jean-Claude Wallach observes that French cultural policy from Malraux through Lang was based on a faith in massive economic expansion and upward social mobility—conditions that no longer hold. Today's outdated system, he argues, serves mainly to finance artists but not to democratize *culture*—which he defines as "the relationships real individuals have with art, artworks, and artists."[54] In place of "an elite theatre for everyone" (following Antoine Vitez's influential but toplofty notion of "*un théâtre élitaire pour tous*"), Wallach calls for "a theatre that embodies equality for all." To attain this goal, he says, policy makers, especially at local levels, must first "identify and understand 'what creates culture' in particular populations and in particular locations, and 'the native talents' ['*les ressources habitantes*'] that need to be mobilized in ways that are responsive and meaningful to themselves and to the world."[55] Wallach's critique chimes fully with that of the sociologist Frédéric Martel, quoted at this chapter's start.

Alternatives to violence

The spring 2006 issue of *Cassandre* showcased numerous pioneering individuals and institutions working within the forward-looking framework Wallach calls for, including the Théâtre de l'Unité in Audincourt (Doubs) and the Nième Compagnie in Vaulx-en-Velin

(Rhône). A profile of the Théâtre Quand Même, established by Joël Beaumont in Seine-Saint-Denis in 1987, describes Beaumont's mighty efforts to ground his stage texts in the authentic words of people in the neighborhood. Among the many other undersung cultural heroes of the *banlieues* not mentioned in the issue are Bernard Bloch, director of the Réseau (théâtre) company, part of the Cartel artists' cooperative in Montreuil, who for the past several years has been working on *Oedipus Rex* with students at the Lycée Jean Moulin in Blanc-Mesnil (Seine-Saint-Denis); and Patrick Sommier, head of the MC93, a much admired *maison de la culture* in Bobigny (Seine-Saint-Denis), who has encouraged the American director Peter Sellars to take part in on-site youth workshops related to Euripides' *Children of Herakles* and who has programmed *raï* music festivals, Berber Days, and pedagogic exercises in cooperation with the Peking Opera. (In fall 2008 Sommier heroically fended off a clumsily managed state-led effort to have the Comédie-Française usurp his authority at the MC93. "It would be the greatest train heist in history to pretend that Paris must go forth to 'civilize' the suburbs," he wisely said during the bitter backlash and show of professional support that followed the revelation of the ministry's plan.)[56]

Soon after the November 2005 riots, Gilberte Tsaï, who runs the Centre dramatique national in Montreuil, noted with pride that at her theatre 60 percent of the audience resides in her district. "At the very moment when cars were aflame," she asserts, "a group of kids in Montreuil were watching a contemporary stage piece, inspired by a Tiepolo painting of Punchinellos, that raises issues of the loss of personal identity and meaningfulness."[57] Yet Guy Bénisty, cofounder of GITHEC (Groupement d'intervention théâtral et cinématographique, or Association for Theatrical and Cinematic Action) in the municipal township of Pantin (Seine-Saint-Denis), notes that when it is addressed to the middle classes, art is typically defined by its *uselessness*, but as soon as the focus moves to art and the disenfranchised, expectations arise (usually from people on the outside) about tangible, quantifiable results. "Must art, when it is produced in marginal locales, have a practical impact?" Bénisty asks. "Are there really fewer torched cars in neighborhoods where artists are at work?"[58] And if the answer to both questions is no, does that invalidate such endeavors?

The editors of *Cassandre* address these knotty points in their introductory column. "Art and culture, by themselves," they write in terms reminiscent of Ariane Mnouchkine's remarks on *Le dernier caravansérail*, "will never solve economic and social disasters. But if we deny possibilities for the artistic expression of people's anger, frustration, dreams, and utopias, then we are promoting a kind of symbolic violence—which can then ignite real violence."[59] From this perspective writers like José Pliya, Marie NDiaye, and Koffi Kwahulé can be seen as part of a vital, larger process of social change in France. In his closing chapter of *La culture, pour qui?* Jean-Claude Wallach writes: "Art and artists share with the political sphere a responsibility to 'give voice to the world' ['*dire le monde*'], to offer up a critical vision of it, and to invite us to imagine and participate in individual and collective change."[60] The Woman's negativism at the end of Pliya's *Nous étions assis sur le rivage du monde . . .* is, indeed, disheartening. But perhaps because of its very extremism it forces those who watch the play to wonder more seriously about the alternatives.

The need is pressing. Four years after the 2005 riots the Observatoire national des zones urbaines sensibles (ONZUS, or National Institute for At-Risk Neighborhoods) reported that the underprivileged outer-city areas, in which over 4.5 million members of France's population reside, are virtually "separate territories detached from the core of the Republic."[61] At the same time, Claude Dilain, the mayor of Clichy-sous-Bois—the site of the police incident that had sparked the nationwide 2005 turmoil—decried the inefficacy of government efforts to improve the situation: "We are now back to exactly how it was before 2005."[62]

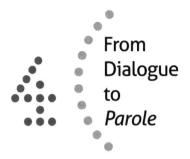

From Dialogue to *Parole*

'*Theatre of* la parole'

The verbally and viscerally scorching performances of Isabelle Huppert in Sarah Kane's *4.48 Psychosis* (chapter 2) and of the six actresses in the staged reading of Koffi Kwahulé's *Misterioso-119* (chapter 3) were a tantalizing foretaste of what I would soon recognize as a distinctive tendency of current writing for the French stage. This style or mode of creation can perhaps best be referred to as theatre of *la parole*, or theatre of the word. The term derives in part from the title of a 1989 collection of theoretical essays, *Le théâtre des paroles* (The Theatre of Words), by Valère Novarina, one of the tendency's most prominent exponents.[1] In programming works by both Novarina (b. 1947) and the novelist-poet Olivier Cadiot (b. 1956), ACT FRENCH showcased a brand of French spectacle making in which actors are called upon less to play a prescribed character in a well-plotted story than to let their bodies function as musical instruments, actualizing texts construed by their authors primarily as scores for intensely embodied, hypersensual stage events.

"Speech," asserts Novarina in *Le théâtre des paroles*, "is something other than having to mutually transmit feelings or share ideas. . . . [S]peaking is breathing and play. Speaking negates words. Speaking is drama."[2] Pointing to the disruptive bodily force that both engenders his texts and determines how actors will perform them, Novarina specifies: "I write in the absence of myself, like a dance without dancing. Undone from my language, unmoored from my thoughts . . . I write by ear, I write backwards. I hear everything."[3] As our experience of *4.48 Psychosis* and *Misterioso-119* made clear, such theatre aims to touch audiences in an equally aberrant manner, jolting our ears, eyes, brains, and guts from their conventional patterns of response.

• • •

Many of the French-language writers associated with this theatrical sensibility—Novarina, Cadiot, Kwahulé, Olivier Py, Michel Vinaver, Nathalie Sarraute, Bernard-Marie Koltès, Philippe Minyana, Jean-Luc Lagarce, Christophe Huysman, Noëlle Renaude, Joël Pommerat, among others—are also part of what is sometimes called a "return of the author" to French theatre. As noted at the end of chapter 2, the late 1960s brought to the fore an influential cluster of director-*auteurs*, such as Ariane Mnouchkine, Claude Régy, and Roger Planchon, whose personalized productions of established classics, of famous authors' lesser-known works, or of collective creations based on nondramaturgic materials tended to reduce opportunities for new writers for the stage. This imbalance continued through much of the 1980s, when Jack Lang's Ministry of Culture appointed a slightly younger generation of director-*auteurs* to head important state-supported theatres throughout France—including Patrice Chéreau, Jean-Pierre Vincent, Jacques Lassalle, Jean Jourdheuil, and Georges Lavaudant. Even when new writers did manage to get produced in such venues, the main artistic mark (and the prime attraction for much of the public) was typically that of the director, whose vision of stage design, performance style, and textual interpretation often diluted or disregarded altogether the inherent attributes of a writer's voice.[4]

The advent of authors engaged in what we are calling theatre of *la parole* has helped to decrease such lopsidedness. In varying ways and to different degrees, these writers aim to inscribe into the very substance of their literary texts—their words on the printed page—a radical manner of performance, a reinvigorated theatrical sensibility, and a readily identifiable writerly voice. While reclaiming the word as theatre's core component, these authors nonetheless conceive of their writing as inextricably tied to the work of an actor's torso, limbs, and vocal and respiratory apparatus in performance. Also paramount for them is the design of the physical and acoustic space within which the actor operates and through which the actor exerts upon an audience the visceral, sensual, and cerebral impact called for by the text.

Laurence Mayor, a veteran Novarinian actress, notes both the freedom and responsibility that such a paradigm confers upon the performer: "When I realized that the actor does not have to transport herself toward some imaginary space intended as an escape from reality but, on the contrary, must discover both the abyss and the limitless power of the real through language alone, I was astounded."[5] Theatre of the word is, indeed, a theatre of the speech act.

• • •

Theatre of *la parole* can also be seen as part of a notable shift that has taken place over the past three decades in France with respect to dramatic dialogue. Many contemporary writers have broken with the tradition of so-called conversation plays à la Chekhov (or for that matter Giraudoux, Camus, and even Ionesco). In those earlier plays, turn-by-turn speaking generally adhered to a dependable standard: through what they said, characters informed other characters and the audience about what and who they were—or at least thought themselves to be, or wanted others to think they were. Since the appearance of such texts as Bernard-Marie Koltès's *La nuit juste avant les forêts* (*Night Just Before the Forests*, 1977) or *Dans la solitude des champs de coton* (*In the Solitude of Cotton Fields*, 1985)—and an even deeper lineage would extend back to Lucky's long speech in Beckett's *Waiting for Godot* (1953)—conversation plays have had to compete with works constructed largely upon other structural formats. These include one-person monologues; alternations of lengthy soliloquies by a cluster of actors; embodied but ambiguously positioned direct addresses to the audience; speeches of totally disembodied provenance; choral deliveries of text ranging from poetic prose to grunts, sobs, and whines; fragmented, elliptical, or overlapping utterances—or any variation and combination thereof.

In and of themselves these dramaturgic techniques are not new to French theatre or even to the Western tradition. But in becoming the main components of a play's construction they have helped bring about a brand of theatre that is qualitatively different from much that went before it. Since speech in these works no longer principally serves to support and advance a logical, continuous, and coherent storyline, it unfolds, as the French theatre specialist Jean-Pierre Ryngaert has observed, virtually "in a textual space without constraints": "The new dramatists . . . use sampling, dissection, suture, graft, and the hybridization of voices and utterances to deliver fragments of fiction to the spectator."[6] Speakers in these plays may sometimes be identified by name, but often they are not. And most times they exhibit multiple, paradoxical, or contradictory traits—thus making inoperative and irrelevant the venerable French notion (central to the neoclassic aesthetic as developed in the mid-seventeenth century and influential ever since) of a character's *vraisemblance*, or consistent plausibility of thought, feeling, and action. In critical discourse about this newer theatre, the very term 'character' ('*personnage*') tends to be replaced by such labels as 'figure' ('*figure*') or 'speaker' ('*récitant*').

   • • •

     In its emphasis on the capacity for an actor to disturb a spectator's somatic and visceral makeup, theatre of *la parole* has clear links with Antonin Artaud's call for a Theatre of Cruelty—a sensory onslaught that unleashes latent, transformative human energies, which Artaud elaborated upon most fully in his essay collection *The Theatre and Its Double* (1938).[7] But in their conviction that playful verbal texts can be created, delivered, and appreciated corporeally, French practitioners of theatre of *la parole* arguably find themselves allied even more closely with the cultural theorist Roland Barthes's notion, set forth in the mid-1970s, of the sensuous "pleasurable text," in which language "granulates," "crackles," "caresses," and ultimately "comes"—attaining and sharing with the receptive reader/auditor/spectator the unspeakable bliss of a *jouissance* that is as physiological as it is mental.[8]

     Thus, Olivier Py in his *Epître aux jeunes acteurs pour que soit rendue la Parole à la parole* (*Epistle to Young Actors, That the Word May Be Restored to the Word*, 2000) reminds thespians and audiences that the signifiers 'incantation' and 'incarnation' are separated by barely a letter, and that an actor's "desire to speak words" is a divinelike gift perhaps best described as "the immortality that inheres in saliva and in the mastication of a text."[9] Valère Novarina, in his *Lettre aux acteurs* (*Letter to the Actors*, 1979), similarly equates performance with ingesting food: "Mastication, sucking, swallowing. Pieces of the text must be bitten off, viciously attacked. . . . other pieces must be quickly gulped down, swallowed, gobbled up, breathed in, guzzled."[10]

     Theatre of *la parole* celebrates not just the musicality but the muscularity of the human voice. It is theatre in which acoustics often outstrip semantics; in which contractions and relaxations of the thoracic diaphragm virtually overtake cogitation; and in which the perceptible stirrings of the uvula, tongue, soft and hard palate, teeth, and lips are frequently what matters most, with oral/aural sensation largely supplanting old-style linguistic realism. It is, as the scholar Clare Finburgh puts it, theatre that furnishes a "revitalizing potential," an "affirmative, even euphoric and utopian relationship between humans and language."[11]

Olivier Cadiot, or textual performativity

Theatre B at 59E59 Theatres in midtown Manhattan is an intimate, small-scale box. For this event it was painted black and dimly lit. Mounted within the floor-level acting space was a set of silvery horizontal and vertical wires that outlined the edges of a three-dimensional rectangle. At the parallelepiped's center stood The Butler (see fig. 4), wearing gray slacks, a long-sleeved gray shirt, and black athletic shoes. At first the actor Laurent Poitrenaux moved and spoke with the robotlike rigidity of Isabelle Huppert at the start of *4.48 psychose*. Soon, however, his hands, arms, and eyes mimicked those of a car driver steering along a perilous curvy road. For the remainder of the quick-paced 100-minute monologue his character, named John Robinson (a wink to Daniel Defoe's resourceful island protagonist), shifted, gyrated, pranced, and swirled virtually nonstop within strict, self-imposed limits. Whether it was a twitching nose, explosively popping lips, an undulating crouched derriere, or legs and feet sprinting wildly in place, Robinson's movements—intricately choreographed by Odile Duboc (1941–2010)—registered as essential components of his storytelling: not so much illustrating the episodes of Robinson's loopy, scrambled narrative, they were more like coequal, symbiotic features of his manic verbalizations.

In this French-language staging of Olivier Cadiot's 1997 seriocomic novel *Le colonel des zouaves* (*Colonel Zoo*), directed by Ludovic Lagarde (b. 1962), neither plot nor character was the primary point. The Butler seemingly oversees, with military rigor, the large staff of a pre–World War II English manor house. Yet his accounts of everyday events— meals served, rooms set up for weekend guests, fish caught in the local river for lunch—are mainly jumping-off points for expansive, euphoric figments of his imagination: improbable conversations, paranoid spying missions, masturbatory erotic fantasies, and ulti-

4. *Laurent Poitrenaux as Robinson crouches in sync with his wild verbiage in Ludovic Lagarde's production of Olivier Cadiot's* Le colonel des zouaves. *Photo © Laurencine Lot.*

mately a psychotic delusion that makes him believe he is the heroic leader of the 2nd regiment of Zouaves (an international infantry unit of the French army that would have served in colonial territories).

Throughout the piece the sonic reverberations, pitch transpositions, and intricate polyphonic and choral effects of composer Gilles Grand's electronic sound design—which Grand, at a console in the rear of the theatre, produced anew for each performance—inflected our aural experience of Poitrenaux's utterances. While this real-time digital wizardry enhanced the fantastical quality of The Butler's fabrications and multiple role-playing, it also paradoxically heightened our alertness to Poitrenaux's awesome natural physical abilities. At one point The Butler babbles:

> I'll know how to do all the voices. The sound of the canon. I'll even do the carrier-pigeon. The ducks in the swamp. The wind in the poplars. The sound of water + the smell of honeysuckle.
>
> I'll make the sound of walking on dry ground. The sound of the blade of grass unfolding after it's been walked on.
>
> Crunch crunch through the snow.
>
> Knock knock.
>
> I go in.[12]

Amazingly, Poitrenaux generated much of what he enumerates here, in large part due to his commanding vocal, pulmonary, and muscular apparatus. A good part of this play's verbal invention is already embedded in Cadiot's text: The Butler pronounces phrases such as "Et là ffffffffff attention ffff bouhhm" or "O' ma' chééééérie' Valantaïne.'"[13] With the self-awareness of a speech act theorist à la J. L. Austin (1911–1960) or John R. Searle (b. 1932), The Butler regularly tosses out propositions like "I say all that I do at the same speed that I do it" or "To say is to do."[14] But in addition to the activation of the text's performative potential via Poitrenaux's elocutionary artistry, it is also true that Gilles Grand's sound design, much like Duboc's choreography, functioned as if it were a natural corollary to the actor's delivery of the verbal text. As spectator-auditors we were prompted to respond not just to the actor's physical body but to that body's technological enrichment, perceiving both as a conjoined seamless whole.

From sense to sensuality

Since the late 1980s Olivier Cadiot has been a leader in French experimental literature. His writings defy generic categories. "My work," the author of the postmodern manifesto *L'art poétic'* (1988) asserts, "is based on the tension between poetry and the novel, and between poetry and theatre."[15] Cadiot, who used to write lyrics for Kat Onoma (a now disbanded English-language underground rock group), compares much contemporary poetry, including his own, to "sound installations, performance pieces that incline toward the conceptual."[16] Although he insists that such poetry demands a storylike component to keep it free from pathos, Cadiot's narratives usually veer toward the nonrepresentational and nonchronological; and they are conspicuously peppered with onomatopoeia, stammered word clusters, and other special phonic effects.

Moreover, by substituting the allusive and the virtual for fixed meaning and stable characterization, Cadiot's works expose human identity and subjectivity as self-constructing entities in perpetual transformation. In this regard a theatregoer's experience of the staged rendition of *Le colonel des zouaves* demands active participation. Along with absorbing and hopefully finding pleasure in the piece's verbal and corporeal torrent of stimuli, our role is also to authenticate and validate, through our sustained attentiveness and within the physical space we share with him, The Butler's feverish efforts to externalize—through words, sounds, and movements—the transient state of his being. Indeed, theatre of *la parole* is also a theatre of *les oreilles* and *les yeux*—namely, *our* ears and eyes. It is a theatre of subtle feedback, with audience response continuously sustaining and transforming the looped circuit of sensory invigoration that embraces performer and spectator.

• • •

Cadiot has authored opera librettos and song cycles for such musicians as Pascal Dusapin (*Romeo & Juliette*, 1989) and Georges Aperghis (*36 prières d'insérer* [36 Inserts], 1995). At the request of Ludovic Lagarde (b. 1962), he once wrote a five-character play, *Soeurs et frères* (Sisters and Brothers, 1993). But Cadiot does not identify as a dramatist: "I try to write books that espouse the spoken word [*l'oral*]; then it's up to [Ludovic Lagarde] to adapt, transform, extend, or cut them. Through modalities of his own, he induces sensations . . . analogous to those found in my books."[17] So far Lagarde has directed six Cadiot works, and in France the two men have rightly been perceived as a formidable creative team. Lagarde counts Claude Régy among his early influences and claims to be emulating the latter in his penchant "for inventing new modes of perception, for creating novel responses in the audience."[18] He also modestly (and accurately) acknowledges how much of what he does is already lodged in Cadiot's texts. Cadiot himself has stated: "I don't write *for* the theatre; I write theatre."[19] Lagarde in turn asserts that his task is simply "to make [Cadiot's] texts ring, to bring out the beauty of the language, the strength and feeling carried by the writing."[20]

In preparing for the 2004 Avignon Festival, artistic codirectors Hortense Archambault and Vincent Baudriller were eager to reinstate the festival's tradition of showcasing living authors whose "writerly voice" (*parole d'écrivain*) had reinvigorated relations between the literary and the theatrical. This Avignon pedigree includes Samuel Beckett, Georges Perec, Armand Gatti, Robert Pinget, and Nathalie Sarraute, and it owes much to the vision of Alain Crombecque (1939–2009), who ran the festival from 1985 to 1992. The 2004 search resulted in the selection of Cadiot, who was represented by three productions, each directed by Lagarde: *Le colonel des zouaves*, which had had its first mounting in 1997 at the CDDB–Théâtre de Lorient (Brittany); *Oui, dit le très jeune homme*, Cadiot's new translation of Gertrude Stein's *Yes Is for a Very Young Man* (1946); and the world premiere of *Fairy queen*, Cadiot's time-bending account (published in 2002) of a twenty-first-century sprite who, as an emerging performance artist, decides to entertain Gertrude Stein and Alice B. Toklas in their prewar Paris salon on the rue de Fleurus.

• • •

ACT FRENCH brought us the Cadiot-Lagarde *Fairy queen* with its original cast. As the agile demi-booted and miniskirted fairy, Valérie Dashwood evinced the ethereality of a Tinker Bell and the spunk of a Peter Pan; Philippe Duquesne, in dowdy drag, was the plump, self-obsessed Stein; and Laurent Poitrenaux, also in drag, played the crabbed, mustachioed Toklas with ace comic flair. Again we were treated to a sensuous mixture of polyphonic, electronically recomposed verbalization (this time David Bichindaritz designed the digital sound), flamboyant body moves, and wacko domestic and aesthetic imaginings.

The tone was mainly playful: though fed up with Alice, Gertrude gorges on the latter's veal sauté to near explosion; Alice, having tired of typing Gertrude's manuscripts, mocks her companion's literary output as pathetic "retirement-home stutterings."[21] Distancing herself from these squabbles, the fairy queen concentrates on her performance, which she believes has the potential to change the world: "There has been bodyart, so why can't there be neuronart? three-dimensional vocalart? live *art-brut* theatre? the label will come later, it's better just to say, 'these are poems.'"[22] Stein, tipsy from lunchtime imbibing, shows little feel for her young guest's project. "Braaaaavo. . . . Bravo, sweetie," she interrupts early on, "but a bit too many images, too many hot images, you need to speak with dead images."[23] The fairy, uncomprehending, sticks to her performance, rhapsodically collapsing barriers between narrator and actor, speech and gesture, dancer and dance: "I am set up for speed, shaped for speed, I am front ahead, she sings, I am a romantic fairy, in front, I am electric, my neurons connect disjointed elements at top velocity, I speak to you at the speed of sound, I guide myself while speaking to you, the stream of my words permanently informs me of my position, I'm set up for speed, shaped for speed, I am front ahead, like a hissing radiator cap, an oiled body, a swimmer's shoulders at the lake's center frozen darkly with everything that can ever be said, a lake streaked with thousands of lightning-thoughts, I slide, I speak, I move forward."[24]

Despite their toying with the real Gertrude Stein (1874–1946), Cadiot and Lagarde implicitly lionize her in *Fairy queen* as a historic forerunner of theatre of *la parole*. Stein's influence on their art is clear: her challenge to fixed genres; her release of language from the requirements of standard syntax, of telling a set story, of delineating sequential thinking; and above all, her vision of a theatre piece as the verbal, sonorous, and spatial equivalent of a Cézanne landscape painting, with the processing of what is essential left largely to spectators immersed in their individual experiences of the ongoing performance.

Yet with *Fairy queen* Cadiot and Lagarde also seem to be asserting that a new kind of theatrical vanguard is alive and well in France today and that there are perhaps specifically twenty-first-century ways to reimagine a fresh rapport between language and the stage. They disclose how new media technologies, and in particular the digital manipulation of spoken discourse for the creation of word-based electronic soundscapes, can advance Stein's now-distant call for a radical shift from sense to sensuality.[25]

'Parole,' New York style

Can such theatre work in English and with a U.S. audience?

The French-born director Marion Schoevaert (b. 1972) issued a strong affirmative response with *A.W.O.L.*, her adaptation of *Le colonel des zouaves* that ran at 59E59 for several weeks following the Lagarde production. Schoevaert, who moved to New York from Paris in the early 1990s, is an alumna of the Lincoln Center Theater Directors Lab. Having presented English-language versions of works by other authors connected with France's theatre of *la parole*—Bernard-Marie Koltès, Jean-Luc Lagarce, Michel Vinaver—Schoevaert was eager to round off ACT FRENCH's Cadiot minifestival (for which she served as producer) with what she announced as an "Americanized" stage rendition of the poet-novelist's book.

While Schoevaert admits that even "sophisticated" American audiences are often averse to plays not grounded in conventional realism, she contends that theatrical expression must stay true to its "sacred roots." "Theatre," she told me, "is the site of a precious exchange, a kind of communion between actors and audience, and such rituals don't necessarily deliver easy pleasures."[26] Still, Schoevaert realized that she had to guarantee a sure level of entertainment when conceiving *A.W.O.L.* for a New York public. Moreover, personal issues were at stake. "After my experience here of September 11, 2001," the French transplant confided, "and then the French-American controversies over the war in Iraq, I told Cadiot that I no longer felt I could do *Le colonel des zouaves* purely as an abstract experimental stage exercise. The rising political tensions between France and the United States were taking a toll on me; somehow I needed to bring out the social humanity that is lodged within Cadiot's text."[27]

• • •

Schoevaert set her bright white-box adaptation in contemporary downtown Manhattan. She depicted Cadiot's protagonist as a homeless man who takes shelter in cardboard boxes and hoards empty beer and soda cans. In the show's early sections the disheveled, stone-faced Robinson—played by Steven Rattazzi—conjures up his past glories as a head butler with a hyperactive vocal and physical athleticism to rival Laurent Poitrenaux's in the Lagarde version. But in Schoevaert's rendition (which has no electronic sound), the passages in Cadiot's text that satirize British class oppression were intoned by an all-male a cappella chorus of tall, squeaky-clean Wall Street types for whom the composer Adam Silverman wrote compellingly sweet music and for whom Schoevaert, assisted by the choreographer Elissaveta Iordanova, supplied boldly patterned group movements and gestures. Little by little these twelve smooth businessmen, who mainly chant clichés and slogans, turn militaristic. The wretched, homeless ex-butler, until now figuratively A.W.O.L. (absent without leave) from social integration and callously ignored by the others, miraculously becomes part of their group: thanks to a battle wound, he soon acquires hero status; he then races up the ranks to become their dictatorial leader, organizing maneuvers and adding the neutron bomb to their arsenal of weaponry.

Much of *A.W.O.L.*'s verbiage and most of its sung lyrics came directly from Cadiot's text as translated by Cole Swensen. But in redistributing the book's discourse among numerous players—while at the same time scrupulously avoiding conversational stage dialogue—Schoevaert stressed how the traces of insanity in *Le colonel des zouaves* attach more to society than to the pitiable protagonist. As she explained to me: "When your life is not going well, when you feel like an invisible outsider, and then the mass media feed you the message that you can turn it all around simply by enlisting in the armed forces, by being part of 'a unified chorus,' so to speak, I think it's the world that's gone mad, not the individual."[28]

For all her effort to make *A.W.O.L.* maximally accessible and relevant to an American audience, Schoevaert's production was no less daring and exacting than Ludovic Lagarde's. The *New Yorker* found it "visually arresting" but slammed it for being "often opaque."[29] Online and alternative press reviews were uniformly ebullient. "You won't find many other theatre pieces in New York that are as challenging as *A.W.O.L.*—and that's a shame," wrote Adam Klasfeld on *Theater-Mania.com*.[30] Helen Shaw in *Time Out New York* called it "postmodern perfection."[31] And Matt Freeman, while confiding to readers of *nytheatre.com* that he never achieved "a firm sense of what exactly was happening," aptly pinned down the essence of the evening's experience: "The play is covered from head to toe in resplendent words. . . . It is a surrealist painting and prose poem, and it demands the attention of those who love language in theatre."[32]

This writer's confession

To appreciate theatre of *la parole* you must approach it with a proper mind-set. My own grasp of its special pleasures occurred almost as an epiphany. I was attending an English-language performance of Valère Novarina's *Adramelech's Monologue* (*Le monologue d'Adramélech*) during its three-day run at the 59E59 Theaters in mid-November. Program notes indicated that the text was an excerpt from Novarina's *Le babil des classes dangereuses* (Babble of the Dangerous Classes, 1978), a play in which 297 characters wage battle over Mouth and Ear's misguided endeavor to silence the 295 others; and that the name 'Adramelech,' deriving from the Hebrew ('*melech*') or the Arabic ('*malik*') for 'king,' probably signifies 'the actor-king.'[33] *Adramelech's Monologue* has frequently been performed to much acclaim in France and elsewhere by the actor André Marcon (b. 1948), who has worked closely with Novarina since the mid-1980s. For ACT FRENCH, Hilario Saavedra, a recent CalArts (Los Angeles) alumnus, bravely delivered the piece in a new American English translation by Guy Bennett (see fig. 5).[34] Both Marcon and Novarina coached Saavedra for this role, in which the protagonist hears multiple voices, responds in multiple voices, and is convulsively traversed by stunning and outlandish words, phrases, pitches, pauses, rhymes, and rhythms.

In all frankness, I was baffled from the get-go. Saavedra's movements were as extravagantly athletic as Poitrenaux's in *Le colonel des zouaves*, and they kept my eyes riveted, occasionally even setting my stomach in knots. But even in English the work's prodigious gush of barely comprehensible verbiage made the Cadiot-Lagarde version

5. *Hilario Saavedra as the eponymous figure of Valère Novarina's*
Le monologue d'Adramélech *(at Bootleg Theater, Los Angeles, directed*
by Joshua Moyse, 2008). Photo © Jennifer Bell.

of *Le colonel des zouaves* seem like a paragon of reason and lucidity. Here, in Bennett's translation, are Adramelech's opening lines, typical of the thirty-minute-long declamation:

Sufferin' sycophant! Sufferin' sulfurous supine simian syllogist! The Adramelech's toil's hit its peak. Adramelech! . . . Sire? I made you of clay. And I go where? To shelter 'neath your splint'ry coat and gnaw your soon-sluiced stump. Hail yes, I'm there lickety-split. So I says to the guy who'd ogle me through spy-like specs. Nine fourths of our lives wasted in inane hours of stanzas, staces, comings and goings! We lift our arms your head falls off. Ah the disappointment of my life's voyage with its lame stations! My head's too triangular, not round enough for my taste: my arms are good, not long enough though and eight short of ten. Adrameon, Ablamelion, Ablame-lech, shut up or step up, but no more words! Marl to my pickaxe, gloss to my heals! We's one thousand below, a handful holds down the fort. They's there in their abode. Their eyes can't see us but we can see them we can, but their eyes can't see us and they can't see us there they can't. Quiet Albert Bellows, crawl quite, lift your head and give ass! Adrameluce. Watch your mug, you old retorter, it'll spring from my head held high, the talker, gush from my hip, slip from the grave and nip at your ears![35]

Saavedra's oral delivery combined a West Virginia backwoods twang, South Central (Los Angeles) raplike rhythms, and grandiloquent flourishes redolent of some public readings of Shakespeare, Rabelais, and Melville I had attended over the years. As I tried in vain to assign meaning to this frequently hilarious verbal puzzle, I found myself thinking of the great double-talking comedian Al Kelly (d. 1966), a featured act on the golden-age television variety shows that I had watched as a child with wonder and wild laughter. In truth there was something pleasingly regressive about this theatrical event. Midway through the show another memory popped into my head. It was of my tenth-grade class trip to the American Shakespeare Festival Theatre for a preseason rendition of *Twelfth Night*. At that performance, just like at the show I was watching, I was able to identify a good percentage of the words being spoken on stage, but the meaning and logic behind the actors' phrases, sentences, and scenes seemed beyond my intellectual reach.

That Shakespeare experience was a shock to my developing ego. It made me—and I suspect other students of my generation—feel culturally and linguistically dumb. For years it squashed any incipient desire I might have had to sample live Shakespeare again. In Theatre C of 59E59, I was once again understanding almost nothing. *But this time I was having a great time!* This is as close as it gets, I was convinced, to Roland Barthes's textual *jouissance*. For here were an actor and a playwright passionately inciting each of us in the audience to confront, revel in, and, yes, even be confounded by a contemporary poetic language whose vocabulary, syntax, and cadences are light-years removed from everyday speech. Rather than transfer set meanings *from* the stage *to* the spectator, this show's main work was to establish a somatically based and mutually respectful field of shared human connectedness *between* actor and audience. In effect, it crystallized for me the useful lesson implicit in all ACT FRENCH events associated with theatre of *la parole*: if you feel discombobulated at the theatre, it is not necessarily shameful evidence of your inferiority. Sometimes you should just sit back, open your ears, and enjoy.

At its best, as in works by Novarina, Py, and Vinaver, theatre of *la parole*—much like Shakespearean theatre in Elizabethan times—draws on festive, popular rituals that encourage playgoers to release themselves from the habits of serious, rational thought and to luxuriate in viscerally *felt* understandings. That is not to say that signification is absent. In the case of the aforementioned writers, profound human meanings attach to their writings, and spectators are enticed to exercise critical thinking skills. Yet to savor these works as a newcomer, you first need to let down your defenses and then gobble up as many productions as possible. *"L'appétit vient en mangeant"* ("The more one has, the more one wants"), goes an old French proverb. Stripped of its moralizing dimension and taken literally—"appetite will come as you eat"—those familiar words apply perfectly to theatre of *la parole*. It is an acquired taste worth developing.

Edgy and Cool

New 'media theatre'

In addition to the dazzling works representing theatre of *la parole*, ACT FRENCH treated New Yorkers to choice specimens of another leading strain of stage pieces, one that might simply be called 'media theatre.' These were experimental works—by such younger creative artists as Philippe Quesne and Pascal Rambert, and by vibrant international collectives like Superamas and WaxFactory—that played with, against, or parallel to contemporary media and information technologies. Almost always they were inventive, iconoclastic, and frolicsome.

Media theatre is akin to theatre of *la parole* inasmuch as it, too, operates within a dramaturgic paradigm that makes our familiar notions of plot, dialogue, and character fairly irrelevant. But where theatre of *la parole* holds as precious the intimate link between staged spectacle and composed written text, media theatre takes as a given that much literary writing for the stage and much theatre-going itself are fairly quaint, if not totally anachronistic, phenomena in a worldwide marketplace saturated with mass-mediated moving images. As a result these idiosyncratic, exploratory stage pieces typically strive to stake out fresh territories for theatre within the larger cultural landscape. They aggressively collapse old barriers between the individual arts (theatre, cinema, dance, video, music, song, painting, architecture, and so on), and they dismiss hoary distinctions between High Art and entertainment. Above all, they engage—in ways ranging from unabashed collusion to ironic complicity to radical critique—with the changed status of actors, spectators, and performance in a mainstream culture attracted to high-tech entertainments that are nominally "live," such as sports events, rock concerts, and most Broadway-style plays and musicals, but that Western and Westernized consumers increasingly experience as mediatized events in which the possibilities for relatively spontaneous and immediate human-to-human interaction are considerably attenuated.

All of ACT FRENCH's media theatre took place at downtown Manhattan and Brooklyn venues. The events were almost always sold out. They shattered the canard that experimental theatre from Europe is too often a weighty, gloomy, and pretentious affair. On the contrary, several of these shows were among the festival's most lighthearted, colorful, and funny. It was also clear that these were the only ACT FRENCH offerings that routinely attracted the Generation Y crowd — young adults in their twenties and thirties who came of age immersed in a digitally driven world of cell phones, laptops, and iPods. For them, the edginess of these quirky imported pieces felt familiar and "cool."

Geek chic

Performance Space 122, at the corner of First Avenue and Ninth Street, has for decades been a prominent East Village hub for emerging stage artists inclined to take risks. It was an apt venue for the weeklong run of *The Itching of Wings* (*La démangeaison des ailes*) — a jaunty performance piece conceived and directed by one of France's fast-rising stars, Philippe Quesne (b. 1970).

The show started in effect the instant we crossed the main entrance to the upstairs theatre. To reach the raked seating area we first had to walk through a patchy plasterboard maze of narrow corridors that led to a small, underequipped recording booth with a Plexiglas window. Through this pane we could view those ticket holders who had already found their places. After exiting on the booth's far side, we then traversed, in whatever path we chose, the main playing space — which resembled the living area of messy college suitemates. Littering the floor were laptop computers, a cheap minifridge, empty bottles of beer and cranberry juice, shoddy chairs, and stacks of used books and CDs. One wild-haired dude seemed to be napping on a worn bare mattress, flush with the floor. Three other guys idled about, studiously inattentive to our presence. Near the fridge was a small video monitor running looped footage of a geeky man, shot in close-up, who twisted his mouth into odd shapes while repeating, with various inflections, the words "*la démangeaison des ailes.*"

Once seated we could take in the full array of screens that filled much of the auditorium's rear and middle spaces: a wall-length vertical surface, stage right; a midsize rectangular one, upstage center, that abutted the sound studio's glass frame; and several feet above the monitor near the fridge, stage left, an oblong horizontal panel for projecting English supertitles. By the time everyone had arrived at their seats and the house lights dimmed to black, it was not hard to surmise that this show was probably going to mimic computer-generated hypertext (see fig. 6).

Indeed, much of Quesne's hour-long spectacle unfolded like a casual perusal of Google and YouTube search results for the topic 'human attempts at flying, legend and reality.' None of it was meant to be taken too seriously. At the start a live actor inside the booth softly recited a select bibliography, offering publication details of titles by such erudite writers as the philosopher Gaston Bachelard (d. 1962), the novelist Georges Perec (d. 1982), and the composer John Cage (d. 1992), as well as of children's tales like Laurent de Brunhoff's *Babar Comes to America* (1965). Another actor, downstage right, gave a wacky, unconvincing demonstration of how, thanks to digital software, sensors attached to his limbs could produce on the wall-length surface opposite him 3D images of his skeletal body in flight. A third nerd tried to skyrocket himself from a stool by igniting a beer can— only to tumble like a modern-day Icarus. Pieter Bruegel the Elder's painting *Landscape with the Fall of Icarus* (c. 1558) was in fact the topic of a capsule disquisition stammered by the videoed mouth-twister we had encountered earlier; and several times throughout the piece live actors meticulously contorted their bodies so that their upturned legs and feet would approximate those of Bruegel's Icarus, half submerged in the sea.

Other videotaped footage included interviews with a dental surgeon who flaunted his passion for miniature model aircraft; a *lycée* philosophy instructor who explicated the passage from Plato's *Phaedrus* where Socrates describes how love can revive the soul's wings— causing the body to itch as the appendages swell and sprout feathers;

6. *In Philippe Quesne's* La démangeaison des ailes, *a spoof of hypertext:* center, midground, *Sébastien Jacobs;* right, standing, *Gaëtan Vourc'h;* seated, *Cyril Gomez-Mathieu. Photo © Vivarium Studio.*

and a tai chi chuan enthusiast who waxed grandiloquent about the way martial arts had turned his hands into metaphoric wings. Midway into the show a live actor read a spellbinding excerpt from the Russian-born conceptual artist Ilya Kabakov's narrative installation about cosmic energy, *The Man Who Flew into Space from His Apartment* (1981–1988). As our attention next shifted to several simultaneously occurring attractions (some live, others virtual), the New York–based punk rock band Mad Cow lugged their gear into the recording booth, performed a powerhouse number, and left the stage as offhandedly as they had arrived.

Near the end of *The Itching of Wings*, the French interactive installation artist and scholar Samuel Bianchini (b. 1971) appeared on the midsize video screen to expatiate upon what he called "the problematic of copying and pasting fragments in *The Itching of Wings*." By referencing Gilles Deleuze and Félix Guattari's "rhizome" concept, set forth in their philosophical tome *Mille plateaux* (*A Thousand Plateaus*, 1980), Bianchini likened Quesne's "hypermediated, hypertextual" piece to an "interactive dictionary" that provides the spectator with multiple, nonhierarchical entry and exit points, thereby enabling each of us, "in a relatively schizophrenic situation," to construct "his or her own composition." As Bianchini's theory-drenched analysis faded out—his lips kept moving but the sound (comically) was cut off—we again saw a computer-generated male human form on the wall-length screen, this time flying ever so gracefully to the strains of Léo Ferré's classic soulful recording of "Les oiseaux du malheur" ("Birds of Misfortune"). These sweet sounds and images, too, dissolved before the song ended, to be replaced by a projected rolling list of detailed credits for *The Itching of Wings*, as at a movie's close.

Meanwhile the sole person, live or simulated, to bring any one act to completion in the entire piece took center stage. He was the (live) nebbishy fellow who throughout the show had been silently ensconced in the sound booth, putting the final touches on an elaborate, feathery bird costume. Now in head-to-toe avian regalia, he moved rhythmically and cheerily to the recorded credit-sequence music—a buoyant music-hall tune, "Mon truc en plumes" ("My Feathered Thingamajig"), warbled in full by the celebrated French dancer-*chanteuse* Zizi Jeanmaire (b. 1924).

The body at risk

Much of the charm of *The Itching of Wings* stems from its gentle tone and self-deprecating humor. A graduate of the Ecole des arts décoratifs (Paris), Philippe Quesne worked in the field of interactive museum display prior to his stint as a stage designer for the director Robert Cantarella (b. 1957). Quesne now places scenography, or a primarily visual dramaturgy whose logic is not subordinated to that of a verbal text, at the center of his creative agenda. "My approach to theatre, my *écriture scénique* [scenic writing]," he told me, "stems from my having been exposed early on to works by Tadeusz Kantor, Bob Wilson, William Forsythe, and Pina Bausch. Much like them, my top priority is spatial composition, the constantly shifting visual relations among objects and bodies in movement."[1] That is one of the reasons Quesne named his company, founded in 2003, Vivarium Studio: "I wanted to create an autonomous, self-contained space in which to observe, and display to others, the processes by which a group of human beings comes together and fabricates a theatrical project." With respect to his smooth assemblage of heterogeneous and fragmentary source materials for *The Itching of Wings*, Quesne points to the influence of Agnès Varda's documentary *Les glaneurs et la glaneuse* (*The Gleaners and I*, 2000) and, especially, of Jean-Luc Godard's fiction film *Pierrot le fou* (1965): "The way in which Godard explicitly quotes works from other media, piecing them all together in the service of a theme and its expression was, for me, pure magic, a true revelation."

Yet I think it is the way Quesne's five live actors set themselves *apart* from moving-image media that is crucial for bringing about the winsome, encouraging feel of *The Itching of Wings*. Jean Cocteau (1889–1963), a pioneer in mixed-media creation, intuited that cinema is the art form that essentially films death at work.[2] Some theorists of electronic media, by contrast, have suggested that information technologies are seductive precisely because they lie "outside of death" — in the sense that users, say, of the World Wide Web operate in a sphere where relations of proximity and distance from other humans have little import, linear temporality is largely dissolved, and other beings exist as, at best, disembodied simulations.[3] According to this view, when we surf from one self-contained media image to another — without resistance, always fairly satisfied, always feeling we can link to another site if we care to—we defuse both human desire and those intimations of mortality that arguably give life its true spark. "The electronic image [on- and offstage]," Hans-Thies Lehmann observes, "[is] pure foreground. It evokes a fulfilled, superficially fulfilled kind of seeing. . . . The electronic image *lacks lack*."[4]

For all their dealings with video, electronic sound, and computer programs, Quesne's bumbling troupe *restored* lack to their (not-so-very) high-tech stage environment. Throughout the show the performers remained as alive with outsize desire and human imperfection as Icarus in his own bungled efforts to fly. "I wanted to do a piece . . . about people who *try* to do things, who *try* to live, just as I *try* to make art," Quesne has said about this work.[5] It was, indeed, his actors' irrepressible clownlike urges to flirt with the unknowable and to put their *real* bodies at risk in *real* time and space that emphatically marked the experience of *The Itching of Wings* as *non*hypertextual, *non*cinematic (in Cocteau's terms)—and *very* theatrical.

Junk-culture overflow

Escape from the media grid is almost unthinkable in Superamas's cheesy and kitschy *BIG: Episode #2 (Show/Business)*, which played at The Kitchen, on West Nineteenth Street in Chelsea—a premiere venue for experimental performance in the United States. Marking Superamas's U.S. debut, *BIG: Episode #2* is the second part of the group's trilogy on how showbiz and ad agency media clichés shape contemporary quests for individual happiness in a *big* way.

The show starts with a clip from Ben Stiller's feature-film parody of the fashion industry, *Zoolander* (2001): the pea-brained male model Derek Zoolander (Stiller)—hoping to figure out how being "really, really ridiculously good-looking" can also make him of service to society—eases his mind by driving with his buddies to a Starbucks for an orange mocha Frappuccino; their kicky fun, including a stop at a service station for a fill-up and a gas-hose squirt fight (shot MTV-style to Wham!'s mid-1980s megahit, "Wake Me Up Before You Go-Go"), ends with a catastrophic cigarette-induced explosion. The remainder of *BIG: Episode #2* is a fifty-five minute multimedia riff on the almightiness of narcissism, consumerism, and arrested adolescence in a pop-culture-glutted world.

Founded in 1999, Superamas is a French-Austrian artists' collective. Its projects have embraced dance, theatre, film, soap opera, live music, and art installation. Based in Vienna, the group receives frequent financial support from institutions in Belgium, Germany, Norway, and France and is well known on the European festival circuit. Having chosen English as its main performance language, it provides supertitled translations for its bookings in non-Anglophone countries. The troupe's name is a deliberate joke, alluding, first, to lofty scientific inquiry: French astrophysicists use the term '*superamas*' to refer to conglomerations of galaxies; and, second, to flagrant corporate globalism: Wal-Mart owns Mexico's Superama supermarket chain.

The *BIG* trilogy shows how desire, shaped in ever-growing measure by junk cultural artifacts, blithely sustains itself even in the face of real-world cataclysms. Such a theme is in no way exotic among alternative and underground theatre companies. But it is Superamas's apparent laissez-faire neutrality toward the issue that makes this work both delightful *and* unsettling. Indeed, watching Superamas in action is like imbibing pomegranate vodka martinis: the hard stuff goes down almost too easily.

BIG: Episode #2 contains two main "live" scenes: one in an upscale boutique for brand-name men's cosmetics and women's lingerie; the other in a glitzy airport lounge where a Superamas member, playing himself, schmoozes with the CEO of Rolls-Royce (who has just fired five thousand workers) in the hope of getting the tycoon to subsidize the troupe. But the liveness is deceptive, for the cartoonish, unvaryingly cheerful actors in these scenes deliver their sitcom-style dialogue entirely in lip-synch to a prerecorded text that is transmitted at high volume via super-high-fidelity directional speakers. (The Marseilles-based performance and research group GMEM–Centre national de création musicale devised the show's sound spatialization.) As if to assure us that the group makes no pretense to genuine liveness, we periodically see large-screen projections of the freelancers (not members of Superamas) who were previously videotaped in the act of recording the players' lines—while the "live" stage actors go about their mouthing.

Liveness in modern theatre has of course always been subject to redefinition with the appearance of new technologies, whether the frame of reference be the machine age of the twentieth century's first decades or the computation age that began after World War II.[6] A long tradition of combining live and projected human images extends from Erwin Piscator's epic-theatre techniques of the mid-1920s in Germany through the work of the U.S.-based Wooster Group and Cyburbia Productions, Italy's Socìetas Raffaello Sanzio, and Poland's Krzysztof Warlikowski—among countless other artists and troupes. In differing ways, the most pathbreaking of these figures and companies have sought to articulate and recalibrate the entanglement between "real" human bodies and those that are screened. But as Philip Auslander usefully notes in *Liveness* (2008), "none of this [history] changes the fact that such performances occur *now* in a cultural context in which the projection is more closely related to the dominant media than is the live body, a fact that undoubtedly has implications for how the audience perceives the whole performance" (my emphasis).[7] Unlike, say, the Wooster Group—for whom manipulations of visual and sonic material via techniques of sampling, cut and paste, layering, and recombining have functioned at least in part as "Brechtian estrangement devices,"[8] Superamas is largely content to employ such media savvy as a means to evoke an antiseptic gee-whiz response in viewers. With Superamas we seem to have, following Auslander (who builds on Jean Baudrillard's paradigm of the hyperreality of simulacra and simulations), "an impossible oscillation" between two poles of what once seemed a clear cultural opposition: "whereas mediatized performance derive[d] its authority from its reference to the live or the real, the live now derives its authority from its reference to the mediatized, which derives its reference to the live, etc."[9]

Both the cosmetics shop and the lounge tableaux in *BIG: Episode #2* mix dazzling gloss—crisp bright lighting, hyperrealistic sets and props, fashionable fitted garments—with the players' barely contained dark erotic urges. Moreover, both scenes are repeated several times throughout the show with slight variations of words and actions. The repetitions themselves are interspersed with fragments from a third scene, prevideotaped in an urban apartment and projected on a midsize screen: dressed as a Catwoman-cum-dominatrix, a female player (whom we have already observed acting "live" on stage) fakes us out by delivering (to another previously seen "live" actor) not the S/M sex workout we are led to expect but a New Age hygiene lesson in proper posture and good-vibe connections with "the space around you."

Some French thinkers have homed in on the reiteration-with-a-difference aspect of these scenes that constantly foreclose on fixed meaning, linking the work of Superamas to the critical theory of deconstruction.[10] But the collective's members are skeptical when it comes to allegations of serious intentions. They much prefer the journalist Helen Shaw's observation, made in the *New York Sun*, that their high-spirited goofiness renders *BIG: Episode #2* "the smartest frat party ever thrown in a downtown venue."[11] In conversation with me, Superamas conceded a wish to show how "mass-media imagery, even at its most blatantly manipulative, never ceases to seduce otherwise intelligent and self-aware people"—including themselves.[12] They were also willing to endorse some of the ideas of Rudi Laermans, a Belgian cultural sociologist who has tagged their spectacles as prime specimens of contemporary *postart*. For Laermans, Superamas shows how the increasingly weak barriers between reality and hyperreality—a blurring that has its early roots in Marcel Duchamp's readymades, Andy Warhol's pop art, and Allan Kaprow's happenings—have now fully imploded, relegating us to that "strange loop wherein it is no longer possible to segregate the influence of the media from the feedback by users of the media."[13] Still, Superamas (surely a bit too sassily) holds that sober discourse about any stage work is itself inevitably ensnared by intellectual clichés: "We use theatre to ask questions. Not to come up with answers. . . . In opposition to faith and demagogy, we foreground montage and research."[14] When I prodded them to name multimedia ensembles with which they share affinities, they pointed—only after much hedging—to Forced Entertainment, based in Sheffield (UK), and to Caden Manson's Big Art Group, a New York–based troupe that, like Superamas, tours heavily throughout Europe.[15]

Superamas's determination to remain free of labels and dogma is at one with their stage playfulness and their desire to entertain audiences in ways that are both polished and provocative. But it also compounds the elusiveness of their project. *BIG: Episode #2* seems satisfied to leave its players—and spectators—stranded in a mindless loop of high-tech, hyperreal simulations without hinting at any strategy for escape. It charmingly but eerily insinuates that we are locked into a creepy video game where the exit button is forever jammed.

State-of-the-art disorder

Technological wizardry was on grand display in WaxFactory's English-language . . . *She Said*—a multimedia take on *Détruire dit-elle (Destroy, She Said)*, Marguerite Duras's celebrated dialogue-driven text that was published as a novel in 1969 and then directed as a film that same year by the French author herself. The performance of . . . *She Said* ran for ten days at the Brooklyn Lyceum, on Fourth Avenue near Union Street, along the west fringe of Park Slope. The Lyceum's scruffy exterior and lobby—the building was once the city's Public Bath No. 7—bore little resemblance to the high-tech trappings set up within the main playing space for this forty-five-minute piece.

Seated at a ground-level horizontal table that spanned the width of a low-raised stage directly behind them, four technicians manned state-of-the-art computers; these served to coordinate an intricate mix of lighting (designed by Jaka Simenc), video work (by Sebastijan Vukusic), film footage (by the collective known as Strup), and surround sound and digital music (by Random Logic). On the platform in back of them, as if floating in a time-space dimension of its own, was a white-walled acrylic pod (designed by the architects Spela Ursic and Nejc Batistic), with a light system embedded in its walls and floor; this "set"—similar to a huge bathtub turned on its side—served as a main site for both live-actor interaction and projected visuals. The piece's three players—an amorous male-female couple and a single woman—were dressed in monochromatic outfits (by Silvio Vujicic) that evoked (for the couple, in white) sci-fi androgyny and (for the single woman, in black) Lower East Side goth.

As conceived and directed by Ivan Talijancic (b. 1969), . . . *She Said* used media technology to explore some of the very subjects that Superamas shut out: complicated feelings, shadowy flights of private imagination, and the often hazardous byways of unfettered creativity. The story is elusive: a redheaded, punkish female fiction writer—who perhaps represents Duras—sits at one of the computer terminals; within the raised pod are two lithe performers who seem to be characters in a novel the writer is working on. However, as . . . *She Said* proceeds, the bounds between ground-level forestage and floating pod fritter away; the unnamed fictional characters physically and psychologically overpower their creator; and in the end the writer is found dead in a forest that has exerted an erotic, obsessive pull on all three figures from the outset.

No less than Superamas, WaxFactory bombards viewers with constant multimediated stimuli. But unlike the experience of Superamas and closer to that of theatre of *la parole*, spectators are primed to work hard in order to construct possible meanings for the highly metaphoric goings-on. Sometimes unvoiced written sentences and odd sets of numbers flash on the pod's rear wall; at various intervals the three characters slink, writhe, and roll about on the pod's floor, creating stunning black-and-white corporeal patterns. At one point the author, having returned to her terminal, sets fire to a page of manuscript that a figure in the pod had folded into a paper airplane and then sent flying beyond the pod's borders. At another moment the house lights suddenly come on, and the writer, with a naturalistic, televisual delivery that jars with the dreaminess of the rest, responds to unseen journalists' queries about her novel: "I was very frightened while I was writing it. I was fear itself. I can't tell you what state I was in. A genuine fear though. Or else the fear of being overcome by this . . . numbness. I had no idea where it would take me . . . or else I was afraid I would wake up. And at the same time I was completely free. But frightened to death of being free."

Marshaled adroitly through the entire piece and resulting in a sensual bath of image and sound are cell-phone rings, answering-machine messages, prerecorded voice-overs, live dialogue delivered by characters simultaneously and in overlap, dialogue delivered so rapidly or so distorted by electronic effects as to be mostly undecipherable, haunting black-and-white film footage of forest scenes, video animation that mimics a homicide police squad's digitized forensics report, and multiple series of blackouts. The following sample of early live dialogue typifies the progressive blurring between narrator and narrated, creator and created—which later peaks in the writer's apparent slip into madness:

WOMAN: You have memories attached to this hotel.
AUTHOR + WOMAN: Haven't you?
MAN: They wouldn't interest you.

AUTHOR + WOMAN: It is up to me to choose.

MAN: I met a woman here.

AUTHOR + WOMAN: She's probably dead.

MAN: Among other possibilities, that's the most likely.

WOMAN: You came back to meet her again?

AUTHOR: He waits before responding.

MAN: No.

AUTHOR: They stop talking. Finally, he looks at her.

WOMAN: Does it hurt?

AUTHOR: Silence

• • •

. . . *She Said* baffled certain New York critics. Jonathan Kalb, in the *Times*, regretted that "the text overlaid on these gorgeous, animated images is even more fractured than Duras's [novel] and extremely frustrating."[16] David Cote, in *Time Out New York*, also felt that the "visual and aural treats" did not fully compensate for a "fail[ed] narrative."[17] Yet as WaxFactory's artistic codirector Erika Latta told the *Brooklyn Rail*, in terms reminiscent of Claude Régy apropos of Sarah Kane's *4.48 Psychosis*: "With our work, we are trying to get at the unexplainable, those moments that language cannot touch."[18]

Like much contemporary exploratory theatre, . . . *She Said* affirms its artistic complexity through strategies of indirection, flux, and ambiguity. Echoing Philippe Quesne and the Superamas team, Ivan Talijancic told me: "The piece gives you clues, but it requires each audience member to make his own interpretation."[19] For audiences unused to such demands it is easy to dismiss . . . *She Said* as elitist and obscurantist. But much like the best theatre of *la parole*, this new-media spectacle dares us to unloose ourselves and to revel in luxuriant sensation rather than precise intellectualization. Viewer bafflement need not always be the sign of a supposed flaw within the work—or in the spectator. In watching . . . *She Said*, our puzzlement, along with that of the performers, is as much a calculated part of the work's endpoint as it is of its start.

Despite taking inspiration for . . . *She Said* from one of France's great twentieth-century writers, WaxFactory, founded in 1998, is less France-identified than even Superamas. Although the ensemble's nominal headquarters are in Manhattan's SoHo district, WaxFactory is essentially a nomadic international troupe that spends as much time developing, rehearsing, and performing its projects in Europe and Latin America as it does in New York or Los Angeles. By inviting WaxFactory to participate in ACT FRENCH, the festival's organizers were in effect recognizing the degree to which experimental media theatre in France, the United States, and elsewhere has become increasingly trans- and supranational, which is to say that—much like ... *She Said* itself—it is exempt from fixed borders and neat identities.

WaxFactory is now proactively helping to arrange exchanges between American audiences and innovative multidisciplinary performers from other countries. In 2010 it launched a curatorial initiative, X-YU, with a festival of genre-exploding dance performances from Croatia, Serbia, and Slovenia, hosted at New York's Dixon Place in association with Dance New Amsterdam.

Beauty deconstructed ... and exalted

Perhaps no work in ACT FRENCH was more ambitiously intricate than Pascal Rambert's *Paradis (unfolding time)*, presented at Dance Theater Workshop in Manhattan's Chelsea district. This powerful piece defies classification. To some degree it can usefully be considered postdramatic, in the sense that it is free of ordinary dialogue, plot, settings, and character psychology. It partakes of media theatre inasmuch as it employs an ingenious dangling-from-the-rafters and sprouting-from-the-ground multiple-microphone concept for its eleven main performers (see fig. 7); and it features a faux-digital musical environment created on site by the composer and electric guitarist Alexandre Meyer. But the piece stands out less by its use of new media technologies than by its media hybridism, or what might be called its self-conscious "intermedialism."[20] For it gives virtually equal weight to spoken utterance, music, song, yoga-inflected acrobatics and body movement, color patterns, sodium and fluorescent light design, sculptural installations, and video. *Paradis* also has affinities with theatre of *la parole* to the extent that there is a recited text whose vibrancy hinges not on the logical clarity associated with fully composed narrative units but on the visceral, incantatory delivery of quasi-oracular sentence fragments, series of unanswered (and unanswerable) questions, rhythmic repetitions of free-floating phrases, and volleys of direct address from player to player (all performers use

7. *Stripped-down and miked-up performers roll, twist, and thrust in Pascal Rambert's* Paradis (unfolding time). *Photo © Sylvain Duffard.*

their real first names). Yet unlike most theatre of *la parole*, Rambert's work openly challenges the primacy of verbal text in theatrical performance. "I don't eliminate text, but I expel it from the center of the scene . . . to the periphery," Rambert asserts with respect to *Paradis*.[21]

In fact, *all* performed elements in this eighty-minute show took place along or outside the perimeter of a pristine 5 × 5 yard square space, midcenter stage. Signaling the show's division into three equal parts, this floor area was successively occupied by square mats of bright solid yellow, green, and pink—whose fruity hues were inspired by Rambert's memories of Noh theatre productions seen in Japan. The players themselves rolled out these mats, unfolded them, and rolled them up again. Five yards above was an equal-size square bank of 200 white fluorescent lights that illuminated the proceedings and, at the show's end, slowly descended to the ground.

Intermittently, voiced fragments of a story about amorous passion and woe—involving an unseen woman named Mathilde and some possibly incriminating videotapes—exerted a mild centripetal pull on the entire piece, even as these same snippets whirled to the outer margins of our comprehension. Midway into the show a swiftly paced slide presentation of details from eighteenth-century European oil paintings, showing fleshy nudity in historic and pastoral settings, was projected onto the side panel of a portable electric heater, downstage right of center; meanwhile, as if in kinesthetic counterbalance, a lengthy video loop of anonymous shoppers slowly traveling up and down escalators in a Japanese shopping mall was screened on a portion of a second heater, downstage left of center.

Loosely knitting all of these de-centered components into a thematic whole were two sorts of recurrent speechifying. The first consisted in self-referential questioning that players (rarely fixed, constantly in movement) seemed to address at fever pitch to (the absent) Rambert himself—though not entirely, since sometimes the utterances were more plausibly tied to Rambert's own thoughts on his relationship with the actress Kate Moran, his real-life partner, for example:

> CLEMENTINE: why don't you write sweet stories any more?
> why is your theatre so cold? are you cold yourself? is it that
> cold? do we fight the cold? are we going to die? are we? are we

starting? . . . are there no more stories? there is nothing else
to tell? why is there no more center? why is there nothing in
the center? why wasn't there anything anywhere when you
started your thing? why kate don't you listen to me when I
speak to you? why don't you love me anymore? why did I pass
from the center to the periphery? why did you expel me from
the center? are you expelled from the center? have we been
expelled? will you expel me forever? will you love me forever?
will you expel me from your center? are you expelled? are you
expellable? do you expel me? will we expel ourselves? are we?
IT IS IN WHAT SENSE? will you? want you? could you? could
we? will we? why are we so alone?[22]

The second verbal patchwork evoked major advances in Western science that have upset humankind's comforting sense of centrality,
especially Copernican astronomy, Darwinian biology, and Freudian
psychology; for instance, apropos of Darwin:

CECILE: yes [this humiliation] arrives pretty quickly after the first
[brought about by Copernicus] in fact exactly 329 years later
same thing charles darwin stops the beagle in the galapagos
islands and there crouching in the grass on all fours and
seeing the beak of the [finches] and the beautiful folds of
the earth he sees clearly that things aren't unchanging and
that they gradually modify in that era he was surrounded by
horrible creatures creationists fixists and catastrophists. . . .
you were picturing yourself if you want in a pretty central
position or if you prefer at the top of the pyramid or even
practically the unique object like the diamond of the creation
you find yourself stuck between the fish and the elephant the
ant fur and feathers and suddenly you feel the cold scales
of the snake against your skin brutally retrograded into the
animal clan. . . . your second expulsion in 1859 from your little
biologically narcissistic paradise baby. . . .[23]

Other players later hinted that new breakthroughs in science and
technology—such as genetic cloning and microchip implants—
will likely foster still more blows to Edenic complacency. Yet *Paradis* ended on a heartening note. In a direct address to the audience,

one player insisted that those of us seated in this theatre at this very time—December 2005—will in all likelihood someday look back on this moment as "a world of love of beauty and of grace where time in the infinite reaches of your imagination you can open close fold open close fold to the right to the left above below fold open close. . . ."[24] Love, beauty, and grace (in both its formal and spiritual senses) are concepts seldom encountered in much current experimental theatre. One might say that straight-from-the-shoulder exaltation of such notions is so *un*cool as to be downright radical. In this respect Pascal Rambert (b. 1962) stands out as one of the more independent-minded of France's contemporary stage artists, for he puts his huge talent for deconstructed, hybrid scenography in the service of some fairly old-fashioned values, including faith in the idea that an aesthetically drenched stage experience like *Paradis (unfolding time)* can strengthen and enrich the shared humanity of those who experience it. As Rambert said during a postperformance discussion at Dance Theater Workshop: "The contemporary artist must speak about the human condition. . . . My job is to do as little as I can, to leave open the space of the imagination."[25]

Exposing the imagination at work

Early in his career Pascal Rambert was viewed as one of the wunderkinder of innovative French theatre. A son of parents who managed a gas station in Nice, he began to direct plays (by Marivaux, and then Dario Fo) in local venues as of 1980, when he was only seventeen. At twenty he startled Parisian theatregoers with a mounting of Georg Büchner's *Leonce and Lena* (1838) at the Théâtre de la Bastille, a major showcase for experimental offerings. He gained national attention in 1989 as the youngest writer-director ever to take part in the official program of an Avignon Festival, with a four-hour abridgment of his self-authored *Les parisiens* (The Parisians). Except for a few months of classes with Antoine Vitez at the Palais de Chaillot (Paris) in 1982–1983, Rambert is an autodidact who, like other French experimental artists of his generation, holds to a creative vision and practice that are as multinational as they are multidisciplinary.

Rambert claims to have been marked in early adolescence by his experience of the works of Pina Bausch, Claude Régy, and Klaus Michael Grüber. Today he speaks of his affinities with the French choreographer-performance artist Myriam Gourfink, the Austrian sculptor-photographer Erwin Wurm, the late Iranian-born American playwright-director Reza Abdoh, and Richard Maxwell, a New York City transplant from North Dakota. For his ideas about Western science in *Paradis*—which premiered as *Paradis (un temps à déplier)* at Paris's La Colline–théâtre national in January 2004—Rambert references works by the German "posthumanist" philosopher Peter Sloterdijk (b. 1947). An avid traveler, Rambert has developed and produced stage pieces in Syria, Japan, California, and New York (where he has taught at New York University); and he has directed operas by the Scottish-born composer James Dillon (*Philomela*, 2005) and the Egyptian-born Marc Monnet (*Pan*, 2005), as well as an updated adaptation, in 2009, of Jean-Baptiste Lully's *Armide* (1686), with Mercury Baroque Ensemble Opera in Houston, Texas. He is also a filmmaker, with several bold shorts to his credit.

Irrespective of their media mix or mode of delivery, Rambert's recent works are all attempts at achieving what he calls "*une écriture en temps réel*," or real-time writing.[26] By this he means that a performed piece will be nothing more—and nothing less—than a display, or an unfolding, of the very processes that bring it into being. In preparing *Paradis*, for example, he drafted about 60 percent of a preliminary text, replete with potential utterances and movements (the latter formulated as detailed stage directions); he then set up intensive improvisation sessions with his players, leaving it to them for months on end to modify what he had already put to paper and to help him come up with the rest. Much of their labor entailed practice in delayed verbalizations and ultraslow motions aimed at keeping the rhythms of "realistic" play-acting at bay.

Just as he shuns conventional stage realism, Rambert (an admirer of Gertrude Stein) rejects symbol and metaphor. He asked his players as they improvised to generate "poetic associations" that would result from a "literal," almost "tautological" succession of concrete words and actions.[27] Each public performance of a finished Rambert stage work is thus a kind of rearticulation—for the spectators' eyes, ears, and sensibilities, as well as for the performers' full bodily apparatus—of creative moments that existed and continue to exist only and always in present time and space.

Rambert's conception of theatre as a fully exposed showing of both the body and the imagination in action helps explain his penchant for stage nudity. At the start of *Paradis* the players—five men and six women, all in their twenties—slowly remove their street clothes and undergarments, which they place in neat piles at the far edges of the playing space. For the rest of the show they remain nude except for orange knit briefs, armbands, and leg warmers that they periodically put on and take off. Yet even as they roll, twist, and perform headstands with legs splayed and genitals in full view, their fit and (apparently) tattoo-less bodies function chiefly as formal elements in the work's scenography.

"I can't dissociate nudity from desire, and I don't want to," says Rambert, who asserts that theatre making has always been a sexually charged activity imprinted with his ardor for the three women who have successively shared his life onstage and off: Narmé Kaveh, Joana Preiss, and currently Kate Moran. "But I also don't want that to be the point of the piece. . . . Rather it's part of its substance."[28] In other words Pascal Rambert sees Dante's muse-driven *Paradiso* as being just as germane to his work as, say, The Living Theatre's *Paradise Now*.[29]

Imagistic New Circus

James Thiérrée descends from a line of creative geniuses. He is Eugene O'Neill's great-grandchild and Charlie Chaplin's grandson. His parents, Victoria Chaplin and Jean-Baptiste Thiérrée, were pioneers in the European development of *nouveau cirque*, or New Circus—an effort begun in the early 1970s to swap poetic vision for big top clichés. By age four, James (born in Lausanne, Switzerland) was, along with his gifted older sister, Aurélie, touring and performing with his parents' company Le Cirque Imaginaire. After studying theatre arts at Milan's Piccolo Teatro and Harvard University, Thiérrée worked as a stage and screen actor for such artistically high-end directors as Peter Greenaway, Coline Serreau, Robert Wilson, and Agnieszka Holland. He continues to appear in films but mainly devotes his energies—as both *auteur* and lead performer—to his own *nouveau cirque* group, La Compagnie du Hanneton (The Junebug Company), whose appellation derives from his childhood nickname. The troupe won popular acclaim with its first full-scale production, *La symphonie du hanneton* (*The Junebug Symphony*) in 1998. Ever since,

Thiérrée has been generally regarded as a major creative and performing artist.

As part of ACT FRENCH, *Bright Abyss* (*La veillée des abysses*), his second full-scale stage piece, thrilled crowds at the Brooklyn Academy of Music's Harvey Theater. It is a stunning art-circus fantasia whose dreamlike imagery is redolent of Jules Verne adventure novels, Little Nemo comic strips, and JJ Grandville's illustrations for *Gulliver's Travels* and *Robinson Crusoe*. (Its French title is a near anagram of that of Maurice Maeterlinck's lyrical treatise on nature's flying pollinators, *La vie des abeilles* [*The Life of the Bee*, 1901].) The piece opens with a large metal-and-rope contraption, presumably a ship at sea, that while slowly crossing the stage succumbs to an equally contrived storm whose violent waves are conjured up via billowing bolts of white cloth (reminiscent of Mnouchkine's technique in *Le dernier caravansérail* and *Les naufragés du Fol Espoir*). For the rest of this ninety-minute spectacle the six survivors, stranded among an array of deceptively ordinary objects, engage with the latter in logic-defying ways: a dining table turns into a giant rolling spool that allows for acrobatic displays; a Victorian-style red velvet couch literally swallows up those who sit on it and then spits them out; a fairy-tale princess pacing about with candelabras that seem swiped from Cocteau's *La belle et la bête* (*Beauty and the Beast*, 1946) metamorphoses into a horse. Other players, with the benefit of still other objects, turn into fanciful quadrupeds and flying bats. When one man (the Swedish dancer-actor Niklas Ek) approaches a lectern and microphone, extreme stage left, his strenuous efforts to speak—in an otherwise wordless show—result only in gibberish. Bodies, alone and in groups, shift from athletic dance to feats of contortion to coursing trapeze stunts carried out via a revolving circular rig hung from the flies. At the show's close the players are again at sea, but they and their ship float suspended, at a safe remove from the swirling waters below.

• • •

The postmodern Rambert and the Victorian-leaning Thiérrée represent distinct theatrical traditions. Yet like Pascal Rambert in *Paradis (unfolding time)*, James Thiérrée rejects story and embraces corporeally based imagistic spectacle. Like Rambert, he offers a hybrid of tried-and-true media—dance, music, vaudeville comedy, mime, acrobatics, aerial arts—in which the finished product is qualitatively richer than the simple sum of its parts. Both he and Rambert partake of a neobaroque vision dominated by centrifugal swerves, sweeping displacements, and frictionless reversals. In both men's pieces, viewers experience creative force as erupting in real time, as if invented at the very moment of enactment. There are, however, clear differences between these two exceptional talents.

Pascal Rambert's poetics is based on literal, concrete alliances among bodies, utterances, and objects. These connect, so to speak, metonymically along a horizontal axis. ("One thing I learned from Pina Bausch's scenography," Rambert notes, "is that the ground [le sol] is the most fundamental thing in theatre.")[30] Thiérrée's poetics, by contrast, favors metaphors, with bodies, sounds, and objects mixing and metamorphosing into chimerical but vaguely identifiable new entities. Be they physical or conceptual, Thiérrée's movements tend to soar upward. ("It's a show," Thiérrée says of Bright Abyss, "that's free as the air, that plays, dances, takes wing, gives a rough ride . . . just for you [the audience]!")[31]

Thus, where Rambert requires us to exercise the mind vigorously in order to discern patterns from which we can then construct possible meanings, Thiérrée largely relieves us of such labor. While Rambert jostles and challenges *our* imagination, Thiérrée transports and enchants us through *his*. And in contradistinction to electronic-age neofuturists who view emerging media technologies as the promising means to solve humanity's social problems, both Rambert and Thiérrée reinstate the value of singular and unreproducible embodied creativity that reaches and enriches what might best be called the viewer's soul.

• • •

Bright Abyss, Thiérrée states in terms similar to those of Philippe Quesne regarding *The Itching of Wings*, "is about people who can't quite make it but they're still doing it."[32] Thiérrée's stress on human fragility and personal risk-taking is telling. It sets his version of New Circus apart from that, for instance, of the entertainment colossus Cirque du Soleil (founded in 1984 and based in Montreal), whose early delicate displays of lyrical inventiveness soon became buried under the weight of high-tech production values, kitschy glitz, and aseptically perfect technique.

James Thiérrée steers clear of splashy new technologies. In the tradition of his celebrated grandfather (who died when James was three), Thiérrée keeps his shows gentle, artisanal, and within a human scale. In fact, James bears a close physical resemblance to Charlie: tight wiry frame, high forehead and cheekbones, thick curly hair, toothy grin, and sad piercing eyes. In *Bright Abyss*, James's comic combats with iron gates, obstreperous newspapers, and his own rebellious limbs tend, like Charlie's, toward the surreal and the balletic. Like the hapless Little Tramp, James, too, seems to be unlucky in love. And while he doesn't exactly waddle, he prances, jumps, slithers, tumbles, and crawls about barefoot with Chaplin's feline grace. Yet one never has the sense of watching an imitation or a nostalgic tribute. James Thiérrée's genius as a theatre-dance-circus performer places him in a class of his own—perhaps neither cool nor edgy, but surely sublime.[33]

Part 2
Paris

I almost moved to Paris, mostly because
I was so unhappy with America. I felt so
much repression. Psychological repression
and puritanical business-oriented American
repression. Now I still feel that way, but of
course it's creeping into France too.
— New York theatre maker
*   Richard Foreman, 2007*

Great Classics Revisited

Playground for aficionados

The variety and quantity of stage performances available on any given day in Paris are staggering. During a typical week of my six-month stay in the City of Light, I was able to choose from 479 events playing at 172 venues.[1] Most of these shows took place in fairly conventional theatre spaces, large and small. Yet just as integral to Paris's theatrical landscape are scores of *café-théâtres*—niches that offer modest plays, stand-up comedy, or poetry readings while you sip, say, a glass of Brouilly—and dozens of *cabaret-dîner-spectacle* spots that present such lavish, tourist-oriented entertainments as the nude shows at Le Crazy Horse, drag parodies at Michou, and splashy Las Vegas–style revues at the Moulin Rouge and the Lido, where your (pricey) tickets come with champagne and a four-course meal. If you add to this the circus tents, puppet-show pavilions, and opera houses strewn throughout the city's neighborhoods and parks (you can take in an opéra bouffe while floating on a barge moored in Paris's largest canal), even the most jaded culture vulture can turn a bit giddy.

Between late December 2005 and the end of June 2006, I attended about ninety French stage events—an average of one show every other day. Conditioned by the bolder segments of ACT FRENCH, I made a point to sample what I suspected would turn out to be unusual and maybe even trailblazing: new playwrights, new experimental companies, new minority voices, *nouveau cirque*, and so on. But I quickly realized that to gain a full sense of the vibrancy of Paris's contemporary theatre scene I would also need to delve into an area not at all represented by ACT FRENCH but one that makes the French capital so intensely pleasurable for theatre aficionados of all stripes: the steady revival of works from the past.

This first chapter on Paris will therefore focus on major new productions of three classic playwrights: Molière, Paul Claudel, and Edmond Rostand. It will also give pride of place to the Comédie-Française—the great state-supported company founded by Louis XIV and whose acting traditions owe a huge debt to Molière himself. In recent years the Comédie-Française—often referred to as the Théâtre Français or simply the Français—has sought to modernize both its repertory and its productions. It has also increasingly drawn on international theatre artists. Yet the Français has no monopoly on reviving the classics. Some of the most interesting new versions of Molière, for instance, often take place in less exalted spaces and sometimes far beyond Paris.

"Public" versus "private" theatre

A fairly strict cultural split exists among Parisian theatregoers. In one camp are those who frequent France's state- and city-supported not-for-profit theatres, known as the *théâtre public*. In the other are those who prefer the *théâtre privé*, the approximately fifty major commercial houses that showcase celebrity players and offer fairly conventional dramatic fare—especially new comedies and plot- and character-driven dramas. It is a division in taste that roughly corresponds, in New York terms, to folks who, on one hand, are strongly drawn to the offbeat and frequently more challenging shows of Off- and Off-Off-Broadway; and, on the other, those who revel in the more familiar and typically less demanding plays and musicals that run at midtown Broadway houses.

'Art' versus 'entertainment' is convenient shorthand for distinguishing between the *théâtre public* and the *théâtre privé*. Within my own circle of Parisian friends I found that—unlike many of their more flexible New York counterparts—very few are inclined to cross the line between the one and the other. I, however, have always enjoyed both the artsy and the "merely" entertaining. So I was determined to do the unthinkable: move freely amid both sectors. After all, boulevard dramas and comedies—named as such because most commercial theatres are found along the *grands boulevards* on Paris's Right Bank—can, at their best, offer intense, even transcendent pleasure. And government-funded projects, for all their artistic pretensions, are sometimes absolute duds.

A national network of theatres

For an American exploring the state of current theatre in France, it is hard not to be awed by the infrastructure that the French subsidized system—much of it funded jointly by national, regional, and local governments—grants to artists who are committed to quality, novelty, and experimentation. Given the paltry government funding available for experimental and noncommercial stage work in the United States, it is little wonder that a good number of international artists and troupes view France, with its exceptionally large cultural budget, with a certain degree of envy.

France has five *théâtres nationaux*, supported entirely by the central government: the Comédie-Française, La Colline–théâtre national, the Odéon-Théâtre de l'Europe, the Théâtre National de Chaillot, and—the only one not in Paris—the Théâtre National de Strasbourg. Also in Paris are various theatres fully funded by the Conseil Municipal de Paris, such as the Théâtre de la Ville, the Théâtre du Châtelet, the Théâtre Silvia Montfort, and the arrondissement or neighborhood theatres, like the Théâtre 13 and the Théâtre 14 Jean-Marie Serreau. Dispersed throughout France are thirty-nine *centres dramatiques nationaux et régionaux* (national and regional dramatic centers, referred to as CDNs or CDRs); seventy *scènes nationales*; more than one hundred *scènes conventionnées*; and over six hundred *compagnies théâtrales subventionnées*—small independent troupes without a permanent institutional base but often lodged in established playhouses. There are also close to thirty *théâtres lyriques* devoted to opera, operetta, and other music-theatre forms; a Conservatoire national supérieur d'art dramatique, in Paris, for the training of actors; an Ecole supérieure d'art dramatique, in Strasbourg, for educating actors, scenographers, directors, stage managers, and dramaturgs; an Ecole nationale supérieure des arts et techniques du théâtre (ENSATT), located in Lyon and run by the Ministry for Public Education; and a Centre national du théâtre, the resource center in Paris that grants general assistance to theatre companies and that promotes contemporary playwriting.[2]

In 2007–2008, the Ministry of Culture and Communication provided 67.8 million euros for the operating costs of the *théâtres nationaux*; 57.6 million euros for the CDNs; and 29 million euros for the *compagnies théâtrales subventionnées*. The euro total of theatre support from regions, departments, and cities exceeded the ministry's grants by over 50 percent.[3] For fiscal year 2010, the ministry's budget allocated 657.7 million euros specifically to the performing arts, and in the preceding year the mayor's office of the city of Paris furnished 28 million euros just for "theatre, dance, circus, and street arts."[4] (The *entire* budget of the U.S. National Endowment for the Arts for fiscal year 2010 was $167.5 million, up $12.5 million from the previous year.)[5]

For creative artists, one of the many appealing features of France's subsidized system is its built-in interconnectedness. In the course of the past fifteen years, for example, the Ministry of Culture appointed a new generation of talented innovators—Stéphane Braunschweig, Arthur Nauzyciel, Pascal Rambert, and others—to directorships of some of the most prestigious CDNs outside of Paris. Many of their new works then went on to tour at other state-supported theatres and festivals throughout France and beyond, often with financial help from the Office national de diffusion artistique (ONDA), a nonprofit organization founded in 1975 with help from the Ministry of Culture. Some of these Young Turks are now heading major public theatres in and around Paris. France's network of government-backed institutions thus provides gifted newcomers to the field with considerable opportunity for risk taking, artistic development, and national recognition.

An American director in the House of Molière

The first stage event I went to that winter in Paris was a choice morsel of cultural opulence. It rolled three national treasures into one: the Comédie-Française, France's oldest and most revered theatre company; Jean de La Fontaine's *Fables*, a beloved literary classic; and Robert "Bob" Wilson (b. 1941), an American director whom the French affectionately view as one of their own. On the surface this is an odd mix. Since its founding in 1680, the Comédie-Française has been the official trustee of France's great dramatic heritage. Yet La Fontaine's *Fables*, a collection of short poems dating from the second half of the seventeenth century, were written not for the theatre but for private reading, recitation, and reflection. Moreover, the Texas-born Wilson—an avant-gardist whose vision has radically altered notions of stage production worldwide—would seem to be oceans apart from the House of Molière, whose conservative praxis has been the stuff of both legend and pique.

To be sure, the Comédie-Française—located on the place Colette across from the Louvre's north wing—is still *the* place to go for flawless versions of canonical plays. On its winter–spring 2006 roster, for example, were new productions of Corneille's *Le Cid* and Sophocles' *Oedipus Tyrannus*; a reprise of Corneille's delightful early comedy *Le menteur* (*The Liar*); and a double bill of Molière and Jean-Baptiste Lully's ballet-farces *L'amour médecin* (*Love's Cure-All*) and *Le Sicilien ou l'amour peintre* (*The Sicilian, or A Painter's Love*). But since at least 2001, when Marcel Bozonnet (b. 1943) took on the post of the theatre's *administrateur général*—a position held by Murielle Mayette as of 2006—the Français has been striving to include more contemporary pieces among the troupe's repertoire and to invite nontraditional international directors to work with the company at rethinking the classics. In February 2011, for instance, the house unveiled its first staging of Tennessee Williams's *Streetcar Named Desire*, directed by Brooklyn-based Lee Breuer, one of the founders (in 1970) of Mabou Mines, the experimental New York theatre company. Under Mayette's aegis, the Français has also aimed to explore newer relations between theatre and cinema, commissioning filmmakers like Mathieu Amalric and the team of Olivier Ducastel and Jacques Martineau to reconceive standard repertory in often audacious ways for the screen.[6]

Initially Marcel Bozonnet wanted Bob Wilson to mount a new version of his first major opus, the seven-hour "silent opera" *Deafman Glance*. That wordless piece, after just two performances at the Brooklyn Academy of Music in 1971, went on to a three-week run (thanks to the financial support of the couturier Pierre Cardin) at Paris's old Théâtre de la Musique, just off the boulevard Sébastopol. The dithyrambic French response catapulted Wilson to superstardom. In the famous "Open Letter to André Breton on Robert Wilson's *Deafman Glance*," Louis Aragon, a former prime mover of the Surrealist movement, hailed Wilson as "what we, for whom Surrealism was born, dreamed would come after us and go beyond us."[7] It was the French, too, via a government subvention, who commissioned the premiere of Wilson's and composer Philip Glass's landmark opera *Einstein on the Beach* for the 1976 Avignon Festival.

Bob Wilson is arguably a more familiar name throughout France than among the general population of his native country. As a token of gratitude, he chose to respond to Bozonnet's offer not with a re-working of *Deafman Glance* but with a new project that would directly honor France's own literary history.

A Zen-like state of "post-anthropocentrism"

Les fables de La Fontaine, which was being reprised at the Comédie-Française after its sellout debut run in 2004 (and which went on to enchant New Yorkers at the Lincoln Center Festival in July 2007), presents 19 of the poet's 245 apologues.[8] For each, Wilson concocts an exquisite stage painting. The show begins with a mute prologue, danced to Michael Galasso's ersatz baroque strains, that presents the full cast of fifteen—including a leaping Frog, a hopping Hare, and a Stag *en pointe*, all choreographed by Béatrice Massin. Some actors wear tuxedos with elaborate animal masks; others are in complete bestial array but leave their human faces visible. The actress Christine Fersen, soon to become the troupe's doyenne, appears in a period black waistcoat, trimmed with white-ruffled linen, and volu-minous hair extensions: she portrays La Fontaine, who, with baton in hand, narrates the start of the evening's first fable, "Le lion amour-eux" ("The Lion in Love").

As in the original poems (some of which were inspired by *Aesop's Fables*), Wilson has his animals speak their own dialogue, but he dis-tributes narrative passages variously to La Fontaine, animals within a fable, and even animals from other fables. In several vignettes Wil-son takes liberties that seem calculated to rile literary purists. The vain Crow, after being tricked by the Fox into dropping his hunk of cheese, speaks the words *"jamais plus . . . plus jamais"* ("nevermore . . . nevermore")—an anachronistic wink to Edgar Allan Poe's ominous raven. Wilson's doomed Frog—the envious one who labors to become as big as an ox and winds up self-detonating—starts out by crooning (in English) the first lines of "Singin' in the Rain." These whimsical grace notes do not cause the piece, as a minority of reviewers felt, to verge on theme-park kitsch.[9] It seems to me that they serve instead the rather useful (and quite American) aim of keeping us, the audi-ence, from taking Great Art too seriously. In this regard Wilson is at one with La Fontaine's neoclassical ideal of human nature, according to which levity and the avoidance of idolatry are princely virtues.

Yet a deeper kinship between the French fabulist and the American director is palpable throughout this work. For Wilson's imagination, like La Fontaine's, has always tilted toward the prerational logic of a mythic world in which animals and plants are just as much agents of events as are human figures. This is why some scholars ally Wilson with the concept of "a post-anthropocentric stage."[10] And it perhaps explains why Wilson closes his *Fables* with the ambiguous "Les compagnons d'Ulysse" ("Ulysses' Companions"), in which the Homeric wanderer's fellow sailors choose to stay under Circe's spell, happy to embrace their metamorphosis into wild wolves, lions, and bears.

Mesmerizing visuals

It is not the moral messages, however, but Wilson's abstract visual style that makes this 110-minute show memorable. Salient traits include mobile panels rearranged for each fable and lit in vivid primary colors or pastel tints depending on the desired mood; the frequent play between brightly illumined bodies and stark silhouettes; traps and windows that suddenly open up so that stories are told, literally, from unexpected angles; and a spare use of objects arranged in geometric patterns, like the three long rods that slowly emerge to suggest the imminent death of the emasculated *lion amoureux* who has foolishly fallen for a shepherdess.

Wilson reaches a height of painterly refinement with his rendering of "Le chêne et le roseau" ("The Oak and the Reed") (see fig. 8). In the first half, as the Oak (in voice-over) conceitedly extols his strength, the stage is totally dark. When the lights gradually return and the lowly Reed (also in voice-over) explains that it has the advantage of bending with the wind, our eyes take in something like a Mondrian canvas infused with powers of subtle animation. Set off against a solid blue background and floor-to-ceiling gray oblong panels that border the wings, a broad black rectangular stripe cuts diagonally upward across the stage. As the oncoming storm gets narrated, this stripe (signifying the uprooted tree) slowly shifts toward the horizontal; downstage, a slim black curvilinear shape (the malleable stalk of grass) holds its own. In serving up a stunning visual complement to La Fontaine's minimalist verbal style and form, Wilson indeed lures us here into an almost Zen-like state of post-anthropocentrism. How

8. *Robert Wilson's set for "The Oak and the Reed" in his* Les fables de La Fontaine. *Photo © Martine Franck/Magnum Photos.*

does this tendency, evident throughout Wilson's *Fables*, impact his actors?

• • •

Christine Fersen, who had been a *sociétaire*, or permanent member, of the Comédie-Française since 1976, died tragically in May 2008. Fortunately we had the chance to chat over drinks two years earlier. Fersen told me that she was initially "miffed" ("*emmerdée*") by Wilson's unusual demand that she, along with all other interested colleagues, audition for participation in *Les fables*—an affront, she felt, to their collective stature and self-regard. Most directors invited to the Français, she noted, choose their casts after observing the company in a number of finished productions. Wilson, however, had each supplicant recite any brief text he or she wanted and then had each take a full two minutes to move toward a chair that stood only six feet away. A chain-smoker, Fersen says she reached for her pack of cigarettes, lit up, and puffed away for those two minutes, deeming the glacially paced exercise to be ridiculous.

Still, Fersen's magnetic presence touched Wilson, whom she soon came to view as "the most courteous, delicious, charming, and vivacious" director she has worked with.[11] "Bob Wilson," she added in her signature throaty voice, "aims for something intangible that emerges from time immemorial, that recreates a state of childhood. He achieves it, and then all you can say is, 'It couldn't have been anything *but* that!'"

The price of tickets

While waiting for the curtain to rise on *Les fables de La Fontaine*, I noted in the program that this production was being underwritten in part by the Fondation Pierre Bergé–Yves Saint Laurent and the Fondation Jacques Toja—whose corporate members include L'Oréal, JPMorgan Chase, and Natexis Banques Populaires. Did this mean, I wondered, that the long-standing distinction between France's *théâtre public* and its *théâtre privé* was disappearing? Not really. It reflected instead what I soon learned were the Ministry of Culture's efforts in a period of growing financial strain to encourage more partnerships with the business community in subsidizing the performing arts.

In fact, the number of French corporate-based foundations for the arts rose from 67 in 2001 to 115 in early 2006, and the corporate sponsorship of culture—very broadly defined—went from 350 million euros in 2002 to one billion in 2005.[12] Nevertheless, France has never had a strong tradition of private support for the public arts. When it comes to culture, business leaders have typically preferred to earmark their philanthropic monies for projects that contribute both to social causes and to smart public relations—for example, bringing the arts to hospitals, increasing youth access to museums and concert halls, or cosponsoring famous established festivals. They are still wary of offering direct support for bold new stage works that might be perceived, rightly or not, as elitist or anticorporate. When foundations do agree to underwrite specific not-for-profit productions, the latter tend to be "safe" vehicles that are guaranteed a broad audience—such as Wilson's *Fables* or another hit of that 2006 season, the St. Petersburg Mariinsky (Kirov) Opera Company's production of Rossini's frolicsome *Il viaggio a Reims* (The Journey to Rheims), which ran at the Théâtre du Châtelet (operated by the city of Paris) with major support from the international banking giant Crédit Agricole.

• • •

Les fables de La Fontaine took place at the Salle Richelieu—the opulent velvet-and-gilt theatre *à l'italienne* that is the Comédie-Française's 862-seat main house. For its 2004–2005 season, the Richelieu—which is part of the Palais-Royal complex of buildings just opposite the Louvre—received a subvention from the Ministry of Culture and Communication equal to 76 percent of its 29.5 million euro annual expenses. The ministry, whose overall budget for the performing arts in 2005 totaled 753 million euros,[13] provided similar measures of support for the Comédie-Française's two affiliated houses: the 300-seat Théâtre du Vieux-Colombier, a rehabilitation of the space off the rue de Rennes (on the Left Bank) made famous by Jacques Copeau in 1913, and which now mounts less costly but often more adventuresome productions than those at the Salle Richelieu; and the Studio-Théâtre, a sparkling 136-seat auditorium nestled in the Galerie du Carrousel du Louvre—a deluxe underground shopping mall accessed from the rue de Rivoli and a stone's throw from the Salle Richelieu—that is dedicated to alternative, low-frill pieces.

In 2004–2005 these three theatres, which have a permanent staff of nearly 400, presented 600 performances to audiences totaling

232,393. *Les fables de La Fontaine*—bested only by the Molière-Lully double bill—played to 98 percent of capacity.[14] Allowing for the euro's fluctuating exchange rate with the U.S. dollar, I found the cost of tickets for most shows at Paris's state-subsidized theatres to be refreshingly within reach when compared with prices for many of New York's Off-Broadway shows. During the 2007–2008 season, seats at the Salle Richelieu ranged from a low of eleven to a high of forty-four euros; top fees at the Vieux-Colombier were twenty-eight euros, and seventeen at the Studio-Théâtre.

Financial troubles

My arrival in France coincided, however, with mounting uncertainty about the Chirac regime's relations to the performing arts. Since June 2003, knotty issues surrounding the eligibility for special unemployment insurance benefits by the nearly 120,000 artists and technicians referred to as *intermittents du spectacle*—freelance contract workers in the cinema, TV, and live-performance industries—had provoked waves of demonstrations and strikes. The turbulence led to a full cancellation of the 2003 Avignon "In" Festival and, following the regional elections of spring 2004, to the ouster of Jean-Jacques Aillagon, then minister of culture.

Aillagon's replacement, Renaud Donnedieu de Vabres, promised to fight "like a lion" to bring this problem to a fair resolution by the end of 2005.[15] Despite his well-intentioned efforts, the conflict—involving labor unions, employer groups, and government agencies—did not get satisfactorily resolved. Throughout my half year in Paris, at least two-thirds of the events I attended were delayed several minutes to enable *intermittents* to appear on stage and give voice to their needs and demands. By March 8, 2006, frustrations had so boiled over that a renewal of strikes caused dozens of Paris theatres to shut down.

The *intermittent* problem relates to broader matters of finance and cultural policy. Ever since President Georges Pompidou launched plans for the great contemporary arts center that now bears his name, the Ministry of Culture has had to expand its administrative purview to accommodate the grandiose projects that Pompidou and his successors pursued as part of their permanent legacy to the French people. For Valéry Giscard d'Estaing, it was the Musée d'Orsay and the Cité des sciences et de l'industrie. For François Mitterrand, it was the Institut du monde arabe, the Opéra Bastille, the Grande Arche de la Défense, the Parc et Grande Halle de la Villette, the Grand Louvre, and the Bibliothèque nationale de France (BNF). For Jacques Chirac, it would be the Musée du quai Branly, a showcase for indigenous arts from Africa, Asia, Oceania, and the Americas that opened in June 2006.

This wondrous burst of new cultural venues shows no signs of abatement. More recent projects underway in Paris and beyond include the Philharmonie de Paris concert hall in the Parc de la Villette, a new Centre des archives nationales in the suburb of Pierrefitte (Seine-Saint-Denis), and the Musée des civilisations de l'Europe et de la Méditerranée in Marseilles. In September 2007 President Nicolas Sarkozy inaugurated a new architectural museum, the Cité de l'architecture et du patrimoine, located in the east wing of the Palais de Chaillot, which had undergone a decadelong makeover costing $114 million. The Ministry of Culture's coffers, however, can be stretched only so far. Of the ministry's 2006 budget of 2.6 billion euros, 25 percent went to maintaining just the BNF, the Opéra Bastille, the Louvre, and the Centre Pompidou.[16] More than ever, culture in France has become big business and big real estate, with the French state its second-largest developer and custodian—just behind local and regional governments. Allocations of public funds for the creation of new art are, as a result, increasingly under stress. In 2010 the ministry's overall budget was 2.92 billion euros; of that, 667.3 million euros went to "the creation, production, and exhibition of *spectacle vivant*" (theatre, music, and dance).[17]

According to some observers, the Ministry of Culture—an invention of the Fifth Republic—has shifted from its earlier mission as a proactive torchbearer for the arts, embodied by such visionary ministers as André Malraux, Jacques Duhamel, and Jack Lang, toward being more of a technocratic apparatus for managing France's vast numbers of cultural workers, agencies, and institutions. Whereas Malraux and Lang often drew upon philosophers, professors, and arts practitioners to fill the ranks of their ministries, "there has been, under Jean-Jacques Aillagon and Renaud Donnedieu de Vabres, hardly any department head or sub-department head who has not come from the Ecole nationale d'administration,"[18] the elite school whose alumni have a near monopoly on access to the highest positions in French industry, state administration, and politics. The time frame of this shift highlights some of its causes: it corresponds roughly to France's transition from *les trente glorieuses*, the "glorious" three decades following World War II that witnessed immense economic reconstruction and expansion, to *les trente piteuses*, the "pitiful" next thirty years that saw rising unemployment, weakened public services, and heightened support for the political far right.

The Sarkozy policy

Soon after he took office in 2007, President Nicolas Sarkozy, who squashed much of the far right's electoral strength, sent a memo of expectations to Christine Albanel, his new Minister of Culture and Communication. An *agrégée* in modern literature and the author of several plays from the early 1980s (most of them unproduced), Christine Albanel (b. 1955) had been Jacques Chirac's speechwriter for nearly two decades and, as of 2003, a controversial president of the museum and domain administration of the Palace of Versailles. After assessing previous regimes' efforts at democratizing culture as "failures," Sarkozy stressed the need for government-supported theatres to "show results" and pay more attention to the "popularity" of their offerings. He especially urged Albanel "to ensure that public assistance to the arts will promote works that respond to audience expectations."[19]

This formulation provoked the ire of many theatre professionals and their allies. "It's like applying a TV ratings system [*l'Audimat*] to the theatre," fumed François Le Pillouër, director of the Théâtre National de Bretagne.[20] "Artistic risk taking and filling the house," cautioned the cultural economist Françoise Benhamou, "do not always coincide."[21] Such perceptions of market demands infringing on artistic privilege, even within France's cushioned public sector, are nothing new. Marc Fumaroli, a member of the Académie Française whose book *L'état culturel: essai sur une religion moderne* (The Culture State: A Modern Religion) caused a stir when it was published in 1991, has repeatedly reproached the ministry for acting like a public relations firm, "collaborating, under the guise of competing, with the market of mass recreation."[22] Jean-Marie Domenach, in *Le crépuscule de la culture française?* (The Twilight of French Culture? 1995), likewise warned: "The role of a democratic state is not to direct culture, not even to subsidize it, but to make sure that a large portion of cultural goods and services remains shielded from the tyranny of profit making."[23] Under pressure from arts professionals who objected vociferously to planned budgetary freezes, Albanel managed to negotiate an unexpected 2.6 percent increase in her overall budget for 2009 and tried to be especially sensitive to the needs of those who work in the area of *spectacle vivant*.[24]

The president, however, became increasingly identified with the antielitist cultural values implicit in his put-down, first articulated the year before he became president, of the required study in many schools of France's first great neoclassical novel, Madame de La Fayette's *La princesse de Clèves* (*The Princess of Cleves*, 1678). Since then, the purchase of a paperback edition of this subtle psychological novel, set in the Renaissance court of King Henri II, has become, for many, a symbolic act of protest against Sarkozy's economic and educational reform policies.

Molière and/as big business

For commercial theatres in Paris, a Molière play can still bring big box-office returns—especially if a celebrity heads the cast. Such was the case for a rollicking revival of *Le bourgeois gentilhomme* (*The Would-Be Gentleman*, 1670) that ran at the plush Théâtre de Paris, in the heart of Paris's ninth arrondissement on the Right Bank. At the Saturday matinee performance I attended, a good part of the audience at this 1,100-seat house was, in appearance, typical of the *théâtre privé* crowd: men in fine suits and ties; well-coiffed matrons, a good number enveloped in furs; teenagers sporting casual-chic Izod or Ralph Lauren, often in the company of parents or grandparents. Ticket prices at the Paris, from fifteen to forty-six euros, are not much more expensive than those at major subsidized theatres. But *théâtre privé* patrons—much like Broadway theatregoers until the late 1960s—still enjoy sprucing up.

Throughout its long history, the Théâtre de Paris has showcased idols of stage and screen: the renowned Réjane, in a 1913 revival of Victorien Sardou's *Madame Sans-Gêne*; the beloved Raimu, in premiere runs of Marcel Pagnol's *Marius* (1929) and *Fanny* (1931); the international movie actress Ingrid Bergman, in a 1956 French-language version of Robert Anderson's *Tea and Sympathy*; the omnipresent Gérard

Depardieu, in a 1999 adaptation of Jacques Attali's best-selling novel about the Holy Roman Emperor Charles V, *Les portes du ciel*.

The Théâtre de Paris's new production of *Le bourgeois gentilhomme* (see fig. 9) featured, in his debut effort at "legit" acting, France's most popular purveyor of smutty stand-up humor, the fifty-one-year-old Jean-Marie Bigard—who in June 2004 had attracted to the Stade de France, normally used for soccer and rugby events, a record-breaking crowd of 52,000 for his one-man show *Des animaux et des hommes* (Of Animals and Men). Bigard, who is a close friend of President Nicolas Sarkozy, has never enjoyed the good graces of France's intelligentsia and its elite cultural tastemakers. He especially outraged many fellow citizens when, as a guest on a radio talk show in September 2009, he declared that much of the September 11, 2001, tragedy was part of a United States conspiracy—thereby echoing sentiments expressed seven months earlier by another celebrity, Marion Cotillard (b. 1975), who had won an Oscar for her portrayal of Edith Piaf in Olivier Dahan's *La Môme* (titled *La Vie en Rose* for English-speaking audiences, 2007). Like Cotillard, Bigard quickly apologized for his "revisionist" statements.[25]

Bigard frustrated journalists who were set to pooh-pooh this show. Savvy and flairful, he conveyed the vulgar materialism of Molière's title character by projecting the same sympathetic gloss he attaches to his raunchy monologues. Director Alain Sachs, who altered not a word of the time-honored text, transformed this Monsieur Jourdain into a contemporary sporting-goods mogul. The arriviste's three tutors, of varied ethnicity, excelled at slamming, kung fu, and break-dancing to the same delightful music that Jean-Baptiste Lully had scored for this *comédie-ballet* centuries ago. Jourdain's sassy servant Nicole, played for broad laughs by Nadège Beausson-Diagne, was an urban black chick who used a Swiffer to wipe up domestic messes. For the mock-Turkish ceremony that elevates the boorish upstart to the honorific rank of "Mamamouchi," Jourdain was wheeled onstage atop a megastore shopping cart as he blissfully snapped digital photos of the assembled crowd. This modish shtick was neither distracting nor detracting. I found that it actually enhanced the grand fun and timelessness of Molière's dialogue, situations, and characters. Roaring with laughter throughout, most fellow spectators seemed to agree.

9. Center front, *Jean-Marie Bigard as the frolicking Monsieur Jourdain in Alain Sachs's production of Molière's* Le bourgeois gentilhomme, *with, in dark suit, Catherine Arditi as his exasperated spouse. Photo © Laurencine Lot.*

Molière as protofeminist

A less glitzy but equally effective updating of a Molière staple was Coline Serreau's *L'école des femmes* (1662), which ran during March at another fashionable commercial house, the Théâtre de la Madeleine. This 728-seat theatre often trots out two plays on its main stage on the same evening. That month, at 7 P.M., it was A. R. Gurney's *Love Letters*, with film stars Anouk Aimée and Philippe Noiret as the epistolary protagonists; and at 9 P.M., Serreau's rendition of the Molière piece.

Coline Serreau (b. 1947) has a sterling theatre pedigree. Her stage-director father, Jean-Marie, was an early champion in France of both Bertolt Brecht and the absurdists; her mother, Geneviève, did major translations of Brecht and Shakespeare. Serreau herself is a multi-talented playwright, actress, filmmaker, and opera director. Known especially for her interest in gender issues—not least as the maker of the movie *Trois hommes et un couffin* (*Three Men and a Cradle*, 1985)—Serreau both directed *L'école des femmes* and took on the starring male role of Arnolphe, a part originally played by Molière and one that Serreau claims to have dreamt of performing since adolescence.[26] (The role has always been a magnet for male movie stars: Pierre Arditi played Arnolphe in Didier Bezace's production at the 2001 Avignon Festival; Daniel Auteuil performed it under Jean-Pierre Vincent's direction at the Odéon-Théâtre de l'Europe in 2008.)

Because she restrained from overmasculinizing her demeanor and voice, Serreau-in-drag was quite credible as young Agnès's misguided guardian. And since Serreau believes that Molière was "five hundred years ahead of his time"[27] with respect to the ideal of male-female equality, she cannily situated the play's action in an unidentifiable era, using only an ingenious network of progressively collapsing heavy drapes for the décor. Yet she gave Agnès's young suitor, Horace, the looks, moves, and speech patterns of a contemporary pop-media-captivated teenager. For some passages—like Agnès's forced recitation of the "Maximes du mariage, ou les devoirs de la femme mariée" ("Marriage Maxims, or A Wife's Duties")—she had her actors deliver their lines in zippy rap fashion.

Some reviewers chided Serreau for tampering with elocutionary tradition.[28] I found, however, that Molière's alexandrines (twelve-syllable lines of rhymed verse) lent themselves well to this ploy and fortified Serreau's (and Molière's) celebration of youth over old age. But what made this production so intelligent was Serreau's decision not to thoroughly condemn the tyrannical Arnolphe but to make us pity him as an almost tragic exponent of a fading, patriarchal world view. Hence her somber, tacked-on coda after the plot's happy resolution—a sung requiem whose first lines were "Oh, malheureux Arnolphe / Agnès n'est pas à toi!" ("O, wretched Arnolphe / You do not own Agnès!").

A darker Molière

Two superb works inspired by the real-life Molière (1622–1673) confirmed that France's subsidized theatres, by contrast with its *théâtres privés*, allow artists substantially increased latitude for risk taking. Each posed challenges, both emotional and intellectual, for willing spectators.

The first was Anne Alvaro's sixty-five-minute *Esprit-Madeleine*, which had a three-week run in the tiny basement Studio of the Théâtre National de Chaillot—the huge multitheatre complex that occupies the eastern wing of the Palais de Chaillot, directly across the Seine from the Eiffel Tower. Alvaro is perhaps best known in the United States for her supporting role in Agnès Jaoui's Oscar-nominated film *Le goût des autres* (*The Taste of Others*, 2000); in 2009 she won a Molière for her performance as the title character in Howard Barker's *Gertrude—The Cry*, which ran at the Odéon-Théâtre de l'Europe. Adapted from a creative prose work by the late Molière scholar Giovanni Macchia,[29] Alvaro's *Esprit-Madeleine* dramatizes an imagined conversation in 1705 between Molière's daughter, Esprit-Madeleine Poquelin (1665–1723), who lived in seclusion for much of her life, and an unnamed admirer of her father's plays, greedy to learn as much as he can about the immortal dramatist's private affairs. The duo's cat-and-mouse encounter transpired amid four wood-framed gauze screens that rotated on hinges to create shifting spaces of passage and obstruction.

The most intriguing moments dealt, inconclusively, with two thorny issues of Molière's enigma-filled biography. Why did Esprit-Madeleine, for whom her father wrote the child's role of Louison in *Le malade imaginaire* (*The Imaginary Invalid*, 1673, act 2, scene 8), fail to play that part and then choose to break with the family tradition of a life on the stage? And is there hard support for the persistent rumor that Esprit-Madeleine's mother, the actress Armande Béjart, may in fact have been Molière's own daughter?

Cryptic answers to both questions may inhere in Esprit-Madeleine's recollection, articulated in Alvaro's play, of why she was unable to play the youngster on stage: "[During rehearsals] I couldn't emit a single sound. . . . I wondered if my father hadn't already discovered within me something that wasn't right . . . as if I'd already been contaminated by the adult world."

• • •

These dark intimations about Molière's life transmute into the core issue of director Arthur Nauzyciel's riveting *Le malade imaginaire ou le silence de Molière* (The Imaginary Invalid, or Molière's Silence) (see fig. 10). A two-and-a-half-hour amalgam of Molière's full play with hefty portions of Giovanni Macchia's speculative text, this production was first conceived by Nauzyciel (b. 1967) in 1999 as his debut creative effort for the CDDB–Théâtre de Lorient in Brittany, where he was an artist-in-residence. Winning much critical praise, the piece toured widely, including a run at Saint Petersburg's Hermitage Theatre in 2000. Since then Nauzyciel has worked on English-language productions with companies in the United States (7 Stages Theatre in Atlanta and the American Repertory Theater in Cambridge), and as of 2007, he has served as head of the CDN of Orléans.

Shortly after my arrival in Paris I learned that *Le malade imaginaire ou le silence de Molière* was being reprised with most of its original ten-member cast at various theatres throughout France. I caught up with it in mid-February at La Passerelle, a *scène nationale* in the center of Saint-Brieuc (Brittany), a town near the English Channel. The tone of Nauzyciel's piece took me by surprise. This is surely one of the rare renditions of a Molière comedy that seems intended to *avert* its audience from bursting into laughter. By intertwining Esprit-Madeleine's supposed memories of her bleak childhood with Molière's ostensible satire of the medical profession, Nauzyciel underscores the rampant physical abuse and emotional blackmail that fluffier productions of the play typically skim over. In making the brief encounter between Argan and his precocious daughter, Louison, the work's central event, Nauzyciel prompts us to hear that scene's final words—

10. *A father-daughter confrontation between Molière/Argan (Jean-Philippe Vidal) and Esprit-Madeleine Poquelin/Louison (Catherine Vuillez) in Arthur Nauzyciel's* Le malade imaginaire ou le silence de Molière. *Photo © Frédéric Nauczyciel.*

ARGAN: Leave me alone, and be on guard against everything; go! . . . Ah, children no longer exist! Ah, there's only deal-making! I don't even have the leisure time to ponder my illness. In truth, I can't take it any longer. . . .

—as a barely veiled expression of Molière's near-paranoid feelings of betrayal and guilt vis-à-vis Esprit-Madeleine and many of the other women who figured in his life.

In line with these disquieting themes, Nauzyciel has Argan's shifty spouse, Béline, appear almost as a soul mate to the infamous heroine of Victor Hugo's Romantic tragedy *Lucrèce Borgia* (1833). Similarly, Toinette projects a moral monstrosity more akin to that of Oenone, the nurse in Racine's *Phèdre* (1677), than to the lighthearted craftiness usually associated with Molière's female servants. Even the tubercular Molière's coughing, retching, and spitting of blood are so graphically and repulsively portrayed that we have scant sympathy for the great writer when we finally see him expire. (Molière died a few hours after the fourth performance of *Le malade imaginaire*.)

Scholars continue to debate whether Molière's darker side had anything to do with incestuous impulses. But Arthur Nauzyciel believes that repressing the hypothesis is itself unhealthy. His Molière project, he explained in conversation, stems in large part from the valuable revelation of his own family secret: his maternal grandfather, despite the tattooed number on his forearm, had stubbornly refused to speak of his having been interned in Auschwitz. It was Arthur's father, Emile, who took pains to break the silence and to explain to his son about the Holocaust and what it means to be a Jew in Europe today. Nauzyciel's company in fact goes by the name 41751, his granddad's serial number.

One of the many pleasures in watching this production of *Le malade imaginaire* is to see the onstage complicity between the octogenarian Emile Nauzyciel, who plays the quack doctor Monsieur Diafoirus, and Arthur Nauzyciel, who plays the doctor's son, the quack-in-training Thomas Diafoirus. In a strangely touching way it is a reinstatement of the real parent-child relationship Molière imagined for his original cast. "I could not have done this production without having my father—who never acted before—take part," says the younger Nauzyciel.[30] Still, the piece does not devolve into self-indulgence. It is instead a profound meditation on the complex character of inheritance—be it biological, political, or theatrical.

Paul Claudel and poetic delirium

The most powerful revival of a classic that I saw was Paul Claudel's *Tête d'or* (1889, first version), directed by Anne Delbée in a new production at the Théâtre du Vieux-Colombier (see fig. 11). Internationally known for her pioneering biography of Claudel's sculptor sister Camille (*Une femme, Camille Claudel*, 1982), Delbée (b. 1946) is one of the rare French female directors regularly called upon to mount major works for the Comédie-Française, including plays by such titans as Racine, Corneille, and now Claudel (1868–1955). She has also served two terms as president of the Syndicat national des metteurs en scène (National Association of Stage Directors).

Taking on *Tête d'or*, however, is a risky effort for any director. The piece, written when the author was only twenty-one, is massive, difficult, and often perplexing. Also, any new production is bound to elicit comparison with Jean-Louis Barrault's legendary 1959 staging at the newly rededicated Théâtre de l'Odéon, which by all accounts featured peerless performances by Alain Cuny (1908–1994) as Simon Agnel, the conquering warrior who becomes known as Tête d'or (Golden Head), and by Laurent Terzieff (1935–2010) as the spiritually tormented adolescent, Cébès. On top of this are the distracting matters of Paul Claudel's faith and politics.

Claudel, who had a mystical religious awakening while writing *Tête d'or*, has long ranked as France's greatest modern Catholic poet and dramatist. He has also been subject to false claims that he, a former career diplomat, was supportive of the occupying German forces in World War II. Because the gatekeepers of Paris's public theatre establishment have tended to be left-leaning and secular humanist, many held Claudel's oeuvre in chilly disregard over the past six decades. *Tête d'or*, whose febrile young protagonist is bent on imposing his will upon all of Europe, has been a special object of anachronistic readings that see the work as celebrating twentieth-century totalitarianism. Anne Delbée tried to preempt such reductionism by making clear in the play's program notes that "Tête d'or is not Hitler . . . nor is he Stalin or Napoleon! This was [for Claudel] above all a play about the overwhelming force of poetry." [31]

11. *The warrior Simon Agnel (Thierry Hancisse) observes the assassinated King (Andrzej Seweryn) and the latter's horrified daughter (Marina Hands) in Paul Claudel's* Tête d'or, *directed by Anne Delbée. Photo © Emmanuel Orain.*

Delbée's efforts were in vain. *Le Canard Enchaîné*'s critic could not refrain from reminding readers that Claudel once dedicated an ode to Marshal Philippe Pétain (whose Vichy policies the author later actively opposed).[32] With respect to *Tête d'or*'s supposed Nietzschean distinction between "the [spiritually] weak" and "the strong," *Le Monde*'s reviewer fingered Claudel (and by implication Delbée) for once again exposing playgoers to "the [racist] rancidness of the France of yore [*la vieille France*]."[33]

At the performance I attended in early April, about a quarter of the audience left the house at intermission. I doubt, however, that their departure stemmed from unease over an imagined crypto-fascist subtext. It was more likely due to their disinclination to engage—for four and a half hours—with poetic declamation delivered at a delirious level of intensity and passion. In the title role, which requires the stamina of a heldentenor performing Richard Wagner's *Siegfried*, Thierry Hancisse was astonishing: he never failed to convince us of Simon's prodigious strength, intelligence, and magnetism. As the frail Cébès, Clément Hervieu-Léger projected feverish emotion with both subtlety and verve; his protracted death throes, followed by Tête d'or's horror at the loss of his friend, gave us a portrayal of tender virile bonding redolent of Homer. Perhaps the most striking revelation was Marina Hands, in her debut role with the Comédie-Française, playing the exiled Princess who endures crucifixion after Tête d'or assassinates her father. From the moment she appeared on stage cloaked in bolts of gold lamé, Hands radiated the deep humanity and inner beauty that make credible Tête d'or's rejection of his hubris at the play's redemptive end. Delbée demanded bold physical as well as vocal gymnastics from this trio of gifted performers. To my mind the interplay of the three leads was flawless.

Most reviewers, however, had little patience for this production. Their main gripe was that the actors' elocutionary manner, as the writer for the weekly *Figaroscope* put it, displayed "bombast" ("*emphase*") bordering on "parody": "We would have preferred more restraint, more discretion, a less grandiloquent style."[34] Yet Delbée, who spoke with me after the play's six-week run, insisted that she (unlike Barrault) chose to work from the earliest version of Claudel's play precisely because it exposes the young poet's incantatory voice "at its most savagely brutal," when he had just fallen under the spell of Arthur Rimbaud's *Illuminations*. "The language of the truest modern poets," she pointed out, "is always scandalously intense. Think of the line of descent that links Rimbaud to Claudel to Jean Genet to Serge Gainsbourg to Valère Novarina."[35]

Regardless of one's opinion about Delbée's success with *Tête d'or*, her production did give evidence of the striking affinities between Claudel and today's theatre of *la parole*. For the basic drama in Claudel does not inhere in characters or in a story line but in the explosively scenic and sensual potential of the spoken word. Marked by the same rhapsodic confidence in the word made flesh found in the works of, say, Novarina and Olivier Py (another unabashedly Catholic playwright), Claudel's prosody—the long, luxuriant lines of free verse known as *le verset claudélien*—aim to convey the performer's very breath and heartbeat in the act of recitation. In a recent overview of twentieth-century French *"poésie de théâtre"* (the term is Jean Cocteau's), one critic astutely noted that Claudel remains "our foremost contemporary."[36] If only to confirm this salient lineage, Anne Delbée's undertaking was both necessary and rewarding.

An old-fashioned Cyrano

At the height of the Paris tourist season, in late June 2006, the Comédie-Française unveiled its new production of Edmond Rostand's beloved *Cyrano de Bergerac* (1897). Preceded by a barrage of media attention, it instantly became the year's hottest ticket. As directed with élan by Denis Podalydès (a *sociétaire* at the Comédie-Française and also an acclaimed actor in films by Bertrand Tavernier, Michael Haneke, and Denis's brother, Bruno Podalydès), Rostand's rompish mix of heroic tragedy, Romantic drama, and Moliéresque farce received nearly unanimous press raves.[37] The three-hour extravaganza went on to nab six Molières, including the award for Best Direction. It also won a Globe de Cristal (the French arts journalists' prize) for the year's Best Play. Over 1.4 million viewers tuned in when it was televised in June 2007.

Famously disdained by many old-style intellectuals for its "cheap" boulevard roots, *Cyrano de Bergerac* did not become part of the Comédie-Française's repertoire until 1938. Prior to this 2006 revival it had enjoyed 873 performances at the House of Molière and thousands of others at theatres large and small, amateur and professional, throughout France. In a nod to the play's rich life, Podalydès (b. 1963) began his show with a photo-film-video montage of notable past Cyranos—from Benoît-Constant Coquelin, who originated the role, to Pierre Dux, Jean Piat, and Daniel Sorano.

This "new media" component then spilled over into the play proper (fig. 12). Early scenes of act 1 depict the seventeenth-century thespian Montfleury as he performs in Balthazar Baro's *La Clorise* (1632) at the Hôtel de Bourgogne. Podalydès chose to give us video images—projected on a large raised screen, stage center—of the actor-spectators as they took their seats for this play-within-the-play. We thus delighted in a magnified close-up of the beauteous Roxane as she tardily settled into her box. Soon we experienced a lively interplay of perspectives: simultaneously we could view Montfleury's performance in on-screen frontal views via live-stream video; and, from the slanting angle of the Bourgogne's off-stage wings area that dominated the downstage space (as called for by Rostand), we could observe his histrionics in the flesh. Such clever use of new technology primed us to suspect that Podalydès was going to bring fresh relevance to the play's central tension between seeing and knowing, between representation and truth.

Was this *Cyrano* therefore going to follow the lead of such companies as the Wooster Group and the Builders Association and explore co-relations of the corporeal and the mediatized, the actual and the virtual? No. After Cyrano bounced on stage in act 1, scene 4, the videography vanished—along with any other sustained attempt to integrate new media. Though it never lagged and always entertained, this production turned out to be rather old-fashioned and unexceptional. In its use of sets, props, costumes, and music that ranged in inspiration from the seventeenth through the twentieth centuries, the guiding directorial principle might best be referred to as razzle-dazzle hodgepodge.

The flashiest bit of staging occurred in the balcony scene: Podalydès had Roxane, enraptured by Christian's/Cyrano's avowal of love, floating amid the starry sky, like Peter Pan. This stunt (done with slightly visible cables descended from the flies) was surely intended as an apt visual metaphor for the sublime potency of the grotesquely long-nosed poet-swordsman's oratorical gifts. Yet the able actor Michel Vuillermoz's command of Rostand's exuberant alexandrines—this play marks the last hurrah for such rhyming couplets in French dramatic literature—never quite justified the gimmick.

Panache and restraint

Audiences did not seem to care. The day I attended there was even repeated applause for the five picture-perfect sets designed by Eric Ruf, who also played Christian; and for the costumes conceived by star couturier Christian Lacroix. Contented murmurs of recognition filled the house when recorded strains of Ravel's *Boléro*—at deafening volume—suffused act 4's battlefield feast scene. As the curtain fell on the final act, the house went wild with vociferous bravos, and the audience soon broke into a brisk unison handclap, the French equivalent of a U.S. standing ovation.

That is perhaps just as it should be for a theatre piece that has long been deemed a popular cultural treasure. Since its inception in the period following France's 1870 defeat to the Germans and Prussians and the country's loss of Alsace and Lorraine, *Cyrano de Bergerac*, it is frequently claimed, has promoted national solidarity, making citizens feel proud to be French. Immediately following the play's inaugural run, Rostand was awarded knighthood in the Légion d'honneur. The cultural critic Jean-Marie Apostolidès has posited "a homology between *Cyrano*'s characters and the unconscious foundational dynamics of the [French] nation," which were especially in play between 1870 and the onset of World War I.[38] According to this view, Cyrano's heroism lies in his ultimate capacity to balance obedience and allegiance to the state (France) with tender love for his native region (Gascony). As France currently debates immigration policies and what it means to be a French citizen in the twenty-first century, this Comédie-Française revival may have coincidentally tapped into a renewed public appreciation of the difficulties attendant upon reaching such harmony in an era of postcolonialism.

Unfortunately, Podalydès's cluttered spectacle overpowered a second factor that accounts for the play's enduring appeal: its delicacy of feeling. The plot's most poignant moment occurs near the end when Cyrano—old, mortally wounded, and semidelirious—inadvertently reveals to the widowed Roxane that it is he, not Christian, who au-

12. *From the wings of the Hôtel de Bourgogne, standing far right, Christian (Eric Ruf) beholds the on-screen image of Roxane (Françoise Gillard) in Denis Podalydès's production of Edmond Rostand's* Cyrano de Bergerac. *Photo © Raphaël Gaillarde.*

thored the fervid love letters that indelibly touched her soul. A single line encapsulates the scene's, and the entire play's, dramatic tension:

CYRANO: No, no, my dear love, I did not love you.[39]

These words should elicit our pity and commiseration for the long-self-sacrificing protagonist. But as delivered by Michel Vuillermoz (and directed by Podalydès), the line provoked—at least at the performance I attended—a rush of audience guffaws.

Rostand had a gift for pushing spectators' emotional buttons at precisely the right time and with exactly the right strength. Essential to the success of any *Cyrano* is the notion of *panache*, or flamboyant style: it is the word Cyrano mouths just before he dies. But equally crucial, as the hero's life story demonstrates, is the concept of *restraint*. To be fully satisfying, productions of *Cyrano de Bergerac* need to coordinate the two.

A matter of expectations

By programming fresh versions of *Tête d'or* and *Cyrano de Bergerac* in the same season, the Comédie-Française bore out its mission to keep alive the multiple strands that make up France's grand theatre history. Should we be shocked that its middling production of the Rostand play won greater critical and popular approval than its inspired mounting of the Claudel opus? I think not. Must we take sides by preferring either Rostand or Claudel? Of course not. We must simply approach productions of these playwrights with different sets of expectations and separate criteria for assessing their validity.

Cyrano de Bergerac is a virtuosic pastiche of the best verse theatre of bygone eras, with echoes of Paul Scarron, Corneille, Marivaux, and Hugo. Much of the pleasure we take in attending a performance of *Cyrano*—whether encountering the work for the first time or having seen it a dozen times over—resides in sensations of *déjà-vu*, *déjà-entendu*, and *déjà-ressenti*: its formal structure, verbal rhetoric, and crystalline themes have a wonderfully familiar ring about them. Rostand's play not only entertains. It also allows us to feel highly cultured.

Tête d'or, which predates *Cyrano* by eight years, is likewise replete with literary echoes—of Aeschylus, Virgil, the Bible, and Shakespeare; of Hugo, Baudelaire, and Stéphane Mallarmé. Yet in watching the play we sense that Claudel is neither repackaging his predecessors nor pandering to mainstream complacency. We perceive instead a young artist driven to add his singular, contemporary voice to a choir of earlier visionaries and to inaugurate a different, more demanding line of poetic theatre—whose boldest exponents still forge ahead today.

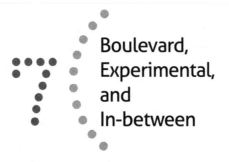

Boulevard, Experimental, and In-between

A spectrum of theatrical pleasures

What visitor to Paris does not respond sentimentally to the sight of a Morris column? The City of Light boasts 733 of these imposing, sometimes rotating, pillars that display eye-catching posters for nightclub shows, concerts, movies, and boulevard plays. They are as much a fixture of the Paris streetscape as are the carts of pretzel and hot-dog vendors on midtown Manhattan street corners.

Soon after my French sojourn began, however, the future of these picturesque structures was in question. The previous June, the Conseil de Paris—the city's main deliberative body—had tucked into its renewed contract with the columns' manufacturers a plan to reduce their number by 35 percent, supposedly to combat growing "congestion of public space."[1] Alarmed by this covert blow to their marketing prowess, the administrative heads of the *théâtres privés* collectively denounced the initiative and demanded that the issue be reexamined. For those of us who cherish French cultural tradition, the city's proposal was likewise unsettling. Not least among the delights of a Paris stroll is chancing upon these visible links back to a golden era of boulevard theatre dominated by such giants as Eugène Labiche, Georges Courteline, and Sacha Guitry.

In this chapter I will direct attention to stage pieces in three categories that are not usually considered together: boulevard comedies of the kind that get splashy advertising space on the Morris columns; literary dramas that sometimes run in commercial venues but when they are more formally inventive play in government-supported theatres; and experimental ventures that leave conventional theatre narrative far behind—and almost never play in commercial houses. This juxtaposition fairly reflects my overall Parisian theatregoing experience in 2005–2006. My internal compass was largely ruled by Voltaire's famous axiom in the preface to his comic play *L'enfant prodigue* (*The Prodigal Son*, 1736): "*Tous les genres sont bons, hors le genre ennuyeux*" ("All styles are good, except the boring kind").

Readers will note that I in fact spend more time with so-called arty or alternative productions than with frothy *divertissements*. Yet I think it is worthwhile to acknowledge the pleasures to be found at all spots along the theatrical spectrum. My somewhat unorthodox commingling will, I think, also bring into clearer focus the rich and varied middle ground that lies between the more sharply marked-off spheres of pure commercialized entertainment and the most progressive vanguard experimentation.

The boulevard

The glory days of French boulevard theatre ended with World War II. Until then, each season's lineup typically featured fifty or so plot-based comedies by such well-known playwrights as Tristan Bernard (1866–1947) and Louis Verneuil (1893–1952); social satires by Georges Courteline (1858–1929) and Jules Renard (1864–1910); psychological dramas by Henry Bernstein (1876–1953) and Henry Bataille (1872–1922); and star turns by the likes of Charles Boyer, Yvonne Printemps, and Victor Boucher. The tail end of the *années folles* (the 1920s) and the unsettled decade leading to France's military defeat and occupation by the Germans (1940–1944) ushered in a new wave of distinguished boulevard writers — Marcel Pagnol (1895–1974), Jean Anouilh (1910–1987), and Marcel Aymé (1902–1967), among others — whose works tended to be more socially probing and biting. In the years following the war, competition from movies and then television worked to the disadvantage of boulevard entertainments. Still, remarkable new pieces by Anouilh, Aymé, Marcel Achard (1899–1974), and the indestructible Sacha Guitry (1885–1957) reinvigorated their thematic scope, infusing boulevard offerings with dreamscapes, playful self-reference, and often polemical treatments of the slippery line between truth and fiction in the modern world.

Yet with the advent of such radical playwrights as Samuel Beckett (1906–1989) and the absurdists, or Jean Genet (1910–1986) and Fernando Arrabal (b. 1932), the call and need for even mild innovation amid boulevard houses virtually disappeared. Within today's Parisian theatre scene, the boulevard stage in content and form probably constitutes, as Michel Corvin puts it, "a regression."[2] But what boulevard fare persists in doing is to provide audiences with engaging, well-made stories about everyday people or exceptional, often historic, figures who are also easy to relate to. These are plays that, without apology, reinforce mainstream values and ultimately expunge moral, social, and existential ambiguities.

While boulevard offerings are thoroughly distinct from theatre of *la parole* and the latter's potent verbal-performative engine, theatre-goers nonetheless mostly identify them by the *playwright*'s name, not by that of a director or company. Indeed, the boulevard supplies a commercial space in which gifted dramatists can ply, on one hand, their rhetorical talent for banter, puns, double entendres, repartee, and winking references to current events and even fellow playwrights; and on the other hand, their skill at constructing scripts replete with unexpected turns, riveting *scènes à faire*, and memorable climaxes.

In today's market, however, it is the star actor, not the playwright, who generally exerts primary box-office pull. Indeed, very few French dramatists, whether they write for the *théâtre privé* or the *théâtre public*, can make a decent living from their writings. The playwright Louise Doutreligne (b. 1948), an officer of the Société des auteurs et compositeurs dramatiques (SACD)—the organization that keeps track of income and royalties received by France's writers for the stage—relates: "In the year 2009, ninety-eight percent of contemporary dramatists earned less than ten thousand euros [about $12,500] annually from their plays."[3] Still, the audience for boulevard pieces remains substantial. In 2008, Paris's *théâtres privés* attracted 3.27 million spectators as opposed to the 1.84 million who attended the city's *théâtres publics*.[4] The seductive pull of light comedy and sentimental drama, performed and consumed "live," undeniably endures.

Laughter and tears

I was especially eager to catch Josiane Balasko, who was starring in *Dernier rappel* (Last Call) at the Théâtre de la Renaissance—a stately house on the boulevard Saint-Martin that in the 1890s had been presided over by the legendary Sarah Bernhardt (1844–1923). Balasko (b. 1950) is a Gallic version of Roseanne Barr: loud and vulgar yet sympathetic and very funny. She is known abroad for her roles in such comic films as Patrice Leconte's *Les bronzés* series (*French Fried Vacation*, 1978, 1979, 2006), Bertrand Blier's *Trop belle pour toi* (*Too Beautiful for You*, 1989), and her self-directed sex farce *Gazon maudit* (*French Twist*, 1995). In winter 2005 Balasko received heightened press attention for having wrested from Audrey Tautou, the lead in Jean-Pierre Jeunet's *Le fabuleux destin d'Amélie Poulain* (*Amélie*, 2001), the title of France's highest-paid female movie star—mainly because of Balasko's current screen hit *L'ex-femme de ma vie* (The Ex-wife of My Life).

In *Dernier rappel*, which Balasko also wrote and directed, she plays a former prostitute who, having died in "a work-related accident," returns to earth in an attempt to redeem a young and profligate showbiz celebrity, played by the stand-up comic Cartouche—a Frenchman of North African descent. Unfortunately the show exhibited some of the worst traits associated with current boulevard comedies when conceived solely as star vehicles. The plot and dialogue were trite, the pacing too often flagged, and Balasko delivered her wisecracks as if on automatic pilot. To her credit she gave Cartouche, a newcomer to so-called legitimate theatre, ample room to show off his talents, especially as a dancer. Balasko's own star charisma was strongest during the curtain calls (*les rappels*), when she milked the audience's good will shamelessly. Still, virtually everyone in the packed house left looking satisfied. I, too, was glad to have seen Josiane "live."

• • •

More artful was the star performance of Jean-Louis Trintignant (b. 1930) in Samuel Benchetrit's *Moins 2* (Just in Time) (fig. 13). This sellout show ran at the Théâtre Hébertot, on the boulevard des Batignolles, for nearly a year. The play's premise is pure whimsy: believing they have no more than two weeks to live, a duo of elderly hospital patients—Trintignant as Paul and Roger Dumas (a longtime staple of French stage, film, and TV, b. 1932) as Jules—escape to the open road, encounter a series of losers much like themselves, and tie up a few loose ends in their private lives. Benchetrit's honed dialogue, along with the endearing chemistry of the two leads—Jules is the excitable mischief maker, Paul the derisive, melancholy dreamer— make up for the implausible plot points. Unlike *Dernier rappel*, *Moins 2* treats its serious themes—child abandonment, death, and the longing for human contact—with a delicacy and intelligence that

13. *As runaway invalids in Samuel Benchetrit's* Moins 2, *left, Roger Dumas (Jules) and, right, Jean-Louis Trintignant (Paul). Photo © Pierre Grosbois.*

outshine less ambitious boulevard shows. It may well figure among the very small pool of today's boulevard properties that will enjoy revivals in years to come.[5]

For many of us in the audience that season at the Hébertot, however, *Moins 2* had an emotional dimension only partly linked to the script's literary caliber. Samuel Benchetrit (b. 1973), who wrote and directed the play specifically for Jean-Louis Trintignant, is the father of Jules, a child he had in 1998 with Trintignant's daughter Marie (b. 1962)—a well-known actress who died of cerebral edema in July 2003 after being punched in a Vilnius (Lithuania) hotel room by her then boyfriend Bertrand Cantat, the lead singer of the French rock group Noir Désir. (Following a high-profile trial, Cantat was sentenced to eight years in prison for manslaughter.) The final episode of *Moins 2* is Paul/Trintignant's surprise reunion with a long-lost adult daughter who just happens to be a professional actress. The overlap between dramatic fantasy and our "insider's" sense of the real-world troubles of certain French entertainers is unmistakable. When this daughter then enacts, in a play-within-the-play, the uplifting final speech of Anton Chekhov's *Uncle Vanya* (1897)—a vision of earthly evil drowned in a sea of universal forgiveness—it is hard not to get misty-eyed.

Thanks to their tactful restraint, neither the playwright-director nor the famous actor-father made me or, I suspect, others feel unduly exploited. Still, laughter, tears, and a knowing self-conscious complicity between stars and the public have since at least the early nineteenth century been standard currency along the wide boulevards that spread westward from the Place de la République to the Place de l'Opéra and beyond.

• • •

Tears *of* laughter were the reigning response at the Théâtre du Palais-Royal, where *Toc toc* (Knock Knock)—Laurent Baffie's comedy about obsessive-compulsive disorder—was one of the season's biggest moneymakers. Baffie (b. 1958), who has long been a sketch writer for the comedian Jean-Marie Bigard, is perhaps best known as a regular panelist on TV talk shows hosted by Thierry Ardisson. He has a sure sense of what popular audiences long for. With an implicit jab toward certain strains of *théâtre public*, Baffie tersely asserts: "I make theatre for people who are afraid to go to the theatre."[6]

The setup for *Toc toc*, which Baffie both directed and wrote, could not be simpler. Six patients, each with a different flamboyant strand of *le trouble obsessionnel compulsif*, or "*le toc*" (OCD), arrive for a therapy session with their inexplicably tardy psychiatrist Dr. Stern. The play turns on their zany interactions within the confines of the doctor's waiting room. Baffie's feel-good surprise ending is almost predictable and—in the fine boulevard tradition of Pagnol and Anouilh—more than a touch mawkish. Yet the playwright's relentless barrage of sight gags, one-liners, zippy ripostes, and burlesque caricatures kept the audience in convulsions for two full hours. With expectations for a good time fully satisfied, ticket holders clearly got our money's worth.

Trouble along the Rialto?

In Paris, as in New York, dramatic theatre written for the so-called general but more discriminating playgoer remains the perennial economic invalid. Odile Quirot, the drama critic for *Le Nouvel Observateur*, took the pulse of the boulevard circuit in 2005. She reported that during the week of March 28, "only fourteen private Paris theatres had ticket sales exceeding 48 percent of capacity."[7] Among the forty-four private houses then eligible for financial aid from the Fonds de soutien au théâtre privé (Support Fund for Private Theatres), overall yearly attendance for 2004 was approximately 2.6 million, compared with a high of 3.5 million in 1990. The Fonds de soutien—monies that are derived from a 3.5 percent tax on ticket sales, municipal and state grants, and help from both the SACD and from the Administration des droits des artistes et musiciens interprètes (ADAMI)—was hard pressed to absorb even a small fraction of its members' annual deficits that year. (In 2010 the then fifty-two commercial theatre members eligible for such aid allied themselves with the Syndicat national de directeurs des théâtres et tourneurs du théâtre privé under a new banner, Théâtres parisiens associés, in part to counteract "the mushrooming of little *théâtres privés* that do not adhere to standard regulations.")[8]

Quirot traced the decline in spectatorship at the major houses to a steady increase of competing smaller events, especially within the public theatre sector; to Parisians' growing penchant for long country weekends, boosted by the introduction for some employees of a thirty-five-hour work week; and to soaring ticket prices in a period of inflation (in some measure a temporary result of the currency change from franc to euro). In calendar year 2006, attendance shot up to a healthier 3 million.[9] Yet in 2008, when attendance was even higher, Quirot saw little improvement in quality and gave an even harsher diagnosis. "The *théâtre privé*," she asserted, "has been stuck in nostalgia for the postwar years; either it looks backward or it desperately tries to find a new sure hit . . . and when it lands upon a hit, it repeats the formula to death."[10] Quirot's assessment is in large part correct. But there are nonetheless numerous successful dramatists who are continually striving to renew themselves. Three of the best—Eric-Emmanuel Schmitt, Jean-Marie Besset, and Yasmina Reza—have considerable stature both in France and internationally, and are the subject of the two next sections.

Middlebrow playwriting: Schmitt and Besset

Eric-Emmanuel Schmitt (b. 1960) has a knack for gratifying the tastes of popular audiences who hunger for rations of cultural enrichment—as opposed to the willfully frivolous entertainments dished out handily by Balasko and Baffie. A novelist and filmmaker as well as a dramatist, Schmitt won the Académie Française's 2001 prize for the entirety of his stage output, which includes *La nuit de Valognes* (*Don Juan on Trial*, 1991); *Le visiteur* (*The Visitor*, 1993), about an encounter in Nazi-occupied Vienna between Sigmund Freud and, possibly, God; and *Oscar et la dame rose* (*Oscar and the Lady in Pink*, 2002), a life-affirming portrait adapted from Schmitt's novella of the same title that deals with an elderly woman's companionship with a dying ten-year-old boy. In fall 2004, when the French literary magazine *Lire* polled its readers about which books had "most affected their lives," *Oscar et la dame rose* was one of the few titles by a living author; it figured right after Gabriel García Márquez's *One Hundred Years of Solitude* and Daniel Defoe's *Robinson Crusoe*.[11]

Schmitt's winning talents were on full display in *Ma vie avec Mozart* (My Life with Mozart), which played at the 700-seat Théâtre Montparnasse on the rue de la Gaîté—the epicenter of a cluster of Left Bank commercial theatres in the fourteenth arrondissement. This project had first taken form as a confessional novel: Schmitt's 2005 best seller told, in letters addressed to the composer, how Mozart's music had kept him from committing suicide at age fifteen and continued to bring him meaning and consolation throughout his life.[12] Schmitt cagily adapted his published text for the stage just in time to have it open during the 2006 celebration of the 250th anniversary of Mozart's birth. Its stage requirements are slight: a charismatic actor; a serviceable soprano, a harpist, and a clarinetist for the occasional musical excerpts; and realistic video projections that help set the scene for some of the quasi-autobiographical episodes. Although the script raises the subject of linkages among art, the body, and the soul, Schmitt—who holds a doctorate in philosophy—treats such matters with a gentle touch. Thus, the protagonist's final epiphany—"It takes so much time to become simple"—is no weightier than any truism found in Antoine de Saint-Exupéry's *Le petit prince* (1943), which was at the very top of *Lire*'s 100 most life-marking books, just after the Bible and Victor Hugo's *Les misérables* (1862). The result is a soothing dose of cultural uplift.

• • •

Jean-Marie Besset (b. 1959) mixes traditional dramaturgy with topics that are more socially and sexually provocative than Schmitt's. Openly gay, Besset does not write primarily for gay theatre-goers. "I never speak about homosexuals," he told me in fluent English. "I speak about homosexuality, which is a much wider theme, a universal variety of human experience."[13] Besset's goal in a number of his plays, he explained, is to reach and affect mainstream audiences that even today often feel uncomfortable with candid portrayals and discussions of sexual desire.

Over the years Besset has translated into French numerous works by gay American playwrights who, like him, target straight, fairly middle-of-the-road audiences: Tennessee Williams, Edward Albee, Richard Greenberg, Jon Robin Baitz, and Moisés Kaufman. He has also written screenplays for film directors whose gay identity is not always central to their work: for example, he cowrote the scenario for André Téchiné's *La fille du RER* (*The Girl on the Train*, 2009), adapted from Besset's play *RER* (2006) and based on the true story of a young white non-Jewish Frenchwoman who pretended to have been the victim of a brutal anti-Semitic assault by six men of African and North African origin on a Paris commuter train. Asked if he objected to my thinking of him as France's leading "*bobo*" (bourgeois-bohemian) dramatist, Besset answered: "A more positive way of saying the same thing is that I have a reputation for bringing back people to the theatre who stopped going, precisely because they thought that what they'd been seeing had gotten too experimental and too obscure."[14]

In spring 2006 Besset's new work, *Les Grecs* (Greeks), opened at the Petit Montparnasse on the rue de la Gaîté. Composed of two acts (Saturday Evening; Sunday Morning) and set in one locale (a married professional couple's trendily posh home just west of Paris), this four-character drama reunites a thirtysomething man and woman, Alain and Léna, who years earlier had become college friends and occasional bedmates after meeting one summer in Delphi, Greece. The plot setup is in some ways similar to that of Besset's *Commentaire d'amour* (Love's Commentary, 2000), which had a semistaged English-language reading at Florence Gould Hall during ACT FRENCH. While most of that earlier play's erotic action occurs in between scenes and gets recounted via dialogue, *Les Grecs*'s depictions of sexual versatility unfold in real stage time. Thus, at the end of act 1, we observe as Alain prepares for oral sex following an unexpected request for this favor by Henri, Léna's husband and the father of their two sons; and we watch Léna, in a spontaneous response to the men's lovemaking, as she propositions Alain's Arab lover, Osman, who has just crashed the dinner party:

LENA (*approaching Osman*): Fuck me.

OSMAN: What?

LENA (*begins to undress*): You like women . . . don't you?

OSMAN: Well, uh, I'm a man, no?

LENA: Fine. So fuck me. Put aside your knife. And fuck me in front of these two queers. (*Pause. Léna undresses completely: Alain and Henri look on, fascinated. Then Alain takes Henri's hand and leads him to the couch. Alain kneels down in front of Henri. Undoes his belt and his pants. Meanwhile, standing in front of Léna, Osman takes off his shirt. . . . Blackout.*)[15]

Throughout *Les Grecs*, Besset sustains savvy parallels between his modern-day story and Homer's *Iliad*. Achilles and Patroclus's same-sex love; the nuclear family as represented by Hector, Andromache, and Astyanax; the libidinal ambiguities surrounding Helen, Paris, and Menelaus; the Trojan horse as homologous to the airliners that carried Islamist terrorists on September 11, 2001—each of these motifs takes on added meaning as the eloquent, self-aware dramatis personae pursue their conversations, disputes, and naughty deeds. In shaping the role of Osman, an illegal Algerian transplant to Paris, Besset wanted, he claims, to remind viewers that, as in ancient Greece, there are ethnic groups today, including some in and from the Maghreb, whose men do not feel duty-bound to confine sex to conjugality or to the homo/hetero dualism. At the play's end, Léna and Henri confirm their love for each other; but they also realize that their prior takes on marriage and fidelity have been transformed and that they are probably the better for it.

Even as Besset deals with aspects of gay and bisexual practices in an open, unembarrassed manner, he is convinced that the distinction between gay and straight cultures, especially among today's French youth, has become so blurred that it is better not to compartmentalize. This view in fact dominates much new French theatre today. Gay-themed plays are almost always well represented in Paris, typically at small commercial theatres away from the *grands boulevards*. In the 2005–2006 season, however, many of these were either belated French-language adaptations of Broadway hits like Harvey Fierstein's *Torch Song Trilogy* at the Vingtième Théâtre in Ménilmontant and Terrence McNally's *Love! Valour! Compassion!* at the Théâtre de la Porte Saint-Martin; or earnest documentations of deadly homophobia like Moisés Kaufman's *Laramie Project* at the Vingtième and Philip Ridley's *Vincent River* at the Théâtre du Marais. Subtler treatments of desire in its most polymorphous and poetically charged guises tend to be found, as we shall see further on in this chapter, among the more experimental offerings of the *théâtre public*.

• • •

  Les Grecs opened in late April, a poor time of year for a new play to break out in Paris. But it reaped strong reviews in major papers like *Le Monde* and *Le Canard Enchaîné*. Philippe Tesson, veteran critic of *Le Figaro Magazine*, found it "brilliantly written," "one of Besset's best plays ever," and "certain to shock many a spectator."[16] Still, Besset regrets that some leading French periodicals snobbishly shy away from productions that are not government funded: "I'd love to attract a larger slice of the younger demographic that *Libération* reaches; but their policy is to ignore all commercial theatre [*théâtre privé*]." Nonetheless, Besset does not regret crafting his plays in accessible, tried-and-true, character- and dialogue-centered fashion. "The term 'avant-garde,'" he quips, "should be limited to the military. Great works of theatre, I think, are all a bit 'arrière-garde': look at Racine's *Phèdre*. I like the tension between highly polished form and raw subject matter."[17]

Besset's wish for greater media attention took on unexpected reality in fall 2009 when Frédéric Mitterrand, minister of culture and communication, named Besset to head the Théâtre des Treize Vents, the CDN of Montpellier and Languedoc-Roussillon. Because it is relatively rare for playwrights to serve as administrators of CDNs, this appointment won applause from such dramatists as Daniel Besnehard and Louise Doutreligne.[18] (Since 1999 Besset, along with his habitual stage director Gilbert Desveaux, has run a summer theatre festival in the Aude Valley [south-central France] that promotes emerging authors; in early 2009 Besset was elected vice president of SACD, the venerable authors' and composers' association that grew from the pioneering efforts of the Enlightenment dramatist Beaumarchais regarding copyright protocols.) But Besset's nomination to the Treize Vents position also triggered a torrent of protests from other seekers of the post, the SYNDEAC (a professional association for administrators of government-funded theatres nationwide), officials in the Socialist Party, and vociferous bloggers.

Many viewed the choice of a successful commercial playwright as insulting to veterans of the *théâtre public* who had been straining for years under budgetary pressures. Others pointed to an arrogant power play by Mitterrand's Parisian circle of associates and superiors against Montpellier's elected officials; the latter had made it clear from the start that they favored the candidacy of Georges Lavaudant (b. 1947), an old hand at directing public theatres. Some critics went so far as to construe Besset's appointment as "the death knell for a certain notion of [French] culture" and further proof of the Sarkozy government's "calculated destruction" of the not-for-profit subsidized system.[19] Moreover, alleged irregularities in the search process flew in the face of Nicolas Sarkozy's much-trumpeted campaign promise to bring greater transparency to all state-government selections.

If this incident exposed a normally veiled quantum of bitterness between the *théâtre public* and the *théâtre privé*, Besset strove to project a spirit of conciliation. He reminded detractors that several of his plays had been produced at government-subsidized houses and that he had frequently applied for CDN directorships in years past. He also suggested that the rigid distinction between public and private is perhaps now obsolete. "Government-sponsored productions," he told Le Monde, "should be encouraged to move on to runs in the commercial sector, which is what often occurs in English-speaking countries."[20] Perhaps the Besset affair will some day be remembered less as a political controversy than as a useful wakeup call for greater flexibility in ways of thinking about the future institutional structure of France's theatre arts generally.

Yasmina Reza's tonal sensitivity

Like Schmitt and Besset, Yasmina Reza (b. 1959) is a highly accessible and popular playwright whose works have been mounted in translation throughout much of the world. Reza has even enjoyed major Broadway success. "Art" (1994), her seriocomic drama about three male friends who dispute the wisdom of spending a small fortune for a white monochrome painting, opened at the Royale Theatre on West Forty-fifth Street in March 1998 and ran for 600 performances. With Alan Alda, Victor Garber, and Alfred Molina cast as the trio of sparring buddies, "Art" won that year's Tony for Best Original Play and has since had over 150 North American productions.[21] Yasmina Reza's later New York forays—The Unexpected Man (L'homme du hasard) at the Promenade in 2000, Life × 3 (Trois versions de la vie) at Circle in the Square in 2003, and A Spanish Play (Une pièce espagnole: théâtre) at Classic Stage Company in 2007—drew varied responses. Still, Reza's visibility and marketability in the United States make her unique among contemporary French playwrights. Charles Isherwood, writing in the New York Times, called her 2009 comeback hit God of Carnage (Le dieu du carnage, 2007) "catnip to Broadway audiences."[22]

Reza also made a splash in the American nonfiction trade sector when, in April 2008, Alfred A. Knopf brought out Dawn Dusk or Night (L'aube le soir ou la nuit, 2007), Reza's memoir about tagging along with Nicolas Sarkozy for the entirety of his presidential campaign. Sarkozy agreed to this arrangement, Reza later said, because of his hunch that she might "heal" what many had taken to be his "cultural deficit."[23] "Even if you demolish me," the politician reportedly told

Reza, "you will elevate me."[24] This view is consistent with the *New York Times*'s chief theatre critic Ben Brantley's slightly deprecating description of Reza's stage stamp: "a raised middlebrow sensibility that presents home truths with a satisfied air of intellectual discovery."[25]

The one Reza piece that ran during my Paris stay was a revival at the Théâtre Antoine (a *théâtre privé*) of her debut venture *Conversations après un enterrement* (*Conversations after a Burial*, 1986). This is the play that brought Reza a Molière for Best Author at the rather tender age of twenty-seven. A depiction of professional-class French Jewish siblings who have just buried their father at his country home, the work discloses themes and techniques that would become hallmarks of Reza's writings: strained family relations, social status issues, and out-of-sync lovers; churning emotions held in check; a multigenerational cast; a diffuse plot shaped by overlapping and often incomplete episodes; multiple strands of conversational dialogue artfully meshed; many silences; and one character's insertion, near the play's end, of a droll fantasy vision within an otherwise prosaic world. *Conversations après un enterrement* also highlights what perhaps counts most in Reza's plays: the metrical pulse and tonal ambiguities of the actors' words and the glimpses into character that such language offers.

Reza (like Schmitt) tends to be dismissed or condescended to by many French (and American) intellectuals, who generally shun the *théâtre privé* altogether. It would be wrong, however, to hold that since she does not belong to the ranks of the vanguard experimentalists Reza must be a reactionary boulevard hack. In *Avez-vous lu Reza? une invitation philosophique* (Have You Read Reza? A Philosophical Invitation, 2005), Denis Guénoun—a Sorbonne professor and former artistic director of the CDN of Rheims—persuasively argues that Reza's theatre stakes out a creative space neither regressively vapid (like much popular stage entertainment) nor nihilistically tormented (like a good number of avant-gardist efforts). Rejecting both the old-fashioned mechanics of the *pièce bien faite*, or well-made play, and the radical formal dislocations inherent in most alternative theatre practices, Reza, Guénoun posits, is a specific kind of postmodernist, in the sense that she is acutely conscious of writing *after* Beckett: "She favors and builds upon modernity's fractures but only on condition that the rupturing will bring to light lines, shapes, and spaces that enable us to see and understand more clearly the human abyss."[26] The intelligentsia's overall disregard notwithstanding, Guénoun proposes that one's relishing the plays of Yasmina Reza need not be viewed as a guilt-filled, downscale pleasure. She arguably belongs to a family of popular contemporary storytellers that includes Milan Kundera, Pierre Michon, Woody Allen, and others, for whom art is a way of asserting the ineffable joy of being alive albeit with full awareness of the insolence such a posture typically holds in the minds of many during a time of deep cynicism.

The "return" of the text-based dramatic author

The artistic middle ground that text-based writers like Schmitt, Besset, and Reza occupy within the *théâtre privé* has a rough equivalent in the *théâtre public*. The decades-long stranglehold by visionary stage directors—and the consequent decline in prestige of contemporary authors—is no longer the reigning dynamic within the domain of subsidized theatres. Many outstanding writers have taken back primary responsibility for renewing French theatre and are now composing innovative texts that present fresh challenges for directors, actors, and audiences alike. All of the authors evoked in chapter 4, on theatre of *la parole*, are part of this more general movement.

The "return" of the *auteur de théâtre* arguably had its first surge in the mid-1980s. But it underwent a major setback with the early deaths of three of its most shining exponents, Bernard-Marie Koltès (1948–1989), Jean-Luc Lagarce (1957–1995), and Didier-Georges Gabily (1955–1996), the first two succumbing to complications from AIDS. While the works of these deceased playwrights are steadily revived throughout France and abroad, the number of writers currently reshaping French dramaturgy is imposing. These include Catherine Anne (b. 1960), Enzo Cormann (b. 1953), Rémi De Vos (b. 1963), Eugène Durif (b. 1950), Fabrice Melquiot (b. 1972), Philippe Minyana (b. 1946), Joël Pommerat (b. 1963), Noëlle Renaude (b. 1949), Christian Siméon (b. 1960), and Serge Valletti (b. 1951)—to name but a few.

For the most part these are artists who would never relegate their verbal texts to peripheral status, as Pascal Rambert does in *Paradis (unfolding time)*. Nor would they align themselves with such media-savvy scenographers as Philippe Quesne or Superamas—although their works are often enriched by recourse to video, live or recorded music, digital sound design, and dance. Some of them are squarely associated with theatre of *la parole*, others not in the least. Yet all of them break with the idolatry of a supposed *belle langue*, the smooth, eloquent discourse that the French stage persistently exhibited from Corneille to Hugo and on to at least Giraudoux and Anouilh. Nonetheless, each views writing for the theatre as a literary activity capable of exerting considerable aesthetic interest in and of itself. In many instances their plays are published long before being guaranteed productions.

In the sections that follow we will discuss three of these contemporary dramatists: Philippe Minyana, Noëlle Renaude, and Joël Pommerat. While all three employ techniques that overlap with those found in theatre of *la parole* and in more extreme experimental works, each has staked out an idiosyncratic territory that prolongs and renews the text-based traditions of French theatre.

Rendering human suffering hyperreal: Minyana

"My theatre is essentially grounded in the written word [*l'écrit*], rather than in a 'story' or even a 'theme,'" says Philippe Minyana (b. 1946), who describes each of his projects as taking shape within his private "*laboratoire d'écriture*," or "writing lab."[27] Upon arriving in Paris from Besançon, where he was born and educated, Minyana began a stage career as an actor. By the early 1980s he turned to writing, and he has since composed over thirty original plays, adaptations, and librettos. In 2010 he won the Académie Française Prize for his collected works. Minyana's most frequently revived works are *Chambres* (Rooms, 1986) and *Inventaires* (*Inventories*, 1987).[28] The former is a series of six self-contained stream-of-consciousness monologues; the latter is a trio of fragmented, intertwined soliloquies set within the context of an exploitative television reality show. Both raise fundamental questions about how to tell stories, how to use theatrical space, and how to position actors on a stage.

Minyana has explored a changing set of formal issues throughout his writing career, but a constant trait of his oeuvre is the voice he gives to human anguish and suffering. As Michel Corvin has written: "With the acuity of an entomologist, Minyana captures every twitch of tortured, mutilated beings; his hyperrealism results in a sort of phantasmagoria whose poetic quality is enriched by the exacting care he devotes to language and phrasing, giving these the appearance of everyday speech in all its spontaneity."[29]

Minyana's *La maison des morts* (The House of the Dead) ran at the Théâtre du Vieux-Colombier in midwinter 2006. Originally radiocast by France Culture in 1995 and then mounted at regional theatres in Quimper (1999), Rennes (1999), and Aix-en-Provence (2000), the play was significantly revised for this Paris production.[30] It starred Catherine Hiegel, the Comédie-Française *sociétaire* for whom Minyana conceived the piece; Robert Cantarella (b. 1957) directed. 'Cantarella-Minyana' is practically a brand name in the French *théâtre public* world. Like Patrice Chéreau and Bernard-Marie Koltès, Claude Régy and Marguerite Duras, or Ariane Mnouchkine and Hélène Cixous, the two men have enjoyed a long and productive though by no means exclusive director-author partnership.

• • •

Minyana's plays deal with so-called ordinary folk. His starting point for writing *La maison des morts* was a real-life document, namely, a correspondence file concerning a middle-aged female custodial worker at a major French university. Because this woman was excessively absent from her job, the university's secretary-general fired her without a hint of compassion for either her illness or her need to take care of aging parents. First engaging in what he calls a "de-realization and de-contextualization of the anecdotal event,"[31] Minyana then imagined—with some help from Dostoyevsky, Faulkner, Brecht, Beckett, and various recent news items—a string of sordid and horrific happenings for which this worker, whom he allegorically names The Woman with the Braid, would, over many decades, be both a participant and a witness. The result, as the work's subtitle indicates, is "a play for actors and puppets in six movements, with prologue and epilogue."

At the Vieux-Colombier, seven actors played twenty-three speaking roles; only Catherine Hiegel had a single part, that of the protagonist. Throughout the piece, on a horizontal screen at the top of the stage, lights of varying colors flashed what Minyana refers to as "inscriptions."[32] These projected words and phrases (a scenographic technique that hearkens back to innovations by Erwin Piscator and Bertolt Brecht) are sometimes explicit stage directions and at other times otherworldly observations about the characters and their actions. They frequently enhance but just as often contradict what we, the audience, watch and hear.

In the prologue an undressed mannequin serving as an effigy for a murdered young girl stands downstage while a disembodied Voice sternly interrogates four seedy, seemingly retarded male suspects who incoherently but with lyric-like repetitiveness speak in what sounds like *ch'ti*, a northern French dialect. In the first movement, set in a sterile furnished abode, The Woman with the Braid reads the letters that will lead to her being sacked; we meet her mother, The Lady with the Little Voice, with whom The Woman has a love/hate codependence; and we watch as The Woman's father, The Man with Canes, has sexual intercourse with his emotionless daughter. The movements that follow, of varying lengths, are set in other times and mainly in other houses where The Woman works or resides: when her (presumably born-of-incest) son is an infant, she yearns to see him killed; she bids adieu to her mother, father, and the family dog, who have inexplicably died together in the parents' bedroom; she encounters a silent Man with a Bundle of Sticks—a soldier who has survived a deadly battle somewhere in southern Europe; in the fancy home of The Woman with a Clay Cast, she looks on as The Man Dressed as a Woman takes refuge after being pelted with stones by villagers and as The Woman with a Clay Cast's ex-lover Walter visits and falls dead; when in the final movement The Woman with the Braid's Son, now a young adult who speaks in an abnormally high-pitched voice, asks his mother to murder him because he has no testicles, she impassively reaches for a rifle in the bathroom and honors the request. In the epilogue, The Woman with the Braid is seated alone at a table, with one hand pressed against her cheek, and intones a rhythmically mesmerizing monologue about waiting for death.

Within Minyana's trajectory as a playwright, *La maison des morts* carries him beyond what he has called "a theatre of precise incidents" toward a more general "human fresco" or "folk opera" ("*opéra des petites gens*").[33] By inflecting ordinary spoken language with the syntactic and acoustic traits of age-old proverbs, oral narrative poetry, and liturgical chant, he aims to tap into "an archeology of our memories."[34] Redolent of modernist black comedy, late-nineteenth-century

Grand-Guignol melodrama, and medieval mystery plays—yet belonging to no preestablished genre—*La maison des morts* proffers a bold and memorable, albeit very grim, theatre experience.

Representation and its limits: Renaude

On a dead-end street at the foot of Montmartre and in the shadow of the Moulin Rouge cabaret sits an arts institution that has possibly done more to encourage the "return" of French writers for the stage than any other. Launched in 1971 at the urging of Jean Vilar, Théâtre Ouvert (Open Theatre) has since 1988 been a Centre national dramatique de création, France's only state- and city-supported CDN specifically charged with the discovery and promotion of innovative contemporary French-language playwrights; to represent its mission more precisely, it was redesignated in 2011 as a Centre national des dramaturgies contemporaines, or CNDC. From its inception Théâtre Ouvert has been lovingly co-run by Lucien Attoun, a stage director turned drama critic, and his wife Micheline, who previously held key positions in the Cultural Services section of the American Embassy in Paris and in the American Center, a hub for U.S. culture in France. Each year Théâtre Ouvert sorts through several hundred submissions and chooses the most promising manuscripts for either a *chantier*, a workshop that allows writers to polish or revise their texts while engaging directly with professional, paid actors and an established director; a *mise en voix*, a public reading of the play, also with professional, paid actors; or a *mise en espace*, a public staged reading with full direction, lighting, and sound design but without costumes and props. Théâtre Ouvert also mounts complete productions and has a vigorous publishing agenda.

In addition to its book imprint, Enjeux, Théâtre Ouvert produces *tapuscrits*, or typed scripts sturdier than spiral-bound photocopies but less formal than fully edited books. These are sent gratis to theatre companies in order to pique interest in new properties. Over the years the Attouns have fostered the writing careers of Jean-Claude Grumberg, Michel Vinaver, Bernard-Marie Koltès, Eugène Durif, Philippe Minyana, Joël Jouanneau, and Serge Valletti, among many others; their *chantiers* and *mises en espace* have attracted many of France's prominent directors, including Daniel Mesguich, Georges Lavaudant, and Alain Françon.

. . .

One playwright who has had a long relationship with Théâtre Ouvert is Noëlle Renaude (b. 1949). Several of her early works, such as *Rose, la nuit australienne* (Rose, the Australian Night, 1987) and *Le renard du nord* (The Northern Fox, 1989), appeared as *tapuscrits* before going on to *mises en voix* and then full productions at Théâtre Ouvert. The Attouns also lent Renaude vital support during the four years she devoted to composing *Ma Solange, comment t'écrire mon désastre, Alex Roux* (My Dear Solange, How Can I Write You of My Disaster, Alex Roux, 1994–1998)—a marathon piece written for the actor Christophe Brault, who plays over two thousand figures or voices; when performed in its entirety, as it was in 2002 at Théâtre Ouvert, the work lasts for approximately eighteen hours. In 2006, for the first time in its history, Théâtre Ouvert organized its winter-spring season around one author, Renaude. The main attraction was a full-blown production of her new play *Par les routes* (*By the Way*)—written for the actors Brault and Jean-Paul Dias and directed by Frédéric Maragnani.

Renaude, who has degrees in art history and Asian languages, became a playwright by personal choice after a decade of writing serious essays for the magazine *Théâtre/Public* and, under a nom de plume, pop mysteries and romance fiction for the women's magazine *Bonne Soirée*. In contrast to Philippe Minyana's works, Renaude's are generally playful, humorous, and optimistic. Yet like Minyana, she explores new dramaturgic issues with each play she writes. Renaude often cites Valère Novarina as a strong influence, and her theatre certainly represents one strain of theatre of *la parole* since her stage speakers construct themselves entirely through their speech acts. But *Par les routes* shows that Renaude's recent works are also veering toward an offbeat *theatre of the written text* in which she attempts to give palpable presence to the visual elements of her drafted pages, whether they are originally set on paper or on a computer screen. Such pieces as *Promenades* (2003) and *Ceux qui partent à l'aventure* (Those Who Set Off Aimlessly, 2006) have been called "landscape plays"[35] not just because their characters are constantly on the move but because these works deliberately engage players and audiences with the physiologically based dynamics of writing and reading no less than with those of speaking and hearing. As the scholar Mary Noonan puts it, Renaude's theatre "charts the [spatial] movement of words [and the self] between interior, auditory space and the exterior visual field of the page/screen/stage." "[Her] desire," Noonan notes, "is to explore, and possibly explode, the frame, the limit of what can and cannot enter the space."[36]

The published text of *Par les routes* consists of ninety-three pages of fairly short lines with no attribution of characters and almost no punctuation.[37] About one-third of these lines suggest dialogue between two males who have each recently lost their mothers and who are now taking a rambling car trip from Ile-de-France across parts of the Loire Valley and then eastward toward the Swiss Alps. Another third of the lines are presumably utterances of the eccentric people the two men meet on their journey, most of whom, curiously, have also recently lost their mothers. Still another third resemble transcriptions of highway signs, tourist information, and roadside advertisements that orient and at times disorient the two wanderers—and the book's readers.

In Frédéric Maragnani's production, Christophe Brault and Jean-Paul Dias played/intoned the main travelers and the secondary figures, a mix of men and women. Sitting in their oversized red car seats, the nomadic duo directly faced the audience while, behind them, the highway signs and commercial ads they were ostensibly passing—some realistic, others whimsical—flashed across a large white screen: "Bear Right"; "Welcome to Loiret: The Spirit of Enterprise"; "Indre: Reduce Your Speed and Be Kind: Population Is Slow, Even Inert"; "Joan and John What's-Their-Names Hospital"; and so on. As in Minyana's *La maison des morts*, where supertitles add a set of messages to be absorbed and possibly decoded, the viewer of *Par les routes* is immersed, along with the play's two central characters, in a profusion of acoustic, written, and pictographic imagery. Unlike the traveling pair, however, we are at least at one remove from their experience. We are thus free to elaborate potential interpretations, including the possibility for retaining greater distinction between the actual physical world we/they claim to move about in—valleys, forests, historic castles, campgrounds, and grocery stores—and the manifold, seemingly inescapable analog and digital representations that mediate the perception of the real.

Renaude holds out hope for maintaining a modicum of unmediated experience. Whereas Minyana in *La maison des morts* places us and his characters within a hermetically sealed space of death and inhumanity, Renaude leaves the audience and her roaming players pleasantly adrift. It is inevitable that they and we will at some point reach the end of the road/our days—and die. Yet within the play's world and by implication our own lives, there seems always to be uncharted territory still to discover and still untouched by cartographic and consumption-driven media. Midway into her play-text Renaude leaves two pages nearly totally blank. When words reinstate themselves, one speaker elatedly says: "Words again. . . . It's good to see words again."[38] This burst of reinvigoration, after some respite from intense information overload, rhymes with one of the men's utterances at the play's end; when thinking again of their recently dead mothers, he says: "Frankly / It's not the end of the world / Of the world, that, no."[39] For Noëlle Renaude, to confront and contest the stagnating margins of conventional representation is to know that one is alive.

A neo-expressionist take on truth: Pommerat

Another text-based playwright of growing importance is Joël Pommerat (b. 1963). No fewer than three of his pieces were scheduled to play in Avignon in July 2006 (see chapter 11). But in Paris that spring, his piece *Cet enfant* (*This Child*) enjoyed its premiere run at the Théâtre Paris-Villette—a city-funded theatre set within the sprawling urban Parc de la Villette at the northern tip of the nineteenth arrondissement. This was an apt site for a play whose text had evolved from interviews that Pommerat, his actors, and a team of social workers had conducted with women living in working-class housing projects near Caen (Normandy) in 2002. (An earlier version of the play, titled *Qu'est-ce qu'on fait?* [What Does One Do?], had been semistaged in various community centers throughout Normandy in 2003.) *Cet enfant* won the prize for Best French Play of 2006 from the Syndicat de la critique dramatique et musicale (Association of Theatre and Music Critics). And it was reprised in Paris the following spring when Pommerat, hand picked by Peter Brook, became the *artiste associé* at the Théâtre des Bouffes du Nord—Brook's home base from the mid-1970s through 2009.

Cet enfant is a series of discrete, short tableaux that dramatize moments of crisis between parents and their children. Since naturalism has no place in Pommerat's neo-expressionist stage vision, all of the children were played, powerfully and convincingly, by adult actors. In one of the ten vignettes a young mother who fears she has no aptitude for raising her infant pleads with strangers to take the baby for themselves. In another a teenage boy viciously mocks his father for being out of work and unemployable. In still another a girl whose parents have divorced coldly informs her disbelieving father that she hopes never to see him again.

Unlike Minyana and Renaude, Pommerat chooses to direct his works himself. Influenced by Claude Régy, his abstract staging for *Cet enfant* was stark and minimalist: it included atmospheric lighting, sustained silences, few props, and lapses between episodes punctuated by muted jazz-rock strains performed by the Prizotos, a five-piece combo positioned on stage behind a scrim. The impact was at once mysterious and frighteningly real. Implicit throughout *Cet enfant* is the notion that people's lives are being ruined because of idealized notions of parenting and domesticity promoted by the mass media and other tradition-bound agencies of "proper" socialization. Yet Pommerat is not a social dramatist per se: he has neither axes to grind nor clear messages to impart. Referencing Chekhov's advice that writers should emulate surgeons in their detachment from patients, he asserts: "I consider the stage not to be a political court of justice but a space for symbolic representations of the world."[40] Like Minyana, he radically transforms his real-world sources through poetic constructs and writerly craft. Since Pommerat rejects what he calls "a moral, Romantic, or compassionate vision of things,"[41] the human truths he distills from life are often as brutal as they are moving.

Praise for Pommerat is not universal. In reviewing *Cet enfant* for *Les Inrockuptibles*, Fabienne Arvers objected to what she perceived as "a kind of sentimental karaoke that refuses to declare itself as such."[42] I think that Brigitte Salino of *Le Monde* was more on target: "You should not go to a Joël Pommerat piece if you expect the kind of theatre that is going to open itself to you all at once. . . . Everything lies in the self-restraint [*la retenue*], a self-restraint that is so exacerbated as to be obsessive and yet, paradoxically, so theatrical [*spectaculaire*] by dint of its not wanting to be."[43]

Exposing the 'ob-scene'

Just a few blocks from the Opéra Bastille, on the lively rue de la Roquette, stands the Théâtre de la Bastille. One of the most inviting midsize not-for-profit houses in Paris, the Bastille (funded by the French government and the city of Paris) quickly became a personal favorite. Since the early 1980s it has been both a launching pad and a coveted showcase for experimental stage artists who work in mixed media and hybrid forms. One of these is Gisèle Vienne, whose dance-theatre diptych *Une belle enfant blonde/A young, beautiful blonde girl* and *I Apologize* ran there for two weeks in February 2006. I was eager to see Vienne's shows since they were among those that had caused so much outrage in Avignon the preceding summer.

Vienne (b. 1976) studied philosophy before attending the Ecole supérieure nationale des arts de la marionnette in Charleville-Mézières (Ardennes). Her first professional production, codirected and choreographed with Etienne Bideau-Rey in 2000, was Jean Genet's posthumously published play *Splendid's* (1948; 1993). In most of her own works Vienne explores unexpected, often eroticized relations between live bodies and life-size dummies. Punning on the French verb '*chorégraphier*' ('to choreograph'), she views her project as centered on "corps-*et*-graphier" ("the body-*and*-making-it-graphic").[44] Nudity and extreme sexual themes, she notes, are necessary elements of her broader program of the '*ob*-scene': to make observable *sur scène* (on-stage) the libidinally charged mechanics of voyeurism, exhibitionism, and cross-identifications—dynamics that are arguably basic to all theatrical and all psychic experience but are usually subject to well-established cultural and social constraints.

As in Avignon, the Théâtre de la Bastille programmed each part of the diptych individually. Both sections loosely deal with an attempt to reconstitute a single horrific crime. What we see and hear, however, leaves us uncertain about the particulars of the supposed offense. What matters most for Vienne is to immerse us, like virtual accomplice detectives, within a world of fluid identities, mutating subjectivities, and interdependent fantasies. The first thirty minutes of *Une belle enfant blonde* are wordless. We watch as the petite and dowdily dressed Catherine Robbe-Grillet (b. 1930) (the famous New Novelist's wife and a writer of erotic fiction herself) plays the dominatrix to the long-legged, somewhat bruised young blonde beauty Anja Röttgerkamp (b. 1969). The two women move about among nine reality-sized mannequins—pubescent girls wearing identical school outfits—who are propped up on shared benches positioned stage center and stage right and who remain eerie, mute witness-participants during the proceedings. Looking herself like a Barbie doll come to life, Röttgerkamp dances robotically (and brilliantly), sometimes dressed and sometimes in the nude, and then interacts—as a partner in dance and in S/M games—with a tall androgynous man (Jonathan Capdevielle, b. 1976) who wears a tailored black suit, matching red lipstick, and stiletto heels and who spits blood, sniffs undergarments, and searches for evidence of a murder.

In the remainder of the ninety-minute piece the bespectacled and severely chignoned Robbe-Grillet recites prose passages about lurid sex from works by the American gay punk/goth novelist Dennis Cooper (b. 1953) and spouts personal reminiscences of her and Alain Robbe-Grillet's (separate) group-sex parties in New York City; she seemingly slits the androgynous man's throat with a broken wine glass; the female dancer ceremoniously lays out one of the schoolgirl mannequins on the floor, as if dead; and then the dancer and Robbe-Grillet, behind gauze curtains, are heard muttering and moaning. *Une belle enfant blonde/A young, beautiful blonde girl* ends so abruptly that many of us in the audience were unsure whether the time for applause had arrived or not. Would *I Apologize* bring this hypnotic but baffling piece to greater closure?

The three-member live cast of *I Apologize* was the same as *Une belle enfant blonde*'s—except for Catherine Robbe-Grillet. Replacing her was the performance artist Jean-Luc Verna (b. 1966), who revealed his astonishing array of tattoos and piercings each time he shifted from hypermasculine to hyperfeminine garb. The show's verbal component now belonged entirely to Dennis Cooper, who declaimed his grisly necrophilic texts written specifically for this piece on a prerecorded sound track. *I Apologize*'s main scenographic conceit was the collective act of slowly removing and re-placing each of the schoolgirl dummies from and into coffinlike wooden crates (see fig. 14). At the play's close Verna, in dominatrix fetish gear, shoots dead the prurient inspector—or is the latter actually a doppelgänger for Dennis Cooper's druggy narrator? The dominatrix then kisses the victim's mouth and walks off stage. In a brief coda the dead man, apparently

14. *Anja Röttgerkamp crawling among bloodied life-size schoolgirl* *dummies in Gisèle Vienne's* I Apologize. *Photo © Mathilde Darel.*

returned to life, rises from a puddle of blood and walks off stage, too. Blackout. End of diptych.

• • •

Gisèle Vienne has a strong gift for putting light, color, sound, fabrics, texts, bodies, and figurines to cohesive purpose. Her diptych is a stunningly executed instance of that strain of alternative theatre in which the performers' most intense visceral energies and somatic urges grab our attention and short-circuit attempts to respond rationally. The substance of Vienne's erotic dreamscapes—the fluid links among sex, crime, and death, and even the added device of mannequins—belongs to a long line of graphic considerations on the transgressive libido that extends from the Marquis de Sade and Leopold von Sacher-Masoch to Georges Bataille, Hans Bellmer, Pierre Molinier, and Jean Genet and on to Alain Robbe-Grillet, Catherine Breillat, and Dennis Cooper (who now lives in France).

It is sometimes said that if there is to be such a thing today as a new avant-garde, it must be the result of a *critique* of the older avant-gardes. According to Günter Berghaus in *Avant-Garde Performance* (2005), for example, this "new avant-garde (or post avant-garde, or whatever it may be called)" will inevitably reinstate components of its predecessors, but at its best it will also "transform them into a new gestalt" that will respond to "contemporary conditions in the culture industry."[45] Gisèle Vienne informed me that she has no qualms about being identified by others as an experimental or even an avant-garde creator; however, she is wary of artists and producers who brandish such labels as marketing devices for self-promotion, just as she finds the commoditization of explicit sex alien to her creative project. Moreover, Vienne stresses that her thematic preoccupations are not at all "innovative" but to the contrary "have existed for millennia." "I think that what makes my works 'contemporary,'" she says, "is the manner in which I *compose* them."[46]

Citing influences that range from Japanese Noh theatre and Bunraku puppet performance to Lewis Carroll and Kafka to Tadeusz Kantor's manifesto *Theatre of Death* (1975), Stanislaw Lem's science-fiction novel *Solaris* (1961), and David Lynch's TV series *Twin Peaks* (1990–1991), Vienne asserts that in structuring her works she aims "to activate the audience's desire to find answers to life's enigmas," but at the same time she wants "to make audiences suspicious of quick and facile solutions." "I offer a network of signs," she says, "but it's up to the audience to play detective as it decodes and grapples with them. I think such intellectual gymnastics are healthy in our times; it is important to misread and make errors and be wary of pat solutions. As a director I do not play God—and I don't want spectators to think I do."[47]

Hyperkinetic flamboyance

I nearly missed one of the more ingenious hybrid projects of the spring season 2006. *Le Figaro*'s theatre critic Armelle Héliot had savaged Gildas Milin's *L'homme de février* (The February Man) for its alleged incomprehensibility and uselessness. "I challenge anyone to understand anything that goes on," she wrote.[48] She also reported that people had walked out in huge numbers. Rather than forfeit my ticket, I went to La Colline–théâtre national, where *L'homme de février* was ending a four-week run. I expected the worst.

The Colline takes its name from its location in the hilly Ménilmontant section of Paris's twentieth arrondissement, just beyond the upper heights of Père Lachaise cemetery. It is dedicated to promoting contemporary modes of stage creation and to creating new audiences for them. Constructed under Jack Lang's aegis in the 1980s, the Colline's unusual glass-and-metal façade on the rue de Malte-Brun and its fluid multilevel interior spaces serve as an invitation to openness and exploration. To cast its net even wider, the Colline—under the leadership of Stéphane Braunschweig—began to experiment, in its 2009–2010 season, with English-language supertitles for selected shows.

I am glad I chose not to boycott the Milin event, since my experience turned out to be quite different from Armelle Héliot's. The Colline's Petit Théâtre, which holds about 200, was swarming with a mainly young (under thirty-five) crowd who clearly reveled in this 130-minute piece. There was not a single walkout. The work, which Milin (b. 1968) refers to as "*une sculpture vivante*" ("a live sculpture"),[49] took place in the round, with the theatre's black-box space set up to resemble a gymnasium stretch room. Some spectators sat on floor-level beanbag chairs; others crouched on low banquettes; still others perched on towering lifeguard lookout seats. We were invited to change places during the show if we cared to. The production, written and directed by Milin for his company Les Bourdons Farouches (The Wild Bumblebees), featured ten lithe actor-dancer-musicians, most of whom wore—and then partly removed—frogman suits and thick knee pads (see fig. 15). The intricate hyperkinetic choreography—pacing, running, flopping, and crawling—was funny and riveting. The delivery of Milin's text—strewn with snatches of dialogue, delirious speechifying, phrases repeated as in a contrapuntal musical canon, and improvisations sometimes directed at specific audience members—was vigorous and often spellbinding.

L'homme de février's plot is steeped in both genuine science and pseudoscience. It focuses on a drug-addled meganeurotic rock singer named Cristal, who engages with her serene psychic double, Christelle, in an attempt to overcome stage fright and chemical dependency. She also undergoes an elaborate brain analysis by a well-meaning team of geeky neuroscientists. But Cristal's problems only get resolved after she meets Mister February, an oracular figure inspired by the clinical research of the controversial twentieth-century American hypnotherapist Milton H. Erickson (1901–1980), who entices Cristal to undergo restorative "TMDM," or "Total Multi Dimensionnelle Musique" therapy.[50] With Cristal apparently cured, the show culminates with a half-hour hard rock concert, its music composed by Philippe Thibault and Vassia Zagar and performed with gung-ho fervor by the full company.

• • •

Flamboyant, visceral, and daringly imaginative without taking itself too seriously, *L'homme de février* is a joy to see and hear. The rational grasp and purposeful utility so regretted in their absence by Armelle Héliot is beside the point. Gildas Milin, who studied jazz composition prior to attending the Conservatoire national d'art dramatique, is clearly exploring untested forms of stage expression. If Günter Berghaus is indeed correct in suggesting that vanguard art of the twenty-first century will have to find a way to merge the formal advances of the various twentieth-century avant-garde movements with "forces that belong to the new age,"[51] then Gildas Milin may well be positioning himself on the frontier of something genuinely new and worthwhile. By integrating both his curiosity about and satiric skepticism toward current trends in behavioral therapy, psychopharmacology, brain imaging, and applied quantum mechanics, he surely

15. *Participants in Gildas Milin's* L'homme de février *trying to help Cristal, center, played by Julie Pilod. Photo © Pierre Grosbois.*

gives a fresh twist to the historical avant-garde's love-hate relationship with new technologies. Milin's *Machine sans cible* (Targetless Machine), which premiered at the 2007 Avignon Festival, likewise recapitulates and enriches the historical avant-garde's pendulum swings between technophilia and primitivism—this time with robotics as a main object of interest. His is an oddball and exceedingly intelligent talent.

In search of the ecological sublime

Impressed so positively by Philippe Quesne during ACT FRENCH, I was pleased to see how his personal stage vision had ripened since *La démangeaison des ailes* (*The Itching of Wings*, originally conceived in 2003). Quesne's new piece *D'après nature* (True to Life) played at the Théâtre de la Bastille for three weeks in January 2006. Even more explicitly self-referential than *Itching*, it is no less gaily mischievous. This time we watch as his company of seven is camped out in tents, stage right. For the first part of this seventy-minute piece the group mainly converses—with most of their dialogue flashed on a screen rather than fully spoken—about how best to put together the very work we are viewing. *D'après nature*, which they refer to as "an ecological fable," will demonstrate, they say, how—through teamwork and a can-do attitude—they can repair the hole in the ozone layer of the earth's stratosphere.

As in *Itching*, a famous Pieter Bruegel painting is part of the mix, this time *The Parable of the Blind Leading the Blind* (1568). Once the players don their gleaming white space suits, they do not immediately scale the ladder that will take them into the skies (actually, the flies). Instead they move to the damp, thick growth of bushes and shrubs that extends stage left, where they reenact, as in a tableau vivant, the content of Bruegel's canvas—which depicts the blind leader just as he falls into a hole in the ground. In Quesne's variant the band of followers are very much in control of their sight (see fig. 16); and with their electrified space-suit helmets illumining their faces with an ethereal glow, they caringly lift up their comrade. Only then do they pursue their collective meteorological exploit, as lush recorded Hollywood movie music by André Previn reverberates through the theatre. Their mission accomplished, the crew return to the camp, stage right; they eat the fresh vegetable soup that has been simmering on a stove

16. *A riff on Pieter Bruegel the Elder's* Parable of the Blind Leading the Blind *(1568) in Philippe Quesne's ecological fable,* D'après nature. *Photo © Pierre Grosbois.*

all the while (and whose intensifying aroma has been tantalizing those of us in the front rows); and they make their own brand of live music—country style, on ukuleles, guitars, harmonicas, and kazoos.

Like Gildas Milin, Philippe Quesne uses his talent to imagine a reality other than one in which men and their machines wreak havoc on nature. With *D'après nature* he creates a work—and a world—of serene beauty where human bodies join with objects, plants, animals (a dog named Hermès is on stage throughout), cultural heritage, and primal terrestrial energies—all healthily connecting anew. Quesne's aesthetic alchemy makes the simplest of elements—his unassuming players, their everyday acts, and their naively pursued missions—combine to yield a most delicate visual and aural poetry. Quesne's professional standing is also crystallizing both in France and internationally. The Avignon "In" Festival programmed his *L'effet de Serge* (*The Serge Effect*) and *La mélancolie des dragons* (The Melancholy of Dragons) in 2009 and his *Big Bang* in 2010. *L'effet de Serge* went on to play in numerous European and North American cities, including a run in 2010 at New York's 3LD Art & Technology Center as part of that year's Under the Radar festival.

Restoring something primordial

It was gratifying to find that Pascal Rambert, too, was in peak form. When it premiered at the 2005 Avignon Festival, Rambert's *After/Before* lent considerable fuel to the discord surrounding that year's offerings. The 105-minute piece was now enjoying, in February 2006, a two-week reprise at the Théâtre de Gennevilliers—a much-admired CDN located in an ethnically diverse industrial suburb northwest of Paris.

The Gennevilliers was just then caught up in a ruckus of its own. Weeks earlier and reportedly without warning or consultation, the Ministry of Culture and Communication informed the theatre's founder, Bernard Sobel (b. 1935), that his post as artistic and administrative director was not going to be renewed. CDN chiefs are typically subject to frequent rotation—and sometimes dismissal. But Sobel, who headed various incarnations of the Gennevilliers for a record forty-three years, had always been the exception. A lifelong Communist, he was especially respected for having introduced the French public to many East European dramatists, including Heiner

Müller. In January 2006 he directed what would be his final production at the Gennevilliers, Alexander Ostrovsky's *Don, mécènes et adorateurs* (*Talanty I Poklonniki/Talents and Admirers*, 1882), a passionate
depiction of nineteenth-century Russian theatre life that won Sobel
that year's Grand Prize from the Syndicat de la critique dramatique et
musicale.

Sobel had always been a supporter of young French theatre artists no matter how provocative. He also brought to the Gennevilliers
some works by the American experimentalist Richard Foreman, including *Café Amérique* (1981), *Pearls for Pigs* (1997), and *Bad Boy Nietz-
sche* (2000).[52] Sobel's having programmed Pascal Rambert's company
for the 2006 winter season was simply further evidence of the sep-
tuagenarian's sustained breadth of vision. A few professionals called
for Renaud Donnedieu de Vabres to reconsider Sobel's termination.[53]
Some were already floating rumors about who might replace him.
Most stayed silent. As an outsider with nothing personal at stake,
I headed up to the Théâtre de Gennevilliers by metro that February with the thought that the cryptic title of Pascal Rambert's new
piece—*After/Before*—had taken on added resonance since I had first
reserved my ticket.

• • •

On the deep, spacious, and nearly bare raised stage of the
Gennevilliers, *After/Before* uncoils in three parts. During the first section we watch a large-screen video montage of individuals from New
York, Tokyo, Paris, and elsewhere who respond to the questions: "In
the event of a great catastrophe, of a new Flood, what would you take
with you from your prior life [*le monde d'avant*] for your subsequent
life [*le monde d'après*]? And what would you absolutely not take from
your prior life for the following one?" Tucked in among the scores
of everyday respondents are a few cultural celebrities such as the
novelist Christine Angot, the choreographer Rachid Ouramdane,
the dramatist-director Olivier Py, the philosopher Marie-José Mond-
zain, and Rambert himself—who says that he would leave behind the
memory of his mother's death, along with all of his clothes.

In the second part, Rambert's company of ten dancer-actors takes
cover under tables on rollers as 650,000 steel marbles crash down-
ward from the flies. After they sweep the silver pellets to the sides of
the performance space, the troupe, all in spotless white sneakers, are

joined on stage by ten nonprofessional dancer-actors from Annecy, the city in the Haute-Savoie where Rambert conceived and fleshed out the piece. The latter players are shoeless and range in age from sixty to eighty-five. They all then proceed to repeat, verbatim, the videoed responses of the first part—mimicking the original delivery while moving acrobatically, intertwining with and embracing one another, standing erect or lying down, and removing items of clothing to expose skin that is for some smooth and taut and for others flabby and wrinkled (see fig. 17). During the final part of *After/Before*, the troupe of twenty once again repeat the original responses, this time entirely sung to the accompaniment both of a Balinese gamelan, which they all play in due order of succession, and of the percussive beats of their wooden clogs, which they all now wear. Throughout this section the performers also slowly drape one another in bolts of brightly colored crepe paper.

· · ·

Like Quesne in *D'après nature* and Milin in *L'homme de février*, Rambert aims to offer a fresh vision of what theatre can be. Compared with *Paradis (unfolding time)*, which in some respects was Rambert's explicit manifesto against traditional theatre practice, *After/Before* shows heightened artistic maturity. Devoid of self-justification and feisty provocation, this beautiful work simply *is*. It gives us the same unwrapping of real time, real words, and real bodies that *Paradis* strove for, but without the earlier work's self-conscious theoretical scaffolding. Indeed, with *After/Before* Rambert eliminates text, action, and character altogether, not just pushing them to the margins as he did in *Paradis*. The shifts from electronically recorded discourse to live speech to sung sounds ultimately place center stage—as if part of a process to reclaim and restore something primordial—the anatomic vibrations that are basic to all vocalization. *After/Before*'s playful central conceit, "What would you take with you . . . ?" defuses the typical twenty-first-century, mostly Western hysteria regarding terrorism, natural disasters, and economic chaos. It replaces mass-media-bolstered anxieties with unhurried ceremonial acts that, disengaged from all specific religious or political reference, are imbued with the natural rhythms of existence, aging, and eventual death. In the tradition of Jacques Copeau, Peter Brook, and Ariane Mnouchkine, it cele-

17. *David Bobée and Gilberte Muguet make physical contact in Pascal Rambert's* After/Before. *Photo © Sylvain Duffard.*

brates theatre as the communion of people in an intensified quest for a renewed sense of human worth.

Rambert clearly takes inspiration from twentieth-century theatre and dance avant-gardisms. These include Gertrude Stein's principle of a continuous, looping present; Antonin Artaud's argument for a ritualistic, transformative theatre; and Pina Bausch's exploration of a democratic physical vocabulary based on everyday bodily movements. He also wrestles with the very possibility of theatre within a high-tech, hypermediated society saturated with electronic reportage. The result is a productive relationship between older and newer experimental practices. Otherwise put, Rambert—like Gildas Milin and Philippe Quesne—points the way to a new avant-garde that is fully aware of its being "post-" avant-garde. It is truly an *after* worthy of the *before*.

Scandal in Avignon, regeneration in Gennevilliers

On the first night of *After/Before*'s premiere run at the Avignon Festival in July 2005, an audience member interrupted the performance and screamed: "Why are you doing this to us? Why are you hurting us? What have we done to merit this? Why are you inflicting this on us?"[54] Many mainstream media pundits construed this outburst as proof positive that the festival's atypical programming that summer was infuriating the general public. What the press failed to indicate, however, was that this indignant spectator—who encouraged others to hiss, whistle, and throw objects toward the stage—was not at all part of the general public but was in fact "a well-known actress."[55] As is typical for opening nights in Avignon, a large part of the audience at the Gymnase Aubanel that evening consisted of theatre or journalism professionals who usually obtain their tickets free of charge.

Members of Rambert's company report that the reception at subsequent performances was "calm" and "appreciative."[56] But Rambert had already become the media's prime whipping boy. The normally even-handed theatre critic Fabienne Darge not only protested in *Le Monde* that "there is not a shadow of a genuine artistic idea" in *After/Before* but also insinuated that Rambert had to have been "high on pot."[57] Rambert later reaffirmed his conviction that true art must always entail, for creators and audiences alike, "a loss of one's bearings": "What happened in Avignon was that the [defamed] offerings, in all their potency and sincerity, were taken to be the work of imposters, whereas the real imposters are those who keep reproducing standardized formats that date from the bourgeois theatre of the nineteenth century."[58]

The French theatre historian Patrice Pavis did not attend *After/Before* in Avignon. But during the festival's initial week he went to eight pieces that provoked nearly as much fuss as did Rambert's, including Jan Fabre's *Je suis sang* (I Am Blood) and *L'histoire des larmes* (*History of Tears*); Romeo and Carla Castellucci's *B. #03 Berlin*; and Jean Lambert-wild and Jean-Luc Therminarias's *Mue—Première Mélopée*.[59] Pavis observed that a common denominator among these works was the expression of "foreseeable and enduring calamity," a mind-set that "lets the audience believe that everything around them is rotten, destroyed, condemned." Pavis admitted that by week's end he felt "overwhelmed by so many universal misfortunes, exhausted by recurring calamities." He specified that these works frequently referred to such topics as genocide, religious fundamentalism, inquisition, and the hatred of women and of bodies.[60]

Rambert's piece ran midfestival and thus after Pavis's short visit. But Pavis's observations perhaps explain why critics less judicious and circumspect hastily and erroneously lumped *After/Before* in with so many of these disheartening offerings. *After/Before* is powerful and moving precisely because it breaks away from the calamitous in order to celebrate the transcendence of bodies rejoicing in themselves.

• • •

Quality has a way of winning out. In June 2006 the Ministry of Culture and Communication announced that Bernard Sobel's successor as director of the Théâtre de Gennevilliers would be—Pascal Rambert. Ironically, the appointment was officially the handiwork of Renaud Donnedieu de Vabres, the very minister who had tried to show a measure of sympathy for those who had angrily protested the more daring productions of Avignon 2005—as epitomized, according to many, by Pascal Rambert's *After/Before*.

Since taking over the reins in January 2007, Rambert has altered the theatre's name to the chatspeak-like *Théâtre2Gennevilliers*.[61] He hired the French conceptual artist Daniel Buren, whose famous black-and-white striped columns grace the courtyard of the Palais Royal, to join with materials science students at the local Lycée Galilée in the construction of eye-catching new signage, in red-and-white striped arrows, for easier automobile and pedestrian access to the theatre. The architect Patrick Bouchain, known for his event-driven public projects, oversaw major renovations of the building's interior. These include a new ground-floor restaurant and bookstore and an upstairs *salon-bibliothèque* intended for informal edification, for socializing with the cast and crew before performances, and for the free use of Wi-Fi-enabled computers. The restaurant, open from late morning to 11 P.M., is called Food'Art and offers organic meals with a gourmet flair for as little as ten euros.

Officially the Gennevilliers is now a Centre dramatique national *de création contemporaine*, with the three added words taken very seriously. Rambert's ten-year plan for the theatre is twofold: to commission the finest French and international artists—in dance, opera, installation, and film as well as in theatre—in order to create new works for and at the Gennevilliers; and to foster novel modes of community participation. Like most of the *banlieue* theatres set up decades ago as part of the French government's efforts at cultural democratization, the Gennevilliers rarely saw more than 10 percent of the local population passing through its doors.

Rambert, whose slogan for the theatre is 'Ecrire ensemble' ('Writing/Creating Together'), foresees a time when those who live, work, and go to school in Gennevilliers will take pride in its theatre and its artists. But this will not result, he insists, from yet another top-down agenda fated to be perceived as elitist and intimidating. Accordingly, Rambert has opened rehearsals to the public, free of charge. He runs a three-hour creative writing workshop once a week, also free of charge. (He recently began sharing this activity with the authors Mathieu Bertholet, Christophe Fiat, and Tanguy Viel.) He and his staff train local adults in their twenties and thirties to serve as *médiateurs*, or insiders who can inform the population about what is happening at the theatre and why it may be of interest to them. And he has joined with Canal+ and France 2 in commissioning filmmakers each year to shoot on location in Gennevilliers.

• • •

Rambert eventually disclosed that Bernard Sobel had personally encouraged him to apply for the Gennevilliers headship and then actively lobbied on his behalf.[62] The fact that a man whose affinities were for the grand literary tradition stretching from Marlowe and Lessing to Brecht and Müller would gallantly pass on the torch to a pluridisciplinarian who positions text at the periphery of the scenic experience betokens the *esprit de famille* that marks so many of the best contemporary French public theatre professionals. The fact that for two decades prior to taking on these new responsibilities Rambert had the time, space, and financial support to hone his talent within government-sponsored houses throughout France is testimony to *théâtre public*'s unique capacity to nurture artistic creativity.

Three
Prodigious
Artists

A towering trio

Among the literary dramatists who are revitalizing French theatre today, three figures stand out for their originality, fecundity, and stature: Michel Vinaver, Valère Novarina, and Olivier Py. Each is a dominant figure in what we described in chapter 3 as theatre of *la parole*. In their resistance to language's debasement by commercial and informational pressures, they actualize the pithy remark of a figure in Novarina's *L'espace furieux* (2006): "We only have speech [*la parole*] to free us from the forest of words [*mots*]."[1]

Each of these artists pursues a complex creative agenda that prevents blanket categorization and that renders the feel and texture of their respective oeuvres entirely distinct from the others. Moreover, their professional personas are extremely dissimilar, with each positioning himself vis-à-vis the institutional structure of France's public theatre in strikingly different ways. By happy coincidence, all three enjoyed special tributes and heightened public visibility during my stay in Paris.

• • •

Chronologically these men belong to separate generations. Michel Vinaver, born in 1927, came of artistic age in the immediate aftermath of World War II. His creative vision owes a substantial debt to the American avant-gardes in music and painting of the 1950s and to the political and cultural upheavals of the 1960s. Vinaver has always thought of himself as not fully belonging to the elaborate network of French theatrical institutions. He is one of France's keenest commentators on the evolving status of text-based theatre within the nation's overall cultural life. Yet he himself has chosen to be something of a loner within the French theatre world.

Valère Novarina was born in 1947 and first gained attention during the 1980s. He confronted the challenge of inventing poetically meaningful language for the stage in the wake of such previous giants as Samuel Beckett and Jean Genet and in an era that had become cynical about language's power. One of Novarina's prime sources of inspiration is Antonin Artaud (1896–1948), whose conception of a replenished approach to theatre Novarina extends in a peculiarly individual manner. Unlike Vinaver, Novarina quickly established long-term working relations with specific directors and actors. He himself often takes part in productions of his works, serving as stage director, set designer, and painter. But like Vinaver, he treasures privacy and the freedom to work at his own pace. Even though he accepted to serve as artist-in-residence at the Odéon-Théâtre de l'Europe for its 2010–2011 season, Novarina has shown little interest in taking on administrative or artistic leadership within the *théâtre public* system.

Olivier Py, born in 1965, experienced as a young man the fall of European communism and the rapid rise of new information technologies. With near-missionary zeal he has strived to safeguard verbal lyricism and the expression of authentic human emotion from the numbing barrage of mass-mediated, homogenized verbiage and poses. He is very much a product of the French institutional theatre apparatus, and now heads one of the great national theatres, the Odéon-Théâtre de l'Europe. Py is a high-profile cultural celebrity: he writes, directs, and performs in his own pieces; he produces major works by others; he enjoys running a large cultural enterprise; and he is an influential voice in French cultural politics. Such extroversion is poles apart from both Vinaver's aristocratic detachment and Novarina's jealously guarded autonomy and private control over his options.

The sensuality of sounds and rhythms: Valère Novarina

East of the Butte Montmartre, in the heart of Paris's Goutte d'or (Gold Drop) district at 35 rue Léon, stands the Lavoir Moderne Parisien (LMP). Until 1953 this unimposing building had stayed a *lavoir*, or washhouse, of the kind depicted in Edgar Degas's paintings of laundresses or in Zola's novel *L'assommoir* (1877). In 1986 an organization named ProcréArt converted the space into a 100-seat no-frills theatre that has retained its mid-nineteenth-century charm.

It has low ceilings, original stone-and-brick walls, and a partially exposed dark timber framework. In winter the little lobby bar serves hot red wine from a large metal basin before and after shows, making more feasible the eventual removal of scarves, gloves, and hats: the LMP's quaint heating system makes visitors feel a bit like characters in Henry Murger's *Scènes de la vie de Bohème* (*Scenes of Bohemian Life*, 1851).

In celebration of its twentieth year as a maverick city- and region-subsidized theatre, the LMP programmed in January and February 2006 an appetizing assortment of works by Valère Novarina, aptly dubbed Les Nourritures Novarina (Novarina Nourishment). This homey smorgasbord was a perfect complement to the more sumptuous Novarina fare being prepared across town. For on January 21, the Comédie-Française would unveil its production of Novarina's *L'espace furieux* (Furious Space)—an event that would place the then fifty-nine-year-old dramatist within the very small number of living authors whose works have become part of the Salle Richelieu's permanent repertory.

To reach the Lavoir Moderne Parisien by subway, you get off at Château Rouge station on metro line 4 (direction Porte de Clignancourt). After walking a few feet northeast on the rue Poulet, you take a sharp right onto the rue Dejan, the site of a lively open-air food market at which you hear as much Arabic and varieties of Caribbean Creole and sub-Saharan languages as you do standard French. You then cross the rue des Poissonniers, go up the short rue Suez until it meets the rue Léon, and turn left. On the corners of each block you can overhear adolescents using street slang, including the latest versions of *verlan* (formed by inverting the order of a word's syllables). You pass a grocery store that advertises Alimentation Afro-Exotique. Your nose picks up scents emanating from Restaurant Ravel, which specializes in Indian food and is a stone's throw from the Ain-El-Hammam, which serves Moroccan delicacies. A wall placard for the upcoming Fête de Tabaski (a post-Ramadan feast) promises "all the *méchoui* [whole roasted lamb] you can eat" and musical entertainment by a well-known Senegalese. Coming from behind the doors of windowless men's eating clubs you hear loud, indistinct chatter and laughter.

Novarina's stage universe has no direct links to this multicultural slice of contemporary French urban life. But each time I traversed the area I could not help but become more attuned to the sounds and rhythms of talk I did not fully understand and to the subtleties of aromatic smells I could not precisely identify. I am sure that this immersion into a sea of unfamiliar language and food primed me for each experience of Novarina at the LMP. I recalled how Ariane Mnouchkine orchestrated ticket holders' exposure to festive music and food before we entered the tent erected at Lincoln Center for *Le dernier caravansérail*. The stimuli met with in the neighborhood of the LMP were of course random and serendipitous. Yet they, too, fashioned a kind of transitional space that sharpened my readiness for the sensually grounded verbalizations soon to emerge from actors performing Novarina.

Hearing with eyes and seeing with ears

Novarina attributes his lifelong fascination with language to his ethnic roots. He grew up in the Savoie (part of the Rhône-Alpes region), where he was exposed to Italian, German, and Savoyard (a dialect of the Franco-Provençal language Arpitan) as well as to French. He is the son of Maurice Novarina, a French architect whose Italian father immigrated to France at the turn of the twentieth century. His mother, Manon Trolliet, was a Swiss-born stage actress. When she became pregnant with him, Trolliet was appearing in a production of Molière's *Tartuffe* and decided to name her child after that comedy's amorous young suitor, Valère. Novarina's first practical contact with the stage was as a boy actor in plays with his mother. Eventually he studied philosophy, philology, and theatre history at the Sorbonne, where he wrote a master's thesis on Artaud.

Novarina's theatrical vision thwarts easy classification. The first time I conversed with him I asked whether he felt comfortable with the labels people habitually use: theatre of *la parole*; postdramatic theatre; theatre of epiphany; theatre of the Word incarnate; logotheist theatre; a theatre of initiation. With the exception of 'postdramatic,' which he found dubious and academic, he said that none of those rubrics was necessarily wrong and that he thought 'theatre of epiphany' was "rather good." For those who insist on fancy tags, Novarina added that he himself sometimes uses the term 'logo-scopic theatre' ('*un théâtre logoscopique*'), which he described as "theatre in which you see language on stage, in which you hear with your eyes and you see with your ears."[2] The eight events programmed at the LMP festival furnished ample opportunity for such a reorientation of the senses.

• • •

L'avant-dernier des hommes (The Next-to-Last Man, 1997) is a self-contained monologue excerpted from Valère Novarina's *La chair de l'homme* (Man's Flesh, 1995)—a "theatrical novel" that includes 3,171 characters and 786 definitions of God, ranging from Saint Augustine's to the German theologian Dietrich Bonhoeffer's (d. 1945). The actor Claude Merlin (b. 1940), who created the role in 1997, reprised it at the LMP. It was as close to genius as a performance can get.

Wearing blue jeans and a nondescript gray smock, Merlin plays a character named The Actor Fleeing All Others, also known as John No-Name (in French, *Jean-sans-nom*). Charged by a paternal voice to "be like Adam when he found his taste for life and discovered stones, iron, the ground, the soil,"[3] he speaks fervently to weeds, snippets of branches, and the scores of items he empties from his shoulder bag—scrap metal, pieces of cardboard, plastic debris, and so on. With equal verve The Actor recites and enacts the stage directions found in the published edition of the piece—which is conveniently among his paraphernalia; for example, "*He dances in order to become a body where his body no longer exists; then he wants to re-dance in order next to become a space where his body will be more him.*"[4] The Actor also mixes anecdotes about his past with rhapsodic ruminations about existence:

> *He hurls his mouth onto the objects and says to them*:
> Is being a blessing? And if not, is *curse* the name of the absence peeled off from being? Are vegetables of the genus plant? Do your eyes see you through your ears yes or no? And this stone that is, the one who says *pebble* to his peers—and may they ever lie on the ground—it, like us, do we hear it? Are eyes [*les yeux*] the plural of eye [*l'oeil*]? Heaven [*Ciel*], are you the plural of here [*ici*]?
> "Stones, how do you manage to hear what you never heard?" Triple-Rooted John-John would always say to the clouds.
> *He throws stones at the stones.*[5]

I asked Novarina what traits an actor must have in order to do his kind of theatre. "You need an actor," he said, "who does not fear being penetrated, being acted upon by the text. The actor must engage in a mysterious state of nonactivity—absolutely free of irony, intentionality, and point of view." "What's required," he continued, "is that the actor assume a kind of 'idiocy' whereby he believes that everything, at every moment, is true."[6] Indeed, throughout *L'avant-dernier des hommes* Merlin resembled a cross between, on one hand, a child earnestly playing with toys and ideas he is sure are alive and, on the other, an escapee from a psychiatric ward. As directed by the Novarinian practitioner Claude Buchvald, Merlin let it all play out like a virtuoso performance of, say, Franz Liszt's *Piano Sonata in B Minor* (1854). It teemed with humor, feeling, and insight. One of the loveliest touches came during final applause, when the actor acknowledged with a reverent bow the sundry objects that had served as his supporting cast.

Divine insanity

A new generation of Novarina performers is stepping forward.

L'opérette imaginaire (The Imaginary Operetta), the writer's sparkling homage to the French cabaret and *café-concert* traditions, is a three-act musical revue that includes burlesque sketches, solo warbling, theatrical parodies, and slapstick dance routines. It premiered in 1998 at Le Quartz in Brest (Brittany), where Claude Buchvald directed a chorus of twenty-two local singers and some of France's finest Novarinian actors, including Laurence Mayor, Elisabeth Mazev, Claude Merlin, and Daniel Znyk. At the LMP we were treated to a scaled-down version (the prologue and act 3) by the Compagnie Air de Lune, a troupe of eight young actors who trained together at the Ecole Claude Mathieu (Paris) and who are dedicated to exploring new alliances between music and theatre. Whereas Buchvald's production featured music composed by Christian Paccoud, a longtime Novarina collaborator, the Air de Lune version, codirected by Marie Ballet and Jean Bellorini, combined new music by Bellorini and Aurélie Verrier with cleverly chosen excerpts from familiar pieces by Handel, Mozart, Schubert, and Gounod.

It was an evening of divine insanity. Air de Lune took a few liberties with Novarina's libretto while never failing to sustain the dizzying hurricane of his verbiage: the neologisms, protracted enu-

merations, and prankish high jinks with suffixes, prefixes, and asso-
nances; the pseudoarchaic expressions and faux-Latin declamations;
the volleys of short staccato and marcato repartee and the endurance
test of each drawn-out monologue—all hilariously covering over the
twinges of anguish that characters are forced to deal with when they
cross paths with death, embodied here by the character Le Mortel.
One memorable highlight was the mock-wedding ceremony between
Dame Autocephalous and The Jack of Diamonds. Into Novarina's already over-the-top nuptials, Ballet and Bellorini inserted an entire
comic miniopera in German that found the bride, the groom, and the
bride's lover negotiating a tangle of plot twists and turns—with bravura singing from all and sidesplitting laughter from the audience.

Novarina has published nearly forty volumes of writings. Although
each of his works is distinct, they all spring from a creative imagination that reworks and pushes in new directions a core set of elements
and concerns. In this regard his pieces—both on the page and in performance—are almost instantly identifiable as his own. (Novarina is
also a gifted visual artist whose distinctive drawings, paintings, and
new-media installations have been exhibited at galleries in France,
Belgium, Italy, and Switzerland.) With its unbridled excess of music
and song—including a percussionist in a tall chef's hat who played
brilliant riffs on a mixing bowl and wire whisk, and another player
who went bonkers with the harmonics and vibratos of his musical
saw—this production of *L'opérette imaginaire* exposed the prime
motor of all Novarinian theatre: body vibrations made visible.

· · ·

Novarina maintains, as did Artaud, that the fundamental task
of an actor is to breathe. Fascinated by Greek Orthodoxy, he points
to the fusion of the physical and the spiritual vividly conveyed in the
title of Nicodemus the Hagiorite's adaptation of Ignatius of Loyola's
Spiritual Exercises (1524)—*Pneumatika gymnasmata* (1800). Novarina's own theatre, he insists, demands that the performer engage in
a "respiratory gymnastics" whereby "human flesh is rendered equally
somatic and ethereal."[7] Some critics have usefully connected Novarina's language practice to early modernist poetic experimentation,
including Italian and Russian Futurism, Dada, Surrealism, and the
French-based OuLiPo group (the Ouvroir de Littérature Potentielle,
or Workshop of Potential Literature), whose members have included

Raymond Queneau, Georges Perec, Marcel Duchamp, and Italo Calvino.[8] A more direct influence is the painter-sculptor Jean Dubuffet (1901–1985), who encouraged Novarina when no publisher and very few producers would consider his manuscripts, and whose interest in art brut, or raw Outsider Art—and above all the creative writings of the severely mentally ill—Novarina shares.[9]

When I asked if he sees himself as belonging to a specifically *theatrical* lineage, Novarina readily mentioned Alfred Jarry, Paul Claudel, Jean Genet, and Samuel Beckett. He also said that he constantly re-reads Shakespeare, Corneille, Racine, and Molière, along with the prose fiction of François Rabelais (d. 1553), the religious philosophy of Blaise Pascal (d. 1662), and the great sermons and funeral orations of the theologian Jacques-Bénigne Bossuet (d. 1704). "I return to these authors," he noted, "as a tonic against the aseptic and anemic writing that is so much the norm today. They inspire me by the energy, the electricity of their language."[10]

On February 15, as a one-night-only contribution to the LMP festival, the veteran Novarinian actor André Marcon (b. 1948) did a reading from *Le discours aux animaux* (Discourse to the Animals, 1987). Marcon is as much identified with this exalted text, which he first performed at the Théâtre des Bouffes du Nord in 1986, as he is with *Le monologue d'Adramélech*, which he introduced at the 1985 Avignon Festival. During a postperformance talk with the audience, Novarina—who is not prone to hyperbole offstage—said to Marcon: "In listening to you tonight, I had the impression that fire was surging forth from the text's very center."[11]

Fast-forward to the 2007 Avignon Festival, July 12. Novarina sits at a small table on a raised platform in the open courtyard of the Calvet Museum. It is midday; the sky is clear and the sun blazes. For the next thirty minutes the dramatist recites pages of a diary he kept during the writing and rehearsals for his latest work, *L'acte inconnu* (The Unknown Act), which had launched the festival a week earlier. As always when he reads in public, Novarina grips the edges of his text and raises his arms so that the page's surface is at a right angle to his larynx. Like a priest engaged in a ritual consecration of the enigmas of Language, his delivery is fervid and incantatory. As Novarina speaks ardently about "*le mystère respiratoire*" ("the respiratory mystery") that for him is the essence of stage performance, the mighty mistral—the dry wind that sweeps through the Rhône Valley on its way to the Mediterranean—blows more forcefully and noisily than I have ever experienced it. It was as if nature itself was ratifying Novarina's insights.

A landmark event at the Comédie-Française

Valère Novarina is only starting to become known in the United States. His works have been translated into at least thirteen languages, including Swedish, Hebrew, Romanian, and Russian. Yet simply a handful of his texts, mainly excerpts, exist in English.[12] In 1999 the California Institute of the Arts (CalArts) in Valencia, California, under the direction of Zaven Paré and Allen S. Weiss, presented *Theater of the Ears*, a high-tech collage of Novarina pieces in English translation. Billed as "a play for electronic marionette and recorded voice," *Theater of the Ears* featured Novarina's speaking and blinking face digitally re-constructed from a life mask and a torso made from X-ray images of his chest.[13] The work then played at La MaMa E.T.C. in New York as part of the Henson International Puppet Festival (2000). More recently Novarina has visited several American universities to deliver readings and lectures and to attend campus-sponsored productions of his works (often in cooperation with the regional French Cultural Services). Such schools include the Massachusetts Institute of Technology (2008), Emory University (Atlanta, Georgia, 2010), and Georgetown University (Washington, DC, 2010).

The American theatre critic Tom Sellar has noted that Novarina's essays, manifestos, and interviews can come off in English translation as "solipsistic" and "self-indulgent."[14] Yet many French critics view these same works as comparable in didactic power and resonance to those of the great teacher-theorists Louis Jouvet and Antoine Vitez.[15] Some of the pieces have even become performance texts. Still, Sellar rightly observes that "in Novarina's case, the proof of his pudding will be better tasted in the dramas themselves."[16] To anyone who doubts that a full-scale Novarina production can be humanely moving and utterly entertaining, the Comédie-Française's mounting in 2006 of *L'espace furieux* puts such concerns to rest.

• • •

L'espace furieux combined *L'opérette imaginaire*'s music-hall and circus antics with *L'avant-dernier des hommes*'s affirmation of the creative synergy between matter and spirit. Philippe Marioge's brightly lit set diagonally sliced the Comédie-Française's proscenium stage into halves (see fig. 18). Dominating stage right was an immense three-dimensional triangular surface (serving as backdrop and floor covering) upon which were painted (based on Novarina's own canvases) swirling designs in vibrant blacks, blues, reds, and whites. Stage left consisted of overlapping eggshell-white panels that traversed their allotted space in a fanlike curve. Middle stage center and positioned midpoint along the oblique seam shared by these two unmatched halves was a small horizontal blue neon sign in cursive writing that read *'Je suis'*—which in French can mean both "I am" and "I follow."

Like the overall set, these two resonant words—*'Je suis'*—encapsulated the dramatic and conceptual tensions that the work's players both embody and interrogate: stasis versus motion; the concrete versus the invisible; the contingent versus the eternal and the infinite. *L'espace furieux* is in fact an adaptation of portions of a 1991 Novarina volume entitled *Je suis*.[17] Embedded within this subject pronoun and verb are allusions to God's saying unto Moses, "I am that I am" (Exod. 3:14); to Jesus and to the followers of His Holy Word (Novarina is fond of noting that *'Je suis'* is a near anagram of 'Jésus'); and to Descartes's *cogito*, which for Novarina morphs into 'I *speak*, therefore I am.'

In effect, *L'espace furieux* is a three-act lyrical exploration of the philosophical issues surrounding man's essence and existence in time and in space. If it stages these matters largely in a tone of turbulent frenzy, it is because the choice between continuing to live or seeking out death is at immediate stake for virtually all of its doleful and conflicted dramatis personae. Yet the play also projects a measure of steady calm and serenity due to its reverberations with and its half-respectful, half-parodic pastiches of famous treatments that these very issues have received by Western philosophers, theologians, mathematicians, and poets over the millennia. With *L'espace furieux*, Novarina gives us a brand-new theatre piece, but its substance is basically ageless. The same can be said of virtually all his works.

• • •

L'espace furieux begins with a Socratic dialogue on the basics of grammar and logic—topics that both fascinate and repel Novarina. Searching for answers are two young androgynous figures dressed in

18. *Philippe Marioge's set for Valère Novarina's* L'espace furieux; *left to right: Christian Paccoud (The Illogician), Catherine Salviat (The Poor Lady), Daniel Znyk (Spitting Image), and Gérard Giroudon (The Meatative Old Man). Photo © Thierry Gründler.*

crisp white, The Traversing Child (L'Enfant Traversant) and The Child from Outer Brevity (L'Enfant d'Outrebref). They intone their words with glowing earnestness:

> THE TRAVERSING CHILD: What are words composed of? And how many are such? What expressly are words composed of?
> THE CHILD FROM OUTER BREVITY: They are composed of syllables.
> THE TRAVERSING CHILD: Which are?
> THE CHILD FROM OUTER BREVITY: Sounds that are heard for an instant and that either cannot or must not be split.
> THE TRAVERSING CHILD: Apply that answer to some examples!
> THE CHILD FROM OUTER BREVITY: The word *opulent* is composed of three different sounds, namely, o-pu-lent; and each of these sounds is pronounced in one single instant that cannot be split. O-pu-lent. Each of these sounds is only composed of instants. The word *Dieu* [God] contains two sounds that are only one syllable because they can only be heard in one single instant: *Dieu!* We must not separate them in our pronunciation.
> THE TRAVERSING CHILD: You have just proved that the word *Dieu* is one syllable only.
> THE CHILD FROM OUTER BREVITY: As a result the word *Dieu* contains two sounds, namely *Di-eu*, however, these two sounds make up only one because they are heard in a single instant and cannot be separated. Neither by science nor by pronunciation. *Dieu* is only one syllable.
> THE TRAVERSING CHILD: What is a word composed of only one syllable called?
> THE CHILD FROM OUTER BREVITY: It is called a monosyllable. Thus 'I fear God' is three monosyllables; 'I am,' two syllables. . . .
> THE TRAVERSING CHILD: Can our speech come from others than ourselves, or be directed toward others than ourselves? Can our speech come from someone else who is speaking to us?
> THE CHILD FROM OUTER BREVITY: I do not believe so.

THE TRAVERSING CHILD: What did your voice just say?
THE CHILD FROM OUTER BREVITY: The voice is in my heart. It
is only its echo in my mouth that you were hearing.[18]

Just as their conversation turns even more theological, the head of The Meatative Old Man (Le Vieillard Carnatif), who is in charge of catering food, pops out from the prompter's box downstage center and puts a damper on their inquisitive ardor by evoking death:

THE MEATATIVE OLD MAN: As voluble as language may be, it
can no longer stir when one's palate is stuffed with earth. A
handful of humus will plug the most eloquent of mouths in
these parts. And a stone will be placed over you, so you have to
shut up. Then you will shut up.[19]

Among the cluster of remaining central figures who will successively appear are First-Person John (Jean Singulier), the play's protagonist; The Poor Lady (La Figure Pauvre); and Spitting Image (Sosie). All three are contemplating taking their own lives. First-Person John claims to have just killed "my father my mother my half-brother his son and his younger brother, his aunt, their recipient, my uncle and their cousins, my son, his father, his sister and his half-sister." But before he can confront death, he makes clear, "I must first search for the space that corresponds to my brain." His comportment makes clear that this space is of the "furious" kind that gives the play its title. The Poor Lady, too, hopes to "leave my body to the ground, but I don't quite know how to." She achieves eternal rest at the play's end, but only after rhapsodically enumerating the seventy-two kinds of leafy herbs she is aware of—and with whose vegetative state she will soon more closely blend. Spitting Image, who is fixated on bodily orifices and is also certain that one does not find oneself until one is dead, comes upon an oversize plaster effigy of his head in a wheelbarrow. Brandishing the likeness and then smashing it, he declares: "Here lies my head: to be consumed preferably before the date indicated on the back of the container."[20]

Each of the play's seven leads performs at least one lengthy monologue; several perform many. In act 1, First-Person John recites his picaresque life story, which goes on for at least ten minutes. Toward the end he says:

FIRST-PERSON JOHN: Then I was a laborer for Jean Urbain, a bouncer at Brute's, a lifeguard for vacation clubs, a snow monitor for Occidorama, then the same for Bicentennial and Secotine, then a supervisor of supervisors for Roc, an affiliate at Chopy's, the vanitor of the vanities at Bricoplaste's, the dust-remover at Lucratives, at Bossey-Vigot, at Fortifiers, then perpendicular apprentice at Enigmas then tourist for vacationers then pump attendant at Payless then dealer for Borghino's, denestifier for Happeny's, then rising businessman, rising consultant, then at last rising business consultant, then at last rising casket.[21]

The Traversing Child, who has clearly learned something about nonmimetic performative language, responds to this verbal avalanche with the question "Can you pull more sounds out for us from the void?" John's reaction advertises pain and scorn: "I would just like to live among cows who are animals that have remained true to their nature, not wavy camels with their cries of melancholy! Will humanity just piss off!" When The Poor Lady completes her soliloquy about an intimate long-term relationship with junk objects, she wards off others' criticism with a rendition of "The Song of People Who Are Going Nowhere," sung to accordion accompaniment. The ballad's plaintive refrain—"Where is the exquisite hour?"—is a nod to both Beckett's *Oh les beaux jours* (*Happy Days*, 1960) and the waltz from Franz Lehár's *Die lustige Witwe* (*The Merry Widow/La veuve joyeuse*, 1861).[22]

As in all Novarina works, *L'espace furieux* offsets the existential turmoil with humor and frolic. The piece brims not only with Novarina's trademark wordplay but with pantomime, trapdoor surprises, entrances on motorbikes, picturesque props ceremoniously brought on stage and then left unused, music-hall-era dances and torch songs—some chanted with Edith Piaf–like vibrato, others intoned in, of all languages, Latin—and fanciful paintings, drawings, and oversize photographs that descend from the flies or creep up from beneath the stage.

• • •

I found three moments in this production to be especially unforgettable. The first came at the end of act 2, just before intermission, when the stage—*la scène*—turned into the quasi-burlesque, quasi-solemn site of *La Cène*—the Last Supper—with six seated players ingesting not only shards of their long wooden table but also a chunk of the House of Molière's gilt stage arch, which came unfixed as readily as a wedge of bread in a medieval farce. It was as if we were watching France's leading troupe of actors taking communion, at once mystical and ridiculous, with the Holy Ghosts of French theatre.

The second indelible moment was Christine Fersen's declamation of The Prophet's monologue (see fig. 19). The tragedienne appeared from the left wing in a shabby black coat and carrying a cheap red handbag. Fersen paced her gait so that at her long speech's end she stood center front with the '*Je suis*' neon sign directly behind her. Just as she was at last physically installed at the set's symbolic junction of chaos and ideal purity, so the personal story she told had moved from spiritual darkness ("*obscurité*") to worldly enlightenment ("*la lumière terrestre*") to an ecstatic fusion with God—which she describes, in language reminiscent of Blaise Pascal at his most paroxysmal, as "nameless Joy" ("*Joie sans nom*"). Then in a final, matter-of-fact declaration—and as if to justify her delusional bluster in case God does not really exist—Fersen tosses out the neo-Pascalian statement: "And even if no one had been listening to the words I was speaking, they were worth imparting, even if just to the floor."[23]

A similar signal of support for humanity's tenuous ontological condition crowned François Chattot's performance as First-Person John. At the play's end, in a last-ditch effort to connect meaningfully with time and space, John dances furiously, desperately, until he drops—to all appearances, dead. But then the omnipresent stagehand, referred to as The Workman of the Drama (L'Ouvrier du Drame) utters his sole lines of the evening:

THE WORKMAN OF THE DRAMA: Get up!
FIRST-PERSON JOHN (*on the ground*): Why?
THE WORKMAN OF THE DRAMA: Death is not true. (*The dancer gets up. In the background the neon sign '*Je suis*' remains lit.*)[24]

In being compelled by himself and others to reset the balance between his body in frenetic movement and his mind in enraged thought, First-Person John has perhaps indeed found the verbal, corporeal, and psychic space that most naturally "corresponds to my

19. *Christine Fersen, center, declaiming The Prophet's tale in Valère Novarina's* L'espace furieux; *looking on are Véronique Vella (The Child from Outer Brevity) and Daniel Znyk (Spitting Image). Photo © Thierry Gründler.*

brain." It is what enables him to stand up and start over in relative calm. *L'espace furieux*, it turns out, is a comedy.

Requiescant in pace

In the months that followed this production, two of its cast members died without warning: in September 2006 Daniel Znyk (Spitting Image) (b. 1959), who had collaborated numerous times with Novarina but was one of the Comédie-Française's most recently appointed *pensionnaires*; and in May 2008 Christine Fersen (The Prophet) (b. 1944), who had enjoyed the longest tenure of any Comédie-Française *sociétaire*. Novarina framed his next major work, *L'acte inconnu* (The Unknown Act, 2007), as a deeply felt homage to Znyk, whose huge puppetlike effigy hovers over the entire proceedings. Many admirers eulogized Fersen. The journalist René Solis noted in *Libération* that while "Queen Christina" had long struggled with private demons, she "found on stage more than just a safe retreat: she found a strong, intense place where, even when besieged by danger, she no longer had anything to fear."[25]

Valère Novarina has said: "Those who are truly dead should not instill fear within us; it is as if there were music playing above them."[26] For those who witnessed Znyk and Fersen at the peak of their vitality in *L'espace furieux* in spring 2006, the play's final words, "Death is not true," now seem doubly appropriate. I continue to see and hear their music.

Olivier Py's cavalcade

Another leading light to enjoy a special Paris showcase that season was the playwright, director, actor, lyricist, drag performer, filmmaker, and novelist Olivier Py (b. 1965). From late April through early June, the Théâtre du Rond-Point ran five of Py's plays and a cabaret show of his songs under the banner La Grande Parade de Py (Py's Big Cavalcade). The Rond-Point is a *théâtre public* that sits at the posh intersection of avenue Franklin D. Roosevelt and the Champs-Elysées. Its elegant circular building, originally conceived by the architect Jacques Ignace Hittorff, has an illustrious history. It was a rotunda for painted panoramas (1860–1893); a famed ice-skating rink, Le Palais des Glaces (1894–1980); and home to the Renaud-Barrault theatre company (1981–1991). Since its major interior reconstruction in 2001 the Rond-Point boasts three auditoriums, the best theatre-arts bookstore in Paris, and a chic restaurant-bar-nightclub. Under the aegis of Jean-Michel Ribes (b. 1946), the playhouse has dedicated itself exclusively to contemporary, living dramatists and enjoys a special working relationship with the Ecrivains associés du théâtre (EAT), a professional association of France's playwrights. It is a theatre complex that programs eclectically and that generally attracts a sophisticated, culturally informed audience.

Ribes's idea for La Grande Parade was to have Olivier Py present a bundle of his pieces that pay explicit homage to the pleasures of theatre. The resulting minifestival was thus heady with self-reference and meta-discourse. It turned out to be a huge critical and box-office success.[27] As luck would have it, La Grande Parade was also a way for Parisians to come to know better the unconventional young artist who, to the surprise of not a few, would by year's end be appointed to run the Odéon-Théâtre de l'Europe, France's most prestigious theatre after the Comédie-Française.

Who is Olivier Py?

Some Americans know Olivier Py from his supporting role as the gay apartment mate, Michel, in Cédric Klapisch's hit film comedy *Chacun cherche son chat* (*When the Cat's Away*, 1996). U.S. theatregoers may have attended his documentary stage piece *Requiem for Srebrenica*, hailed by the *New York Times* as "powerful and chilling"[28] during the 2000 New Wave Festival at the Brooklyn Academy of Music. In early 2007 Py's *Epistle to Young Actors, That the Word May Be Restored to the Word* played at the Massachusetts International Festival of the Arts (Holyoke) before moving on to New York City's French Institute/Alliance Française. International opera fans are likely to be familiar with his innovative productions of Wagner's *Tristan und Isolde* at the Grand Théâtre de Genève (Switzerland) in February 2005 and Benjamin Britten's *Curlew River* at Edinburgh's Royal Lyceum Theatre in August 2005.

Among movers and shakers in the contemporary French theatre world, Olivier Py is unapologetically Catholic, openly homosexual, and politically outspoken. Born in southern France, he comes from a family of *pieds-noirs*, Algerian settlers of European origin who relocated to France when Algeria became independent in 1962. In two of his plays, *Théâtres* (1998), and *L'exaltation du labyrinthe* (2001), Py's protagonists obsess over their fathers' former roles as colonizers or combatants. In 1995 Py took part with other French performing-arts figures in a protracted hunger strike to decry the way that Western policy makers were dealing with Serbian barbarity in Bosnia. In May 2006, during the run of La Grande Parade de Py, he defended Marcel Bozonnet's swift decision to drop a planned Comédie-Française production of the Austrian playwright Peter Handke's *Voyage to the Sonorous Land, or The Art of Asking* (1989); the cancellation occurred when it became known that Handke had given a eulogy at the funeral of former Yugoslav president Slobodan Milosevic—who at the time of his death was being tried on charges of genocide. Some public figures accused Bozonnet of "sectarian" high-handedness that amounted to censorship.[29] But Py—in a published statement endorsed by 150 intellectuals, artists, and political figures—affirmed, with pointed reference to the cultural legacy of such Nazi sympathizers as the German philosopher Martin Heidegger (d. 1976) and the French novelist Louis-Ferdinand Céline (d. 1961): "There comes a time when one can separate the work from the man. But in the case at hand, that time has not yet arrived."[30]

In late February 2008 Py was again in the headlines when he flung open the doors of his national theatre to accommodate on the Odéon's stage a history-making gathering of over 150 prominent French theatre artists: their common purpose was to impugn the Ministry of Culture's new budgetary freeze decisions. Py declared that the latter bespoke "a staggering absence of sound cultural policy."[31]

• • •

Artistically Olivier Py is an anomaly. He views himself as a lyric poet with a mission to counteract the residual taints of theatrical modernism and the so-called avant-garde—especially the flight from storytelling and the grimness that suffuses much contemporary fare. "I am modern in the sense of being a product of the aftermath of the Renaissance and its humanism," he asserts. "But modern in the twentieth-century sense, no. The latter [*la modernité*] implies ruptures, breaks, and an abyss between words and things. It is based on despair. And upon such despair I cannot dance freely."[32] For all his political engagement, Py opposes so-called didactic theatre: "I'm not at all a rebel [*un homme révolté*]. . . . Theatre must be affirmative, not reactive. It must say, show, and bring to life everything that is deeply missing from a market society. . . . My dream is of an insurrection of the word [*la parole*] not against the world's evils, but against a more terrifying enemy, boredom [*l'ennui*]."[33] Py has as little sympathy for identity politics as he does for feel-good consensus, both of which he sees as dominating TV and movies and as giving rise to narcissism and complacency: "In live theatre, certain actors—not directors, but actors—can make us understand that before being gay, female, black, poor, or rich, we above all belong to humanity."[34]

With respect to the brouhaha of Avignon 2005—where his trilogy *Les vainqueurs* (The Conquerors) had a week's run—Py's stance, too, is at odds with that of many of his peers. He feels that the festival programmers did overly brush aside text-based plays in favor of image-based performance pieces. "If outraged spectators clamor for a stage with actors and [verbal] poetry, should they automatically be deemed reactionary?" he asked soon after the event.[35] Apropos of the supposed salutary shock value of dance and hybrid pieces by the likes of Jan Fabre and Gisèle Vienne, Py notes that the subversive force of The Living Theatre, which truly jostled middle-class French sensibilities in the late 1960s, has for at least the last quarter century been recast as little more than a theatre-establishment "marketing strategy."[36] The Avignon debate, he now insists, was not so much about a distinction between text-based and non-text-based theatre as it was about the competing appeals of, on one hand, brute instinct ["*la pulsion*"] and realism ["*le réel*"] and, on the other hand, dream, metaphor, and desire ["*le libidinal*"]: "A suffering body [on stage] that is [actually] shivering, naked, and smeared with genuine blood is the polar opposite of metaphor."[37]

His generation of artists, Py asserts harshly, has been quick to accept public funding while refusing to acknowledge that "public service," not "narcissistic comportment," is due in return.[38] La Grande Parade de Py offered some fine illustrations of Olivier Py's concept of civic purpose.

The mystic thrust of a profane métier

Epître aux jeunes acteurs pour que soit rendue la Parole à la parole (Epistle to Young Actors, That the Word May Be Restored to the Word) was originally a dramatized lecture that Py gave in 2000 to stu-

dents and staff of the Conservatoire national supérieur d'art dramatique, of which he is an alumnus. At the Rond-Point, John Arnold—
who trained with Ariane Mnouchkine at Théâtre du Soleil before
attending the Conservatoire—performed the main role of The Poet,
who plays the harassed Muse of Tragedy (see fig. 20). Samuel Churin,
who set the night's tone with barrel-organ carnival music, took on the
parts of Tragedy's numerous interlocutors.

At the play's start—and in full sight of the audience—Arnold
changed out of his black business suit, white shirt, and men's briefs
into an ivory-colored, flowing feminine gown; applied damp flour
makeup and red lipstick to his face; and plunked a fake laurel wreath
onto his blonde-bewigged head. He/she then embarked on a frenzied
and often uproarious hourlong plea to resist "this utter degradation
of our civilization that no longer speaks of the Word [*la Parole*] except
as hogwash, puts the poet on the same level as a seal trainer, and re-
duces words to the barnyard of charitable and promotional shows
that are very entertaining."[39] Wielding Novarina-like concepts and
Claudel-inspired prosody, Tragedy passionately asserts:

> What is essential in the word, words cannot express, granted.
> But is that a reason to seal your lips? . . .
> When I speak to you, I display the boundless expanse of those
> things which, because they can't be expressed, are shown, are
> shown in the very act of speaking.
> The Word is the manifestation of Being.[40]

Throughout the piece, Tragedy proffers quick and confident rejoin-
ders to a series of rogue defenders of mediocrity who include The
Cultural Official, The Policeman of Desire, and The Killjoy:

> THE KILLJOY: Who has ever seen a man saved by a word?
> [THE POET] AS TRAGEDY: I have. And I believe in the
> resurrection of the dead. And I also believe in the real
> presence in the Eucharist, and that makes me something
> other than a maker of plays.[41]

In Tragedy's final remarks the simple yet "miraculous" deed of an
actor's walking on stage to utter words takes on a generalized social
dimension, namely, the gift of human compassion and empathy—
with clear spiritual overtones: "One never says anything but 'I suffer

20. *John Arnold as The Poet playing The Muse of Tragedy in Olivier Py's* Epître aux jeunes acteurs pour que soit rendue la Parole à la parole. *Photo © Alain Fonteray.*

with you.' 'I suffer with you' is healing. I suffer with you. That's all. . . .
And it doesn't matter if it's spoken clumsily if it is spoken in truth."[42]

Py firmly rejects the notion that he is "a Christian poet" and, as
some critics claim, a "proselytizer": "I have never confused the Catholic mass with the theatre. Theatre is the site of the profane [*le païen*].
Hence the debauchery, the nudity, the music [in my shows]."[43] Nevertheless Py insists that theatre is also a precious site of spiritual activity, which he defines as "the incarnation of the word in the actor's
body" and which he considers to be "*sacré*" (holy): "The stage is, at
bottom, this miraculous place in which the body and the soul are one
and the same."[44] Formulated this way, Py's idea of the mystic thrust of
theatrical activity seems close to that of Valère Novarina. Their plays,
however, reflect the difference between a true believer and a probing
agnostic.

In Novarina's *L'origine rouge* (2000), a character called The Evange-
list asserts that "God made man in the image of His nothingness. No
more than that."[45] Throughout Novarina's writings God is a necessary but negatively marked theatrical and philosophical foil defined
variously as "a void," "a vacant food," "the presence of a hole," or "a
hollowed name."[46] As one commentator notes, "the Novarinian God
is the precise inverse of the God of the faithful."[47] Indeed, the dense
theological paradoxes, contradictions, and oxymora found in *L'espace
furieux* make *Epître aux jeunes acteurs*'s declarations of faith in the
mystery of the Word seem, for all their sincerity and heat, like Novarina lite. This contrast may account for the relatively greater popularity Py has with large audiences regardless of their religious convictions. For although both Py and Novarina are exceedingly playful
and entertaining dramatists, Novarina packs his theatrical universe
with linguistic and conceptual complexities of an order that is absent
from Py's.

Also separating these two major artists is Olivier Py's dismissal of
modernism. Py's verbal brio is sharp, clever, and often dazzling, but
it is never self-consciously problematic. Novarina by contrast is as
much a descendent of Beckett as of Claudel. The pathos we feel for
his characters is rooted not in the melodramatic (as is often the case
with Py) but in the Beckettian tensions between man's yearning for
verbal expressiveness and an acknowledgment of its futility, between
affirmation and despair, plenitude and the abyss. Novarina's theatri-

cal world is vastly more joyful and life-affirming than Beckett's, but both writers' works are haunted by the post-Auschwitz pull of silence and extinction. Py's are not.

Children's plays and adult marathons

La Grande Parade's roster included two delightful musical adaptations of fairy tales by the Brothers Grimm: *La jeune fille, le diable, et le moulin* (*The Young Girl, the Devil, and the Mill*) and *L'eau de la vie* (*The Water of Life*). Py's longtime stage designer Pierre-André Weitz set these familiar stories within sleek, visually striking décors dominated by blacks, whites, and reds. Scene changes relied upon an ingenious metallic cubelike unit whose sections folded inward and outward. A permanent backdrop grid of music-hall-style white stage lights underscored the overall artifice. Variations on each of these scenic elements were part and parcel of all of the shows in La Grande Parade and are basic to virtually all of Py's theatre and opera productions.

Py believes that well-made children's theatre can be "a perfect initiation to theatrical mystery."[48] What is most impressive about these two plays for youngsters is the complete absence of condescension to the material and to the audience—about one-third of which was made up of children on the night I attended. The actors, all veteran (adult) members of Py's troupe L'Inconvénient des Boutures (The Trouble with Plant-Cuttings, founded in 1988), were funny, silly, and—at the same time—amazingly moving. Py is just one of many distinguished French playwrights who regularly author scripts that specifically target youngsters but equally aim to please adults. Among their number are Joël Pommerat, Catherine Anne, Fabrice Melquiot, Christophe Honoré, Jean-Claude Grumberg, and Joseph Danan. France has several theatres that program exclusively for children, like the Théâtre Nouvelle Génération in Lyon, the Atelier de la Bonne Graine in Paris, and the Théâtre Massalia in Marseilles. Of the thirty-nine national and regional dramatic centers (CDNs and CDRs) in the *théâtre public* network, four are officially charged with producing works for young people: the Grand Bleu in Lille, the Théâtre Jeune Public in Strasbourg, the Théâtre des Jeunes Années in Lyon, and the Préau in Vire (Lower Normandy).[49]

The CDN of Sartrouville, a suburb northwest of Paris, has since

1997 mounted a traveling biennial festival, Odysseys in Yvelines, that commissions writers and directors for new works and then visits eighty communes in the region. "What I find amazing," says the program's administrator Dominique Bérody, "is that the artists we use, whether it's Joël Jouanneau or Olivier Py, Jean-Yves Ruf or Emmanuel Demarcy-Mota, when they address children they remain themselves. . . . Those who go and see a play of Olivier Py for children are seeing Olivier Py's theatre *tout court*."[50] Indeed, Marie Bernanoce, a scholar of children's theatre, notes that "whether it is sexual orientation, death, war, madness, the Holocaust, or violence," French plays for youngsters, while often taking artistic inspiration from the Symbolists and Surrealists, are emphatically uninhibited in their treatment of hard subjects: "I see here a form of ethical commitment in addressing young people, which doesn't mean sentimentality or facility."[51]

• • •

Py likes theatrical marathons. His breakthrough production at the 1995 Avignon Festival was his self-authored *La servante: histoire sans fin* (The Servant: An Endless Story), a set of five full plays and five small "*dramaticules*" that together last twenty-four hours. (The "servant"—which among its other French meanings is the lonely 'ghost lamp' lit on stage when the house is dark—is, above all, theatre itself.) In 2003 at the CDN Orléans/Loiret/Centre, which he headed as of 1997, Py staged Claudel's twelve-hour *Soulier de satin* (*The Satin Slipper*)—only the third time, after Barrault's staging in 1943 and Vitez's in 1987, that this masterwork had been produced since its completion in 1929. For La Grande Parade, Py reprised *Les vainqueurs* (*The Conquerors*), the trilogy that had been part of Avignon 2005 and that runs for nine hours forty-five minutes, including intermissions.

Les vainqueurs's prologue triggers the improbable saga that follows. A young man hiding in the armoire of a prostitute's bedroom observes how she transfers a beatific smile to two of her clients: Florian, a fallen prince, and Axel, a gravedigger. Like the stolen Rhinemaidens' gold in Richard Wagner's four-opera *Ring of the Nibelung*, this smile, and the young man's quest to retrieve it, links each of the ensuing dramas, with the young man becoming the protagonist of each full-length play. In *Les étoiles d'Arcadie* (The Stars of Arcadia) he is Prince Florian, at odds with post-Communist political foes and allies. In *La Méditerranée perdue* (The Lost Mediterranean) he is Cythère, a legendary whore of Antiquity who manages a Dionysian music hall where sex and poetry run wild. And in *La couronne d'olivier* (The Olive-wood Crown) he is the one-legged, necrophilic, plurisexual Axel, entangled in a series of life-or-death struggles that take place in Grasse (coincidentally Py's home town in Provence). The epilogue unfolds in the prostitute's room where the fable began, and the young man learns that the sought-after smile was a red herring. Joy, he is instructed, resides solely in an appreciation of the very act of living: "Joy, joy, joy! All the joys! All the joys!"[52]

There is much to admire in *Les vainqueurs*: its enormous ambition, its baroque sweep, its creative sets and lighting, its sustained and effortless mix of the carnal, the political, and the poetic. Passages of great verbal beauty segue with total artistic plausibility into comic episodes of graphic profanity. Nonetheless, the plotting and dialogue of *Les vainqueurs* are too often unfocused, ponderous, and slow going. Despite moments of inspired éclat, it is not Py at his very best.

Great performances

The minifestival's major revelation was Olivier Py's new piece, *Illusions comiques* (Theatrical Illusions). It is pure enchantment. The title is a wink to Corneille's *L'illusion comique* (1636), a reflexive tribute to the actor's craft and a play that exploded neoclassicism's stodgy rules via a cat's cradle of plays-within-plays. Py also takes inspiration from Molière's *L'impromptu de Versailles* (1663), a comedy in which Molière's royal troupe—like Py's government-subsidized company here—play themselves playing an assortment of roles; and in which Molière, also playing himself—as does Py here under the guise of Myself (Moi-même)—parodies Louis XIV's pretensions to direct the planet's affairs. The tongue-in-cheek premise of *Illusions comiques* is that the twenty-first-century world, no longer able to solve its problems, clamors to enlist the dramatic poet Myself as its leader and savior (see fig. 21). Pressured to accept by his overbearing mother, Myself comes to learn—three acts and three hours later—that the theatre can retain its art and soul only by keeping a safe distance from commerce, technology, and established religion.

Illusions comiques culminates with a group recitation of "100 defi-

21. Standing right of center, *Olivier Py in the role of Myself, being photographed next to the Mayor of Paris in Py's* Illusions comiques. *Photo © Alain Fonteray.*

nitions of theatre" that Myself's Aunt Genevieve requests as wrapping inserts for her line of handmade candies:

> AUNT GENEVIEVE: It's unlikely that [the enumeration] will give a human face to globalization, or bring about fairer distribution of wealth, or repair the ozone layer. But who knows, some adolescent may find something to decorate his bedroom wall with. . . .
>
> MYSELF [*who gets the final word, with definition number 100*]: Theatre is the prize for having expected nothing.[53]

Olivier Py is slight and wiry with dark wavy hair and irregular facial features that bring to mind a softer-looking Nicolas Sarkozy (who is ten years Py's senior). Although Py generously claims that the actors of his troupe "have taught me everything I know,"[54] he is a natural-born showman with superb stage presence, and *Illusions comiques* demonstrated this vividly. From the moment after we hear the bouncy trumpet and piano melodies that open the show, Py and his kinetic cast hop from role to role—including the Pope, the President of the Republic, the Mayor of Paris, Bertolt Brecht, a philosopher, a theatre usherette, Death, and God.

Even among such sterling company, the actor Michel Fau stole the show with his impersonation of Myself's provincial Aunt Gene-vieve, whom we first see garbed in a shocking pink faux-Chanel suit set off by inordinate strings of pearls. Later, Aunt Genevieve removes her skirt in a brazen display of thick thighs in sheer pink tights and a nylon-covered crotch that is indisputably male. In a tour de force episode in act 2, Aunt Genevieve's acting coach requires her to voice the line "Even the Gods cannot undo what has been" in thirty-seven ways: these range from "absentmindedly" and "with wicked irony" to "licentiously," "sententiously," and "while holding back a little fart."[55] Just as opera divas once upon a time inspired composers to tailor transcendent arias for them, Michel Fau here becomes Py's ideal *porte-parole*, or mouthpiece, in a virtuoso celebration of the blazing, demented energy with which a prima donna can ravish a grateful audience. The minor fact that this particular goddess is a he in heels—much like Py when he performs as Miss Knife in his drag cabaret act—simply reinforces the special madness that is basic to theatre. Deservedly, Michel Fau won the year's Best Actor prize from the Syndicat de la critique théâtre, musique et danse.

• • •

Illusions comiques was not immune from negative criticism. One journalist, annoyed by the play's speeches that urgently call for Py's own brand of dramatic lyricism, begged him to refrain from "beating his own drum."[56] Another commentator decried Py's pose of complicity with Corneille's L'illusion comique, which in her view is a "pre-revolutionary and visionary" work; Illusions comiques, she argued, belongs to a "counter-revolutionary" "theatre of dandys" that, in its hostility to modernism, is unable to "relate to social realities."[57]

Py has defended himself against such charges many times. In an interview published just as La Grande Parade de Py got underway, he said:

Theatre no longer needs "new forms." It should leave that to the visual arts and fashion industries. Theatre does not require that sort of legitimacy. What it must do . . . is constantly observe the way older artists worked in order to invent a theatre for today. Poets have always been reactionaries. Even the Surrealists went in search of the archaic. . . .

If there is anyone who challenges the cant of leftist discourse, it is me—because you simply cannot spout old formulas that no longer correspond to anything. You cannot content yourself with thinking "we are going to educate the working masses," because we do not address ourselves to defined social groups. Contemporary society is both socially fragmented—notions of "proletarian" and "bourgeois" have become meaningless—and culturally uniform: whether someone earns one thousand or ten thousand euros a month, we are all part of the same television culture. That is what a man of the theatre has to respond to.[58]

In a thoughtful book entitled Quel théâtre pour aujourd'hui? (What Theatre for Today? 2007) Jean-Pierre Siméon (b. 1950), a poet, novelist, critic, and playwright, considers why French "alternative" or "art" theatre has regularly failed to attract broader audiences. He points to three factors: an overly serious attitude; a loathing for sentiment; and a disdain for old-fashioned ideas. "People do not go to the [public] theatre," he says, because, among other reasons, "they are afraid. Of two main things: of not being up to it intellectually (that they lack sufficient knowledge); and of being bored."[59] Siméon lays blame for this climate of intimidation not just upon creative personnel but upon programmers, publicists, and even theatregoing regulars, whom he takes to task for cliquishness, puffed-up solemnity, and partisan whispering. One remedy, Siméon suggests, is for the subsidized theatre establishment to reclaim a "lightness of being" that would inject humor, humility, simplicity, and childlike directness into the cement that binds the stage with its public.[60]

Whatever one may think about Olivier Py, there is little question that he is committed to a jubilant, inviting, and even self-deprecating theatre. As the head of the Odéon-Théâtre de l'Europe, he has explicitly espoused Jean Vilar's vision of a public theatre—one that is popular, antielitist, and above all convivial: "If I were not confident in theatre's capacity to appeal to people of every social stratum, I would give up!"[61] In his first year at the Odéon's helm, Py programmed productions of Melville's *Moby Dick* in Italian, Chekhov's *Ivanov* in Hungarian, and Hanoch Levin's *Krum* in Polish; in French there were Molière and Maeterlinck, Joël Pommerat's *Pinocchio*, and Py's own new translation of Aeschylus's *Oresteia*. But ever the consummate showman, Py launched the season with *Illusions comiques*. It was a smart choice.

Alias Michel Grinberg, CEO

In New York I often asked ACT FRENCH attendees for tips on major playwrights I ought to become familiar with. One name that cropped up regularly was Michel Vinaver (b. 1927). Some even said that Vinaver may be France's greatest living dramatist. One of Vinaver's works, *11 September 2001*, had been slated for ACT FRENCH but was canceled in the wake of a political tangle that undermined its funding. I was thus pleased when, soon after arriving in Paris, I came across advance notice for a new production of his *A la renverse* (Bending over Backwards, 1979), to take place in early April. The newspaper item specified that the show would be staged by the seventy-nine-year-old author himself—*in his solo directorial debut*. Thanks to a friend, I secured a seat for the press opening. I also began to seek answers to questions that had been quietly vexing me for months: Who is Michel Vinaver? And why—in my long career devoted to French culture—had I never heard of him?

• • •

Vinaver's real name is Michel Grinberg. His Russian-Jewish parents had, individually, left Russia for Paris in the wake of the Russian Revolution of 1917 and married in 1925. Michel's father was an antiques dealer; his mother, a jurist. The family fled France during the Nazi occupation, and Michel finished his secondary education at New York's Lycée Français. In 1944 he joined the French Free Forces. At the war's end he returned to the United States, adopted his mother's maiden name—Vinaver—and soon graduated from Wesleyan University (Middletown, Connecticut) with a bachelor's degree in English and American literature. One day in New York he had a brief encounter with Albert Camus (1913–1960), who encouraged his literary efforts and later smoothed the way for publication by Gallimard of his two novels, *Lataume* (1950) and *L'objecteur* (1951). *L'objecteur* won the Prix Fénéon, which honors emerging artists: Vinaver was barely twenty-four. He went on to earn another degree, this time at the Sorbonne and in French literature. Then, virtually through a misunderstanding, he accepted a job in 1953 as a managerial services officer with the Gillette Corporation, the safety razor manufacturer, at its new French offices in Annecy, near the Swiss border.

From that moment on he pursued a dual career. As Michel Grinberg, he climbed the corporate ladder and eventually became CEO of Gillette Belgium, Gillette Italy, Gillette France, and S.T. DuPont: he introduced, among other products, Teflon-treated Gillette Extra Blue Blades and Right Guard deodorant. As Michel Vinaver, he switched from novels to plays. His first major stage piece was politically controversial: *Aujourd'hui ou les Coréens* (Today, or The Koreans) dealt with a deserter from the volunteer French batallion of the UN fighting forces during the Korean War and demystified crusades of so-called liberation. The then up-and-coming vanguard director Roger Planchon (b. 1931) mounted this bold work in Lyon in 1956. Vinaver's subsequent creative efforts, such as *La demande d'emploi* (*The Interview*, 1973) and *Par-dessus bord* (*Overboard*, 1974), increasingly focused on the power dynamics of corporate culture and on the cold-bloodedness and insecurity that are built into the capitalist system.

At first Vinaver found his dual allegiances troublesome: they triggered seven years of writer's block as of 1960. During those same years Vinaver began to raise a family; one of his four children is Anouk Grinberg (b. 1963), the accomplished stage and movie actress. Eventually Vinaver reconciled his callings, viewing each as reinforcing the other. "I was both a very faithful agent of the system and a traitor to it," he told me. "And I tried to 'decipher' this contradiction in my writings."[62] Indeed, a central dynamic in Vinaver's plays is the pull between belonging and disengagement—both in one's personal life and in the workplace. As lucid as he remains about the downside of corporate practices, Vinaver is genuinely grateful for its many qualities. Regarding the Gillette Corporation, he confided: "I felt that something mystical was being generated among employees. It was more like a church than anything else. There was a sense of vocation, solidarity, and belonging to something bigger than myself. That's one of the reasons, I think, why capitalism is superior to the bureaucracies of totalitarian systems."[63]

Vinaver had to leave Gillette at the end of 1979: his being both an able captain and an artsy rebel of industry did not sit well with certain board members. He continued to write new plays, revise his older ones, and translate Shakespeare and Botho Strauss (b. 1944). He found a new vocation as a professor of theatre studies at the University of Paris III (1982–1988) and Paris VIII (1988–1991), where he introduced some of France's first classes in creative writing for the stage. His essay collections on classic and contemporary French plays became essential reading, exhibiting the high level of critical insight and literate prose style that André Bazin and François Truffaut had brought to their landmark writings on French cinema.

A forceful advocate of the playwriting profession, Vinaver served from 1982 to 1986 as the first chair of a separate theatre committee within the Ministry of Culture's Centre national des lettres (CNL). In his CNL-commissioned *Le compte rendu d'Avignon: des mille maux dont souffre l'édition théâtrale et des trente-sept remèdes pour l'en soulager* (Report from Avignon: On the Thousand Ills of Theatre Publishers and Thirty-seven Remedies for Bringing Relief, 1987), he investigated the diminished status of plays within the publishing industry and made recommendations that have helped to reverse the trend.[64]

The bugbear that Michel Vinaver has most consistently decried is a director's theatre, whereby director-*auteurs* impose their vision on contemporary dramatic texts and in the process distort and debase the playwright's fundamental literary contribution. With few exceptions Vinaver has not been pleased with productions of his plays, even (and especially) when directed by such luminaries as Roger Planchon, Jacques Lassalle, and Alain Françon. These artists, he bitingly claims, have turned *mise en scène* into *"mise en trop"* (*trop* is French for 'too much').[65] This provocative stance made me all the more eager to attend the man's directorial premiere on April 3, 2006.

The discreet charm of the free enterprise system

Among the keyed-up ticket holders swarming the lobby that warm spring evening were longtime Vinaver friends and fans, members of the press, theatre artists of all stripes, and surely no more than a handful of folks like myself who had never attended a Vinaver play. The sole prior production of *A la renverse*, directed by Jacques Lassalle in 1980, had taken place at the mighty Théâtre National de Chaillot. This new rendition ran at the more modest Théâtre Artistic Athévains, a semisubsidized theatre on the rue Richard Lenoir in the eleventh arrondissement, and it was based on a major 2002 rewrite in which Vinaver had increased the cast from six actors playing twenty roles to twenty-three actors taking on twenty-nine parts. The venture grew out of a series of professional actors' workshops that Vinaver had been invited to run in 2004 with Catherine Anne—the playwright-director who then headed the Théâtre de l'Est Parisien.

As I entered the midsize auditorium and searched for my seat, I was struck by the hall's setup (see fig. 22). Except for circus events and Gildas Milin's *L'homme de février*, I had not seen any Paris productions that—like this one—took place fully in the round. The acting space, arranged specially for this show, was a floor-level ellipse framed by tiers of spectator seats on two opposite sides and a single row of seats on each perpendicular side. The spare gray set consisted of one square table, stage center, and three small, identical oblong platforms, each with an attached bench, set equidistantly from one another. Wherever you sat, you therefore viewed the same symmetrically arranged pattern—but from an angle and a distance that no one but you could lay claim to. As showtime approached, a number of actors took front-row seats in scattered reserved spots along the stage's periphery. Once the show began, The Voice of the Narra-

22. *In Michel Vinaver's production of* A la renverse, *corporate executives, factory managers, laborers, and,* seated midground center, with headscarf, *a dying princess. Photo © Marion Duhamel.*

tive gave a long expository speech while striding clockwise, over and over, along the ellipse's border. His words, however, were interrupted when actors, still seated among the audience, spouted short staccato phrases. The immediate auditory effect was similar to that of multi-channel surround sound though devoid of electronic support. Players and audience alike were thus embedded within the work's natural acoustic substance: Vinaver's written words vocalized.

I can best compare the next ninety minutes to listening to a perfectly executed set of Bach three-part inventions. (In the play's published edition Vinaver divides the work into two sections labeled "Prelude" and "Fugue.")[66] Continuously and exuberantly, words, phrases, and sentences overlapped and intertwined. Short, distinct motifs were set off, seconds later, by countermotifs, new expositions, repeated themes, and on occasion robust choral passages. This patterning of language—whether we think of it as baroque or modernist—was swift, intense, and crystalline; there was no place for Romantic-era rubato, metaphor, or psychologizing. An additional contrapuntal dimension came from the actors' precisely gauged movements from bench to table, from table to the edge of the ellipse, from standing alone to meeting in pairs to converging in groups. Because they wore either gray business suits or white workers' smocks, their motions registered as a continuous flow of muted tones with a few splotches of color (a tie, scarf, or head covering) as if in an early Robert Rauschenberg canvas come to life. This was theatre like none I had experienced.

• • •

Unlike Novarina's and similar to Py's (minus the melodramatics), Vinaver's brand of theatre of *la parole* typically gives us a substantive, complicated plot. *A la renverse* follows events in the life of Bronzex, a small French pharmaceuticals firm that manufactures tanning cream and is planning a switch in product name from Mi Fa Sol to Si Do Ré. Its destiny, however, depends less on decisions by its executive and managerial staff than on the whims of American honchos at the Cincinnati-based conglomerate that is its parent company and on the strike potential of its production-line workers. The firm's fate is also intertwined with that of Princess Bénédicte de Bourbon-Beaugency, a Frenchwoman dying of skin cancer because she sunbathed too much: each week Princess Bénédicte appears on a popular reality TV series that charts her agony. Short scenes that at times overlap or occur simultaneously take place in Ohio and in France; in board rooms, office suites, airports, factory workspaces, and sundry gathering places; and *chez la princesse*. At what appears to be a climactic finish but is in fact a deceptive cadence, the workers take over the firm as a cooperative, buying it for a symbolic one franc. In a coda, The Voice of the Narrative returns to inform us—as he again strides along the fringes of the ellipse, this time counterclockwise—that a certain David Siderman, a global marketer of solar energy who was once connected to the old parent company, is just now jetting from Beijing in the hope of executing a hostile takeover.

Vinaver had the cast take bows while holding hands in a circle and skipping clockwise, ring-around-the-rosy style. This final touch was formally exquisite and perfect in its implied irony: the self-perpetuating market system, it seemed to say, will neither "all fall down" nor find itself irrevocably *à la renverse*.

Theatre for our times

"I never felt that I belonged to the theatre community," Vinaver informed me. "Artists I feel close to are John Cage, Merce Cunningham, Claes Oldenburg, and Robert Rauschenberg."[67] Vinaver's compositional method relies on juxtaposed verbal assemblages and on the connections and spaces between disparate elements; except for question marks, he writes without punctuation. This approach to literature is rooted in his experience of T. S. Eliot's *The Waste Land* (1922), which he discovered as a Wesleyan undergraduate and translated into French as *La terre vague* in 1947.[68] "I was struck," he said during a rare recent visit to New York, "by Eliot's mix of trivia with mythology and world literature, and how all this heterogeneous material ends up being polyphonic."[69]

Vinaver's mix of formal innovation with an insistent focus on the simple details of people's lives led critics, as of the 1970s, to place him within a loosely defined category of *théâtre du quotidien* (theatre of the everyday)—a label that included such playwrights as Jean-Paul Wenzel (b. 1947), Michel Deutsch (b. 1948), Michèle Foucher (b. 1941), and Daniel Besnehard (b. 1954). In various ways each of these writers "reenvisioned the political dimension of theatre and the theatrical representations of the political."[70] Yet Vinaver prefers the notion of *ordinariness* to 'quotidian': one of his finest plays, based on accounts of the Uruguayan rugby players who survived a plane crash in the Andes by eating bodies of dead passengers, is ironically titled *L'ordinaire* (1982).[71]

Michel Vinaver's chief subject is the trials and tribulations of *homo economicus*. In *L'ordinaire*, for example, he transforms the rugby players into a team of U.S. corporate types on a South American business trip. (*L'ordinaire* was Vinaver's first play to enter the repertory of the Comédie-Française, in spring 2009, with the author codirecting the piece with Gilone Brun.) Nonetheless Vinaver aims to write plays that have no obvious message or ideological stance. "In all of my plays," he says, "writing is used as research. It endeavors to *know*—not to expose or to illustrate what's already known."[72] He likes to speak of each play as a "landscape" or "the mapping of a territory" that triggers in the spectator a "drive towards meaning" but never imposes "one single meaning."[73]

Vinaver's meticulous arrangement of the space at the Théâtre Artistic Athévains—especially his effort to erase barriers between audience and players—affected me in a curious way. I almost felt as if Vinaver had cunningly arranged the "landscape" of *A la renverse* so that we, the spectators, would figuratively function as an assembly of the company's stockholders, observing and assessing the firm's "performance" as it unfolded in real time. In making us complicit with what took place on stage, our strong final applause that night became trickily ambiguous. We were of course congratulating Vinaver and the troupe. But by providing the acoustic beat for the actors' ring-around-the-rosy strutting, were we not also approving the symbolism inherent in their posture, namely, the firm's allowing itself to be gobbled up once again by a multinational—and the cost to human lives be damned? Such an interpretation may seem impressionistic and idiosyncratic, but personal constructions of meaning and a consideration of their impact on real life are precisely what Vinaver wants his plays to elicit from every ticket holder.

• • •

I saw *A la renverse* on Monday, April 3. The next day, France experienced the third round (in as many months) of massive, disruptive demonstrations as students and workers united to protest controversial legislation concerning the *contrat première embauche* (CPE, or first job contract). The de Villepin government was promoting the CPE as a way to provide a greater number of jobs; the protesters saw it as giving employers an easy way of firing them. The points of congruence between the political clashes played out on the streets that Tuesday in 2006 and those that Vinaver had explored in his riveting play, conceived twenty-six years earlier, were striking. Not the least attractive aspect of Michel Vinaver's entire oeuvre (twenty plays) is the extent to which he presciently addressed the ways in which transnational economics and the mass media, especially television, have complicated life as we know it today. Two outstanding instances are *La demande d'emploi* (*The Interview*, 1973), which follows the plight of a middle-aged out-of-work manager who seeks new employment, and *L'émission de télévision* (*The Television Programme*, 1989), a frightening comic take on the insidious impact of reality TV on ordinary people.

• • •

Lightning almost struck twice. The second week in June 2006, at the Théâtre Nanterre-Amandiers in the industrial suburb just beyond La Défense, Vinaver's *Iphigénie Hôtel* (Hotel Iphigenia) had a five-day run in a production again directed by the author and featuring the same actors who had played in *A la renverse*. Before the show started, Vinaver—who is trim and wiry with a delicate, birdlike face—spoke to the audience, once more positioned in the round. He told us that although he wrote the play in the immediate wake of the May 1958 events that led to Charles de Gaulle's return to political power, the piece was not produced until Antoine Vitez mounted it in an abridgment at the Pompidou Center in 1977. Vinaver stressed, as if to apologize, that the rendition we were about to see was only "*une esquisse*," or first sketch, of an ideal mise-en-scène and that his budget for costumes and props amounted to just a few hundred euros.

In fact Vinaver's direction was nearly as masterful as that of *A la renverse*. The dominant geometric pattern this time was a square, and the total absence of a set—when necessary, actors wheeled in chairs, beds, and steamer trunks—enhanced our engagement with the verbal polyphony that is basic to Vinaver's theatre. *Iphigénie Hôtel* deals with a group of French tourists marooned at a hotel in Greece and only vaguely aware of the military and political turmoil taking place in France and Algeria. In its steady rotation and overlap of scenes that focus on the hotel's servants, on glamorous well-to-do guests, and on the two groups' interacting with each other, the play's open structure is reminiscent of Jean Renoir's *La règle du jeu* (*Rules of the Game*, 1939). Vinaver told me that he admires Renoir's films but "was not conscious of an influence."[74] Still, Vinaver's manner of presenting multiple conversations that take place at the same time but retain their individual clarity—even as they inflect the meanings we attribute to the others—is highly Renoir-like. It results in deep-acoustic scenography that is comparable, I think, to Jean Renoir's pioneering use of deep-focus cinematography.

An international hot potato

The production of Vinaver's *11 September 2001* that had to be withdrawn from ACT FRENCH for political reasons in fall 2005 went on a European tour in June 2006. The show was the offspring of a collaboration between the Center for New Performance at CalArts and the Théâtre Dijon Bourgogne. Directed by Robert Cantarella (who then headed the Dijon Bourgogne), it premiered in April 2005 at the Roy and Edna Disney/CalArts Theatre (REDCAT), the center for innovative performing arts at the Walt Disney Concert Hall complex in Los Angeles. Along with the Cultural Services of the French Embassy of the United States, the Center for New Performance at CalArts project had been funded in part by Etant donnés: The French-American Fund for Contemporary Art and the Association française d'action artistique (AFAA), an agency under the purview of the French Ministry of Foreign Affairs but also supported financially by the Ministry of Culture. Prior to its ten-day Paris run at La Colline–théâtre national in mid-June 2006, the piece played at the Frictions Festival in Dijon and at the Théâtre des Treize Vents in Montpellier. The only other time *11 September 2001/11 septembre 2001* had been mounted in France was in July 2004 at Avignon's Théâtre du Balcon, as part of the summer "Off," or fringe, festival. Even then, according to Vinaver, the play's director Jean-François Demeyère and his Belgium-based company Le Théâtre tu (The Silenced Theatre) ran into "numerous obstacles on the part of the programmers."[75] Why is this work so controversial? Vinaver wrote *11 September 2001* in English during the weeks that followed the Twin Towers catastrophe. The play is primarily an assemblage of excerpts of media coverage of the disaster. It presents, in their own words, Islamist terrorists, staff workers at the World Trade Center, Wall Street brokers, airline pilots and passengers, survivors, spouses of the dead, journalists, George W. Bush, Donald Rumsfeld, and Osama bin Laden. Vinaver says he composed the piece in order to "retain the grain of the event" in advance of memories that would become "increasingly associated with agreed upon images."[76] He rearranged his notes and clippings in a form he describes as "close to that of the cantata and oratorio," made up of "arias (for one, two or three voices)," "choral parts," and "recitatives."[77] Just prior to the World Trade Center attack, Vinaver had been talking to the experimental music theatre composer Georges Aperghis (b. 1945) about a possible collaboration. When Aperghis read *11 September 2001*, however, he was unable, Vinaver says, "to find his way into it": "And I think that's for the best, because today I really don't want music to accompany the words."[78] The play's published version gives us Vinaver's French translation on pages facing the original English, and the scripts are respectively labeled "*Libretto*" and "*Livret*."

Robert Cantarella's mise-en-scène of *11 September 2001* exhibited artful touches (see fig. 23). In theory, Vinaver's complete text should take no more than about a half hour to perform. Cantarella chose to repeat it three times seriatim, with his cast of eleven American actors switching roles for each restatement. The iterations displayed distinct tones ranging from neutral to melodramatic to solemn, and each staging diverged from the others in actors' placement, gestures, and movements. Like the actual TV coverage in 2001 that constantly looped images and accounts of the calamity, Cantarella's reprises worked to engrave the players' words in our heads; yet their varied delivery shrewdly hindered us from according fixed meanings or interpretations to them. In the initial round, just before Bush says,

> Freedom itself
> Was attacked this morning by a faceless coward
> And freedom
> Will be defended,

the Chorus sing-songs, to the tune of the nursery rhyme "London Bridges,"

23. *The Chorus in motion during the CalArts Center for New Performance production, in April 2005, of Michel Vinaver's* 11 September 2001, *directed by Robert Cantarella. Photo © Scott Groller/CalArts.*

Twin Towers
Falling Down Falling Down Falling
Gone
The Twin Towers Are Falling Down Falling Down Falling Down.

Just after Bush says,

The United States will hunt down
And punish
Those responsible for these cowardly acts,

the Chorus utters, in advertising jingle fashion,

U.S. Terror Alert Networks
Were Looking in the Wrong Direction
Warnings
Went Unheeded for Years.[79]

These same lines, like all others in the text, are delivered in a different fashion later on. A terrorist, for example, first reads his lengthy Instruction Sheet to Hijackers with a folding chair balanced precariously on his head; second, while jumping in place; and third, with his back to the audience, his arms extended like an airplane's wings, and his head and hair covered with scores of Post-it Notes. Sporadically throughout the proceedings, haunting chords were plunked on an electric guitar and slides of supermarket aisles and office corridors were flashed on the auditorium's stage-left wall; each ticket holder eventually received a matte-finish print of one of the slides.

While writing *11 September 2001*, the former Gillette CEO felt that he was functioning a bit like the ancient dramatists who adapted mythic stories for the stage—with the difference that the destruction of the Twin Towers had taken place just days before. He also sensed that George W. Bush and Osama bin Laden were akin to the irascible, feuding gods that we find in Homer and the Greek tragedies.[80] The play's next-to-last section gives us parallel statements by these two leaders in a format that imitates the classical Greek dramatic technique known as stichomythia, or the quick alternation of short lines:

BUSH: Good afternoon on my orders the United States military
has begun strikes

BIN LADEN: Here is America struck by God almighty in one of its vital organs.

. . .

BUSH: In the face of today's new threat the only way to pursue peace

BIN LADEN: The wind of change is blowing

BUSH: Is to pursue those who threaten it

BIN LADEN: To remove evil

BUSH: The name of today's military operation

BIN LADEN: I swear to God

BUSH: Is Enduring Freedom

BIN LADEN: That America will not live in peace

BUSH: Our patience in all the sacrifices that may come

BIN LADEN: Before all the army of infidels depart the land of Mohamed

BUSH: The battle is now joined

BIN LADEN: God is the greatest

BUSH: We will not waver

BIN LADEN: These events have divided the world

BUSH: We will not tire

BIN LADEN: Into two camps

BUSH: We will not falter

BIN LADEN: The camp of the faithful

BUSH: And we will not fail

BIN LADEN: And the camp of the infidels

BUSH: Peace and freedom will prevail

BIN LADEN: May God shield us

BUSH: May God continue to bless us.[81]

In the first iteration of these lines, George W. Bush, played by a man, comes off as silly, whereas Osama bin Laden, played by a woman, is subdued and dignified. In the next, Cantarella reverses the genders and the two leaders individually indulge themselves in toying with large plastic cylinders that they try to keep balanced upright. The final time, Bush (played by a woman) and bin Laden (played by a man) face each other, chest to chest, and speak their lines with equal gravitas as the rest of the cast echo their words in whispers.

The Paris critics were respectful of the play but less than enthusiastic about the production. The *Figaro* reviewer titled her piece "Exercises sans style" ("Style-*less*-tic Exercises").[82] *Le Monde* found Cantarella's "chic and sophisticated" rendition too steeped in "the clichés of a certain American avant-garde" and lacking "the modesty and simplicity" the text calls for.[83] Antoine de Baecque, writing in *Libération*, compared Vinaver's work to a "memorial shrine" whose strength resides in its "immediacy" and "fragility" and not in Robert Cantarella's show of "sophistication."[84] I, too, wondered whether this was perhaps another instance of "*mise en trop*." It would be fascinating to see how Vinaver might direct the piece. Until he does, however, the Cantarella version stands as an inventive, ambitious rendering of this important play.[85]

• • •

Why didn't *11 September 2001* play in New York?

According to Vinaver, the French Embassy in Washington came down with a case of "cold feet" ("*frilosité*").[86] A few weeks before the play's Los Angeles opening, Jean-René Gehan, the embassy's New York–based cultural counselor, read the script and feared that right-wing Americans and relatives of the dead would construe the juxtaposed quotations from bin Laden and Bush as French government endorsement for equating the two men's mind-sets. With the assent of ambassador Jean-David Levitte, who had been working to repair Franco-American relations, Gehan canceled $5,000 of last-minute funding to the Center for New Performance at CalArts, reneged on an offer to pay for Vinaver's travel to Los Angeles, and asked that the center expunge from its publicity all acknowledgment of support from the Ministry of Foreign Affairs.[87] Travis Preston, the artistic director of the Center for New Performance at CalArts, asserts that "there was the suggestion that if we could see cutting [the quotations in question], the situation could be different."[88] Preston informed the Los Angeles cultural attaché, Alain Belais, that a compromise of that sort was out of the question. Gehan later apologized to Vinaver for the embarrassing diplomatic predicament they found themselves in. But it was clear that the prospect of receiving an official blessing for the show to move on to ACT FRENCH that autumn was nil. "The piece did not open in New York," Preston says, "because the French Embassy didn't want it to happen. They had created a situation that spiraled out of control."[89]

In retrospect Vinaver sees this imbroglio as confirmation that he does not write political message plays but that by "immersing [his works] in the topical," he allows them to exert unlooked-for political impact:

> The act of censorship fell on a play which did not tally with any political position. . . . In the case of *11 September 2001*, the fact of "de-hierarchising" the words, whatever their sense, putting them on the same level, on the same level of interest, of creativity—what an office employee who is going to die says, another who slides down the stairs toward the exit, a trader, a terrorist, Bush, bin Laden— without any scale of importance or value is, without doubt, a political act. . . . For me, what the theatre does is to disturb the smoothness of experience, the smoothness of reality, or what is perceived as smoothness. . . . What disturbs the smooth surface? It's the events, the hitches, the roughness. It's the catastrophes, both big and small. That's the material of theatre. . . . And that's perhaps what makes for politics in the theatre.[90]

In 1959 the cultural critic Roland Barthes detected in Vinaver "that beauty of language that is never an imitation of bygone beauties, but which is the foundation of an in-tune language [*un langage juste*], equally distinct from the literary and the natural."[91] A half century later, the political journalist Edwy Plenel dubbed Vinaver "the tireless narrator . . . of our era's havoc": "Nothing that was and is still at the heart of our immediate history has been overlooked or spared by Vinaver: unemployment, industry, television, the workplace, agencies, strikes, competition, money, the rat race, capital, labor, neighborhoods, crime, freedom, disasters. . . . In years to come anyone who will want to understand our times and acquire a feel for our language and its rhythms . . . must read this man's oeuvre over all others."[92]

Astonishingly, Michel Vinaver's works are barely known in the United States. His texts certainly pose challenges for translators, producers, actors, and audiences. Yet the potential rewards for all who engage with his genius are stupendous.

Cultural Diversity (I)
Ethnicities

Hoary notions of culture versus a changed population

Just after ACT FRENCH began in New York, I saw a remarkable new French-language film that was showing at the IFC Center near Washington Square: Abdellatif Kechiche's *L'esquive* (*Games of Love and Chance*, 2004). The Tunisian-born Kechiche (b. 1960) would become better known in this country two years later when his next movie, *La graine et le mulet* (*The Secret of the Grain*), became a popular success along the U.S. art-house circuit. *L'esquive* is a motion picture whose subject matter stayed with me throughout my initial exploration of the French theatre scene. More directly than any French-language stage work I would see in the following twelve months, this stunning movie—which had already garnered four Césars (France's equivalent of Oscars)—treated the thorny and timely issue of whether France's grand theatre tradition has pertinence for minority youth in today's Paris suburbs and, by extension, for all French citizens in the years to come.

L'esquive deals with a group of multiracial high schoolers whose white French teacher is prepping them for an end-of-year performance of Pierre de Marivaux's comedy *Le jeu de l'amour et du hasard* (*The Game of Love and Chance*, 1730)—a staple of the Comédie-Française repertoire and a prize example of France's vaunted theatrical *patrimoine*, or legacy from the past. The movie's most salient trait is the linguistic divide between the refined, precious Enlightenment idiom of Marivaux's script and the youngsters' rough, slang- and hip-hop-laden street talk. As the story progresses, however, Kechiche cleverly makes us alert to the elaborate artifice—and the lyrical charm—inherent in both ways of speaking.

The well-intentioned teacher (played by Carole Franck) labors valiantly to convince her pupils that by performing such archetypal characters as Silvia and Harlequin they will "find pleasure in getting out of themselves." Yet she holds back from cautioning that unless they acquire a good command of standard modern French, their chances for social mobility are slim. Kechiche's screenplay perhaps makes a stronger case for Marivaux's curricular appropriateness simply by exposing multiple parallels between the anxieties and awkward encounters of the playwright's fictive young lovers and those of the contemporary teens who hang out, flirt, and squabble with one another amid the concrete hallways and plazas of their housing project. Near the film's end, a sequence of the students' public performance at the local community center shows the young thespians joyfully acting out their roles to the obvious delight and pride of family and friends.

Yet *L'esquive* is not a naive defense of the often-heard precept, triggered by supposed French republican values, that one cultural canon happily fits and uplifts all. In a chilling anticipation of the police misconduct that allegedly triggered the 2005 suburban riots, Kechiche gives us a powerful sequence—just before that of the Marivaux performance—in which a local police squad stop, search, and strong-arm the film's innocent lead characters without due cause. Moreover, Kechiche's main male protagonist, the lovesick introvert Krimo (Osman Elkharraz), who was born in France to Algerian parents, is thoroughly resistant to the supposed allure of eighteenth-century prose and dramaturgy. By the film's close, Krimo's inability to don the masks of neoclassic French comic theatre leads to his feeling even more alienated from his peers than he had been at the movie's start. *L'esquive* thus discloses the inadequacy of the ideal of a wholly shared cultural *patrimoine* in a nation whose demography is increasingly diverse.

In chapter 3 we explored how some of the ideological tensions and paradoxes concerning the fuller recognition of France's ethnic diversity make themselves felt in three French-language playwrights of African and Caribbean descent or affiliation who were on the roster of the ACT FRENCH festival in New York. In the pages that follow we will examine how several minority theatre makers and show people encountered in Paris have dealt with these same matters, especially through humor.

An indictment of so-called integration

As of early March 2006, you could not take a subway ride in Paris without seeing billboards for *Bambi, elle est noire mais elle est belle* (Bambi, She's Black But She's Beautiful) plastered along the system's connecting corridors. These eye-catching posters depicted the face and exposed shoulders of a gorgeous black woman whose photo was doctored so that half of her face and body looked white. *Bambi* played throughout April 2006 at the Tarmac de la Villette. This small theatre complex stands adjacent to the Grande Halle in the Parc de la Villette. Formerly called the Théâtre International de Langue Française (International French-Language Theatre, or TILF), it enjoys financial support from the Ministries of Culture and Foreign Affairs as well as from the city of Paris and is a showcase for interdisciplinary artists from French-speaking areas around the world. The Tarmac aims, in the words of its director Valérie Baran, "to help construct the foundation of a clear-sighted, vigilant, and responsible society."[1] Its operations are now so extensive that plans are afoot to move the Tarmac to larger quarters, currently occupied by the Théâtre de l'Est Parisien, on the avenue Gambetta.

Bambi, elle est noire mais elle est belle is a semiautobiographical one-woman piece. It was written and performed by the vivacious Maïmouna Gueye—the woman on the subway posters—who emigrated from Senegal to France in 1988 after marrying a white Frenchman from Auvergne. Gueye's show takes its title from the patronizing words Bambi's mother-in-law regularly uttered when introducing her to friends and relatives. Her Disney-inspired nickname, 'Bambi,' was coined by Gueye's father, who abandoned the family when she was a girl to seek a better life for himself in France.

A good-humored entertainment full of plot-propelling songs composed by Quentin Sirjacq, the play does not cover up the more painful episodes in Bambi's quest for autonomy. These include her violent rape by a neighbor during her teen years and her husband Antoine's wrongheaded suspicion that she married him only to acquire naturalization papers. The event that triggers her breakup with Antoine occurs one night at dinner when Bambi picks up her food with her hands "just for the fun and sensual pleasure of it": her spouse's reflex is to slap Bambi for exhibiting "savage" behavior. *Bambi* is ultimately a deft indictment of the French government's habitual call for immigrants to "integrate" into traditional society. "'Integrate!' ['*Intègre-toi!*'] means 'Be like everyone else,'" Gueye told a reporter. "And I don't want to be like everyone else!"[2] In a variation on the famous line from Sartre's *Huis clos* (*No Exit*, 1944), Bambi asserts midway into the play: "To integrate is to adapt to other people, and other people are hell!" The work's hilarious final episode finds Bambi encountering a new lover—in the Paris metro. Referred to by her as yet another "*toubab*," or white man, he soon discovers that for all his attraction to Bambi he is unable to get an erection in her presence. Bambi turns to African folk apparatus and magic potions for her frustrated partner—without success. Only when she gives up trying and re-becomes her "natural" self, neither entirely Senegalese nor entirely French, does the miracle happen. The play's last line is: "*Alléluia, il bande!*" ("Hallelujah, he's hard!").

At the performance I attended, about one-quarter of the audience appeared to be black or racially mixed, and many of these were teenagers. Seated behind me were some black *lycéennes* who, each time Bambi posed a rhetorical question, answered her back. No one minded, Maïmouna Gueye least of all. In fact *Bambi* was such a crowd-pleaser (the critics loved it, too) that after its run at the Tarmac it moved to the Lavoir Moderne Parisien, where it played in late June and early July 2006. It has since been reprised several times.

The reality of discrimination

My sojourn in Paris coincided with the incipient erosion of France's longtime reluctance to acknowledge its ethnic diversity. A year earlier, on January 18, 2005, members of various activist groups issued an online manifesto provocatively titled "We Are the Republic's Natives [*Indigènes*]!" Their statement, directed at "the sons and daughters of colonized peoples and immigrants," urged these French citizens and residents to become involved in "the struggle against the oppression and discrimination produced by the post-colonial Republic."[3] Ten months later, the November 2005 riots fortified the claim of the "*indigènes*" that France's suburban housing projects mirrored the old colonial scheme whereby a white French upper class in the city center lorded it over blacks and North African Muslims on the periphery. With controversy still brewing over legislation that would require history textbooks to underscore "the positive role" of France's colonial ventures, sixty organizations—whose members are mainly French people of African or Caribbean origin—united to form, in November 2005, the Conseil représentatif des associations noires (Representative Council of Black Associations, or CRAN).

CRAN's express purpose is to lobby for "the recognition and the remembrance" of the full history of French slavery and colonialism.[4] One of its early initiatives was to press the market researchers at TNS Sofres to conduct the first survey of France's black population. The results showed that "fifty-six percent of France's estimated two million black adults say they suffer from discrimination."[5]

• • •

A major hit of the May 2006 Cannes Film Festival was Rachid Bouchareb's *Indigènes* (*Days of Glory*), one of the rare films to depict the heroism of the North African soldiers who fought on French territory in the final battles of World War II. Although it leans heavily on war-picture clichés, *Indigènes* points out the scandal of the paltry pensions these African veterans had been receiving over the years in contrast to their European-born counterparts. The movie in fact pushed President Jacques Chirac to make good on his promise to redress this wrong, even though the institutional mechanism for disbursements was not put in motion until January 2011, during the Sarkozy presidency.

One of the stars and coproducers of *Indigènes* was Jamel Debbouze, the popular comedian born in Paris in 1975 to impoverished Moroccan parents and raised in the Parisian suburb of Trappes. After rising to prominence via the Canal+ hit sitcom *H* (set in a hospital), he toured France and Europe with a phenomenally successful one-man show, *100% Debbouze*, which in 2004 sold over a million copies on DVD. In late December 2005, Debbouze was noisily touted as the country's highest-paid male movie actor. After supporting roles in blockbusters like Jean-Pierre Jeunet's *Le fabuleux destin d'Amélie Poulain* (*Amélie*, 2001) and Alain Chabat's *Astérix & Obélix: Mission Cléopâtre* (*Asterix and Obelix Meet Cleopatra*, 2002), he gained star status in Luc Besson's *Angel-A*, a bittersweet fable about love and self-acceptance, released in December 2005. The following May, Debbouze shared the Cannes Festival's Best Actor prize with his male costars Samy Naceri, Roschdy Zem, Sami Bouajila, and Bernard Blancan for their dramatic efforts in *Indigènes*.

Debbouze concedes that a single motion picture cannot undo decades of ethnic tensions and resentments. "If at some moment [Charles] de Gaulle [1890–1970] had recognized the contribution of Algerians, Moroccans, Senegalese and others in the war, there would now be less racism [in France]," he told one reporter.[6] Still, the thirty-one-year-old was confident that *Indigènes* would make French-born youths of immigrant extraction—who live, he said, "a terrible crisis of identity"—feel prouder of their history.[7]

The empowering force of stand-up comedy

The biggest news about Jamel Debbouze that spring was his imminent return to Canal+ to host a new Saturday-night summer show, *Jamel Comedy Club*. This half-hour pay-per-view telecast would feature emerging urban comics doing five-minute routines in front of a live audience at Le Réservoir, a club in Paris's eleventh arrondissement. The show went on to launch a nontelevised version—a showcase for twelve of the best newcomers—that played in various venues during fall 2006 and winter 2007. The Jamel Comedy Club now has a permanent home on the boulevard Bonne Nouvelle, along one of the more concentrated stretches of the *théâtre privé* circuit. From the outset, Debbouze's troupe embraced women (Amelle Chahbi, Claudia Tagbo), Asians (Frédéric Chau), blacks (Patson, Thomas N'Gijol), and Arabs (Fabrice Eboué). Eboué, whose semi-improvised act includes imitations of Romanians faking disabilities and one-liners like "A Jew is nothing other than a Muslim who's moved up in the world," observes offstage: "We are the first generation that can joke about blacks, whites, and Asians. We have legitimacy! If [the white comedian Jean-Marie] Bigard did the jokes we do, he'd be accused of racism."[8]

Stand-up is huge business in France. A 2005 study ascertained that it accounted for 21 percent of all ticket sales for live-performance shows, outdone only by rock concerts and festivals.[9] In Paris alone there are scores of stand-up gigs on any given evening. A visitor to the Marais district, for example, inevitably stumbles upon the long line of ticket holders outside Le Point Virgule (The Semicolon), a 120-seat theatre on the rue Sainte-Croix-de-la-Bretonnerie that schedules a dozen acts each week, with as many as five different attractions per day.

In addition to Jamel Debbouze, the current young ethnic explosion takes inspiration from other established comedians like Smaïn, Gad Elmaleh, and Michaël Youn and from comic duos like Kad Merad and Olivier Baroux (known as "Kad et O") and Eric Judor and Ramzy Bédia ("Eric et Ramzy"). African American funnymen, from Richard Pryor to Eddie Murphy to Chris Rock, are also common figures of idolatry and close scrutiny for this new breed of French entertainer. Debbouze's sketch writer Kader Aoun, who mentors the Jamel Comedy Club players, notes: "Today, being 'subversive' has no purpose. The sole value is success. If you don't fill the seats, no one is going to hear you, and you're dead!"[10] Consequently, the humor of these budding celebrities, like Debbouze's, may often be trashy but is rarely offensive. These comics want to be loved.

• • •

Booder (b. 1978)—whose real name is Mohamed Benyamna—is a gifted Debbouze disciple. I caught his *One Man Show* in early May at the Théâtre Le Temple, a converted movie house on the rue du Faubourg du Temple in the eleventh arrondissement. This neighborhood currently boasts more new midsize commercial theatres than any other part of the city and now competes with the Marais, on its west border, as the most "happening" district in Paris.[11] The evening I attended Booder's seventy-five-minute show, the 300-seat house was nearly full; in terms of age and race the audience was visibly diverse.

Booder is *literally* a natural-born showman. At birth his respiratory and bone disorders were so severe that he had to be flown from Morocco to a major hospital in France. His physical appearance on- and offstage is odd: at five feet two inches, in jeans and a floppy wool cap, he could be taken for a preteen; his facial features—wide puffy lips, droopy eyes, and a schnozz as expressively doleful as it is long—call to mind a cross between Bashful and Sleepy in Walt Disney's *Snow White and the Seven Dwarfs*. In his opening routine he reenacts his birth and his parents' horror at first seeing him: "For years they just called me 'half-price.'" The nickname he chose when he was six, 'Booder,' comes from his worship of the Moroccan soccer legend Aziz Bouderbala.

Booder's show recounts the misadventures of his childhood and schooling. With astounding vocal dexterity and rubbery body moves, Booder dishes out cartoonlike impressions of the Chinese, Cameroonian, and Guadeloupean kids he grew up with. The only time rancor tinges his words is when he talks about how he trained to be an accountant and no one would give him a job: "Today, in any kind of work, you've got to have the right look. Did you *ever* see a banker with a gashed face and missing teeth?" Even when Booder tells hard truths about ghetto life—"If you say 'street,' you know it leads to 'mischief'; and if you say 'mischief,' you know it leads to 'cops'"—he is never abrasive. From the moment he comes on stage, the crowd senses that this young man abhors discrimination of any kind. As he told Macha Séry in an interview for *Le Monde*: "I am against racism regardless of where it originates, because it comes not just from the Frenchies; there's also racism among *beurs* toward *blacks*, and so on down the line."[12]

    • • •

A more established humorist of North African origin goes only by his last name, Fellag. Born Mohand Saïd Fellag in 1950—in Tizi Ouzo, a village in Algeria's Kabylie region—Fellag studied acting and European dramatic literature in Algiers at the National Institute of Dramatic Arts, where Stanislavskian techniques were still prized. He then joined the National Theatre and performed Shakespeare, Molière, and Chekhov throughout Algeria. But eventually, Fellag explains, "I found true theatre to be right on the Algerian streets, where people talked about politics and social problems in an incredibly inventive language, a mix of colloquial Arabic, Kabyle, and French. That's what I wanted to bring to the stage."[13] Fellag soon put together comic monologues such as *Un bateau pour l'Australie* (A Boat for Australia, 1991) and *Djurdjurassique Bled* (Djur-Jurassic Middle of Nowhere, 1995), which he performed at major venues in both Algeria and France.

Fellag's satiric pieces tend to deal with the ups and downs of belonging to multiple cultures and the risks of being straitjacketed by any one identity. He is overtly critical of radical Islamism. In 1995, when Algeria clamped down on free expression, Fellag exiled himself to Paris, where the radio station France Culture signed him for weekly broadcasts. The author of several novels and story collections,[14] Fellag often performs his stage pieces in a polka-dot shirt, clownlike suspenders, and porkpie hat. This casual façade is deceptive, for Fellag meticulously prearranges each word and gesture. The goal of his comic storytelling, he says with heartfelt emotion, is "not to cheer the lonely immigrant but to tell young *beurs* about their background."[15] His recent show, *Tous les Algériens sont des mécaniciens* (All Algerians Are Garage Mechanics, 2010), is a joint effort with his Euro-French companion Marianne Epin and treats the headaches endured by a mixed-race couple discriminated against on both sides of the Mediterranean; it exhibits the same blend of lightheartedness and critical umbrage found in Maïmouna Gueye's *Bambi*. Apropos of the Sarkozy-Besson "conversation" on national identity, Fellag says: "Why waste time fixating on such an old-fashioned notion when all signs indicate that the entire world is creolizing?"[16]

Mixing cultures, mixing power

Souria Adèle's one-woman *Marie-Thérèse Barnabé, Négresse de France!* took place at the Comédie Bastille, a small theatre tucked away amid a housing complex in the eleventh arrondissement. It was the only event I went to during my Paris stay where the better part (at least 80 percent) of the audience was black and of which a plurality were women of Caribbean background, most of whom appeared to be in their midthirties. The show's premise is that the comedienne Souria Adèle is—as always—late for appointments, and her aunt Marie-Thérèse is stepping in to mark time until Souria arrives. Marie-Thérèse (played by Adèle) appears from the back of the theatre costumed as a stereotypic Martiniquais woman of a certain age—overweight, nappy hair, humongous breasts, a colossal derrière, and giant spectacles. As she waddles down the aisle and then climbs up to the stage, Marie-Thérèse speaks in a Creole dialect that many in the audience, judging from the laughter, understood. By the time she settles into a large cushioned armchair, Marie-Thérèse modulates into standard French and lets us know that she is a "sit-down" rather than a "stand-up" comic.

For the rest of this tongue-in-cheek show Marie-Thérèse pokes fun at Caribbeans, Africans, French blacks, and European whites. She mocks *Elle* magazine for its latest politically safe feature on how "black professional women are opting for the 'power look' in fashion." She pooh-poohs Caucasian celebrities who Botox their lips and have implants set in their rear ends—just to look more like her! And she sternly warns whites in the audience to buy property quickly. Why? Because thanks to their dark pigmentation, blacks will survive the ozone-layer crisis better than whites, and in holding the new reins of power they will be very reluctant to rent to minority folk.

From the get-go Souria Adèle wins us over by her impromptu quips. She asks for the names of audience members, jokes about our backgrounds and appearances, and makes us feel that she is *our* good-hearted, caring relative. When "Marie-Thérèse"—who claims to have gone through seven husbands—found out that I was a New Yorker, she asked if I would marry her on the spot. When I played coy, she made me a running joke throughout the show.

Yet very serious issues simmer beneath the comic surface. Upon entering the theatre we had each been handed a page called Marie-Thérèse Barnabé's Glossary of Martinique-Creole Phrases. A bold-faced note explained that the term '*nègre/négresse*' "designates a black man or woman in all his or her nobility—as long as one doesn't precede it by the word 'dirty.'" In the show, Marie-Thérèse jokes about how she was part of the first wave of the BUMIDOM, a French-government plan implemented between 1962 and 1981 by the Bureau des Migrations d'Outre-Mer (Bureau of Overseas Migrations) to transfer thousands of people from the allegedly overpopulated regions of Guadeloupe, Martinique, Guyana, and Réunion to cities in mainland France; unfortunately, government promises of work and housing often went unfulfilled, and the program's bureaucrats could be shamelessly racist. On stage Marie-Thérèse keeps her cool about this scandal. In her glossary, however, she refers to BUMIDOM as "the second deportation" and she quotes Aimé Césaire (1913–2008), the Afro-Martinican poet, dramatist, and politician who called this initiative "alternative genocide." As Marie-Thérèse asserts in her final remarks—just before her "niece" Souria finally "arrives" and we see that she is a shapely, beautiful woman: "A true mixing of cultures [*métissage*] must also be a true mixing of power."

In an interview, Souria Adèle confided that she has written an adaptation of Jean-Philippe Bacri and Agnès Jaoui's hit play and movie about a dysfunctional middle-class (white) family, *Un air de famille* (*Family Resemblances*, 1994, 1996). Adèle sets the new version in a small town in Martinique. Having won the original writers' approval, her script has been read by many actors who would be pleased to play one of the roles. "All we need are a hall and a producer," Adèle says. "But so far I've gotten the cold shoulder. Six blacks on [a non-musical] stage, well, I guess that's a bit too much for some people!"[17]

Outrageous talk and freedom of expression

I landed in Paris on the morning after Christmas 2005. Three days earlier the comedian Dieudonné (born Dieudonné M'Bala M'Bala in 1966) announced his intent to run for president of the Republic in 2007. As in the United States, where comics Pat Paulsen and Stephen Colbert have made bids for the White House, there is in France a tradition of jokesmith hopefuls. Typically their platforms are less whimsical than those of their American peers. In 1981, for example, the much beloved Coluche (Michel Colucci, 1944–1986), who was very anti–Giscard d'Estaing (b. 1926) and a vocal opponent of anti-immigrant sentiment, was pressured to pull out of his race for the Elysée Palace when it became clear that he was a real threat to the chances of François Mitterrand (1916–1996), the Socialist party favorite. In the 2002 elections Dieudonné had made a first bid to get his name on the ballot but failed to win the necessary sponsorship of five hundred local politicians. Now he was more optimistic.

I was vaguely aware of the controversies swirling around Dieudonné, who is the son of a Cameroonian father and a white French mother and is the father of four children whom he raises with his longtime white partner. In December 2003 Dieudonné had made a surprise appearance on Marc-Olivier Fogiel's popular TV talk show *On ne peut pas plaire à tout le monde* (You Can't Please Everyone). Dieudonné—who claims to be "an atheist reared as a Catholic"[18]—walked on camera wearing a black ski mask, a Hasidic Jewish hat with fake earlocks, and an army camouflage jacket. He urged the audience to join "the Americano-Zionist Axis—the only one . . . that offers you happiness, and the only one to give you a chance of living a bit longer." He finished his skit by raising his arm Nazi style and shouting "Isra-heil." The audience gave him a standing ovation. Host Fogiel looked perturbed. Other comedians on the panel, including Jamel Debbouze, laughed heartily. Within days the French government and Jewish groups sued Dieudonné for "defamation of a racial nature."[19]

Earlier that year Dieudonné had declared in an interview with the magazine *Lyon Capitale*: "Jews are a sect, a fraud [*une escroquerie*], and one of the worst because they were the first."[20] Those words also spurred a legal suit.

Would this prevent me, an American Jew, from purchasing a ticket for Dieudonné's New Year's Eve show *1905*? The show, I gathered from its title, was part of France's centennial celebration of the French law on the separation of church and state, the backbone of France's *laïcité*, or humanist secularism. Were not Dieudonné's outrageous remarks, as he and his supporters insisted, simply an instance of the cherished Enlightenment-based right to freedom of expression? And was that not a principle vital to the art of comedy? That past October the Denmark-based Mohammed cartoon controversy triggered worldwide debate—and significant violence—over just this matter. France itself would get caught up in the furor when on February 8, 2006, the French satiric weekly *Charlie Hebdo* saucily reprinted the twelve editorial caricatures in question.

Indeed, 2006 turned out to be a year filled with threats to free speech. In Geneva (Switzerland) and Saint-Genis-Pouilly (France), public readings of Voltaire's play *Le fanatisme ou Mahomet le prophète* (*Fanaticism, or The Prophet Mohammed*, 1736) required special police protection. In March the New York Theatre Workshop postponed indefinitely its production of *My Name Is Rachel Carrie*, a monologue about a pro-Palestinian American activist killed by an Israeli bulldozer in the Gaza Strip. In June a major Canadian chain of bookstores banned sales of an issue of *Harper's* magazine that had a cover story by Art Spiegelman about racial stereotypes. Fearful of a terrorist attack, a leading German opera house, the Deutsche Oper Berlin, canceled its October performances of Mozart's *Idomeneo* (1781) because Hans Neuenfels's production depicted the severed head of the Prophet Mohammed along with those of Jesus, Buddha, and Poseidon. In November, Russia blocked the distribution of Sacha Baron Cohen's mock documentary comedy *Borat: Cultural Learnings of America for Make Benefit Glorious Nation of Kazakhstan.*

Given this volatile climate I thought that the only way to judge Dieudonné responsibly was to see his work firsthand. Accordingly I made *1905* part of my New Year's Eve agenda.

The disingenuousness of "equal treatment"

Dieudonné owns the 250-seat Théâtre de la Main d'Or, located on a quiet dead end near the bustling Place de la Bastille, in the eleventh arrondissement. The theatre has a spacious lounge area and bar. When I arrived I took close note of the entering crowd. They were mainly well-dressed people under forty and ethnically diverse: whites, blacks, Arabs, Eurasians, and other métis. There were dozens of interracial couples—not an oddity in Paris, but I had never seen so many in one public space. I noticed very few children and no obvious gays or lesbians, and it seemed as if everyone was smoking. (France's ban on smoking in public spaces would not take effect until January 2007.)

Conspicuously displayed above the bar was a framed black yarmulke mounted atop a certificate that read: "A Yarmulke for Dieudonné, Benevolently Offered by The Store-keepers [*les Commerçants*] of the Rue des Rosiers [the main street of the Marais's Jewish quarter], Wednesday, September 14, 2005." At the bottom of this document were several merchants' signatures. A promising sign, I thought. I would soon learn, however, that Dieudonné also enjoys the support of several rabbis belonging to Neturei Karta [Jews United against Zionism], whose members call for a dismantling of the state of Israel and whose leaders would travel to Iran in December 2006 for the International Conference to Review the Global Vision of the Holocaust, called by the Iranian president Mahmoud Ahmadinejad.[21]

Dieudonné's show revealed a major talent. Copper-toned, goateed, and sporting a medium-length Afro hairdo, Dieudonné has a brilliant imagination and a quick-as-lightning delivery. His deep-set eyes periodically give off a mischievous glint, as if he wants us to know that not only is he pushing the envelope but he is going to get away with it scot-free. *1905* alternates between onstage sketches and supposedly backstage musings about those sketches. Mixing the latest news with historical events, Dieudonné is a thinking person's comedian. One sketch deals with Galileo as he is forced to make abject apologies for his theories while standing before his Inquisitors. "The Problem with the Veil" depicts a high school parent-teacher meeting at which mothers and fathers vent opinions about the 2004 law prohibiting religious garb in public schools, including headscarves for Muslim girls: with awesome mimicry Dieudonné satirizes the special agendas of France's African, Asian, Arab, and Jewish communities. I was not certain that "Monsieur Blumenthal," obsessed with the fear of his people's extermination, fared any worse than "Madame Wong," who harped tediously on the fate of Vietnamese boat people. However, I was troubled near the show's start when Dieudonné contemptuously spat into the face of his female stage manager. At evening's end I was glad that she got to spit back at him. Was Dieudonné telling us that just as he skewers every special interest, he is prepared to receive equal treatment? Was that a mark of courage? Or was it bluster, since it was he who was obviously pulling all the strings?

Afterward Dieudonné invited the audience to join him for champagne in the lobby bar. I chose not to indulge, mainly because I needed to hurry off to a party. But I also found the comedian's generosity a bit disquieting. As I walked along the rue du Faubourg-Saint-Antoine toward the Place de la Bastille, I kept wondering if this disarming entertainer had just played me—and everyone else—for a sucker.

A few weeks later I returned to the Main d'Or to see *Emeutes en banlieue* (Suburban Riots), a comic revue Dieudonné wrote for two actors who went only by the names America (a pretty white blonde) and Eric (a handsome black Frenchman). The script is thin, but the show makes its points with fierce clarity. The gruff offstage voice of "Monsieur Birenbaum," the head of a TV operation and clearly marked as Jewish, demands *"images choc"* ("sensationalist images") for his station's coverage of the 2005 race riots. Birenbaum's compliant, self-serving female reporter becomes complicit with ghetto drug dealers who sell her dope as well as hot tips; she soon turns into an addict for, as we are told none too subtly, "information is the new opium of the people." Further farcical relief comes from a recently appointed "Minister of Integration," a black Oreo with stinky breath, who trumpets his plan to rehabilitate teenage delinquents by teaching them to make crêpes suzette. The show climaxes with the murder of a local rap artist known as Sony, killed by the police; meanwhile the female reporter and drug dealer blithely dance a sensual tango.

Is there a "Dieudonné effect"?

Dieudonné started his career as a darling of the media, especially when he partnered (1991–1997) with Elie Semoun (b. 1963), a Jewish boyhood friend. Their wildly successful act mocked all minority pretense and prejudice with equal élan. But once Dieudonné gave freer rein to raw anti-Semitic and anti-Israel sentiment onstage and off, most television stations and newspapers denied publicity and coverage to him and his shows.[22] Semoun cut off all personal contact with his ex-partner when in 2008 Dieudonné chose the extreme-right politician Jean-Marie Le Pen to be godfather to one of his daughters.

Dieudonné has blamed the press for misconstruing his statement, made in Algeria in February 2005, that Holocaust remembrance amounts to "memorial pornography."[23] He publicly defended the concept's legitimacy by attributing it to an Israeli historian, Idith Zertal. It turned out, however, that Zertal, who is in fact a revisionist scholar of Israeli culture, never used such a crude term.[24] Given Dieudonné's repeated distortions concerning the Shoah and his growing chumminess with leaders of the Front national (FN), it is not surprising that the philosopher Bernard-Henri Lévy wrote a scathing piece in the news weekly Le Point titled "Dieudonné, fils de Le Pen" (Dieudonné, Son of [Jean-Marie] Le Pen [founder and president of the FN]).[25] But the journalist Anne-Sophie Mercier, who has written an entire book on Dieudonné's political stances, makes the case that in spite of certain resemblances to Le Pen, Dieudonné is more exactly an "improbable cross" between Jacques Doriot, who in 1931 founded France's ultranationalist Fascist party, known as the Parti Populaire Français (PPF), and Louis Farrakhan, the Supreme Minister of the Nation of Islam.[26]

Three weeks after I saw Emeutes en banlieue, a major national news story broke. The mutilated body of Ilan Halimi, a twenty-three-year-old French Jewish cell-phone salesman, was found near a train station south of Paris. A police investigation showed that Halimi, who worked in Paris, had been kidnapped and brought to the cellar of a housing project in Bagneux, a banlieue in Hauts-de-Seine (the area Dieudonné hails from), where he was slowly tortured. The alleged perpetrators were part of a gang of youths known as The Barbarians, whose members include blacks, Arabs, Persians from Iran, and whites from Portugal and France. They were apparently motivated by Halimi's religion, believing that "Jews have money" and that the man's family or rabbi would therefore pay big bucks for his release.[27] Just a month and a half earlier a report published by the Commission nationale consultative des droits de l'homme (National Advisory Commission on Human Rights) disclosed that racially motivated violence in France had in fact dropped by 38 percent in 2005, compared with 2004, and that anti-Semitic violence had fallen by 48 percent.[28] An editorial in *Le Monde* applauded these findings but also deplored what it called the growing "liberation of racist speech."[29]

Two weeks after the discovery of Halimi's body, Julien Dray—a spokesman for the Socialist Party and a founder of the nongovernmental antiracism organization S.O.S. Racisme—appeared on the TV program *Parlons-en* (Let's Talk about It). Dray opined: "There are certain 'symbolic personalities' who are vehicles for the anti-Semitism that has become encrusted on French society. . . . We are witnessing the deferred impact of all that Dieudonné has done these past years. There is 'a Dieudonné effect' . . . a 'stupid assimilation effect' visible in the acts of the young people who have guffawed at such humor."[30] Offended at being portrayed as somehow responsible for Ilan Halimi's murder, Dieudonné filed a defamation suit against Julien Dray. In public pronouncements the comedian placed blame for the Halimi tragedy upon the "American drift in French society," which promotes "the cult of profit" as a central value.[31] Wielding the diversionary tactic of victim competitiveness, Dieudonné also accused the media for paying less attention to tragedies involving blacks, Algerians, and Armenians than to those pertaining to Jews. In late spring 2008 the courts ruled in Julien Dray's favor, acquitting him of all charges.[32]

• • •

Amid this uproar I again went to the Main d'Or to see Dieudonné in his newest opus, *Dépôt de bilan* (Voluntary Liquidation). The general press boycott notwithstanding, there was not an empty seat in the house. (Dieudonné and his associates maintain an extensive online outreach structure, and hard-core fans are aware of the comedian-candidate's every move.) As the show's title suggests, its premise is that Dieudonné is folding up business; we watch as he composes his "last show"—though in an early quick aside he asserts with a wink, "last *for now*."

In technique, delivery, and creative power Dieudonné was to my mind even stronger here than in *1905*. But this time his tone veered insistently toward the macabre. He of course took his usual jolly jabs at Chinese, Caribbeans, and Muslims. In a tasteless but not un-expected riff on his nemesis Bernard-Henri Lévy, he portrayed the well-to-do philosopher as "jewing down" a greengrocer for a bag of potatoes: "With six million dead, you could at least give me a good price!" the comedian-as-Lévy moans. Yet I had the impression that Dieudonné was, above all, crying out for recognition of his own sup-posed victimization. Straining to be perceived as the martyr of mar-tyrs, he repeatedly flirted with Death. In one sketch he was Hitler in the bunker, ingesting his cyanide tablet. In another he was Jesus on the cross, asserting that "Love's message will survive." As the chief of a Bureau of Extinct Species, he fired off jokes about giant pandas and mako sharks but also somberly prophesied that *Homo sapiens* would soon disappear. Dieudonné, it occurred to me while watching this last skit, was arguably as brilliant—and just as paranoid—as the anti-Semitic apocalyptic novelist Louis-Ferdinand Céline (1894–1961).

Despite *Dépôt de bilan*'s galloping speed, I was able to exert greater critical distance—and skepticism—than when I had seen *1905*. I noted that one of Dieudonné's techniques is to have his most con-temptible lines delivered by a made-up character, with Dieudon-né—"as himself"—then chastising that person for bigotry, vileness, or whatever. Such blatantly insincere mimicry of a "correct" moral stance points to the bad faith that underlies Dieudonné's entire project. Souria Adèle, for example, also mocks, taunts, and lampoons others throughout her act. But she sustains a healthy distinction be-tween herself and "Aunt Marie-Thérèse," even though both personas overflow with a generosity of spirit and an authentic love of people that are alien to Dieudonné. Dieudonné by contrast has locked him-self into a pitiful loop of victimizing himself as well as everyone else.

Jamel Debbouze says that during Dieudonné's infamous "Isra-heil" routine on Marc-Olivier Fogiel's talk show, he could not fully see or hear what was going on from where he was positioned on stage: "I didn't truly understand the situation until I rewatched the broadcast. In my opinion, even though [Dieudonné] is surely the most talented of us all, he has gone insane [*fou*]."[33] The two men are no longer friends.

In *1905*, Dieudonné bragged that out of the twenty lawsuits brought against him in the previous two years, he had never failed to be exon-erated, at least on appeal. That streak of luck ended on February 16,

2007. After a series of appeals and reversals the Cour de Cassation—France's highest and final Court of Appeals—ruled that Dieudonné's 2003 remarks in Lyon about the Jewish religion being an *escroquerie*, or fraud, constituted "racial abuse . . . whose suppression is a necessary constraint on freedom of expression in a democratic society."[34]

Cultural Diversity (II)
Operas and Circuses

Rounding out the survey

Socially driven plots and neo-expressionist scene painting. The boulevard and the experimental. Tradition-bound revivals and provocative riffs on the classics. One-person stand-up and big-cast spectacles. Extolments of the Word and dance-text-video hybrids. As the preceding four chapters have shown, the variety of contemporary French theatre in Paris is energizing, and one's experience of the array can bring about both heightened enlightenment and richly textured pleasures. Before moving on to the final stretch of our three-city tour of the current French theatre scene, I want to share my observations on two more spheres of Parisian *arts de la scène*: opera and circus.

At first glance these areas may seem beyond the frame of our main concerns. To be sure, each stands at an opposite end of the "Art versus Amusement" spectrum: on the one hand, a music-theatre medium generally linked today with a cultural elite, and on the other, an entertainment that speaks to the unschooled sense of wonder within us all. In point of fact, however, the Paris opera establishment is increasingly preoccupied with reaching out to greater segments of the overall populace. And performers associated with the *nouveau cirque*, or New Circus, are exhibiting higher, even rarefied levels of artistic originality that appeal to new and more sophisticated audiences. Moreover, we have seen that traditionally constructed stage works are increasingly sharing the spotlight in France with hybrid, mixed-media performance pieces. Opera and circus are in effect historical forerunners of this current trend. For these reasons the 'cultural diversity' evoked in this chapter's title—in contrast to that of the previous one—is mainly a label for embracing two components of current French theatre practice that are generally viewed by professionals and theatregoers alike as full-fledged partners among the *arts du spectacle vivant.*

Opera in and for the suburbs?

In the aftermath of the autumn 2005 riots, Gérard Mortier, then the director of the Opéra national de Paris, decided it would be a good thing to take affordable opera to the *banlieues.* Mortier (b. 1943) is recognized internationally as an artistic visionary and an intellectual powerhouse. His costly and inventive programs have, however, sometimes been critiqued for appealing only to connoisseurs. After being tapped in 2007 to become the next general manager and artistic director of the New York City Opera, often called 'the people's opera house' and an affordable alternative to the Metropolitan, Mortier precipitously resigned from the post in November 2008 before mounting even one production. He claimed that the budget he was given, compared with that of the Opéra national de Paris, was insufficient to allow for a truly innovative first season. (In 2010 the Opéra national de Paris received 113 million euros of state monies.)[1]

Nonetheless, Mortier has regularly pointed to his boyhood as a baker's son from Ghent (Belgium) in support of opera's populist potential: "In our neighborhood, working people were open to beauty. . . . Many went to the opera."[2] Every operatic venture, Mortier insists, "must have a public function and be more than elitist entertainment. . . . It is a question of transmitting this enormous tradition to the young."[3] During his tenure at the Opéra national de Paris, Mortier launched a Youth Pass initiative, demanded that standing-room tickets be sold at no more than five euros per spot, and reduced the average age of the audience from fifty-six to forty-two years old.[4]

The Opéra national de Paris's forays into working-class areas like Créteil, Bobigny, and Nanterre took place after my six-month stay. But Anthony Tommasini, the *New York Times* music critic, attended a performance of Mozart's *Le nozze di Figaro* (*The Marriage of Figaro*, 1786) that ran at the 900-seat Théâtre Nanterre-Amandiers in April 2008. He reported that "the house was packed . . . with a diverse and noticeably young audience"; the final ovation, he added, was "uncommonly vigorous."[5] I saw this production of *Le nozze di Figaro*, directed by Christoph Marthaler and conducted by Sylvain Cambreling, when it debuted at the Palais Garnier—the "old" home of the Opéra national de Paris—in March 2006. (It was originally designed for the 2001 Salzburg Festival.) Christoph Marthaler (b. 1951), who had been chief of the Zurich (Switzerland) Schauspielhaus for several years, is known for his irreverent staging of classics. He is part of a trend that began in the 1980s to lure high-concept stage director-*auteurs*, such as Patrice Chéreau, Robert Wilson, and Robert Lepage, into French opera houses.

I can imagine young audiences responding well to aspects of Marthaler's rather radical updating of *Le nozze di Figaro*. He sets the action in the lobby of a contemporary marriage license bureau. Frisky Cherubino wears work boots, a T-shirt with an ironic design, and cargo pants whose deep pockets are stuffed with the undies of women he pines for. The older generation—Bartolo, Don Basilio, and Marcellina—suffer from flamboyant tics that make them endearingly ineffectual. Recitatives are accompanied by a dorky instrumentalist who wanders about playing bottles, glass harmonicas, and a synthesizer. The act 3 sextet is done as a break dance. Marcellina invites the audience to clap rhythmically on the second chorus of her bouncy act 4 aria "Il caprio e la capretta" ("The billy goat and the she-goat"). The whole experience was, in its way, emphatically "democratic."

Marthaler's concept, however, too often kept the libretto's period details dangling without reference. More seriously, it virtually eradicated an aspect of the opera that would surely have appealed to an ethnically mixed and lower-income *banlieue* audience: the class tensions between the servant Figaro and the arrogant Count Almaviva. Mozart and his librettist Lorenzo Da Ponte purposefully stressed this story element in their adaptation of Beaumarchais's *Le mariage de Figaro* (a play whose debut production at the Odéon was in fact held up for six years, until 1784, because of threats by royal government censors). Updates of opera, like those of all stage classics, can be marvelous if they spark new insights into the original work or if they coherently bestow new topical relevance to it. Marthaler's *Nozze*, while often delightful, did neither.

A satisfying modernization

In the long history of the Opéra national de Paris, Mozart's *Don Giovanni* (1787) had already enjoyed 722 performances. Yet word that the Austrian stage and film director Michael Haneke (b. 1942) would be making his debut voyage into operatic waters with a new production of this grand warhorse caused it to be the hottest ticket not just for an opera but for *any* French theatre event of midwinter 2006. It was also among the more controversial. Could a movie director who specializes in getting art-film audiences to squirm at the sight of torture and kinky sex (*Funny Games* [1997], *La pianiste* [2002]) do justice to Mozart's sublime lyric masterpiece—even though its subject, one sometimes forgets, is sexual harassment and erotic transgression?

The first-night audience on January 27, a date chosen to coincide with the 250th anniversary of Mozart's birth, was reportedly split—as is customary on opening nights in Paris—between those who booed and those who cheered.[6] On the evening I attended, the crowd was uniformly enthusiastic—rightfully so, I think. Haneke's updating is coherent, intelligent, and dramatically gripping. He has the entire opera take place, from dusk to dawn, in the sterile, dimly lit corridors of a major transnational corporation whose headquarters are in a high-rise business district not unlike La Défense, on Paris's western border. Giovanni is the corporation's ruthless general manager. Leporello is his adoring personal assistant and, we are led to infer, occasional bedmate. The Commendatore is the self-righteous board director; Anna, an arrogant junior director; Elvira, an alcoholic, self-loathing executive from Giovanni's prior place of work; and Zerlina and Masetto, part of a cadre of hardworking janitors who have varied ethnicities and skin colors. Haneke thus puts us squarely within an economic milieu familiar to fans of Tom Wolfe (*Bonfire of the Vanities*, 1987), Oliver Stone (*Wall Street*, 1987), and Michel Vinaver (*Par-dessus bord*; *A la dérive*). In its hypernaturalism, the principal players' acting style is also viewer friendly, evoking TV's *Desperate Housewives* more than, say, Joseph Losey's stately 1979 cinematic version of *Don Giovanni*, which was shot in period dress and décor.

By presenting the Don as both a sex addict (his libidinal misadventures are graphically staged) and a golden boy of the world marketplace, Haneke does away with the legend's metaphysical dimension. It is not a statue come to life but rather the Commendatore's preserved corpse that is rolled out in an office chair near the opera's end. It is not by divine intervention but by Elvira's knife thrust that death greets Giovanni, with Elvira's fellow victims aiding her by hurling the double-dealer from the skyscraper's open window to his demise on the asphalt streets below. This take on *Don Giovanni* succeeded, I think, because in exploring the darkness of the protagonist's psyche as well as that of his enablers, Haneke did not put forth pat solutions concerning their makeup. Moreover, his substitution of a corporate empire for the feudally based social structure found in the Mozart original was not a routine retread of the Marxist angle that previous opera director-*auteurs*, such as Patrice Chéreau in his pioneering *Ring* cycle (1976), had so often chosen.

One of the eerier motifs in this new production were the Mickey and Minnie Mouse masks and ears that the servants wear during act 1's celebration of Masetto and Zerlina's marriage and again for act 2's collective murder—where they engage in Busby Berkeley–like nightmare choreography (see fig. 24). What was Haneke trying to say? During intermission I felt stumped for a sure response—as did the handful of strangers I casually chatted with. But by the end of act 2 it became clearer that Haneke was using the Disney icons as a further way to make this eighteenth-century opera tap into the cultural and economic anxieties that people in France (and other parts of Western Europe) were at that very moment feeling.

The period 2005–2006 in fact marked the high point in a perception, shared by many dispirited citizens, of France's economic fragility, geopolitical decline, and supposed lack of cultural influence—the latter regularly attributed to the unbeatable primacy of American pop culture. Just weeks earlier, in his January 2006 New Year's speech, Prime Minister Dominique de Villepin, straining to be upbeat, sternly branded such pessimism as the misguided work of "*déclinologues*," or "specialists in France's [alleged] decline."[7] Part of Mozart's genius, as Eric-Emmanuel Schmitt showed so effectively in *Ma vie avec Mozart* (discussed in chapter 7), is his way of releasing us from all sorts of personal pressures, real or imagined. In Haneke's production the victorious servants—after annihilating the Don—strip off their lurid Disney masks and warble the glorious act 2 finale. It is almost as if "European culture," as represented by both Enlightenment opera and Haneke's unabashedly brainy, auteurist stage direction, were reasserting its artistic pedigree against the Walt Disney Company, whose ubiquitous products arguably epitomize a global leveling of old cultural hierarchies. As one political observer wrote

24. Back to audience, *the scoundrel/general manager (Peter Mattei) confronts*, in office chair, *the propped-up corpse of the Commendatore/board director (Robert Lloyd) and a throng of peasants/office workers in Michael Haneke's staging of Mozart's* Don Giovanni. *Photo © Pascal Victor/ArtComArt.*

in, aptly, *Le Figaro*: "With this *Don Giovanni* . . . the Austrian director Michael Haneke, the French conductor Sylvain Cambreling, and of course the Belgian head of the Paris Opéra, Gérard Mortier, have given us the best antidote imaginable for [the current epidemic] of nihilism."[8]

New opera and social commitment

The 2,700-seat Opéra Bastille is one of Paris's more spectacular pieces of modern architecture. The brainchild of President François Mitterrand, it was meant to fulfill a vision originally set forth by the composer Pierre Boulez and the choreographer Maurice Béjart, who wanted France to have a new opera house that would truly democratize classical music. The sleek, high-luster venue (designed by Carlos Ott, a Uruguayan who lives in Canada and whose proposal won out over 756 competing entries) opened to much fanfare on July 13, 1989, the eve of the two hundredth anniversary of the storming of the Bastille. To the chagrin of some Parisian *citoyens*, however, good seats at the Bastille turned out to be as costly as those at the Palais Garnier—the Beaux Arts–style house at Place de l'Opéra, inaugurated in 1875, that continues to present opera, ballet, and concerts. Administratively the Bastille is simply an additional venue for an old institution—the state-supported Opéra national de Paris. Its initial airy goal of democratizing opera has had mixed results. Still, it is almost always possible to purchase cheap remaining tickets a few minutes before the curtain rises at the Bastille. And every seat in this new theatre, unlike the horseshoe-shaped Garnier, enjoys unobstructed views of the stage.

• • •

In early spring 2006, the Bastille was the site for a vigorous blend of lofty political statement and vanguard music theatre. Commissioned by Gérard Mortier, *Adriana Mater* has a prestigious international pedigree: the composer, Kaija Saariaho (b. 1952), is Finnish; the librettist, Amin Maalouf (b. 1949), is originally from Lebanon and now resides in France; and the director, Peter Sellars (b. 1957), is from the United States. This creative trio had previously worked together on the Salzburg and Santa Fe Opera productions of Saariaho's earlier opera *L'amour de loin* (Love from Afar, 2000), a work commissioned by the Santa Fe Opera and the Théâtre du Châtelet, one of Paris's municipally funded concert and opera houses. They would also join forces on Saariaho's *La Passion de Simone* (The Passion of Simone, 2006), an oratorio for solo soprano, choir, orchestra, and electronics that deals with the ideas and life of the French philosopher and Christian activist-mystic Simone Weil (1909–1943). According to Saariaho, both *Adriana Mater* and *La Passion de Simone* are responses to the sense of social commitment she acquired after the attacks of September 11, 2001: "I felt that I must somehow open into the world."[9]

Adriana Mater's seven tableaux present a parable on violence and compassion. The setting is unspecified, although the characters' names suggest that we are somewhere in the Balkans. George Tsypin's main set—a labyrinth of stone walls, huts, and domes—is equally generic. The opera's plot is austere and simple. A village is at war with The Others, and Adriana (a mezzo-soprano), in spite of the urgings of her sister Refka (a soprano), does not terminate the pregnancy that resulted from her rape by a local bully, the soldier Tsargo (a baritone). Seventeen years pass, and Adriana's son Yonas (a tenor), learns of his paternity, searches for Tsargo, and is about to kill him. But he finds himself unable to do so. Relieved that her son did not inherit his father's barbarity, Adriana sings: "We are not avenged, Yonas / But we are saved."[10] The opera ends with Adriana's resting her head on the shoulder of a son who is now, she proudly says, "a man."

The idea for this opera first occurred to Saariaho after examining a sonogram taken while she was pregnant. She began to reflect on the strange and intimate relationship between mothers and their unborn children. Amin Maalouf, a journalist and novelist who was raised as a Catholic and served as director of the Beirut daily *an-Nahar* until the start of the Lebanese civil war in 1975, amplified Saariaho's idea by crafting a libretto that drew on his own experiences. "In today's world," he says, "the most important barrier is not that which separates one religion from another, but that which divides those who favor dialogue, regardless of their religion, from those who favor confrontation."[11] The duty of contemporary art, Maalouf asserts idealistically, is "to advocate the harmonious coexistence of people, in spite of their differences, and to struggle against intolerance and beastly human acts."[12] At the end of the opera's third tableau, he has the pregnant Adriana ask herself the awful question, "Will he be Cain or Abel?"

I found that one of the challenges posed by *Adriana Mater* was reconciling, on one hand, the tale's simplicity and Peter Sellars's extreme directorial restraint with, on the other hand, the overwhelming force and complexity of Saariaho's orchestral music—magisterially conducted by her fellow Finn Esa-Pekka Salonen. Saariaho, who makes her home in Paris, has long been associated with IRCAM (Institut de recherche et coordination acoustique/musique), the electronic-music institute that Pierre Boulez founded in 1977. A major influence on her composing style is a process called spectralism, which builds on the computer analysis of overtones that accompany resonating notes. The result is, as one music critic puts it, "masses of sound" that buzz with "inner activity": "[Saariaho's] music evolves in heaving, essentially atonal swells, with fragments of melody and instrumental riffs sometimes coalescing into long thematic lines."[13] In *Adriana Mater* the orchestration for eighty-two instrumentalists and the many passages for a large offstage chorus called for substantial electronic design, credited to IRCAM, and computational realization, overseen by the IRCAM-based researcher-musician Gilbert Nouno.

The *New Yorker*'s Alex Ross, who also attended this production, points out that "the Bastille is not made for electronic effects" and that as a result the "greatness" of Saariaho's new opera was perhaps "more sensed than heard."[14] Yet Ross also offers an intriguing gender-related reason why the barrage of dissonant sound that pervades the work's early sections may lack the "mystery" and "sensuousness" that he had found integral to *L'amour de loin*. It is perhaps that after centuries of male composers' subjecting female characters to humiliation and death onstage, Kaija Saariaho wanted to distinguish herself in *Adriana Mater* by foreclosing on any traditional element of masculinist "fantasy" about women and sensuality in her music, thus making Adriana's final internal triumph all the more authentic.[15] While this interpretation is subject to debate, it is a useful reminder that gender issues are now being addressed by many of France's most prominent women of the theatre, as we saw in the treatments of Molière by Anne Alvaro and Coline Serreau; of Claudel by Anne Delbée; and of autobiographical theatre by Maïmouna Gueye.

Old-fashioned one-ring circus

In recent years France has seen an explosion of circus companies of diverse stripes. Between 1990 and 2008 the number went from 93 to 415.[16] Spectator interest in circus has never been higher: nearly fifteen million tickets were sold in 2005.[17] This has led to serious financial issues. In 2004, for example, the Ministry of Culture earmarked nearly five million euros for a select number of circus schools, including the university-level Centre national des arts du cirque (CNAC) (National Center for Circus Arts) in Châlons-en-Champagne, founded in 1986; but total state allocations to individual companies amounted to only four million euros.[18] A 2006 report by Territoires de cirque (Circus Territories), one of several national associations that view circus as an art form as well as a craft, voiced concern for small companies that, for lack of adequate funding, have had to move their shows from tents to conventional theatre spaces, thus compromising big-top tradition and creative potential.[19]

Back in the early 1970s, traditional French circus was moribund. Unable to compete with movies, television, and sports events, many major circus troupes folded. But in 1974 this weakened form of popular culture received a huge boost from Annie Fratellini (1932–1997), heiress to a famous clown dynasty, and Alexis Gruss (1909–1985), heir to France's last great equestrian dynasty. With the aid, respectively, of the filmmaker-comedian-clown Pierre Etaix (b. 1928) and of the stage tragedienne Silvia Monfort (1923–1991), Fratellini and Gruss opened the first French circus conservatory, providing an unprecedented training ground for students who had no links to the notoriously closed network of family-based outfits. The result was an influx of new ideas and energy that revitalized the time-honored components of classical circus. Furthering this reinvigoration were the creation of high-profile annual festivals—such as Prince Rainier of Monaco's International Circus Festival of Monte-Carlo (begun in 1975) and Paris's Festival Mondial du Cirque de Demain (World Festival of Tomorrow's Circus, launched in 1977)—and the influence of innovative foreign companies, such as Germany's Circus Roncalli and Canada's Cirque du Soleil.

These changing conditions spawned the two leading types of traditional circus that are practiced today. One expert has identified these as nostalgia circus and transitional circus.[20] The first self-consciously flaunts its roots in tradition and fosters an idealized, romanticized experience for the spectator. Examples include the companies of Alexis Gruss, Alexandre Romanès, and the Bouglione brothers. The transitional circus—represented by such troupes as the Arlette Gruss Circus and Valérie Fratellini's Ô Cirque company—shares certain traits with the *nouveau cirque*, such as cross-disciplinarity and collaborative vision, but maintains the classic structure of one act following upon another and pays only minimal attention to the *nouveau cirque* preoccupation with subtle visual poetry and storytelling. Instead, transitional circus takes cues for its typically flashy atmosphere, costumes, and music from extravaganzas like the staged epics of director Robert Hossein (b. 1927), the arena concerts of rock star Johnny Hallyday (b. 1943), and Holiday on Ice touring shows.

• • •

Perhaps no traditional circus compares to the Cirque d'Hiver Bouglione for nostalgia. Its home base is the elegant Cirque d'Hiver (Winter Circus), a building that is worth a special visit all its own. Located on the rue Amelot, a few blocks east of the Place de la République, the cream-toned, yellow-and-crimson-trimmed Cirque d'Hiver has hosted circuses since 1852, when it was known as the Cirque Napoléon in honor of Louis-Napoléon Bonaparte. Shaped as a twenty-sided oval polygon, the exterior façade has Corinthian columns and intricate bas-relief by James Pradier, the Swiss sculptor whose figures of Fame grace the Arc de Triomphe. The architect Jacques Ignace Hittorff, who created the two fountains at the Place de la Concorde, designed the Cirque d'Hiver's interior space to resemble a steeply banked coliseum whose self-supporting dome would ensure unblocked views for all. It is here that Henri de Toulouse-Lautrec and Georges Seurat found inspiration for a number of their most vivid sketches and paintings.

The Bouglione family—four original brothers and many of their descendants—have operated their one-ring circus at the Cirque d'Hiver since 1934. The 2006 edition was titled *Audace* (Daring). Its name comes from Jean Cocteau's quip: "Tact in audacity consists in knowing how far you may go too far" (*Le coq et l'harlequin/The Rooster and the Harlequin*, 1918). *Audace* gave us prancing white steeds, double-humped camels, and six trained poodles (plus a mutt that outwitted the fancy canines); clowns, tightrope walkers, and jugglers; *truly* death-defying trapeze artists who worked without nets; and a human cannonball who—for the first time in Bouglione history—was a woman (Robin Valencia, from the United States). Linking these classic acts—and occasional calls for audience participation—was a slight narrative that featured two hapless clowns, overweight Mimi and hunched Angelina, who yearned to be dazzling big-top stars. All of this took place under the trained eye of Sergio, the dignified Monsieur Loyal (Ringmaster), and amid the tuneful melodies of an eleven-piece orchestra. The only major concession to Las Vegas–style glitz was a gang of eight stunning showgirls whose routines stood out like a crate of Coca-Cola in a Loire Valley vineyard.

Still, at how many circuses other than the Bouglione can you actually purchase crêpes and champagne at intermission (along with the more usual popcorn and cotton candy) while mingling with costumed clowns and daredevils?

Nouveau cirque

The true renaissance of French circus today is found among the many companies that since the 1980s have eliminated trained animals; have performed in nontraditional spaces (including *théâtres à l'italienne*); have prioritized poetic imagery over glossy spectacle and fluid, interlocking tableaux over a succession of discrete acts; and have blurred the lines between performance art, dance, theatre, mime, and feats of circus bravado. Among the most notable pioneers of the *nouveau cirque* are (in addition to the Thiérrée family discussed in chapter 5) Pierrot Bidon and his Archaos circus, renowned for its dangerous, heavy-metal aesthetic and its social critique; Bernard Kudlak and his Cirque Plume, whose delicate dreamscapes often have the feel and logic of a Marc Chagall painting; and Christian Taguet, whose Cirque Baroque has found narrative source material in the literary works of Voltaire (*Candides*, 1995) and of the Japanese novelist Yukio Mishima (*Ningen*, 1998). Of 415 French circus companies inventoried in 2008, 375 identify themselves as producing *nouveau cirque*.[21] Critics, moreover, are increasingly evaluating circus presentations less in terms of the virtuosity or fearlessness of performers than in the strength of a director's or a company's *écriture scénique*.[22]

* * *

Rain, a popular touring *nouveau cirque* show by the Quebec-based troupe Cirque Eloize, took place on the proscenium stage of the Trianon, a boulevard theatre that since 1893 has been variously a music hall, an operetta house, and a movie palace. *Rain* had tumblers, contortionists, and mimes but no animals, clowns, or brass bands. Its Italian-born director, Daniele Finzi Pasca (who had just created the closing ceremonies for the winter Olympic Games in Turin), aimed to paint via lighting, costumes, anecdotes, and dance-hall piano music a cinematic mood evocative of 1920s working-class Italy. The spectacle's saving grace was that it did not take itself very seriously. Midway through, an acrobat-actor-singer asks, "Can someone explain this show to me? I don't understand this '*new*' circus." When another player rushes to her aid and suggests that "it's metaphor . . . it's the unconscious," a torrent of work boots swoop down from the flies to deliver the point more concretely. The piece culminated with rain flooding the stage while the cast of eleven men and women skidded, toppled down, and mock-urinated—as they might have once done as kids during a summer storm.

To debate whether this last device is cliché or "poetic" is probably beside the point. As far back as 1983, Tommy Tune, in tribute to Gene Kelly, frolicked amid puddles in his Broadway show *My One and Only*. Similar setups among *nouveau cirque* events include the Cirque Désaccordé's *Après la pluie* (After the Rain, 2005) and Jérôme Thomas's *Arc après la pluie* (*Rain/Bow*, 2006). What Cirque Eloize's creative team understood was that—originality be damned—a water-soaked finale is always great show business.

* * *

Philippe Genty (b. 1938) is one of France's great modern puppeteers. He helped promote the practice now known as *théâtre d'objets* (object theatre), in which manipulators—who are typically visible to spectators and on occasion speak to them directly—make inanimate objects the focus of a work's dramatic action. French examples of object theatre, which is also an outgrowth of Tadeusz Kantor's explorations of the dialectic between animate and inanimate beings on stage, currently include Christian Carrignon's Théâtre de Cuisine and Michel Laubu's Turak Théâtre. At their best, such works allow for a sophisticated probing of the nature of theatre and a rethinking of the standard boundaries between theatre, sculpture, and dance. Genty's recent works have in fact blended dance, mime, magic, and acrobatics with everyday objects that function much like Sigmund Freud's notion of the *Unheimliche* (uncanny), being ordinary and strange at once. (Genty recently disclosed that much of his life's creative work stems from his having blamed himself since age seven for his father's death.)[23]

Genty's *La fin des terres*, codirected with Mary Underwood, played at the Palais de Chaillot's Salle Jean Vilar, a conventional proscenium-stage auditorium that seats 1,250. The piece is essentially a ninety-five-minute wordless dreamscape in which a man attempts to enter the private space of a woman he desires. Its crisp scenography is visually arresting: life-size mannequins become confused with genuine humans; huge inflated cellophane bags ensnare and enfold cascading players; trapdoors and sliding panels alter our frames of reference; shifts between identical props in miniature and on a gigantic scale pique the imagination. Genty memorably stages a nightmarish snowstorm of written letters that will never reach their destination and a human-sized spider with a real man's head that incorporates a woman into its web and then melts away with her into a dark blue void. Throughout we observe a Surrealistic realm of psychic symbolism, with Genty exploiting the abstract possibilities of concrete objects given animated life on stage.

Yet because Genty's stage mechanics are so meticulously controlled, the result is fairly frigid. There is little chance for spectators of *La fin des terres* to identify viscerally with anything pertaining to human emotion, wonder, or vulnerability. Too often *La fin des terres* seems to be saying, "Look how 'poetic' this image is!" It is an example of the New Circus spirit turning overly robotic and self-conscious. Consequently it lacks the element of human risk that is essential to circus, be it traditional or *nouveau*.

New Circus and cultural democratization

My relative discomfort with *La fin des terres* may have resulted from having seen, one day earlier, the Collectif AOC's new show, *Question de directions* (A Question of Directions). This was as joyous, vibrant, and unpretentious as a New Circus event can be. The Collectif AOC was launched in 2000, when its original seven members graduated from the CNAC. The troupe's name sparks an immediate link with fine French wines certified as *appellation d'origine contrôlée* (AOC, or Appellation of Controlled Origin). But the initials can also be construed as Artistes d'origine châlonnaise (Graduates of Châlons, where the circus university CNAC is located) or—as the players themselves prefer—Artistes d'origine circassienne (Performers of Circus Descent). This playful ambiguity squares with the company's overall project, which aims to celebrate fluidity and uncertainty.

Question de directions took place in the Parc de la Villette's Espace Chapiteaux (Big Top Space), a genuine circus tent that is regularly altered to meet the needs of each visiting troupe. For this show there was a midsize arena with six concentric tiers of benches. Linked to the big top was a smaller tent that housed a restaurant serving French-style comfort food: piping-hot lentil soup; spinach or salmon quiche; a plate of *charcuterie*. Such artisanal cuisine—like that of Ariane Mnouchkine's company at the Vincennes Cartoucherie—was in full accord with the resourceful character of the show that followed. In fact, *Question de directions* was a near-flawless instance of what might best be called New Age *nouveau cirque*. A large, raised circular platform filled with traps and minielevators blurred the lines between onstage and off (see fig. 25). Trampoline, aerial, and tightrope artists, along with a DJ/sound-effects operator and his equipment, popped into and out of sight at irregular moments. There were no fancy costumes and no big finishes to milk applause: the start of each new routine tranquilly overlapped with the final minute of the previous one.

Acts of courage in *Question de directions* advertised their modesty: the high wire was only five feet off the floor; an ace tumbler-dancer followed up his amazing cartwheels and *kazatsky* with some Raggedy Andy–like flops and blunders. Performers connected with individual audience members via winks, gentle glances, and toasts offered with a raised Heineken bottle. The show's only thematic thread was the fresh exploration of unusual spatial patterns and human relations. A kaleidoscope of solos, duos, trios, and ensembles kept the spectator's eye on the move. The gymnast-trapezists Marc Pareti and Marlène Rubinelli-Giordano gave alluring new anatomic meaning to having a workout partner *join* you in squats, push-ups, and dips. Yet despite the varying combinations and permutations, each of the nine performers projected through his or her body language a consis-

25. *A tumbler-dancer does his number as,* left, *a DJ operates turntables and sound mixer in the Collectif AOC's* Question de directions. *Photo © Christophe Raynaud de Lage.*

tent, quirky persona—the romantic, the rogue, the smart aleck, the grouch, and so on. This entire show was a smooth blend of newness and tradition.

. . .

At the spectacle's end, one of the players made the usual appeal for solidarity with the entertainment industry's *intermittents*. The response, however, was anything but ordinary. I had never witnessed greater applause and cheering in support of this political *cause célèbre*. Typically such appeals are greeted with faint handclapping and polite detachment. Why was this reaction so different? Looking around the arena, I noticed that almost everyone in the audience was, like the AOC troupe members themselves, in their mid-to-late twenties. Most, but by no means all, were white, and there were at least 10 percent more women than men.[24] It then occurred to me that these young adults, on this Thursday, April 6 at the Espace Chapiteaux, roughly belonged to the same demographic as the well-educated, middle-class street demonstrators who had brought turmoil to Paris two days earlier in what turned out to be a final and successful protest against the government's expansion of the "first job contract" (CPE) and the lack of security that this legislation would potentially create for them during their first two years of work. It was likely that many in this audience had in fact taken part in the recent rallies and marches.

Regardless of the accuracy of the protesters' perception of the impending legislation, it was clear to most political observers at this time that the government of Dominique de Villepin had failed to assess adequately the pulse of public opinion, especially that of its younger citizens. It was also clear that France was in urgent need of major social reform but that government leaders and the French population as a whole had been conditioned, almost reflexively, to be suspicious of it. In its gentle, unaffected play with flux, instability, and uncertainty, the Collectif AOC's show may well have offered a measure of catharsis for this younger generation's anxiety and sense of powerlessness—just as Michael Haneke's *Don Giovanni* had done for another demographic.

In their program note for *Question de directions*, the Collectif AOC offered an explanation of the show's title: "[The *question* becomes,] how can we speak about the real world while doing our somersaults?

. . . [The *response* is] by being together and by enlarging the range of spaces in which life is possible."[25] That answer seemed to resonate with France's newer breeds of activists and searchers for social justice. It also chimed with a faith in theatre as a privileged, symbolic, and empathic space, much extolled, as we have seen, by such current theatre luminaries as Ariane Mnouchkine, Enzo Cormann, Philippe Quesne, Pascal Rambert, Arthur Nauzyciel, and others. Here at the Espace Chapiteaux was a strain of twenty-first-century theatre that addressed the concerns and feelings of a central segment of the French populace often disregarded by those of an older generation who currently wield political and economic power. This modest *nouveau cirque* piece was a grand slam for cultural democratization.[26]

Part 3
Avignon

It is a magical spot with
perpetual astonishments.
— Avignon Festival director
Alain Crombecque, 1986

A Festival Turns Sixty

Who and where?

Each July a small medieval-walled city in Provence hosts one of the grandest theatre jamborees on the planet. For three and a half weeks, from 10 A.M. to well after midnight, its winding streets and picturesque public squares swarm with festivalgoers of all ages and of numerous nationalities. Avignon's year-round population is about 96,000—and most of its citizens live beyond the ramparts that enfold the city center. At festival season, many times that number come to visit and perform, injecting nearly 2.75 million euros into the local economy.[1]

Wealthy visitors may choose to stay at the chic Hôtel La Mirande in the shadow of the Popes' Palace, a towering Gothic fortress where the absentee Bishops of Rome resided in the fourteenth century; or at the Hôtel d'Europe, a converted Renaissance townhouse a stone's throw from the Rhône River; or perhaps at the Hôtel Cloître Saint-Louis, part of a sixteenth-century complex that serves as headquarters for the Avignon Festival. The most budget-conscious pitch tents at camps on Barthelasse Island, across from Avignon Bridge—the tourist site famous for its missing arches and for the children's ditty about those who dance on it *"tout en rond"* ("round in a circle"). Moderate-priced hotel rooms and apartments are plentiful within the city ramparts but are best reserved at least six months in advance.

Jean Vilar (1912–1971) launched this bustling festival as part of a modest Semaine d'art en Avignon (Arts Week in Avignon) in late summer 1947—three years after the liberation of Paris from Nazi rule and one year after the first Cannes Film Festival. The impetus came from two art dealers, Christian and Yvonne Zervos, who had the un-precedented idea of exhibiting modern paintings and sculpture in the Grand Chapel of the Popes' Palace that September. The poet René Char (1907–1988), a friend of the Zervoses, suggested that they ask Vilar if he might augment the festivities by bringing to Avignon his recent French-language production of T. S. Eliot's *Murder in the Cathedral* (1935), which had had a notable Paris run at the Théâtre du Vieux-Colombier in 1945. Vilar declined to revive *Murder in the Cathedral*. Instead he proposed to direct, act in, or coordinate three new productions in three distinct venues: the palace's open-air Honor Court, its Pope Urban V Gardens, and Avignon's Municipal Theatre. Vilar's choice of works was a harbinger of the kind of programming that would come to define the early years of the Avignon Festival: William Shakespeare's *Richard II*, a grand English classic never before performed in France; Paul Claudel's *L'histoire de Tobie et de Sara* (*The Story of Tobie and Sara*, 1939), a little-known play by a great living author; and *La terrasse de midi* (The Noon Terrace), an unpublished politically themed piece by the young writer Maurice Clavel (1920–1979).

The Arts Week in Avignon soon evolved into the summer residency of the Paris-based Théâtre national populaire (TNP), which Vilar headed as of 1951. The TNP's mission was to build a more democratic audience for theatre. Vilar hoped that the yearly festival in Provence would likewise appeal to a wide spectrum of French men and women regardless of their social class and that it would especially benefit those who had previously been deprived of the pleasures of theatregoing. In accord with this founding vision were Georges Pons, Avignon's Communist mayor at the time of the first Arts Week, and Jeanne Laurent (1902–1989), a senior state official in the short-lived Ministry of Youth, Arts, and Letters and then a guiding force in the Fourth Republic's project of *décentralisation théâtrale*, which aimed to have permanent regional theatres function as a counterbalance to Paris's abiding supremacy in the field.

Certain left-wing thinkers—including Jean-Paul Sartre (1905–1980)—deemed Avignon and the TNP to be failures because they did not attract many factory or farm workers. Vilar, however, was proud of what he thought of as the distinctly popular quality of his audiences: Avignon festivalgoers tended to be unpretentious, uninhibited, and open-minded, and they were alert to and comfortable with their diversity of social standing and educational background. To make the relatively less sophisticated participants feel at home, Vilar kept ticket prices low and surrounded performances with free concerts and informal talks with artists.

• • •

Today, according to recent surveys, the festival is perhaps not so demographically broad as Vilar had hoped for. Elite professionals (such as lawyers, doctors, university professors, and upper corporate managers) and midlevel business and government workers (such as commercial artists, high school teachers, nurses, and lab technicians) make up a majority of the audiences for both the official "In" festival and the "Off" fringe festival (67.1 percent and 67.2 percent, respectively). Audiences for the "Off" are slightly more socially varied and include a greater number of students (18 percent) than those for the "In" (13.9 percent). The least represented social groups at Avignon overall are manual laborers (0.3 percent at the "In" and 0.4 percent at the "Off," from a total of 14.9 percent in France's general population) and farmers (0.1 percent at the "In" and 0.3 percent at the "Off," from 1.4 percent of the general population).[2] Until the late 1960s over half of the Avignon festivalgoers were under thirty. In recent years the two largest blocks of participants are between thirty-five and sixty-four years old (58.7 percent) and twenty-five and thirty-four (17.9 percent). Persons under twenty-four account for 17.1 percent of the total; those over sixty-five, 6.3 percent.[3] Not surprisingly, middle-aged and older folks tend to order tickets weeks in advance, especially for the "In" program, whose schedule is announced in early June. Younger audiences are more often drawn to the "Off" because tickets are cheaper and can frequently be purchased just minutes before a show. At most "In" and "Off" events female spectators outnumber men, 62.6 to 37.4 percent.[4]

Contrary to popular rumor, the Avignon Festival is not a playground mainly for the Paris theatre crowd—who can now reach the City of the Popes in just over two and a half hours by the TGV (France's high-speed railroad). The Paris-area constituency is sizable, representing 23.2 percent of festivalgoers. But the largest group of Avignon ticket holders (34.3 percent) are "local" residents of the Provence–Alpes–Côte d'Azur region; a similar number (35.9 percent) hail from other areas throughout France.[5] Non-French attendees comprise 6.6 percent of the total. This figure includes a large cohort of French-speaking Belgians and Swiss; a good number of Germans, English, and Italians; a growing number of Asians and Eastern Europeans; and—alas—a mere sprinkling of people from the United States.[6]

Given the increasingly international character of the "In" festival's offerings, a good number of productions are now conducted in "foreign" languages with French supertitles assisting audience comprehension. In May 2009, the "In" launched its first e-newsletter in English; it also updated the English-language version of its website and announced that ten offerings that summer would have either supertitles or handout synopses in English. Nevertheless, the festival's lingua franca remains the language of Molière. For those who have no French, the many dance-, circus-, and multimedia-inflected attractions are a safe bet, as are the informal street performances (magic and puppet shows, acrobatics, musicales) that take place near the Place de l'Horloge and on the borders of the Popes' Palace. To savor the full range of events in Avignon, however, some French is . . . well, *de rigueur.*

A singular esprit de corps

Regardless of class, geographic, and linguistic differences, the reigning mind-set in Avignon is egalitarian. Partly due to the democracy of choice afforded by the range and diversity of offerings and partly because of the relaxed codes of dress and protocol that prevail everywhere in the city, festival pleasures truly seem to undo some of the barriers that too often isolate people. As you line up in front of playhouses large and small, you can sense a bond forming between, say, the noted European architect and an anonymous French shopkeeper, or the famous Paris fashion designer and a *lycée* instructor from Rouen. It is an infectious camaraderie that stems from shared high hopes for the fast-approaching stage piece and the awful tedium of the wait: doors typically open only minutes before showtime and the summer heat is often extreme.

If you "do" Avignon, you cannot be averse to crowds or to narrow cobblestone walkways. The "In" program's forty-odd theatrical offerings and the nearly 1,100 "Off" shows (in 2010) take place in about 140 venues scattered throughout the circular city. Some "In" events occur beyond the ramparts—for example, on nearby Barthelasse Island or in the historic town of Villeneuve-lès-Avignon, a vigorous half hour's walk. A few sites require that you take a car or bus. One such place is

Boulbon Quarry—a majestic stone pit fifteen kilometers southwest of the city where Peter Brook's *Mahâbhârata* played from dusk to dawn in 1985 and where the equestrian Bartabas (b. 1957) displayed in 2006 his early-morning workout with his trained horse, Le Caravage, in the awe-inspiring *Lever du soleil* (*Sunrise*).

The liberty of setting up and following your own itinerary of events is very much a part of the Avignon experience. Since participants rarely follow identical routines, festivalgoers move about in crisscrossing patterns like thousands of ants carrying on their daily tasks within and occasionally beyond a busy colony. We are all doing the same thing—going to shows—but each at our own pace and in our own way. Fortunately, people's paths and theatrical choices frequently overlap, and it is not unusual to make new friends easily.

Something similar holds for all city arts festivals. So what makes Avignon special? The feeling of overwhelming intimacy is key. In Edinburgh, for instance—home to Europe's other great performing arts summer festival—the regularly intense daily life and commerce of the Scottish capital (population 460,000) carry on fairly much as usual. Moreover, Edinburgh's festival is just one of numerous major cultural and tourist events that this large, cosmopolitan city hosts each August. In Avignon, by contrast, virtually every visitor comes to the little town in July for only one of two reasons: some are there to take a quick tour of the Popes' Palace and other historic sites; the majority have come solely to feast on theatre. Small enough to generate a quick grasp of its captivating layout, Avignon seems to exert a near-spiritual pull that makes many festivalgoers return year after year, almost like devoted long-distance lovers.

Another distinguishing mark is Avignon's nearly complete absence of modern buildings. Since the City of the Popes has only a relatively small number of year-round theatres, many of its magnificent churches, chapels, and cloisters (as well as its school gymnasiums and museum courtyards) mutate into stage venues each summer. Seated indoors or alfresco, we are almost continuously immersed in a space that is at once centuries old and as fresh as the performance in progress. The intoxicating perception of superimposed past and present is perhaps strongest when an aggressively experimental production takes place within sites as venerable as the Popes' Palace or the Carmel Cloister, both dating from the fourteenth century. Yet the festival tricks our sense of ordinary time in still other ways. If, for instance, you take a fifteen-minute stroll southwestward from the farmers' market at Place Pie and head to the Contemporary Art Museum on the rue Violette, you are likely to glance at your mobile smart phone to confirm the time and place of the next show indicated on your twenty-first-century daily agenda. You are also bound to run into gallant street jugglers, acrobats, puppeteers, and processions of costumed actors doing their pre-show *parades* in the hope of creating a buzz for their "Off" productions. In other words, Avignon brims with time-honored outdoor amusements and marketing ploys that are as charmingly effective today as they were in the Middle Ages.

Still another defining trait of the Avignon festival is that it is as much about education as it is about performance. Because of the milieu's informality, strangers in Avignon will spontaneously chat among themselves about how they reacted to a show just moments after it ends. Even theatre professionals from Paris will often "catch up" in meaningful ways when they inevitably run into one another on Avignon's streets. But since community dialogue was a key element in Jean Vilar's conception of the Avignon experience, the "In"—and to an increasing degree the "Off"—designs events expressly to promote more structured participant interaction. Morning "In" press conferences, for instance, are open not just to reporters (as in Cannes) but to the general public as well. Roundtable debates with critics and scholars on the plays being shown occur throughout July, and questions and comments from the crowd are not just tolerated: they are genuinely valued.

The "In" festival also sponsors seminars led by that season's featured artists and, as of 2004, a weeklong Theatre of Ideas program in which major intellectuals from France and elsewhere offer afternoon lectures on subjects of contemporary interest inspired by that edition's slate of offerings, for example, "What Does Resistance Mean Today?" with Edgar Morin, "Can Work Reassert Its Value?" with Richard Sennett, or "Marginals and Society" with Arlette Farge. Since 1955, the Centres d'entraînement aux méthodes d'éducation active (CEMEA)—a national association for promoting on-site educational complements to established school training—has provided over one million young and not-so-young people from France and elsewhere with inexpensive tickets, dormitory facilities, a meal plan, and work-

shops with festival artists. In 2009, 700 French *lycéens* took advantage
of the program.[7] For some of them, this is a life-changing experience.

Two festivals in one

If Avignon turns into a Republic of Theatre each July, it is in
large part because of the friendly coexistence between the high-toned
"In" and the more down-to-earth "Off." Taken together, these autonomous entities constitute—as one state official has put it—a "magnified image of the profession, the media, and the politics" that shape
the French theatre landscape more generally.[8] Indeed, their missions
and modi operandi could not be more divergent.

Officially known as Le Festival d'Avignon, the "In" is a resplendent showcase for *théâtre public*. It mostly programs new projects
conceived by visionary stage artists, either established or emerging.
In any given year, the selection of its approximately three dozen attractions is based entirely on the taste, discernment, and savvy of its
artistic directors, currently Hortense Archambault and Vincent Baudriller, with input from that year's *artiste associé*. Its budget for 2009–
2010, which included the 2010 festival, was 10.5 million euros, with
about 65 percent coming from subsidies by the Ministry of Culture in
Paris, the City of Avignon, the Vaucluse County Council, the Provence-
Alpes-Côte d'Azur Regional Council, and the European Commission.
Another 30 percent or so results from ticket sales, with the rest derived from private support. The ticket prices in 2010 ranged from thirteen to thirty-eight euros; ticket sales in recent years have numbered
typically between 100,000 and 150,000, with 20,000 to 40,000 additional seats offered free to students, theatre professionals, the press,
and others.[9]

Grandeur and artistic ambition are the hallmarks of the "In." It
foots the lavish bill for the performance costs of all works on its
roster. Although it also functions as the main producer for a small
number of major pieces each year, it encourages coproductions with
other public theatres, festivals, and performing arts organizations
and with international government agencies. Thus, by the time a new
work premieres at the Avignon "In," it will often already have a hefty
number of advance bookings elsewhere in France and Europe. In
this respect many offerings of the official Avignon festival smoothly
work their way into the wider network of contemporary *théâtre public*,

with the festival serving as a rarefied breeding ground for the *théâ-tre public*'s ever-expanding canon. Sometimes referred to jokingly as France's sixth *théâtre national*, the Avignon Festival is emphatically not about reviving France's centuries-old legacy of dramatic litera-ture. That task is primarily the business of the Comédie-Française. The Avignon "In," as codirector Hortense Archambault notes, is "a site for new creation" with an accent on "*écriture contemporaine*," artistic "risk," and scenographic "experimentation."[10]

The "Off" fringe festival, by contrast, is a crazy quilt of old and new theatrical entertainments, each one struggling for audience atten-tion. It began in 1966, when the Marseilles-born actor-director-author André Benedetto (1934–2009) decided to program his play *Statues* in-dependent of the official festival. Legend has it that an American the-atre critic in attendance that July quipped to Benedetto that the piece would be Avignon's version of New York's Off-Broadway.[11] The term "Off" stuck. Indeed, Benedetto's vision was boldly antiestablishment. He soon issued a manifesto that called for relegating "the Classics to the stake and Culture to the sewer."[12] Companies from through-out France heeded his call, and under Benedetto's aegis the Avignon "Off" grew exponentially. Of its 933 offerings in 2009, a majority were shoestring productions by fledgling troupes with little-known actors and directors. Yet with 656 plays by living writers on the July 2009 pro-gram, the "Off" is arguably, as one high official puts it, "the world's largest contemporary playwrights festival."[13]

On July 13, 2009, the day before his seventy-fifth birthday, André Benedetto died of a stroke. Frédéric Mitterrand, then France's new minister of culture, lauded Benedetto's "teeming rebelliousness" and extolled him as "a great voice in theatre history."[14] After found-ing Avignon's Théâtre des Carmes in 1963, Benedetto went on to pro-duce and direct hundreds of provocative plays and authored nearly eighty of his own—including *Napalm* (1967), the first French play to denounce the American presence in Vietnam. One week prior to his death I saw my first Benedetto play—and his last for the Théâtre des Carmes: *La sorcière, son sanglier, et l'inquisiteur lubrique* (The Sorcer-ess, the Wild Boar, and the Lecherous Inquisitor). It is a fable about a woman's struggle to maintain freedom over her body against the hypocritical moral fanaticism of the Catholic Church. In its use of puppets along with live actors, its appeal to the invisible, and its respect for the audience's power of imagination, this funny, modest production was reminiscent of the story theatre format pioneered by Paul Sills (1927–2008) in the early 1970s. Yet its message is as fresh as the latest headlines about the plight of women in much of the world today.

For fans of the rhetorical tradition, the "Off" provides innumerable takes on stage classics (Sophocles, Molière, Musset, Feydeau), the modern masters (Alfred Jarry, Fernando Arrabal, Eugène Ionesco, Dario Fo), and established contemporary playwrights (Olivier Py, Carole Fréchette, Jean-Claude Grumberg, Koffi Kwahulé, Enzo Cormann, Victor Haïm, Howard Barker, Martin Crimp). Along with often intriguing adaptations of poetry and prose by the likes of Baudelaire, Henry James, and Pablo Neruda—and in addition to new short plays by scores of under-the-radar budding dramatists—you can also enjoy raunchy stand-up and sketch comedy, delightful puppet theatre, virtuoso circus acts, bouncy music-hall variety shows, serious modern dance, cheesy Bollywood-derived musicals, and pleasant revivals of recent hit boulevard dramas and comedies.

One "Off" venue, the Théâtre du Verbe Incarné, is housed in a seventeenth-century chapel on the rue des Lices and specializes in productions originating in France's overseas territories as well as in other predominantly nonwhite regions of the world. Among its 2010 offerings was *J'ai pas cherché* (I Wasn't Asking for It), a dance adaptation of Koffi Kwahulé's *Jaz* conceived by Soraya Thomas, who is a member of Eric Languet's company Danses en l'R (La Réunion). The "Off" also caters to children. In 2009 it listed nearly 120 of its shows as "family fare," scheduled mainly in the morning and midafternoon.[15]

• • •

To appear in the "Off," amateur and professional troupes typically rent a monthlong daily time slot and a compatible venue through Avignon Festival & Compagnies (AF&C)—a clearinghouse set up in 2007 after three years of strife between competing organizations that were challenging the longtime sway of Avignon Public Off (APO, established in 1982 by Alain Léonard). Although many of the visiting groups enjoy financial support from regional arts agencies, rental fees for Avignon venues are fairly steep.[16] Some players and technicians associated with the "Off" (over 6,000 in 2009) frequently can afford to live only in pup tents at campsites on Barthelasse Island. The hope of all "Off" performers is to win recognition from the public and garner attention from one of the many programmers and producers who descend upon Avignon from all corners of France in search of bankable new talent and shows. In 2010, 3,700 programmers reportedly were present.[17]

While only a few "Off" companies go on to immediate runs elsewhere, each year at least one show attracts massive critical praise and audience adulation. Such was the case in 2007 for Darina Al-Joundi's *Le jour où Nina Simone a cessé de chanter* (The Day Nina Simone Stopped Singing), a one-woman piece about coming of age in Lebanon during the civil wars. Directed by Alain Timar, who runs Avignon's Théâtre des Halles, the show went on a two-year tour throughout France and in several other European countries.

AF&C publishes a free, well-indexed program of all "Off" events. Beyond that, most groups are on their own when it comes to publicity. While France's national print media run feature articles and reviews for almost all of the "In," only regional dailies cast a steady spotlight on the "Off"—and just on a tiny fraction. So by the time the "Off" festival starts (usually a few days prior to the "In"), every metal grate, drainpipe, and street lamp along the city's main walkways is plastered with eye-catching posters, and for hours each day, tireless thespians pound the pavement as they ply potential ticket buyers with fliers, postcards, and greetings. This nonstop outdoor spectacle—part street theatre, part merchandising campaign—winsomely revivifies the basic tie between Western theatre's origins and the agora, or ancient Greek marketplace.

Moreover, through its ceaseless hawking, its sale of discount membership cards (30 percent off all shows, most of which, in 2010, were fifteen euros at full price), and its unembarrassed display of the sweat and toil of the trade (just seconds after applause and bows, for instance, actors must often undo the sets and sweep the playing area in order to make way for the following show), the "Off" festival insistently reminds us of the precarious economic status of most of the devoted souls who are driven to pursue a life on today's stage. Except for our purchase of tickets on the web, at FNAC (the entertainment retail chain), or at festival headquarters, the "In," by contrast, shrewdly conceals from spectators the enormous financial machinery that keeps it afloat.

．．．

In terms of numbers, it is logical to view the carnivalesque "Off" as more popular than the lordly, high-flown "In." In 2007, for instance, the "Off" reportedly sold over 710,000 tickets, as opposed to the approximately 100,000 seats filled by the "In."[18] "Off" sales rocketed to over one million tickets in 2010.[19] In terms of quality, both festivals are always uneven—as should probably be expected. Bernard Faivre d'Arcier, a longtime head of the "In," posited that for every ten summer theatre seekers in Avignon, "there are two who go exclusively to the In, two others who only attend the Off, [and] a majority who happily split their time between both." He was quick to add—rightly, I think—that the ambidextrous majority is "more demanding of the In, and more indulgent toward the Off."[20] (A more formal study determined that, in 2009, the average festivalgoer came to Avignon for an eight-day stay and bought tickets to eleven "Off" and two "In" shows.)[21]

Over the past few summers I have mainly frequented the offerings of Avignon's "In." But in 2006 I tried to attend as much of both jubilant festivals as was humanly possible, and I indeed found myself fairly forgiving of the numerous clinkers encountered at the "Off." Still, I had the good luck to catch some superb "Off" shows. Among the best were Patrick Blandin's bewitching, midmorning performance of Michel Tournier's dramatic monologue *Le fétichiste* (*The Fetishist*, 1978), with only three of us in the audience; a surprisingly witty two-woman rendition of Philippe Minyana's *Chambres* (1993) by Mélanie de Diesbach and Caroline Weiss; a virtuoso staging of Koffi Kwahulé's *Blue-S-cat* (2005), directed by the playwright; and *De nos jours, les saintes vierges ne versent plus de larmes* (Nowadays, Holy Virgins No Longer Shed Tears), a spellbinding French-language fusion of Pasolini's stage works *Porcile* (1968) and *Affabulazione* (1977) by the Montpellier-based company Machine Théâtre. No text-based work, either at the "In" or the "Off," was to my mind more affecting and more perfectly executed that year than Marguerite Duras's *Agatha* (1981), directed by Jacques Kraemer at the Théâtre du Balcon: as the incestuous lovers, Lara Guirao and Nicolas Rappo were luminous.

Nonetheless, experience shows that for overall quality and complexity of artistic ambition, the "In" simply cannot be beaten. Moreover, the "In" is a precious barometer of new creative trends in contemporary French and European theatre. That is why, in the sections that follow, I focus steadily on it.

Homage to Jean Vilar

The 2006 edition marked the "In" festival's sixtieth anniversary. To celebrate, Hortense Archambault and Vincent Baudriller asked Olivier Py to conceive and mount a gala homage to its charismatic founder. The stirring result took place on July 27, the festival's final night, in the Honor Court of the Popes' Palace. Titled *L'énigme Vilar* (The Vilar Enigma), this two-hour piece traced the legendary actor-director's thoughts, feelings, and aspirations regarding theatre's artistic and sociopolitical potential, from the mid-1940s until his sudden death in 1971.

This sold-out production was a tight fusion of staged biography and theatre of *la parole*. It included a number of Py's trademark set-design concepts, themselves partly derived from Vilar's penchant for abstract, uncluttered stages: light-bulb-studded makeup tables; small, mobile trestles; shiny black bleachers that pivoted and folded in on themselves. Py's artistic indebtedness to Vilar was also obvious in that the focus of our attention always fell on the actors' bodies and their words, the latter assembled almost entirely from Vilar's published and private writings. Adding to the sense of occasion was Stéphane Leach's incidental music, consisting of variations on the celebrated brass fanfare by Maurice Jarre (1924–2009) that over the decades has heralded the start of every Honor Court performance.

L'énigme Vilar put Py's creative fortitude to the test. Allotted only three weeks for rehearsals during the hottest summer France had experienced in decades, Py prepped his actors—from the CDN Orléans/Loiret/Centre, which he then headed—to deliver polished portraits of fabled performers from the festival's early years, such as Maria Casarès (1922–1996) and Gérard Philipe (1922–1959), and of literary-theatrical giants with whom Vilar had interacted—sometimes amiably, at other times less so. These included Camus, Sartre, Cocteau, Beckett, and Jean Genet, who, as played by Michel Fau, appeared in flamboyant bishop drag (a wink to Genet's *Le balcon/The Balcony*, 1956). Embodied by the superb thespian Philippe Girard, Jean Vilar's own voice—wise, humane, passionately idealistic, and always self-questioning—dominated the evening.

The piece climaxed with a broadly satiric evocation of the chaotic events of Avignon 1968. Actors dressed as student radicals raced up and down the Honor Court aisles, noisily chanting the now infamous rhymed slogan equating *Vilar* and the regularly invited choreographer Maurice *Béjart* (1927–2007) with Portugal's longtime dictator Antonio de Oliveira *Salazar* (d. 1970); a few moments later an ersatz reassembling of Judith Malina and Julian Beck's Living Theatre company, notorious for having smashed bourgeois prudery, engaged in an awkward onstage orgy.

Some left-leaning critics took Py to task for his supposed "reactionary" bias in this latter portion of the show and for having more generally "projected his own life" onto that of his subject.[22] Yet I think that Py's intent throughout *L'énigme Vilar* was not so much self-serving or nostalgic as it was pragmatic and forward-looking. At bottom the production was a heartfelt call for today's French theatre community to reexamine Jean Vilar's central convictions and to reapply them prudently to France's current cultural context. Among these are Vilar's notion of theatre as no less a public service than a fine art; his dream of creating spectacles to nourish the souls of factory workers and university graduates alike; and his view of the Avignon Festival as an almost hallowed time and place for honest artistic and political reflection, confrontation, and hope.

Serenity restored

Most of the issues inflaming Avignon attendees in July 2006, unlike the previous year, had nothing to do with the festival itself. Upsetting our otherwise firm absorption in matters theatrical were the televised head-butt that caused French soccer star Zinédine Zidane to be ejected from the World Cup final match, hard-boiled directives from Interior Minister Nicolas Sarkozy that heightened the risk of undocumented immigrants in France being forcibly separated from their school-age children, and the destruction of much of Lebanon's civil infrastructure and the many civilian deaths in the new conflict between Hezbollah militants and the Israeli army. The sole festival-based turmoil occurred on Monday, July 17, which had been designated a special day to honor France's six decades of *décentralisation théâtrale*. When Culture Minister Renaud Donnedieu de Vabres arrived at the Pope Urban V Gardens to take part in a late-afternoon roundtable on the *next* sixty years of French theatre, scores of *inter-mittents*—many wearing T-shirts lettered INTER*LUTT*ANT-E-S (PART-TIME *STRUGGLERS*)—booed, heckled, and threw tomatoes, forcing the minister to retreat to an indoor area of the Popes' Palace. That evening, about one hundred *intermittents* occupied the Honor Court's stage for an hour and a half until they were satisfied that Donnedieu de Vabres would not be present for the premiere of Eric Lacascade's new production of Gorky's *Barbarians* (1905).

Still, Avignon 2006 did not spark furious debate over which kind of stage works the "In" should showcase. Even before the festival began, *Libération* expressed pleasure that the announced program had been "swept of explosives"; *Les Inrockuptibles* called the roster "principled."[23] The following October the Ministry of Culture and Communication (still under Donnedieu de Vabres) renewed Archambault and Baudriller's codirectorship for a second term, through 2011. A consensus held that the newfound serenity surrounding the festival's workings owed something to the influence of Josef Nadj (b. 1957), the Vojvodina (Serbia)-born dancer and choreographer who served as artist-in-residence for that summer of 2006. Along with the festival's two directors, Nadj judiciously allotted ample room to such esteemed literary playwrights as Gorky, Bernard-Marie Koltès, and Edward Bond. He thereby negated the fears of critics and spectators who, in July 2005, felt that media hybrids had gained a permanent stranglehold over text-driven creations.

Nonetheless there were, as always, numerous unclassifiable mixed-form shows on the 2006 bill. Among the most outstanding were those of Nadj himself.

Creativity and otherness

For opening night at the Honor Court, Josef Nadj presented the world premiere of *Asobu* (Japanese for "to have fun"), a grandly conceived homage to the Belgian poet and graphic artist Henri Michaux (1899–1984). Performing this abstract exploration of subjective and far-flung geographic spaces were twenty-four players, including two circus performers, one puppeteer, one actor, four musicians, and numerous dancers, six of whom were Japanese with ample practice in the Butoh dance forms that shaped several parts of this ninety-minute fantasia. Simple objects—pails, poles, ribbons, blow darts—were put to poetic and often funny use: at one point the full ensemble chewed on an immense bolt of flowing cloth. Near the end Nadj performed a breathtaking solo that, in the spirit of the entire work, was at once playful and precisely controlled. Central to Nadj's mixed-media vision were Vladimir Tasarov's bass-violin and percussion music, played by the four onstage musicians, and Thierry Thibaudeau's black-and-white video images of Nadj's hometown of Kanjiza, projected onto the courtyard's exposed stone wall.

Rather than illustrate specific Michaux texts and drawings, Nadj's kaleidoscopic spectacle sought to capture the writer's attachment to foreignness and to fluid cultural identities. The spaces traversed by the players became the symbolic equivalents of faraway journeying and the embrace of otherness. Yet it was the performers' enactment of interdisciplinary porousness that truly distinguished the piece. It was near impossible for viewers to identify who was trained in dance, acting, puppetry, or circus since disciplinary markers seemed to be irrelevant for onstage participants. The piece, as one commentator notes, was "not so much 'hybrid' as continuously 'other'": "In *Asobu* [theatrical] genres are undifferentiated, and [performance] disciplines fuse to bring forth the 'elsewhere' that resides within each performer's body. We no longer perceive separations between forms but rather a permanent process of 'de-formation.'"[24]

• • •

Nadj's subtle genius was even more apparent in *Paso doble*, a performance-installation work fabricated with the Majorca-born painter and sculptor Miquel Barceló (b. 1957) (see fig. 26). This duet for dancer and sculptor—which later opened the 2007–2008 season at St. Ann's Warehouse in Brooklyn, New York—took place at the Celestine Church, located on the Place des Corps-Saints. To find your spot among the tiered seats set up within the narrow nave of this restored Gothic church, you first had to walk in front of the chancel, where a perfectly smooth ochre wet-clay floor and a tall, flat, white wet-clay rectangular surface had been erected. Once the show began, bubbles swelled on the white canvas and fingers soon appeared through its tiny perforations. In the hour that followed, and to Alain Mahé's cunning percussive soundscape, Nadj and Barceló created a living, breathing two-toned sculpture in which their bodies were both the means to and an integral part of the resulting work of art. Along

the way they mutated into figures suggestive of roosters, pigs, and foxes. Toward the end a pulsating mountain of refashioned clay literally swallowed up the two men.

Paso doble was messy and methodic, primal and sophisticated. As a work of abstract formalism it was devoid of any narrative content other than the tools and acts of its production. Nadj explained in an interview why he so enjoyed conceiving this piece for the Celestine Church, which he referred to as "an already de-sanctified space": "To some extent we were re-sanctifying it by inventing another kind of worship, not so far removed from the original—we, too, transform clay into flesh, into life."[25] Paso doble's emphatic play with orifices, penetrations, secretions, and expulsions also backs up the venerable hypothesis that libidinal energy propels the greater part of human creativity. It gives testimony as well to the spiritual richness that can infuse such efforts at their best. Fortunately, two performances of this ephemeral masterpiece—which Nadj and Barceló reinvented from scratch thirteen times for Avignon audiences—were recorded and released on a commercial DVD.[26]

The festival and internationalization

Nadj settled in Paris in 1980 and now holds a French passport; he currently directs the Centre Chorégraphique National d'Orléans (France). Barceló splits his time between Majorca, Paris, and Mali (West Africa) and often shows his works in Naples, Boston, and New York. Both artists embody the international spirit of the 2006 "In" festival, one of whose explicit aims was to feature works that explore the enduring worldwide impact of colonialism and the continuing clashes of cultural, social, and racial identities. Among the pieces dealing directly with such themes were a French-language adaptation of Athol Fugard's Sizwe Bansi Is Dead (1972), directed by Peter Brook; the young hip-hop artist Hamid Ben Mahi's autobiographical Faut qu'on parle (We Gotta Talk, 2006), coconceived with Guy Alloucherie, who heads the Compagnie Hendrick Van Der Zee, known for its circus- and dance-influenced probes into the social injustices endured by the working classes of northern France and Belgium; and Frédéric

(opposite) 26. Josef Nadj, right, and Miquel Barceló give shape to a breathing sculpture piece in their Paso doble. Photo © Christophe Raynaud de Lage.

Fisbach's Japanese-language mounting (with French supertitles) of Oriza Hirata's play about the anxieties of a Japanese family living in Korea in 1909, *Gens de Séoul* (*Citizens of Seoul*, 1991).

The "In" festival's emphatic swerve toward internationalization began under Bernard Faivre d'Arcier's first administration (1980–1984) and took on added momentum during Alain Crombecque's leadership (1985–1992). Faivre d'Arcier introduced Avignon spectators in the early 1980s to such virtually unknown (in France) artists as the dance-theatre pioneer Pina Bausch and the Japanese Butoh dance troupe Sankai Juku. From Western Europe in the 1990s came Jan Fabre (Belgium), Romeo Castellucci (Italy), and Pippo Delbono (Italy). Eastern European participation included the Lithuanian director Eimuntas Nekrochius, the Russian Anatoli Vassiliev, and the Pole Krzysztof Warlikowski. In more recent years an African presence has increased thanks to such performer-directors as Dieudonné Niangouna and Faustin Linyekula, both Congolese. Several of these non-French artists have virtually become festival regulars.

But where is the United States of America?

Despite the Avignon Festival's efforts to be broadly international in flavor and scope, stage works by United States writers and theatre companies have been sorely underrepresented. In the 1980s the "In" Festival hosted numerous U.S. dance troupes and even invited the American Repertory Theater (Cambridge, Massachusetts) to perform, in 1982, its English-language production of Molière's *Sganarelle/Le médecin malgré lui* (*Sganarelle/A Doctor in Spite of Himself*, 1660/1666), directed by Andrei Serban and featuring the U.S.-based actors Tony Shaloub, Thomas Derrah, and Jeremy Geidt. When I asked Hortense Archambault to explain the near-total absence of American voices in the 2006 edition, she noted that she and codirector Vincent Baudriller are always on the lookout for new U.S. pieces. But, she added, "the American framework for doing theatre" does not readily lend itself to the kind of "*recherches*" ("experimentation" or "investigation") that is a defining feature of Avignon programs.[27]

It is true that, having scant government support and being so greatly yoked to individual sponsorship and box-office receipts, much mainstream American theatre perpetuates a brand of naturalistic production that, viewed from the Avignon perspective, is stale and uninteresting. The difficulty of raising funds for exporting productions is, moreover, a big disincentive for American companies. Still, one can make the case that there are many ambitious, risk-taking artists and companies throughout the United States that are worthy successors to the Wooster Group, Mabou Mines, and Richard Foreman's Ontological-Hysteric Theatre—American experimental ensembles that French tastemakers have long supported and continue to extol.

Recent stateside productions of works by such outstanding young United States playwrights as Suzan-Lori Parks and Sarah Ruhl and by innovative multimedia directors like Pavol Liska and Kelly Copper (who run Nature Theater of Oklahoma), Jay Scheib (*Addicted to Bad Ideas: Peter Lorre's Twentieth Century*, 2009), and Caden Manson (*House of No More*, 2005) would, I think, fit beautifully in the Avignon context and would help to expand the somewhat dated French and European view of America's alternative and exploratory theatrical terrain. Scheib is already known elsewhere in Europe, and Manson's Big Art Group has been a frequent guest of Paris's annual Autumn Festival, long run by Alain Crombecque (who died in 2009); Nature Theater of Oklahoma performed *No Dice* (2007) at the invitation of Pascal Rambert's Théâtre2Gennevilliers in spring 2010. Yet nothing more fully ratifies creative stature in the eyes of many French theatregoers, professionals, and the press than a run at the Avignon Festival. Ironically, the site of several brilliant Sarah Ruhl productions has been the Yale Repertory Theatre in New Haven, Connecticut—Avignon's "sister city" in the United States.

A bold transatlantic endeavor

The 2006 Avignon Festival did showcase an intriguing experiment in Franco-American collaboration. Under the meticulous and insightful direction of Arthur Nauzyciel, a team of American actors from 7 Stages, a nonprofit company in Atlanta, Georgia, performed—in English, with French supertitles—a classic piece of contemporary French theatre: Bernard-Marie Koltès's *Combat de nègre et de chiens* (*Black Battles with Dogs*, 1981).

For all its potential richness as an instance of cross-cultural dialogue, a project as daring as that of Nauzyciel and 7 Stages runs the risk of raising, among spectators and practitioners alike, chauvinist claims concerning artistic "genuineness." It is the equivalent, say, of a French troupe's being invited to perform Edward Albee's *The Goat or*

Who Is Sylvia? at the Brooklyn Academy of Music in a French-language version—and for a mainly American audience obliged to read the original dialogue on electronic signboards. As noted in chapter 2, a good number of New Yorkers did not take well to such a scheme when Claude Régy presented his French-language version of Sarah Kane's *4.48 Psychosis* during ACT FRENCH. In the Koltès case, however, the theatre gods proved more benign and protective.

Bernard-Marie Koltès, who died of AIDS in 1989 at age forty-one, remains one of the most imposing French playwrights of his generation. (Both the "In" and the "Off" editions of Avignon 2009 commemorated the twentieth anniversary of his passing.) By reinstating the primacy of finely crafted verbal expression on stage, Koltès helped to reverse the sway of the director-*auteur* that prevailed in much of the high-profile public theatre of his times. Although he shunned psychological realism, Koltès used theatre to explore the mysteries of human relations with a depth and incisiveness that arguably hark back to the great French poetic tragedian Racine. He was also among the first of his times to grapple with contemporary issues of race, gender, and postcolonialism. Perhaps Koltès's most distinctive trait—and the one most influential for French theatre today—was his international vision. Koltès took inspiration from kung fu films, the music of Bob Dylan and Lou Reed, the poetry and journals of Allen Ginsberg, and the American novelists Jack London, James Baldwin, and J. D. Salinger, among others. (One of his earliest plays is *Sallinger* [sic], 1977.) Koltès spent some of his most intensely lived months exploring the wild side of New York City. His travels to Africa, Central America, and the Soviet Union enhanced his sensitivity to otherness and the sense of his own existential marginality. In fact, Koltès rarely treated themes, characters, and locales that could be identified as specifically French. His plays focus on foreigners, exiles, and the displaced—individuals who are literally always *en route*. As one critic has noted, Koltès's theatre is global in essence and appeal because "its very substance is the transversal of borders."[28]

Koltès's plays have been translated into nearly forty languages, including English. His plays are performed worldwide. Yet given both his renown and the impact he still has on much current French and European theatre, his work is far less often produced in the United

States than it ought to be. As early as 1982 Françoise Kourilsky introduced Americans to Koltès via her production at La MaMa Annex of *Combat de nègre et de chiens* (under the title *Come Dog, Come Night*). Two decades later, in 2003, the French-born directors Marion Schoevaert and Doris Mirescu joined Robert Lyons of the SoHo Think Tank to present Koltès/New York at the Ohio Theatre, on lower Manhattan's Wooster Street. This three-week-long festival of Koltès plays in new American translations won strong critical notice. The *New York Times* remarked approvingly that thanks to the team of translators, "Koltès now sounds like Dante with the voice of Sam Shepard."[29]

Efforts to publish these new translations were, however, blocked by François Koltès, who holds the rights to his brother's works. The English-language translations currently available in book format are mainly British.[30] In spring 2010, the Yale Repertory Theatre mounted *Combat de nègre et de chiens*—under the title *Battle of Black and Dog*—in a translation by Michaël Attias that was originally written for Koltès/New York. Still, the lack of readily accessible renditions in colloquial American English may help explain what Travis Preston—who staged Koltès's final play, *Roberto Zucco*, at the New Federal Theatre (New York City) in 1997—has referred to with regret as the "short-term but unsustained interest [by much of the U.S. theatre community] in the playwright's work."[31] Also at play, as Stéphane Patrice suggests, is Koltès's intrinsic opposition to the history of Northern (or so-called Western) imperialism and the continued postcolonial exploitation carried on in most areas of Africa, Latin America, and South Asia.[32]

Nauzyciel's solution

The plot of *Black Battles with Dogs* is at once exotic and familiar. The action takes place at a European company's construction site located "in West Africa, somewhere between Senegal and Nigeria."[33] A local black character, Alboury, searches for the cadaver of his dead brother, whose murder by a young white racist engineer, Cal, is being covered up by the project's arrogant but insecure manager, Horn, also white. Augmenting the tension is the sixty-year-old Horn's newly arrived young bride-to-be, Léone, from Alsace, who arouses erotic desire in the other two men.

The idea of hiring a French director for the play's Atlanta production in 2001 originated with Del Hamilton and Faye Allen, the artistic and producing directors, respectively, of 7 Stages. With help from both Cécile Peyronnet, Atlanta's cultural attachée, and AFAA (the France-based government organization that promotes French culture internationally), the American team eventually chose Nauzyciel. His work with the Georgia company started with a revision of the play's standard English translation: Nauzyciel is fluent in English and carried out the modifications with the company's full participation. In his view the play's fine British translators, David Bradby and Maria Delgado, had overly adhered to a "sociological interpretation" that sacrificed the musical quality of Koltès's sentences for the sake of narrative transparency: "If Koltès had wanted to write a realistic play about class struggle, he would have done so. . . . It was our job to reinstate the play's more poetic and mysterious relationship to the world." [34]

A second challenge was to bypass the usual expectation among American actors that a play's director will help them grasp the motivations supposedly driving their characters. Perhaps because 7 Stages has a long history of performing international works, Nauzyciel was able to shift the emphasis from psychology to lyric vocalization with little difficulty. "European actors," the French-born director notes, "tend to be more cerebral and attentive to formal subtleties than their American counterparts. But I've found that American actors are generally much better in exerting their physical, bodily presence. Koltès's writing is very sensual, and its articulation requires the mobilization of the performer's entire body. Working with the 7 Stages troupe was a real advantage in this regard." [35]

Another immediate task was to rein in the African American actor Isma'il ibn Conner (Alboury), who at first wanted to draw extra attention to the play's themes of racial conflict (see fig. 27). Nauzyciel intuited that in mounting this particular play in Atlanta, a Southern city closely identified with the American civil rights struggle, any special stress put on the play's sociopolitical implications would unduly gild the lily. Thus, although the word "nigger" ("*nègre*" in Koltès's text)

(opposite) 27. *Isma'il ibn Conner as Alboury in the 7 Stages production of Bernard-Marie Koltès's* Black Battles with Dogs, *directed by Arthur Nauzyciel. Photo © Frédéric Naucyziel.*

appears in the dialogue translated by the 7 Stages team, Nauzyciel thought it politic to keep this term out of the play's title—in this instance conforming to the British rendition.

The 7 Stages production of *Black Battles with Dogs* was a critical, commercial, *and* civic success. At the start of its monthlong run in Atlanta the audience was 90 percent white; at the end it was 80 percent black.[36] Before reaching Avignon in 2006, the production played in Chicago and at the CDDB–Théâtre de Lorient in Brittany. It was later reprised in Greece at the Athens International Festival. During Avignon 2006, French reviewers responded openly to the acting, the translation, and Nauzyciel's mise-en-scène. Many were attuned to the fresh layers of meaning that the play takes on when performed by Americans.[37]

I attended two of the five Avignon performances, which took place on the large indoor stage of the Gymnase Aubanel. They were mesmerizing. Nauzyciel's Rembrandt-like visual design—flickering candelabras and harsh splashes of light from electric torches against a severe black backdrop—appropriately created an overall aura of existential and psychological murkiness. In sync with Koltès's cinematic imagination, the director had Léone and Alboury's nervous first embrace occur in slow motion; and he had the tense, prolonged drinking scene between Horn and Alboury unfold like a CinemaScope version of the final shootout in Fred Zinnemann's *High Noon* (1952), with the antagonists initially opposite each other at the far ends of the proscenium and ultimately meeting stage center.

The entire 7 Stages cast was in strong form, but Janice Aker's portrayal of Léone's descent into suicidal madness was especially affecting. It exposed how much *Black Battles with Dogs* owes to Shakespeare's *Othello* and *Hamlet*. Like Desdemona and Ophelia, Léone finds herself, in Koltès's words, "alone, and incapable of articulating the meaning or nature of her condemnation."[38] Koltès in fact wrote a short adaptation of *Hamlet* early in his career, in 1974; and his full French-language rendition of *A Winter's Tale* (*Le conte d'hiver*) was mounted at the Théâtre du Rond-Point less than a year before his death, in 1988. Translating Shakespeare, he once told an interviewer, "showed me how to free myself from the so-called rules of the [French] theatre."[39]

••••

Arthur Nauzyciel is the only major French director today to mount French plays in France with professional American actors. He is currently planning an English-language production of Jean Genet's posthumously published *Splendid's* (c. 1948), using mostly the players and artistic collaborators he worked with at Harvard University's American Repertory Theater for an outstandingly innovative *Julius Caesar* in 2008—a show that went on to play at the Maison des Arts de Créteil as part of the 2009 Autumn Festival in Paris before touring elsewhere in France. The impact of Nauzyciel's gutsy leaps back and forth across the Atlantic has proved to be even greater than first expected. With support from French government agencies and Etant donnés: The French-American Fund for the Performing Arts, and with the blessing of François Koltès, 7 Stages is now pursuing a ten-year "U.S. Koltès Project." It will result in five more American productions of his plays, each translated by Isma'il ibn Conner, and each staged at two-year intervals by a different French director. To date, 7 Stages has produced Koltès's *In the Solitude of Cotton Fields* (*Dans la solitude des champs de coton*, 1986), directed by Eric Vigner in 2008, and *The Day of Murders in the History of Hamlet* (*Le jour des meurtres dans l'histoire d'Hamlet*, 1974), under Thierry de Peretti's direction.

This long-term collaboration between French and American artists offers an emphatic and salutary signal to the French theatre establishment. It says that there are, indeed, unorthodox, chance-taking theatre companies in the United States whose tastes and goals are not that far removed from those of the European, Asian, and African countries more regularly represented at the Avignon "In" festival. In addition, it serves as a model for other American stage organizations that are seeking fresh ways to internationalize their contemporary repertory but may be hesitant about making a French connection.

A history of transplants

Throughout the twentieth century France has been a magnet for theatre artists from around the world. In the 1950s and 1960s the most performed modern playwright in Paris was not a French writer but Bertolt Brecht (1898–1956).[40] The visit of Brecht's Berliner Ensemble to Paris in 1954 was a signal event in sparking the French public's new appetite for foreign-language stage productions. Facilitating this ecumenicalism was the Théâtre des Nations, an international drama festival that as of 1955 took place in Paris under the auspices of UNESCO, with French state and municipal support. Coordination of the two-month annual festival was largely in the hands of the leadership and staff of the Théâtre Sarah-Bernhardt (now the Théâtre de la Ville) located on the Place du Châtelet. Between 1957 and 1965 the Théâtre des Nations organized visits by about 150 companies from some fifty countries. These included the Piccolo Teatro della Città di Milano (Italy), the Living Theatre (United States), the Royal Shakespeare Company (United Kingdom), and the Peking Opera (China), as well as the Berliner Ensemble. In a similar vein it is useful to recall that the leaders of the post–World War II theatre of the absurd, so often thought of as quintessentially French, were writing in a language that was not the tongue of their native lands: Ionesco came from Romania; Beckett was Irish; and Arthur Adamov (1908–1970) had been born in Kislovodsk, Russia.

As of the mid-1960s, when cultural theorists like Roland Barthes and Michel Foucault were announcing the death of the author and the philosopher Jacques Derrida was launching his call to "overthrow the tyranny of the text,"[41] many of France's theatre festivals became havens for a new wave of international artists and troupes exploring image-based theatre. These included Bread and Puppet Theater (United States), Tadeusz Kantor (Poland), and Pina Bausch (Germany). An especially strong bond between French theory and non-French performance practice came from Argentina with the relocation to Paris of such bold directors as Jorge Lavelli (b. 1932), Victor García (1934–1982), and Alfredo Arias (b. 1944).

Avignon 2006 saluted the Argentina-France interchange with a cluster of stage works inspired by the writings and drawings of Raúl Damonte Botana (1939–1987), the Argentine exile better known to the French public as Copi (diminutive for *copa de nieve*, or snowflake, in Spanish). A taboo-breaking humorist-cartoonist-novelist-playwright-director-actor and a pioneering gay rights instigator, Copi arrived in Paris in 1963 and died of complications from AIDS in 1987. The Avignon tribute was the brainchild of the prolific performer-director Marcial Di Fonzo Bo (b. 1968)—also an Argentine transplant to

France—and his extraordinary actors' collective, Les Lucioles (The Fireflies), based in Rennes (Brittany).

Two rollicking Copi events took place in a specially built circus tent erected in the parking lot of the Lycée Mistral. The first, *Les poulets n'ont pas de chaises* (Chickens Don't Have Chairs) (see fig. 28), was a musical extravaganza featuring life-size digitized animations of several of the comic-strip characters Copi regularly sketched in the 1960s for the weekly *Nouvel Observateur*—including his pouting Seated Woman and the suicidal out-of-work snails. Think Charles Schulz's *Peanuts* but with as much smutty double entendre as sweet philosophy. The second was *Loretta Strong* (1974), Copi's sci-fi monologue about a murderous female astronaut who watches as planets explode around her. Di Fonzo Bo played Loretta (just as Copi had done decades earlier) and delivered most of her demented lines while swooping and gliding above the big top's audience thanks to an intricate cable-and-wire system. Imagine a cross between Georges Méliès's 1902 *A Trip to the Moon* and a Carmen Miranda production number directed by Busby Berkeley—viewed while on hallucinogens.

Across the river, on Barthelasse Island, we were treated to a one-night-only performance of *Eva Perón*, Copi's drag-drenched five-character satire of Evita's dying days—performed in Spanish with French supertitles. When Copi premiered this play in Paris in 1969 (with Alfredo Arias directing), a mob of outraged Peronistas stormed the theatre, trashed the set, and released stink bombs. Di Fonzo Bo's hilarious, sleazy rendition—he both directed the show and portrayed the expiring First Lady—made plain that Copi's subversive plays have outlasted his fiercest enemies and that for all their entertainment value they remain confrontational. "With the rightward shift that is overtaking Europe today," Di Fonzo Bo noted, "these works by Copi are a discreet weapon against mounting self-righteousness."[42]

A blend of political conviction, camp sensibility, and insight into the human condition, Copi's radical queer theatre appeals to a relatively wide French audience today. In this regard he is akin to such current U.S. drag-*auteurs* as Charles Busch (*Vampire Lesbians of Sodom*, 1984, and *The Divine Sister*, 2010), Joey Arias (*Christmas with the Crawfords*, 2001, and *Arias with a Twist*, 2008), and the Boston-based Ryan Landry (*All About Christmas Eve*, 2004, and *Of Mice and Mink*, 2009).

28. *Casual mingling of the human and the digital in Marcial Di Fonzo Bo's homage to Copi,* Les poulets n'ont pas de chaises. *Photo © Pierre Grosbois.*

Copi's fierce social and political bite, however, sets him perhaps more closely among the coterie of Jean Genet, Fernando Arrabal, and the Living Theatre. Might this militancy explain why Copi is at present barely known and performed in the United States?

In the early 1980s a few of Copi's plays were available in American translation from the Riverrun Press. He was also one of the scores of French-language playwrights to enjoy English-language productions by New York's Ubu Repertory Theatre (1981–2001), under the artistic and administrative aegis of Françoise Kourilsky and housed mainly at La MaMa Experimental Theatre Club in the East Village. In 2008, with aid from the French Cultural Services, Beata Pilch, the artistic director of Chicago's Trap Door Theatre, produced Copi's *Eva Perón*. Eight years earlier she presented his *The Homosexual, or The Difficulty of Sexpressing Oneself* (*L'homosexuel ou la difficulté de s'exprimer*, 1971). Still, Pilch notes: "I'm just perplexed as to why we are not open to this kind of material in the United States, or why we are not even taught it at our fancy universities."[43]

A haunted imagination, beyond French

One of the current French playwrights who *is* being taught more and more in French literature and theatre courses in the United States is Joël Pommerat (b. 1963), the midcareer dramatist who had three works on the Avignon 2006 roster. Asked about his artistic trajectory, the author of *Cet enfant* says with optimism that he would like to write "one play per year for the next four decades" — not as a string of separate works but as a cohesive oeuvre.[44] Pommerat's forty-five-minute *Le petit chaperon rouge* (*Little Red Riding Hood*, 2004) played to children and adults in Avignon's Salle Benoît XII, on the rue des Teinturiers. With grim lighting and eerie amplified clicks of stiletto heels on pavement, this ingenious retelling of the Perrault fairy tale probed the sometimes terrifying relations among daughters, mothers, and grandmothers. Programmed as afternoon and evening doubleheaders at the Municipal Theatre on the Place de l'Horloge were two other, more ambitious Pommerat pieces: *Au monde* (In the World, 2004) and *Les marchands* (The Merchants, 2006).

The Municipal Theatre (recently renamed Opéra-Théâtre d'Avignon) is a stately nineteenth-century structure that boasts the festival's most comfortable seats, but its sight lines are atrocious if you are at either end of its U-shaped balcony—as I was for *Les marchands*. Still, the play's dark magic was discernible. *Au monde* and *Les marchands* are two panels of a triptych: the third is Pommerat's *D'une seule main* (With One Hand, 2004). On the surface these two-hour plays depict how contemporary financial and business crises are weathered by families and friends of captains of industry (in *Au monde*) and by the working classes (in *Les marchands*). Yet in form and mise-en-scène these plays are antinaturalist explorations of cryptic misdeeds and the lure of the occult. Pommerat's main aim is to immerse the spectator in a world of verbal mystery and visual ambiguity—a project that calls to mind Maurice Maeterlinck's haunting manner in such pathbreaking plays as *L'intruse* (*The Intruder*, 1890) or *Les aveugles* (*The Sightless*, 1890). In 2007, *Les marchands* won the Grand Prize for Dramatic Literature from the Société des auteurs et compositeurs dramatiques (SACD).

Joël Pommerat is an autodidact who never finished high school. Over the past decade he has taken to directing his plays. Like Michel Vinaver, he deplores the "injustice" that has long made French playwrights subservient to director-*auteurs*.[45] In public remarks delivered midfestival at Avignon's Calvet Museum, he spelled out details of his artistic credo. "I think it is impossible," he said, "to become a true *auteur de théâtre* today without tightly tying the writing of a text to its direction." Convinced that this fusion is the way toward a healthier theatre in France, and one that will finally resolve the tension between writers for the stage and director-*auteurs*, Pommerat predicted a "new dawn" for a large number of fellow writers.[46]

Pommerat's principles overlap with those of several stage practitioners we have encountered in this book. Like Olivier Py, Pommerat relies upon a core team of actors for whom he tailors roles. Like Py and Valère Novarina, he insists that his performers be "in the word, not in the recitation or reproduction of a text." Like Pascal Rambert, Pommerat believes that theatre's "sole and essential purpose" is "not to disguise, not to concoct" but "simply to be."[47] Like Philippe Minyana and Bernard-Marie Koltès, his characters—Pommerat prefers the term 'figures'—are more given to soliloquies than to simple dialogue. And in the low-key manner of Philippe Quesne, Pommerat sees himself as "a sculptor or painter searching obstinately to capture the real, to put pressure on it so that it reveals itself."[48] Other artists who have taken on the amalgamated role of author and director include Py, Rambert, and Gildas Milin, along with Christophe Huysman (b. 1964), Pierre Meunier (b. 1957), Hubert Colas (b. 1957), and Joël Jouanneau (b. 1946).

But it is Pommerat's relation to language that perhaps makes him most representative of a certain tendency in current French theatre. Each of his plays tells an intriguing story. Thus, each marks a swerve back toward narrative-based theatre, a trait we noted in the works of Marie NDiaye, José Pliya, and Yasmina Reza, and one that also informs the plays of other prominent post-Beckettian writers such as Jean-Luc Lagarce, Enzo Cormann, and Noëlle Renaude. Yet Pommerat crafts his words so that utterances are both plain and puzzling: they drive a plot, but they withhold a sure progression of events. Referring to his works as "dramatic poems," Pommerat asserts: "I can very well imagine a wordless theatre—which is not at all the same thing as a theatre without a text."[49]

Pommerat approaches this ideal in *Les marchands* (see fig. 29). Throughout the play's thirty-nine brief sequences, his onstage figures are entirely mute. Their every gesture carries storytelling weight because their mimed situations are often, but not always, at variance with the play's verbal text. This spoken component is delivered in the first-person singular by one of the two main female characters whose offstage words we hear through loudspeakers as in a cinematic voice-over. Her opening lines (the whole script is in free verse) are:

The voice you are now hearing
is my voice
where I am at the moment of talking to you has no importance believe me
it's me you see there
and that's me getting up
I am the one who is about to speak
[*pause*]
there, that's me speaking
[*pause*]
I was her friend
the person you see there sitting beside me[50]

29. *In Joël Pommerat's* Les marchands, *actors miming their roles and situations. Photo © Christophe Raynaud de Lage.*

Pommerat's contrarian stance toward standard dramatic language (not to speak of his full rejection of a declamatory *belle langue*) is also evident in *Au monde*. None of this play's seven family members is able to communicate with The Hired Woman, since she speaks a foreign tongue adapted from the Basque:

THE MIDDLE DAUGHTER: Did you hear someone shout?
I wonder if I really heard someone shouting or crying.
THE HIRED WOMAN: Gauar iz dinan arrikatzen samarki burutu garalako.[51]

The Youngest Son fears that this woman represents Death and Evil: "With every means available I'm going to keep you from being what you are."[52] Yet Pommerat's script and stage direction render her the least gruesome and most sensual and attractive character of the lot. Periodically, with mike in hand and a cabaret spotlight directed at her, she lip-synchs to familiar pop songs—entirely in the nude except for her spiky cutaway shoes. The Hired Woman's unembarrassed "foreignness" highlights what appears to be the others' collective slide toward delusion and delirium. By play's end we sense that getting *beyond* the French language may be this group's only hope for redemption.

Beyond France: experimental form, popular content

The 2006 "In" festival's surprise crowd-pleaser and darling of a majority of critics was the documentary installation-theatre piece *Mnemopark: un monde de train miniature* (Mnemopark: A Mini Train World, 2005). It went on to receive the 2008 European Theatre Prize for New Theatrical Realities. Conceived by Stefan Kaegi (b. 1972 in Solothurn, Switzerland), this multimedia work featured a nebbishy group of authentic (nonactor) Swiss miniature-train aficionados aged sixty-five to eighty and one professional actress, Rahel Hubacher, who served as MC.

For an hour and ten minutes they all related, in native German or in rudimentary French, facts and figures about the current economy of rural Switzerland, fragments of their nation's history, and memories from their lives as obsessive hobbyists. Concurrently, miniature video cameras, positioned upon moving electric trains set up on utility tables midstage, traversed a made-to-scale toy landscape of a Swiss canton: the audience viewed these electronic images on a giant screen, stage rear. For comic relief Kaegi threw in some Surreal visual effects, such as a live chicken in its coop or real goldfish swirling in their bowl, which the roving camera also duly recorded. But mainly, spectators perceived a near-perfect picture-postcard simulation of Europe's most self-consciously picturesque haven for tourists, financiers, and Bollywood film directors. Kaegi's drably dressed hobbyists informed us that these cinéastes often shoot glamorous outdoor musical numbers in the safety of the Alps as a substitute for Kashmir's more politically risky Himalayas. Midshow in *Mnemopark* they performed a karaoke-like parody of just such a number.

I was bored after five minutes.

Despite occasional leaps into a back-to-the-future fictional subplot and jabs at Switzerland's protectionist farm policies, this cavalcade of cutesy banalities pandered, I felt, to the worst instincts of undemanding audiences. It invited us to take on the mind-set promoted by most reality TV shows: self-complacency and a phony pose of empathy. It is certainly possible that I just did not "get" it. In hitching the earnest celebration of a marginalized fan community to a vaguely ironical critique of Switzerland's anti–European Union isolationism, *Mnemopark* may well have offered "an original perspective situated at the improbable contact point of avant-garde form and popular content," as a critic for *Les Inrockuptibles* observed.[53] But like *L'Humanité*'s Marie-José Sirach, I would have preferred a piece with greater "muscle" and "irreverence."[54]

•   •   •

Fortunately my qualms with *Mnemopark* did not stop me from partaking in Kaegi's other festival offering, *Cargo Sofia-Avignon: un voyage en camion bulgare* (Cargo Sofia-Avignon: A Bulgarian Truck Ride, 2006). Twice daily over five days, this roaming site-specific installation enabled forty-eight spectator-passengers to board a specially altered trailer truck that took us on a two-hour multisensory excursion (see fig. 30). The vehicle, which departed from the Cours Président Kennedy, near the central post office, drove mainly through Avignon's industrialized suburbs. But Kaegi fashioned the show as a condensed documentary reenactment of the 3,000-kilometer trip that a pair of genuine Bulgarian truckers, Ventzislav Borissov and Svetoslav Michev, regularly make as they haul fresh produce from Sofia

30. *In Stefan Kaegi's* Cargo Sofia-Avignon, *a ticket holder views the real-cum-spectacle through multipaned windows on the side of a trailer-truck-cum-theatre. Photo © Christophe Raynaud de Lage.*

to various West European locales, including the City of the Popes. These two men were in fact the driver-hosts for this festival event that later played in and around thirteen other European cities, including Vienna, Dublin, and Strasbourg.

Cargo Sofia-Avignon was never less than riveting. We took places in long rows of blue seats that faced the trailer's left panel. As soon as the truck started to move, this lateral surface functioned as a screen for the live video and audio feed coming from the truck's cab. Ventzislav spoke in broken English; Svetoslav, in Bulgarian; a young woman from Sofia who was studying viticulture in Avignon sat with us in the trailer and translated the men's semi-improvised remarks into French. Kaegi, too, was aboard: he mainly oversaw a fellow at the computer controls, set up on a platform behind the last row of seats. Throughout the show the two truckers' comments alternated with film footage of the European highway system, as seen mainly from their up-front vantage, and documentary sequences about SOMAT— the scandal-plagued Bulgarian trucking firm that the notorious German mogul Willi Betz purchased from the state in the 1990s. The trip's most savory moments, however, took place each time the beige shades suddenly rose, allowing us to view "reality" directly through the floor-to-ceiling multipaned windows that lined the trailer's side.

After weeks spent within the cocoonlike environs of Avignon and its theatre venues, I found this abrupt shift of viewpoint to be invigorating. We stopped at a freight railroad station to observe a mighty crane lift a container wagon and edge it onto a trailer truck's chassis. We went for a truck wash. We pulled into a vast warehouse that supplies vegetables to retailers. We passed by Europcar and Hertz outlets, Yamaha and Toyota dealers, Best Western hotels, Esso service stations, and Quick burger franchises. Here were slices of the material world in all their uniform, consumption-driven ugliness. We could have been on any stretch of highway in almost any country on the planet. Yet because the mix of interlinked sounds and visuals was so compellingly consistent, we could also almost believe—and this is why the project succeeded as an artistic exercise—that we were en route from Sofia and moving along the expressways of Serbia, Slovenia, and Italy.

Of course, we were never really far from Avignon, France. And yes, Stefan Kaegi had choreographed nearly every detail, from the drive within a run-down trailer park while Ventzislav casually recounted his experience of the plight of Romanian gypsies to the Bulgarian song-stress we repeatedly espied standing at traffic circles or amid clumps of roadside bushes and whose sweet live singing registered in two separate dimensions—from a visual distance (perceived through the windows) and in acoustic close-up (via the earphones we were asked to wear for the entire trip).

• • •

Kaegi, who began his professional life as a journalist, is a graduate of the Institute for Applied Theatre Studies at the University of Giessen (Germany). He often refers to his works as "theatre ready-mades" in which "people who are alien to theatre productions but . . . [who] are the experts on perspectives on reality come to serve as suppliers of materials and as actors."[55] Yet for me what was most rousing about this entire experience was how the material-world-made-theatrical also cropped up in ways that could not have been prearranged—as when we stopped for a red light and two young truckers, pulling up beside us, gawked in amazement and some of us, gawking back, smiled broadly and waved. Just as Kaegi and his collaborators meticulously molded normally unframed reality into spectacle and performance, so we, the ticket holders, became the show's co-players. In other words this was theatrical interactivity pried away, at least in part, from its usual mediated, top-down manipulation.

To some extent my enjoyment of *Cargo* may simply have been a sophisticate's frisson at safely slumming within the "exotic" territory of the laboring classes. The complacent and pseudoempathic attitude that I deplored with respect to *Mnemopark* may well have been at work in my favorable response to *Cargo*—although the latter's "muscularity" and "irreverence" struck me as more impressive. Moreover, it must be conceded that even as site-specific theatre, *Cargo Sofia-Avignon* is neither unique nor pioneering. For example, in a caustic response to the 500th anniversary of the New World's "discovery," Christof Nel, Wolfgang Storch, and Eberhard Kloke mounted *Aufbrechen Amerika* (*Opening Up America*, 1992)—a three-day blend of "'journeys' by bus, train, and ship through the heterogeneous diversity of the industrial landscape between Bochum, Duisberg, Gelsenkirchen and Mülheim [Germany]."[56] The French director André Engel (b. 1947)— known in the early part of his career for creating *événements-*

spectacles (event-shows) in outdoor, nontheatrical spaces—mounted *Dell'inferno* (From Hell, 1982, inspired by Virgil, Dante, and Rilke) in an abandoned factory of the Plaine Saint-Denis, just outside Paris. In fall 2009 the New York–based Foundry Theater mounted *The Provenance of Beauty*, a theatricalized bus tour of the Bronx. Similar public-space theatre events have occurred worldwide.

Still, among the works showcased at the 2006 Avignon Festival, Stefan Kaegi's opus stands out for its deterritorialized boldness. Kaegi is Swiss, not French. His production company, Rimini Protokoll (a collective venture with directors Helgard Haug and Daniel Wetzel), is based in Berlin. As *Cargo* travels literally and figuratively throughout Europe, it glories in its hybrid and deconstructed "foreign" dimensions. With little fuss it recasts its mix of languages, target audience, and site-specific environments according to wherever it is contracted to play. Kaegi's *Cargo* thus points to one way of approaching an ambitious ideal that operates as an implicit structuring force in much contemporary French theatre and that is especially evident in the programming of the Avignon "In" over the past few years: the creation of world theatre for world audiences.

• • •

Near this chapter's start we took special note of the supranational aspect of Josef Nadj's contributions to the Avignon Festival. We now end our view of today's French theatre with a piece that cannot be identified as specific to any one nation. Readers should not construe this final pirouette as perversely erratic. On the contrary, I think that *Cargo*, in its Avignon incarnation, reminds us of how very much of the identifiably *French* theatre discussed in these pages is, in ways both obvious and subtle, also working to extricate itself from strictly Gallocentric coordinates and traditions. As the final chapter will suggest, notions of migration and intercultural influence offer a useful conceptual grid for summing up a number of the threads we have traced throughout this overview.

Recap and Coda
French Theatre
Tomorrow

Centrifugal sweep

The snapshot of Stefan Kaegi's *Cargo Sofia-Avignon* in chapter 11 returns us to the multilingual, transnational masterwork with which we began this exploration of contemporary French theatre: Ariane Mnouchkine's *Le dernier caravansérail: odyssées* (*The Last Caravan-Stop: Odysseys*). By coincidence, Mnouchkine's film adaptation of that epic work enjoyed a sneak preview in the Honor Court of the Popes' Palace on the night of July 10, 2006, just days before Kaegi, previously unknown in France, made his splash with Avignon audiences and with the national press.

Kaegi explicitly distances himself from such older, ideologically driven theatre artists as Mnouchkine and Peter Weiss (1916–1982, born in Germany): "I stay away from that. For me, to be political today is to be a documentarian . . . [with an emphasis on] the economy, not ideology."[1] Yet as we have seen, *Le dernier caravansérail*, too, sprang from Théâtre du Soleil's intense engagement with primary real-world documents, and its episodes often shed damning light on current economic inequities. Conversely, just as Mnouchkine squarely indicts the relentless violence of religious fundamentalism, so Kaegi — with a lighter hand and more ironic distance — exposes the soulless impact of multinational corporate capitalism on everyday life. More important, both *Cargo* and *Le dernier caravansérail* offer us shared voyages *to* the other, and *with* the other. Their common artistic aim is to promote human empathy without regard to fixed national identities. Structurally and dramaturgically, their sweep is centrifugal: *Cargo*'s truck-cum-bus literally steers us away from a familiar starting place, and *Le dernier caravansérail*'s mobile dollies — brought briefly on stage, precariously held to frame each sketch, and then swiftly wheeled off stage—simulate the vertiginous, never-ending motions of diaspora.

In their insistence on border-crossings and the erasure of frontiers, these two pieces bring to the fore an underlying dynamic that shapes many of the writers, directors, and works discussed in *French Theatre Today*. We can refer to this dynamic as a renewed cosmopolitanism. Its components include intense, explicit engagement with non-French artists and subjects—Claude Régy, Pascal Rambert, Michel Vinaver, Amin Maalouf; a markedly transatlantic vision—Fabrice Rozié, José Pliya, WaxFactory, Arthur Nauzyciel, Vinaver, Marcial Di Fonzo Bo; immersion in a multiplicity of cultural and national traditions—Koffi Kwahulé, Pliya, Vinaver, James Thiérrée, Di Fonzo Bo; a preoccupation with hybrid and fluid human identities—Jean-Marie Besset, Coline Serreau, Nauzyciel, Noëlle Renaude, Olivier Py, Gisèle Vienne, Maïmouna Gueye, Booder, Josef Nadj; a recourse to languages other than standard French—Valère Novarina, Superamas, Philippe Minyana, Souria Adèle; and considerable stage experience with nonnative languages—Marion Schoevaert, Robert Wilson, Nauzyciel, Di Fonzo Bo. In harmony with this renewed cosmopolitanism is a second, more explicit dynamic traced throughout much of our survey: the embrace of expressive media other than spoken, text-centered theatre as seen in the formally hybrid and often unclassifiable works of Philippe Quesne, Superamas, WaxFactory, Thiérrée, Vienne, Gildas Milin, Novarina, Rambert, and Philippe Genty.

All of these currents are consistent with Joël Pommerat's ideal of operating above and beyond the French language, in a "wordless theatre." As noted in chapter 11, Pommerat does not intend to have us take this formulation literally. His is more a statement about an impulse to keep French theatre moving toward a condition where its basic elements—its "vocabulary" and "syntax"—will be ever evolving; a theatre that will resist reduction to simplistic categories and that will fly in the face of an expectation of pristine "Frenchness."

Contemplating the future

The plays of Bernard-Marie Koltès (d. 1989) remain an inspiration and a benchmark for the centrifugal and cosmopolitan tendencies in today's French theatre. Midway into *Combat de nègre et de chiens* (*Black Battles with Dogs*, 1981) is a moving scene about breaking free of the barriers to understanding imposed by differing languages. It presents the first intimate encounter between the two characters most marked as outsiders—Léone, who hails from Alsace and speaks German with the same facility as she does French; and Alboury, the African protagonist whose native tongue is Wolof:

> LEONE: Es ist der Vater mit seinem Kind [translation: *It is a father with his child*; Léone quotes from the first lines of Goethe's ballad, "The Erl-king"]. (*She laughs.*) You see, I can speak foreign too! We'll manage to understand each other in the end, I'm sure we will.
>
> ALBOURY: Yow dégguloo sama lakk waandé man dégg naa sa bos [translation: *You don't understand my language but I can understand yours*].
>
> LEONE: Yes, go on speaking like that, you'll see, I'll get it eventually. . . . I've always thought that if you look at people very carefully, for a long time, while they're talking, you can understand them. You just need to take your time. I speak foreign, and you too, so we'll soon be on the same wavelength.[2]

Later on, these two characters fall prey to mutual mistrust. But their effort here is symbolic not only of one of Koltès's artistic aspirations but of that of many innovative French stage practitioners—from Quesne and Rambert to Kwahulé and Pommerat—who in diverse ways are following in Koltès's footsteps: to transcend Gallocentrism.

Over the past few years, France has been recalibrating its political and economic bearings vis-à-vis an enlarged European Union, fast-moving global power shifts, and domestic population changes stemming from decades of nontraditional immigration flows. Similarly, contemporary French theatre has been loosening itself from nation-bound cultural traditions perceived as dated and confining. Drawing on and contributing to practices that have marked much experimental stage work in Europe and North America since at least the early 1990s, today's French theatre, as noted throughout this book, is increasingly fluid and porous, crossbred and crossbreeding. To maintain this cosmopolitan momentum, intercultural exchange is imperative. The ACT FRENCH festival was a precious affirmation of the curiosity for and receptivity to new currents in French theatre among

U.S. audiences. In order for such openness to avoid the sad fate of Koltès's Léone and Alboury, however, it needs to be sustained, reciprocated, and financed.

• • •

Various recent signals emanating from France's central government have been troubling with respect to the future of national subsidies and of the French artistic climate overall. Much like his top rival Ségolène Royal, Nicolas Sarkozy managed to evade concrete talk about most cultural matters during his campaign for the presidency in 2006–2007. It was not until twenty months after taking office that Sarkozy addressed the issue head-on. In a New Year's speech delivered in Nîmes (on the border between Provence and Languedoc) and aimed at "*les acteurs de la culture*" (cultural operatives), Sarkozy loftily affirmed on January 13, 2009, that "without artists, society would die." Yet the head of state also underscored that the arts have potent "economic value" not only because they foster "creativity and innovation" but because "piggybacked on cultural industries, they add to the competitive attractiveness [of French cities and communities]."[3]

This view is fully in line with the memo of expectations (referred to in chapter 6) that Sarkozy, soon after his election, sent to his then minister of culture, Christine Albanel. In that document the president stressed the need for state-supported theatres to "show results" and to conform more closely to "audience expectations."[4] This bottom-line, businesslike mind-set rankled many creative artists in the public theatre sector. Some observers now wondered if Sarkozy was trying to sabotage Albanel's authority altogether. For he also announced on January 13 the creation of a Conseil pour la création artistique (Council for the Creative Arts), ostensibly a think tank on government and the arts, to be presided over by none other than Sarkozy himself. The council's mission, in the president's words, would be to "propose new cultural policies geared toward excellence" and to "reorient [*recentrer*] the granting of state subsidies." "Given the [poor state of the current] economy," Sarkozy declared, "we must make choices, and they must be the right choices."[5]

In its inaugural makeup, this twelve-person council inclined heavily toward arts administrators (already beholden to and in varying degrees complicit with the ruling administration), not creative artists. These included Dominique Hervieu, a choreographer and then codirector of the Théâtre National de Chaillot (and the sole female on the council); Laurent Le Bon, a curator at the National Museum of Modern Art/Centre Pompidou; the sociologist Emmanuel Ethis; Jacques Blanc, director of the Quartz, scène nationale de Brest (Brittany); Jean Vinet, chief of the Lower Normandy Center for Circus Arts; and most conspicuously Marin Karmitz (b. 1938), the founder of the MK2 film production company and movie theatre chain, who was named the group's secretary-general.

The council's imprint remains to be seen.[6] Dominique Hervieu insisted that it would in no way replace the ministry but might well serve as "a trigger for making certain [new] things possible."[7] Pascal Rogard, who heads the Société des auteurs et compositeurs dramatiques (SACD), deplored the choice of Karmitz as the council's chief official: "He is a very fine businessman and a strong defender of vested interests; but I have never seen him support the common good."[8] The very establishment of such an entity prompted Olivier Py to remind fellow citizens of what would be lost if France's Ministry of Culture, celebrating its fiftieth anniversary in 2009, were to be dissolved or supplanted. In a piece written that February for Le Monde, Py reviewed the ministry's accomplishments and extolled its genius at having "organized, if not actually invented" such dearly prized entities as "a popular culture distinct from mass entertainment," "artistic freedom liberated from commercial stakes," and a capacity to be "respectful toward audiences and protective of artists." Looking forward, Py urged that the ministry remain "a tool of intellectual and aesthetic speculation" and that it play a crucial role not just in France's and the European Union's economy but in education, diplomacy, and human rights. "Culture," the director of the Odéon-Théâtre de l'Europe concluded, must stand "at the very center of political life, of our plan for the future."[9]

President Sarkozy, however, is basically suspicious of and uninterested in much inventive contemporary culture. He is, as Antoine de Baecque observes, "uncultivated [*peu cultivé*] and proud of it."[10] Sarkozy's main set of values, de Baecque notes, bolsters a domestic climate of law and order and the populace's unbridled consumption of material goods. In June 2009, Sarkozy indeed fired Christine Albanel as minister of culture and communication. The head of state had become especially displeased with Albanel's handling of the so-called

Hadopi bill, a legislative measure to protect the financial interests of creative artists and industries, especially those of film and popular music, against illegal Internet downloading. Although the bill won approval from Parliament, a good part of it was then rejected by the Constitutional Council, which claimed that punitive actions taken against Internet abusers were the domain of the judicial, not the executive, branch of government.

Sarkozy replaced Albanel with Frédéric Mitterrand (b. 1947), the former Socialist president's nephew and a well-known charismatic TV host, writer, and documentary film producer. While the younger Mitterrand supported his uncle in the 1980s, his political ideology now tends toward the center-right, making him a fit ally for Sarkozy. Mitterrand's longtime personal rapport with many in the French theatre arts community inspires cautious optimism. During his first visit as minister to the Avignon Festival on July 12, 2009, Mitterrand promised "always to lend a ready ear to *artistes*" and asserted that "the central issue for the performing arts" is "salaries."[11] But the need for an overhaul of the Ministry of Culture will require more than Mitterrand's charm and unobjectionable short-range plans. As several heads of cultural institutions collectively—and anonymously—wrote in the professional journal *La Scène*: "For over a decade, [the ministry] has repeatedly demonstrated an incapacity to rethink seriously its mission, its organization, and its modes of intervention; to build respectful, demanding, and sustainable relationships with other public organisms; and to plan for the future by encouraging and promoting the experimentation and innovation our nation urgently needs."[12]

The indispensable imponderable

In December 2007, a two-day colloquium called Teatro Europa took place at the Teatro Nacional in Porto (Portugal). Its sponsors were the Union of the Theatres of Europe, an alliance of European public theatres established in 1990 to promote coproductions and intercultural exchange, and the European Theatre Convention, a project founded in 1988 to encourage young theatre professionals to reach out to new audiences within today's European society. The conference's goal was to examine Europe's cultural policies primarily as they affect theatre. The event featured stage artists, politicians, social scientists, humanists, and others involved in cultural activities. The remarks of two French participants are of particular interest.

The philosopher Bernard Stiegler, head of the Department of Cultural Development at the Pompidou Center (Paris), addressed the digital revolution and its impact. Stiegler, who authored the multivolume *La technique et le temps* (*Technics and Time*, 1994, 1996, 2004), cheered the advent of digital technologies as "the equivalent of writing at the time of the Greeks, the writing which was the origin of the appearance of theatre and which gave rise to the whole great Western cultural tradition."[13] Convinced that spectators no longer simplistically "consume" plays and other works of art, Stiegler urged that we "cultivate ourselves with these objects," "participate in their evolution," and "become involved . . . in the way [these works] are accepted."[14]

Stiegler thus seemed to endorse the aspect of much contemporary French theatre that stresses the productive, fluid interaction between performer and spectator—as seen in the work of Quesne, Novarina, Vinaver, Rambert, Pommerat, Milin, Kaegi, and others. Stiegler's frequent, although highly nuanced enthusiasm for the U.S. model of "a cultural policy that [is] also an industrial policy"[15] is not fully compatible with the temperament of these same artists who, as we have noted, are in large measure reacting, if not entirely against, then more surely as a needed corrective and alternative, to the exorbitant reach of new technologies and transnational cultural industries. Still, Stiegler's contribution to the Porto colloquium articulated an intriguingly broad, if not to say populist, strategy for the future: "We Europeans must invent a new industrial model . . . no longer based on the consumption and production of CO_2, but on sublimation, and what I call contribution, in fact the production of culture by everyone. . . . [T]he required technologies are already available."[16]

Emmanuel Wallon, an expert in French and European arts policies (and professor of political sociology at the University of Paris Ouest Nanterre La Défense), sought to clarify a number of conceptual imprecisions that have clouded many of the well-intentioned statements recently set forth by European cultural agencies. For example, the buzzword 'innovation' (used by Sarkozy in his January 2009 speech) certainly chimes well with the European Union's economic development plan for the first decade of the twenty-first century, known as the Lisbon Strategy; the latter, whose first draft dates from 2000, holds that innovation is the prime means for countering low productivity and promoting competition in a knowledge-based economy. Yet in the realm of theatre arts, Wallon noted, *innovation*, or "the introduction of new features of a technical or practical nature into the sphere of production and distribution," is of far less import than *invention*, or "the irruption of the unprecedented, the unformulated, the unknown, of something unexpected that will never be fully contained by the styles and media through which it takes form."[17]

Similarly, the terms 'creativity' and 'creation' are too often used synonymously. For Wallon, *"creativity* [also evoked by Sarkozy in his 2009 speech] is merely an aptitude that awaits to be applied in any given undertaking, whether abhorrent or excellent," whereas *"creation* is the production of a work of art and of the mind" (my italics).[18] Wallon also affirmed that theatre, like other art forms, "cannot be reduced to a stock of heritage wealth nor to a [self-perpetuating] entertainment industry." Genuine theatre creations result instead from "a succession of operations of transformation which escape any possibility of calculation."[19]

Wallon conceded at Porto that European theatre is currently "a David facing the Goliath of the communication industries." But he was confident that today's theatre practitioners can rise to the main challenge confronting them: to articulate persuasively what makes their art distinct and original, and to contribute thereby to the construction of a public space that will be in tune with the full range of needs of "the citizens of the times we live in." "The most important thing about Europeans' shared capital," Wallon said, "is not their total net or gross income, but what the [French] poet Michel Deguy [b. 1930] calls the 'incalculable,' that which escapes [computation] and resists measure—in other words, *the necessity of the imponderable.*"[20]

• • •

Many of the leading French figures treated in these pages, from Mnouchkine, Quesne, Rambert, and Py to Novarina, Minyana, and Pommerat, among others, have given brilliant voice to "the imponderable" not only via their exceptional stage pieces but through their public statements about the urgency, importance, and uniqueness of their calling. These individuals and their teams are already actualizing a good part of Wallon's vision. They exemplify what Robert Lepage, quoted in the introduction, sees as key to the contemporary theatre's process of renewal: "expressing things that have yet to be expressed."[21] In this regard, French theatre today is at the forefront of theatre for tomorrow.

Notes

Preface

1. To permit easy identification by the reader, I have chosen to place ACT FRENCH in uppercase throughout this book.

2. Among the prime movers of ACT FRENCH were Emmanuelle de Montgazon, then *attachée culturelle*, and her associate Nicole Birmann-Bloom of the Cultural Services of the French Embassy in New York; Paris-based artistic liaison Denise Luccioni, assisted by Professor Philippa Wehle (SUNY/Purchase); New York–based artistic advisor Mark Russell, founder of the Under the Radar festival; Elisabeth Hayes, executive director of the French American Cultural Exchange (FACE), based in New York; and Jean-Marc Granet Bouffartigue and Marie Raymond of the performing arts department of AFAA, based in Paris. Eighty percent of the festival's $3.7 million budget came from participating New York theatres, ticket sales, and individual and corporate sponsors, while 20 percent came from AFAA and the French Cultural Services; see Alison James, "Gotham speaks 'French,'" *Variety.com*, 10 July 2005, http://www.variety.com/, and Claire Derville, "'Act French': les trois coups ont retenti," *France-Amérique*, 16 July 2005.

3. In October and November 2004 the Cultural Services of the French Embassy of Chicago hosted a festival of twenty-three contemporary French plays in English translation, performed by Chicago-area theatre ensembles. Unlike New York's ACT FRENCH —which aimed to showcase alternative and hybrid stage forms along with more traditional works, and whose organizers invited France-based companies to perform in New York—the emphasis in Playing French: Chicago's First Festival of Contemporary Plays from France fell squarely on literary playwriting in new translations. For an overview, see Yannick Mercoyrol, "Playing French: Notes and Reflections," *Entr'actes* (Paris), no. 20 (January 2005): 151–55.

Introduction

1. Donald Morrison, "The Death of French Culture," *Time*, 21 November 2007, European edition. A revised and updated version of this text, with a reply by Antoine Compagnon, was published as *Que reste-t-il de la culture*

française? (Paris: Denoël, 2008) and as *The Death of French Culture* (Cambridge, UK: Polity, 2010).

2. Bernard-Henri Lévy, "American Talk of French Culture Says More about Them Than Us," *Guardian* (London), 8 December 2007. Random House (New York) published Lévy's *American Vertigo* in January 2006.

3. John Lichfield, "The Death of French Culture? I Don't Think So," *Independent* (London), 6 December 2007.

4. Frédéric Martel, "*Time Magazine* et le débat sur la mort de la culture," *nonfiction.fr*, 21 December 2007, http://www.nonfiction.fr/article-420-time_magazine_et_le_debat_sur_la_mort_de_la_culture_francaise.htm.

5. *Les Echos*, 7 July 2005, quoted in Nathalie Mauret, "Festival d'Avignon: l'été de toutes les attaques," *La Scène*, no. 38 (September 2005): 31.

6. Frédéric Ferney, *Le Point*, 21 July 2005, quoted in Mauret, "Festival d'Avignon," 31.

7. Armelle Héliot, *Le Figaro*, 21 July 2005, quoted in Mauret, "Festival d'Avignon," 31.

8. René Gonzalez, *L'Humanité*, 18 July 2005, quoted in editorial, "Une partie du public et des critiques contestent la direction prise à Avignon," *Le Monde*, 24 July 2005.

9. Odile Quirot, "On danse sur le pont d'Avignon," *Le Nouvel Observateur*, 7 July 2005.

10. Renaud Donnedieu de Vabres quoted in Emmanuelle Loyer and Antoine de Baecque, *Histoire du festival d'Avignon* (Paris: Gallimard, 2007), 546.

11. Régis Debray, *Sur le pont d'Avignon* (Paris: Flammarion, 2005), 98–99.

12. Georges Banu and Bruno Tackels, eds., *Le cas Avignon 2005: regards critiques* (Vic-la-Gardiole: L'Entretemps, 2005), 16.

13. Ibid., 222. Jean Vilar's statement originally appeared in his 1968 piece "Théâtre et révolution," which was reprinted in Jean Vilar, *Le théâtre, service public et autres textes* (Paris: Gallimard, 1986).

14. See Antoine de Baecque, *Crises dans la culture française* (Paris: Bayard, 2008), 222–28.

15. See Olivier Donnat, *Les pratiques culturelles des français à l'ère numérique: enquête 2008* (Paris: Editions de La Découverte/Ministère de la Culture, 2009), 181.

16. Emmanuel Wallon, "Le théâtre et les spectacles," in *Politiques et pratiques culturelles*, collection "Les Notices," ed. Philippe Poirrier (Paris: La Documentation Française, 2010), 126.

17. Wallace Fowlie, *Dionysus in Paris: A Guide to Contemporary French Theatre* (New York: Meridian Books, 1960), 7.

18. Ibid., 202. Fowlie's book was one of a cluster of scholarly overviews of French literary playwrights that appeared in the United States around the same time. These include David I. Grossvogel, *The Self-Conscious Stage in Modern French Drama* (New York: Columbia University Press, 1958); Jacques Guicharnaud, with June Beckelman, *Modern French Theatre from Giraudoux to Beckett* (New Haven, CT: Yale University Press, 1961); and Leonard Cabell Pronko, *Avant-Garde: The Experimental Theater in France* (Berkeley: University of California Press, 1962), which examines works by Samuel Beckett, Arthur Adamov, Jean Genet, and Jacques Audiberti, among others. The first American edition of Martin Esslin's *Theatre of the Absurd* (Garden City, NY: Doubleday, 1961) targeted a more general public and embraced, along with the leading French-based exponents (Beckett, Adamov, Ionesco, and Genet), British and other European playwrights engaged in what was then viewed as an emergent new tendency. Since the early 1960s, Bettina Knapp's *French Theater since 1968* (New York: Twayne, 1995) stands out as one of the rare attempts by a U.S.-based specialist to offer an updated panoramic view of the field, devoting special attention to Ariane Mnouchkine, Patrice Chéreau, Michel Vinaver, and Valère Novarina, among many others. The London-based scholar David Bradby has authored two valuable overviews, *Modern French Drama, 1940–1990*, 2nd ed. (Cambridge: Cambridge University Press, 1991), and, with Annie Sparks, *Mise en Scène: French Theatre Now* (London: Methuen, 1997). To the best of my knowledge, my book is only English-language effort to explore in depth the various tendencies that make up French theatre and stage performance in the first decade of the twenty-first century.

19. For an elaboration of these thoughts by a contemporary dramatist, see George Hunka, "The Booking of the Play," *Theater* (New Haven, CT) 40, no. 2 (2010): 19–31; also, in the same issue, Tom Sellar, "The Unscripted Future": 1.

20. With explicit reference to the French-language publication in 2002 of Hans-Thies Lehmann's *Postdramatisches Theater* (Frankfurt am Main: Verlag der Autoren, 1999), Antoine de Baecque, in *Crises dans la culture*, dubs the 2005 edition of the Avignon Festival "the postdramatic Festival," 224.

21. See Michel Guerrin and Nathaniel Herzberg, "Internet bouscule les choix culturels des Français," *Le Monde.fr*, 14 October 2009, http://www .lemonde.fr/, and Donnat, *Les pratiques culturelles*, passim.

22. Václav Havel, *Disturbing the Peace: A Conversation with Kavel Huizdala* (New York: Knopf, 1990), 51.

23. De Baecque, *Crises dans la culture*, 202.

24. Havel, *Disturbing the Peace*, 51.

25. Robert Abirached quoted in Catherine Robert, "Un ministère à la dérive," *La Terrasse*, special issue (July 2010): 14–15.

26. Tony Judt, "Crossings," *New York Review of Books*, 25 March 2010, 15.

27. Christopher P. Pinet, "From the Editor's Desk," *French Review* 83, no. 5 (April 2010): 960; see also Olivier Todd, "Ce que Sarkozy propose, c'est la haine de l'autre," *Le Monde*, 27 December 2009.

28. See Philippe Bernard, "De la diversité à l'identité, le virage de Nicolas Sarkozy," *Le Monde*, 21 January 2010.

29. Eric Besson, "Je n'ai pas fait le jeu du Front national," *Le Monde.fr*, 6 March 2010, http://www.lemonde.fr/cgi-bin/ACHATS/acheter.cgi?offre=ARCHIVES&type_item=ART_ARCH_30J&objet_id=1116883.

30. Didier Fassin, "La France a du mal à se confronter à sa réalité sociale," *Les Inrockuptibles*, no. 747 (24 March 2010), http://www.lesinrocks.com/actualite/actu-article/article/la-france-a-du-mal-a-se-confronter-a-sa-realite-sociale/.

31. Robert Lepage, "Théâtre des métamorphoses," interview by Jean-Louis Perrier, *Mouvement*, no. 45 (October–December 2007): 121.

Chapter 1. Border-crossings

1. Nigel Redden quoted in Robin Tabachnik, "Festival Arts," *PlaybillArts .com*, 1 April 2005, http://www.playbillarts.com/features/article/1657.html.

2. Ariane Mnouchkine, remarks at symposium "Does Art Matter?" Kaplan Penthouse, Lincoln Center for the Performing Arts, New York, 19 July 2005.

3. See Steve James, "France: Growing Desperation amongst Sangatte Refugees," *World Socialist Web Site*, 5 September 2001, http://www.wsws.org/articles/2001/sep2001/asyl-s05.shtml.

4. Mnouchkine, remarks at "Does Art Matter?"

5. Ariane Mnouchkine, *L'art du présent, entretiens avec Fabienne Pascaud* (Paris: Plon, 2005), 70.

6. See David Bradby, *Modern French Drama, 1940–1990*, 2nd ed. (Cambridge: Cambridge University Press, 1991), 95.

7. Joseph Loach, "Kinesis: The New Mimesis," *Theater* (New Haven, CT) 40, no. 1 (2010): 2.

8. Ariane's Russian-Jewish immigrant father was the versatile French movie producer Alexandre Mnouchkine, and she herself has directed several films, most notably her extraordinary *Molière* (1976). Mnouchkine's more recent stage piece, *Les naufragés du Fol Espoir (aurores)* (Shipwrecked of the Wild Hope [Dawnings], 2010), is in large part an extravagant celebration of early cinema.

9. Charles Isherwood, "Never Touching the Ground in a Constant Search for Refuge," *New York Times*, 19 July 2005.

10. Michael Feingold, "Ariane Mnouchkine Tells an Epic Story of Millions of Lives—But Does She Make Us Care?" *Village Voice*, 27 July–2 August 2005.

11. Mnouchkine, *L'art du présent*, 58.

12. Ibid., 64.

13. Nicolas Sarkozy in "Nicolas Sarkozy présente les axes de sa politique d'"immigration choisie,'" *Le Monde*, 11 July 2005.

14. Editorial, "Immigration choisie," *Le Monde*, 13 July 2005.

15. Sarkozy quoted in "M. Sarkozy veut expulser les imams 'radicaux,'" *Le Monde*, 17 July 2005.

16. Mnouchkine, *L'art du présent*, 60.

17. Robert Brustein, "Theatre of the Mushy Tushy," *New Republic*, 5 September 2005.

18. Mnouchkine, remarks at "Does Art Matter?"

19. See Mnouchkine, *L'art du présent*, 169.

20. Redden quoted in Jonathan Kalb, "Better Hope the Seats Are Comfortable," *New York Times*, 10 July 2005.

21. David Kornhaber, "Taking the Show on the Road: The 2005 Lincoln Center Festival," *New York Sun*, 12 July 2005.

22. Kalb, "Better Hope the Seats."

23. Margo Jefferson, "The Avant-Garde, Rarely Love at First Sight," *New York Times*, 8 July 2005.

24. Mnouchkine quoted in Jean-Louis Perrier, "A la Cartoucherie, les flux et les reflux de la misère des hommes," *Le Monde*, 16 January 2003.

25. John Rockwell, "Behind the Masks of a Moralist," *New York Times*, 27 September 1992.

26. Mnouchkine, *L'art du présent*, 77.

27. André Gide quoted in Michel del Castillo, *Sortie des artistes: de l'art à la culture, chronique d'une chute annoncée* (Paris: Le Seuil, 2004), 97.

28. Mnouchkine, *L'art du présent*, 78.

29. Charles Dullin quoted in del Castillo, *Sortie des artistes*, 102.

30. Mnouchkine, *L'art du présent*, 125.

31. Ibid., 82.

32. The principal reference is Hans-Thies Lehmann, *Postdramatic Theatre*, trans. Karen Jürs-Munby (London: Routledge, 2006). Three probing critiques of Lehmann's controversial study are Elinor Fuchs's book review in *TDR: The Drama Review* 52, no. 2 (Summer 2008): 178–82; Christophe Bident, "Et le théâtre devint postdramatique: histoire d'une illusion," *Théâtre/Public*, no. 194 (September 2009): 76–82; and Bernd Stegemann, "After Postdramatic Theater," trans. Matthew R. Price, *Theater* (New Haven, CT) 39, no. 3 (2009): 11–23.

33. Enzo Cormann, *A quoi sert le théâtre?* (Paris: Les Solitaires Intempestifs, 2003), 118.

34. Ibid., 12.

Chapter 2. Star Power, Gallic Style

1. See Simone de Beauvoir, *A Transatlantic Love Affair: Letters to Nelson Algren*, ed. Sylvie Le Bon de Beauvoir (New York: The New Press, 1998).

2. Fabrice Rozié, conversation with the author, New York City, 23 December 2005.

3. Marie-France Pisier, postperformance panel discussion, Florence Gould Hall, New York City, 2 October 2005.

4. See Rudi Chelminski, "Rad-Fem Marie-France Pisier Takes a (Heavy) Breather in *The Other Side of Midnight*," *People*, no. 25 (1977): 78.

5. Pisier, discussion at Florence Gould Hall, 2 October 2005.

6. Ibid.

7. See Colette Godard, *Patrice Chéreau: un trajet* (Paris: Rocher, 2007), 169.

8. Patrice Chéreau, *J'y arriverai un jour* (Arles: Actes Sud, 2009), 12, 59. Chéreau launched his public readings of *Les carnets du sous-sol* (*Notes from Underground*) at the Barcelona Festival in 2001 and performed the piece in numerous other European cities before bringing it to Peter Brook's Théâtre des Bouffes du Nord in Paris in spring 2005. He has since done dramatic readings of works by Bruno Schulz, Hervé Guibert, Marguerite Duras, and Pierre Guyotat, as well as of the Grand Inquisitor section of Dostoyevsky's *Brothers Karamazov* (1879–1880).

9. In a slightly modified mise-en-scène, this production of *4.48 psychose* with Isabelle Huppert premiered in October 2002 at the Théâtre des Bouffes du Nord in Paris; it then toured to other cities in France, Switzerland, Portugal, and Brazil; finally, it played in Los Angeles and New York.

10. Hans-Thies Lehmann, preface to the English edition, *Postdramatic Theatre*, trans. Karen Jürs-Munby (London: Routledge, 2006), ix.

11. See, for example, *New York Times*, arts section advertisement, 21 October 2005.

12. A.G., "People Are Talking About/Theatre: Heart of Darkness," *Vogue*, October 2005.

13. Jesse McKinley, "Sending a Warning on an Unusual Play (Pack Your Pocket Larousse?)," *New York Times*, 8 October 2005.

14. James V. Melillo, letter to *4.48 psychose* ticket buyers, 20 September 2005.

15. Susan Sontag in presentation at the French Institute/Alliance Française's Trophée des Arts Gala honoring Isabelle Huppert, New York City, 5 November 2003; a version of Sontag's text is included in Ronald Chammah

and Jeanne Fouchet, eds., *Isabelle Huppert: Woman of Many Faces* (New York: Harry N. Abrams, 2005), 41–43.

16. Sarah Kane, *4.48 Psychosis*, in *Complete Plays*, ed. David Greig (London: Methuen, 2001), 206–7.

17. Ibid., 207, 299, 242.

18. Ibid., 224–25.

19. Claude Régy, "BAMdialogue with Claude Régy," BAM Rose Cinemas, Brooklyn, NY, 26 October 2005.

20. Charles Isherwood, "Existentialist Musings, Clinically Pondered in French," *New York Times*, 21 October 2005.

21. Adam Feldman, "4.48 Psychose," *Time Out New York*, 27 October 2005.

22. Frank Scheck, "Lost in Lack of Translation," *New York Post* online, 28 October 2005, http://www.nypost.com/.

23. Régy, "BAMdialogue."

24. Régy in *Claude Régy, le passeur*, directed by Elisabeth Coronel and Arnaud de Mesamat, produced by ABACARIS Films and La SEPT-ARTE, 1997; screened at Bruno Walter Auditorium, Lincoln Center for the Performing Arts, New York City, 10 December 2005.

25. Régy quoted in Jean Chollet, "Claude Régy, militant de l'obscur," *Théâtre d'aujourd'hui*, no. 10 (2005), 182.

26. David Bradby and Annie Sparks, *Mise en Scène: French Theatre Now* (London: Methuen, 1997), 40.

Chapter 3. Three Fresh Voices

1. Frédéric Martel, *Theater: sur le déclin du théâtre en Amérique (et comment il peut résister en France)* (Paris: La Découverte, 2006), 225–26.

2. Koffi Kwahulé, *Misterioso-119/Blue-S-cat* (Paris: Editions Théâtrales, 2005).

3. Judith G. Miller, "Thinking about Theater within World Literature in French," *Contemporary French and Francophone Studies* 14, no. 1 (January 2010): 45.

4. The collection of seven Kwahulé plays, with an introduction by Judith G. Miller, is forthcoming from Indiana University Press.

5. Koffi Kwahulé in roundtable discussion, "Francophone African and Caribbean Playwrights," Symposium on Francophone Theatre, La Maison Française, New York University, 28 October 2005.

6. Koffi Kwahulé, public remarks following reading/performance of *Misterioso-119* at the New York Theatre Workshop, 24 October 2005.

7. See "Pour une 'littérature-monde' en français," *Le Monde*, 3 March 2007; and Michel Le Bris and Jean Rouaud, eds., *Pour une littérature-monde* (Paris: Gallimard, 2007).

8. See Sylvie Chalaye, *Afrique noire et dramaturgies contemporaines: le syndrome Frankenstein* (Paris: Editions Théâtrales, 2004).

9. Koffi Kwahulé at Lark Play Development Center, 27 October 2005.

10. Koffi Kwahulé quoted in Gilles Mouëllic, "Koffi Kwahulé Jazzman," introduction to Kwahulé, *Misterioso-119*, 5.

11. Judith G. Miller in public discussion of Francophone theatre following the Lark Center reading/performance of Kwahulé's *Misterioso-119*, 27 October 2005.

12. Sylvie Chalaye, "Contemporary Dramaturgies of the Black Francophone World: The Detours of Orality," lecture at Symposium on Francophone Theatre, La Maison Française, New York University, 28 October 2005.

13. Miller, "Thinking about Theater," 42.

14. See editorial, "Chirac l'historien," *Le Monde*, 31 January 2006.

15. Jacques Chirac, quoted ibid.

16. Craig Smith, "France Has an Underclass, But Its Roots Are Still Shallow," *New York Times*, 6 November 2005.

17. Since the beginning of the Third Republic, the French census process does not allow for the collection of religious or ethnic data. Estimates suggest that within a total current population of over sixty million, there are about six million persons of Muslim descent living in France, and that ten million inhabitants fall into the category of ethnic minorities, which include Muslim North Africans, Muslim Turks and Near Easterners, Muslim black Africans, and Christian black West Indians, Africans, and Reunioners. It is estimated that 35 percent of all French inhabitants under the age of twenty and 50 percent of all inhabitants in and around the major urban centers belong to ethnic minorities. The jobless rate among French Arabs and French Africans is as high as 30 percent in some neighborhoods, triple the national average; see Smith, ibid. According to the report of a 2007 Pew Research Center study of Muslims born in France, "forty-six percent define themselves firstly by their religion, while forty-two percent declare themselves, above all, to be French"; see Cécilia Gabizon, "Les musulmans restent très attachés aux rites collectifs," *France-Amérique*, 20 January 2007. Yet other polls show that "French Muslims overwhelmingly endorse Republican values"; see Henri Astier, "France's *banlieues*: Year of the Locust," *openDemocracy*, 8 November 2006, http://www.opendemocracy.net/democracy-protest/france_riots_4074 .jsp. French researchers and policy makers have only recently begun to debate seriously the uses of ethnic and so-called racial statistics; see the special issue of *French Politics, Culture, and Society* 26, no. 1 (Spring 2008).

18. Koffi Kwahulé, *Jaz* (Paris: Editions Théâtrales, 1998), 65; my translation here and elsewhere.

19. Koffi Kwahulé, "Eloge de l'hérésie," interview by Sylvie Chalaye in Chalaye, *Afrique noire*, 41.

20. Chalaye, "Contemporary Dramaturgies."

21. Sylvie Chalaye, "Des dramaturgies qui ont du corps ou la musicale culbute de la langue," *Revue des littératures du Sud* 51 (July–September 2003): 7.

22. Marie NDiaye, interview by Catherine Argand, *Lire*, April 2001.

23. Marie NDiaye quoted in press release by the Studio Theater, Washington, DC, where *Hilda* had its East Coast premiere, 5–23 October 2005.

24. Frédéric Ferney, "L'ogre et la servante," *Le Figaro*, 9 February 2002.

25. The day before the play's New York opening at 59E59 Theaters, another production—directed in French by Guila-Clara Kessous at Manhattan's United Nations International School—accentuated the play's supposed "racial tension" (Kessous's words) by casting black Haitian actors in the roles of Franck and Corinne (Hilda's sister); Kessous, who is white-skinned, portrayed the manipulative employer. NDiaye reportedly "gave her blessing" to this one-night undertaking. But Kessous concedes that the playwright declined to make any statement about the actors' or the characters' skin tones: "She told me she was content with having written the play and that it now had to lead a life of its own"; Maeva Bambuck, "*Hilda*: un autre regard et une pièce à débat," *France-Amérique*, on page 35 of production dossier provided by Kessous in e-mail correspondence with the author, 14 August 2010. I saw Kessous's version when it was reprised, with similar casting, as part of the Avignon "Off" festival the following summer (2006). Well-intentioned and often entertaining, Kessous's experiment came off, I thought, as a bit heavyhanded in its insistence on a white-black dichotomy.

26. See Marie NDiaye, *Hilda* (Paris: Editions de Minuit, 1999), 34. Erika Rundle's American-language script, used in the 59E59 production, omits the first sentence of this telling piece of dialogue; Rundle's rendition of the play has been published in *PAJ: A Journal of Performance and Art* 28, no. 1 (2005): 32–104.

27. NDiaye, *Hilda*, 63–64 (French edition).

28. Marie NDiaye, *Papa doit manger* (Paris: Editions de Minuit, 2003), 11. I quote the English translation of these lines as found in Liesl Yamaguchi, "Marie NDiaye: Translating the Surface," *Columbia Journal of Literary Criticism* 4 (2006): 43.

29. See Marie NDiaye, "Les soeurs," preface to Pap Ndiaye, *La condition noire, essai sur une minorité française* (Paris: Calmann Lévy, 2008), 11–18.

30. Marie NDiaye quoted in Nelly Kaprièlian, "Marie NDiaye aux prises avec le monde," *Les Inrockuptibles*, no. 716 (18 August 2009): 32.

31. See "Affaire NDiaye: Eric Raoult nuance ses propos," *Le Monde*, 12 November 2009.

32. See Nelly Kaprièlian, "Marie NDiaye: je persiste et signe!" *Les inRocks* .*com*, 11 November 2009, http://www.lesinrocks.com/actualite/actu-article/ t/1257963000/article/marie-ndiaye-je-persiste-et-signe/.

33. Nelly Kaprièlian, review of Marie NDiaye's *Papa doit manger*, *Les Inrockuptibles*, no. 376 (12 February 2003).

34. José Pliya, "Inventer sa langue," interview by Sylvie Chalaye in Chalaye, *Afrique noire*, 91.

35. Jean-Michel Ribes, "Entretien," interview by Sylvie Chalaye in Chalaye, *Nouvelles dramaturgies d'Afrique noire francophone* (Rennes: Presses de l'Université de Rennes, 2004), 121.

36. Pliya, "Inventer sa langue," 94.

37. Ibid., 91.

38. See Judith G. Miller, "Dramaturgies des errances: le cas de José Pliya," in Chalaye, *Nouvelles dramaturgies*, 32.

39. José Pliya, remarks to audience following the performance of *Trapped* (*Le complexe de Thénardier*), Ohio Theatre, New York, 6 November 2005.

40. Ibid.

41. Ribes's Théâtre du Rond-Point production, filmed in December 2002, is available on commercial DVD in the Collection COPAT [Coopérative de Production Audiovisuelle Théâtrale] (Paris: Sopat, 2004).

42. Ribes, "Entretien," 123.

43. Pliya, "Inventer sa langue," 94.

44. See Pliya's remarks at "Une famille ordinaire," *Theatreonline.com*, http://www.theatreonline.com/guide/detail_piece.asp?i_Region=&i_Pro grammation=12571&i_Genre=&I_Origine=&I_Type=.

45. Pliya, "Inventer sa langue," 94.

46. See Hannah Arendt, *Eichmann in Jerusalem: A Report on the Banality of Evil* (New York: Viking, 1963), and Daniel Goldhagen, *Hitler's Willing Executioners* (New York: Knopf, 1996).

47. José Pliya quoted in Véronique Hotte, "La reconnaissance parisienne d'une écriture universelle," *La Terrasse*, no. 134 (January 2006): 10.

48. José Pliya, program note for his *Une famille ordinaire*, Théâtre de la Tempête, Cartoucherie de Vincennes, Paris, directed by Isabelle Ronayette, 13 January–12 February 2006.

49. José Pliya, conversation with the author, New York City, 5 November 2006.

50. José Pliya, *Les Effracteurs/Nous étions assis sur le rivage du monde . . .* (Paris: L'Avant-Scène Théâtre/Collection des Quatre-Vents, 2004), 104.

51. For The Woman's final lines, I quote from *We Were Sitting on the Shores of the World . . .* , trans. Philippa Wehle with the help of Ellen Lampert-Gréaux,

in *Act French: Contemporary Plays from France*, ed. Philippa Wehle (New York: PAJ Publications, 2007), 37.

52. José Pliya quoted in Thomas Hahn, "Banlieue, rivage du monde," *Cassandre*, no. 65 (Spring 2006): 29.

53. Jules Michelet quoted in Jean-Claude Wallach, *La culture, pour qui? essai sur les limites de la démocratisation culturelle* (Paris: Editions de l'Attribut, 2006), 35.

54. Ibid., 62.

55. Ibid., 82.

56. Patrick Sommier quoted in Fabienne Arvers, "MC93: on ne joue plus," *Les Inrockuptibles*, no. 672 (14 October 2008): 10.

57. See Magali Jauffret, "A-t-on besoin de culture pour vivre en banlieue?" *L'Humanité*, 11 March 2006; and Antoine de Baecque, Mathilde La Bardonnie, and René Solis, "Contre l'apartheid culturel," *Libération*, 5 January 2006.

58. Guy Bénisty quoted in "Actes du 1er atelier Arcadi-*Cassandre*/Horschamp," *Cassandre* 65 (Spring 2006): 46.

59. Valérie de Saint-Do and Nicolas Roméas, "Présumés 'sensibles,'" *Cassandre* 65 (Spring 2006): 5.

60. Wallach, *La culture, pour qui?* 107.

61. See editorial, "Ghettos français," *Le Monde*, 1 December 2009.

62. Ibid.

Chapter 4. From Dialogue to *Parole*

1. Valère Novarina, *Le théâtre des paroles* (Paris: P.O.L., 1989). In choosing the term 'theatre of *la parole*' to refer to this tendency of current French theatre, I am selecting a rubric that does not yet have wide currency among its practitioners and commentators. But the phrase has been used, typically without special emphasis or systematization, by numerous scholars who work on this brand of theatre. See, for instance, Florence March, *Ludovic Lagarde: un théâtre pour quoi faire* (Besançon: Les Solitaires Intempestifs, 2010), 132, and Jean-Pierre Ryngaert's entry "Personnage (crise du)," in Jean-Pierre Sarrazac, ed., *Poétique du drame moderne et contemporain, lexique d'une recherche*, a special issue of *Etudes Théâtrales* (Louvain-la-Neuve, Belgium), no. 22 (2001): 88. In their *Le personnage théâtral contemporain: décomposition, recomposition* (Montreuil-sous-Bois: Editions Théâtrales, 2006), Jean-Pierre Ryngaert and Julie Sermon use the phrase "*les théâtres de la parole-action*" (164), underscoring by the word '*action*' the performative rather than mimetic nature of such works, and by the plural '*les théâtres*' that these works do not belong to or constitute a particular "genre," but can be associated with many; these two scholars are also authors of the entry "Théâtres de la parole," in

Michel Corvin, ed., *Dictionnaire encyclopédique du théâtre à travers le monde*, 4th ed. (Paris: Bordas, 2008), 1036–37.

2. Novarina, *Le théâtre des paroles*, 163. I am using Leslie Wickes's English translations as found in Josette Féral, "Moving Across Languages," *Yale French Studies*, no. 112 (2007): 50–68.

3. Novarina, *Le théâtre des paroles*, 72.

4. See Tom Bishop, "Whatever Happened to the Avant-Garde?" *Yale French Studies*, no. 112 (2007): 9–10.

5. Laurence Mayor quoted in Alain Berset, ed., *Valère Novarina, théâtres du verbe, l'offrande imprévisible* (Paris: José Corti, 2001), 241–42.

6. Jean-Pierre Ryngaert, "Speech in Tatters: The Interplay of Voices in Recent Dramatic Writing," *Yale French Studies*, no. 112 (2007): 18, 25.

7. Antonin Artaud, *The Theater and Its Double*, trans. Mary Caroline Richards (New York: Grove, 1994).

8. See Roland Barthes, "Le bruissement de la langue," in *Le bruissement de la langue* (Paris: Seuil, 1984); the English-language translation is by Richard Howard, *The Rustle of Language* (Berkeley: University of California Press, 1989).

9. Olivier Py, *Epître aux jeunes acteurs pour que soit rendue la Parole à la parole* (Arles: Actes Sud-Papiers, 2000), 33–34.

10. Valère Novarina, *Lettre aux acteurs* (Paris: L'Energumène, 1979), 95.

11. Clare Finburgh, "*Voix/Voie/Vie*: The Voice in Contemporary French Theater," *Yale French Studies*, no. 112 (2007): 100–101.

12. Olivier Cadiot, *Colonel Zoo*, trans. Cole Swensen (Copenhagen: Green Integer, 2006), 142. The New York production used Swensen's translation for its supertitling.

13. Olivier Cadiot, *Le Colonel des Zouaves* (Paris: P.O.L., 1997), 121, 167.

14. Ibid., 32, 168.

15. Olivier Cadiot, interview by Nelly Kaprièlian, *Les Inrockuptibles*, no. 321 (15 January 2002).

16. Ibid.

17. Nicolas Truong, "Entretien avec Olivier Cadiot et Ludovic Lagarde," press materials for the 2004 Avignon Festival; this interview is reprinted by *theatre-contemporain.net*, http://www.theatre-contemporain.net/spectacles/Le-Colonel-des-zouaves/ensavoirplus/idcontent/4876.

18. Ludovic Lagarde quoted in March, *Ludovic Lagarde*, 20.

19. Olivier Cadiot in Eric Mangion, "Olivier Cadiot, recherche d'une voix," *Mouvement*, no. 43 (April–June 2007): 148.

20. Lagarde quoted in March, *Ludovic Lagarde*, 137.

21. Olivier Cadiot, *Fairy queen* (Paris: P.O.L., 2002), 47; my translation here

and elsewhere. English supertitles for the New York production were by Cole Swensen.

22. Ibid., 18.

23. Ibid., 62.

24. Ibid., 66.

25. The Avignon Festival chose Cadiot as one of the two *artistes associés* (the other was Christoph Marthaler) for its 2010 edition. Among Cadiot's offerings were a nine-character adaptation of his novel *Un nid pour quoi faire* (A Nest What For? 2007) and a new solo piece for Laurent Poitrenaux, *Un mage en été* (A Summer Sorcerer), both directed by Ludovic Lagarde.

26. Marion Schoevaert, conversation with the author, New York City, 1 December 2005. Schoevaert had already mounted two very different English-language versions of this text: *Colonel of Fools*, at the Ohio Theatre, New York City, in July 2000, and *The Unknown Guest*, part of the HERE/American Living Room Festival, New York City, in June 2001. Schoevaert described the first version as having "a single character, lots of props, and substantial video work by Irina Patkania" and the second as being "close in feel and concept to Lagarde's rendition"; both earlier renditions featured the actor Steven Rattazzi.

27. Ibid.

28. Ibid.

29. Theatre listing, "*A.W.O.L.*," *New Yorker*, 28 November 2005, 34.

30. Adam Klasfeld, "*A.W.O.L.*," *TheaterMania.com*, 14 November 2005, http://www.theatermania.com/off-broadway/news/11-2005/awol_7099.html.

31. Helen Shaw, "*A.W.O.L.*," *Time Out New York*, 17 November 2005.

32. Matt Freeman, "*A.W.O.L.*," *nytheatre.com*, 22 November 2005, http://www.nytheatre.com/.

33. See Valère Novarina, *Le babil des classes dangereuses*, in *Théâtre* (Paris: P.O.L., 1989); *Le monologue d'Adramélech* appears on pages 239 to 254.

34. Valère Novarina, *Adramelech's Monologue*, trans. Guy Bennett (Los Angeles: Seeing Eye Books, 2004).

35. Ibid., 7.

Chapter 5. Edgy and Cool

1. All quotations in this paragraph are from Philippe Quesne, conversation with the author, Paris, 23 February 2006.

2. In his film *Le testament d'Orphée* (1960), when asked to define cinema, Cocteau, in the role of The Poet, says: "A film revives dead acts"; see James S. Williams, *Jean Cocteau* (Manchester, UK: Manchester University Press, 2006), especially 17 and 161.

3. The phrase "outside of death" comes from Hans-Thies Lehmann, *Postdramatic Theatre*, trans. Karen Jürs-Munby (London: Routledge, 2006), 167. See also Vivian Sobchack, "The Scene of the Screen: Envisioning Cinematic and Electronic 'Presence,'" in *Film and Theory: An Anthology*, ed. Robert Stam and Toby Miller (Malden, MA: Blackwell, 2000), 67–84.

4. Lehmann, *Postdramatic Theatre*, 171.

5. Philippe Quesne in "Flight Paths," interview and translation by Tom Sellar, *Theater* (New Haven, CT) 37, no. 1 (2007): 42.

6. The impact on theatre of these two "technological frames" is elaborated throughout Chris Salter, *Entangled: Technology and the Transformation of Performance* (Cambridge, MA: MIT Press, 2010). Salter's initial evocation of this temporal mapping occurs in his preface (xv).

7. Philip Auslander, *Liveness: Performance in a Mediatized Culture*, 2nd ed. (London: Routledge, 2008), 43.

8. Salter, *Entangled*, 136.

9. Auslander, *Liveness*, 43.

10. See, for example, François Frimat, "Les sorciers de la déconstruction," *Droit de cités*, no. 3 (May 2007): 3.

11. Helen Shaw, "Not Quite Fluent French," *New York Sun*, 4 November 2005.

12. Anonymous members of Superamas, conversation with the author, Avignon, 20 July 2007. Because of their belief that notions of "authorship," "originality," and "the personalities" of those making up the collective are of no relevance to a consideration of their work, the half-dozen core members of Superamas studiously refrain from revealing their individual names.

13. Rudi Laermans, "Art versus Mass Culture, Episode 4579945 (a [Culture Sociological] Fragment on the Work of Superamas)," http://www.superamas .com/pagesTexts/texts.html.

14. Superamas quoted in Peter T'Jonck, "Montage and Research versus Faith and Demagogy: French-Austrian Group Makes Contaminated Theater with 'Big 2,'" *De Tijd* (Utrecht), 18 June 2004.

15. Artistic director Caden Manson, dialogue writer and sound designer Jemma Nelson, and other members of Big Art Group presented a "hyperlecture" titled "This Is the Show" for ACT FRENCH's Carte Blanche: French-American Theatre Dialogue Series at the Martin E. Segal Theatre, CUNY/ Graduate Center, New York, on 28 November 2005. They discussed and illustrated their technologically ingenious *Real-Time Film Trilogy: Shelf Life* (2001), *Flicker* (2002), and *House of No More* (2004)—which combines live video layering, green screen technology, split-second choreographed movement, and dense sound design with live performers; *House of No More* was about to en-

joy a New York reprise (after its debut at Performance Space 122, followed by a European tour) at Dance Theater Workshop, where it ran from 14 to 22 December 2005. For commentary on the contrasting use of filmic conventions in the stage work of Big Art Group and Superamas, see Jeroen Versteele, "Performance and Cognitive Narratology," *Image [&] Narrative*, no. 9 (October 2004), http://www.imageandnarrative.be/inarchive/performance/versteele .htm.

16. Jonathan Kalb, "Who Are We? Where Are We? What Are We Doing? You Decide," *New York Times*, 8 November 2005.

17. David Cote, ". . . *She Said*," *Time Out New York*, 10 November 2005.

18. Erika Latta in "He Said . . . SHE SAID: WaxFactory Reconstructs Duras," interview by Jason Grote with Erika Latta, Ivan Talijancic, and Simona Semencic (the troupe's executive producer and production dramaturg), *The Brooklyn Rail: Critical Perspectives on Arts, Politics, and Culture*, November 2005, http://www.brooklynrail.org/2005/11/theater/he-said-she-said-waxfactory-reconstructs.

19. Ivan Talijancic, conversation with the author, New York City, 16 December 2005.

20. In the opening essay of their edited collection *Intermediality in Theatre and Performance* (Amsterdam: Rodopi, 2006), Fred Chapple and Chiel Kattenbelt describe the intermedial as "a space where the boundaries soften—and we are in-between and within a mixing of spaces, media and realities" (12). They also note: "Although at first sight intermediality might appear to be a technologically driven phenomenon it actually operates, at times, without any technology being present. Intermediality is about change in theatre practice and thus about changing perceptions of performance, which become visible through the process of staging" (12). This understanding applies fairly closely to Rambert's piece.

21. Pascal Rambert, postface, *Paradis (un temps à déplier)* (Besançon: Les Solitaires Intempestifs, 2004), 72.

22. I quote here and elsewhere from the unpublished English-language script (minus stage directions) titled *Paradise (a time to unfold) (sic)*, as translated by Kate Moran and performed at Dance Theater Workshop; 8 in script; 26 in Rambert, *Paradis (un temps à déplier)*. Except for question marks, Rambert's creative writings are almost always devoid of punctuation.

23. Ibid., 7; 22–23.

24. Ibid., 31; 67.

25. Rambert, postperformance discussion with audience of *Paradis (unfolding time)*, Dance Theater Workshop, 7 December 2005.

26. See Laurent Goumarre, *Rambert en temps réel* (Besançon: Les Soli-

taires Intempestifs, 2005), passim. This is a book-length transcript of Goumarre's interviews with Rambert about his life and his art.

27. Ibid., 75.

28. Ibid., 85–86.

29. At the Théâtre2Gennevilliers in April 2009, Rambert presented *Libido Sciendi*, a dance piece for two performers, Ikue Nakagawa and Lorenzo de Angelis, in which physical lovemaking—including nonsimulated fellatio and vaginal penetration—was the sole content. The piece had earlier been done in Paris at the Ménagerie de Verre's Festival Les Inaccoutumés in late 2006. In a 2010 interview with *Théâtral Magazine*, Rambert signaled his intention to reprise the work, this time with two player-dancers in their sixties.

30. Goumarre, *Rambert*, 62.

31. James Thiérrée, "Le mot de l'auteur," in "Dossier pédagogique: *La Veillée des Abysses*," Le Théâtre/Scène Nationale de Narbonne, http://www.letheatrenarbonne.com/saisons/04-05/dossierspedagogiques/laveilleedesabysses.htm.

32. James Thiérrée in David Adams, "Circus inspires leading stage shows," *icWales: The National Website of Wales*, 28 October 2005, http://icwales.icnetwork.co.uk/0900entertainment/0050artsnews/tm_objectid=16305372&method=full&siteid=50082&headline=circus-inspires-leading-stage-shows-name_page.html.

33. In *Raoul*, his solo piece that ran at the Théâtre de la Ville in late 2009 and early 2010, Thiérrée reportedly staged a dialogue between "his own image and its troubling resemblance to that of his grandfather"; see Patrick Sourd, "Dans la tête de James Thiérrée," *Les Inrockuptibles*, no. 763 (16 December 2009): 84.

Chapter 6. Great Classics Revisited

1. I calculated these figures from the listings in the 8–14 February 2006 issue of *Pariscope*, a weekly guide to the city's cultural offerings available for purchase at Parisian newsstands.

2. In 2008 the Théâtre National de Chaillot became redeployed as a house primarily for dance, not theatre, but it continues to program theatre events. For figures on various categories of public theatres, see "Organismes du secteur théâtral," appendix to Emmanuel Wallon, "Le théâtre en quête de repères," *Esprit*, no. 335 (June 2007): 126–47; Chantal Lacroix, ed., *Chiffres clés 2009: statistiques de la culture* (Paris: La Documentation Française, 2009), 126–31; the website of the Réunion des Opéras de France, http://www.rof.fr/; and Emmanuel Wallon, "Le spectacle vivant en chiffres (2010)," in *Politiques et pratiques culturelles*, collection "Les notices," ed. Philippe Poirrier (Paris: La Documentation Française, 2010), 128–35.

3. See Lacroix, *Chiffres clés 2009*, 126–31.

4. See Yves Pérennou, "Des réformes en vue à moyens constants," *La Lettre du Spectacle*, no. 237 (9 October 2009): 1; and Yves Pérennou, "Mairie de Paris: un budget culturel stable mais des lieux en déficit," *La Lettre du Spectacle*, no. 246 (19 February 2010): 1–2.

5. See Robin Pogrebin, "Broadway Producer Chosen to Lead Arts Endowment," *New York Times*, 13 May 2009; and Robin Pogrebin, "Congress Approves Budget Increase for Arts and Humanities Endowments," *ArtsBeat* blog, 30 October 2009, http://artsbeat.blogs.nytimes.com/2009/10/30/congress-approves-budget-increase.

6. The series of films to date includes Pierre Corneille's *L'illusion comique*, directed by Mathieu Amalric; Paul Claudel's *Partage de midi*, directed by Claude Mouriéas; and Jean-Luc Lagarce's *Juste la fin du monde*, directed by Olivier Ducastel and Jacques Martineau. See Olivier Joyard, "Amalric, cinéaste pressé," *Les Inrockuptibles*, no. 752 (28 April 2010): 12.

7. Louis Aragon, "An Open Letter to André Breton on Robert Wilson's *Deafman Glance*," *Performing Arts Journal* 1, no. 1 (1976): 40.

8. A PAL-format DVD of Wilson's *Les fables de La Fontaine*, filmed by Don Kent, was released in 2007 by Editions Montparnasse, "Collection Comédie-Française." Shot in July 2005, this version exhibits slight differences in mise-en-scène from the live performance I saw in January 2006.

9. For example, see Jean-Pierre Léonardini, "Quand la grenouille s'éclate," *L'Humanité*, 27 December 2005.

10. See, for instance, Elinor Fuchs, *The Death of Character: Perspectives on Theater after Modernism* (Indianapolis: Indiana University Press, 1996), 107; also, Hans-Thies Lehmann, *Postdramatic Theatre*, trans. Karen Jürs-Munby (London: Routledge, 2006), 77–81.

11. Christine Fersen, conversation with the author, Paris, 18 April 2006.

12. See Ariane Bavelier, "Les mécènes s'invitent au spectacle," *Le Figaroscope*, 5 April 2006, 4–6. In the wake of the recent global financial crisis, French corporate sponsorship of culture declined to 380 million euros in 2010, as compared with 975 million euros in 2008. See Y.P., "Mauvais temps pour le mécénat culturel," *La Lettre du Spectacle*, no. 260 (22 October 2010): 6.

13. See Clarisse Fabre, "Le ministère de la culture veut développer le CDD de longue durée dans le spectacle," *Le Monde*, 18 October 2004. In the United States, the National Endowment for the Arts in 2008 granted a total of $72 million to all the creative arts combined, with another $48 million sent to state arts councils to make their own allocations; see Daniel J. Wakin, "National Endowment Salutes Opera," *New York Times*, 5 April 2008.

14. The figures in this paragraph come from summary documents included in a house-generated public relations folder, "La Comédie-Française,

saison 2005–2006, une troupe, trois théâtres." I am grateful to Isabelle Baragan for access to this material.

15. See Clarisse Fabre, "'RDDV,' ministre des transitions culturelles," *Le Monde*, 26 March 2006.

16. See Michel Guerrin and Emmanuel de Roux, "La planète culturelle bouleversée," *Le Monde*, 7 January 2006.

17. See Wallon, "Le spectacle vivant," 133.

18. Emmanuel Wallon, "L'ami des arts: absolument moderne ou résolument modeste?" in *Culture publique*, opus 3, *L'art de gouverner la culture* (Paris: Skite/Sens & Tonka, 2005).

19. Nicolas Sarkozy quoted in Clarisse Fabre, "La feuille de route de l'Elysée à Christine Albanel inquiète les professionnels de la culture," *Le Monde*, 12 September 2007.

20. François Le Pillouër quoted in Fabre, "La feuille de route."

21. Françoise Benhamou quoted in Fabre, "La feuille de route."

22. Marc Fumaroli, "The State, Culture, and 'L'Esprit,'" *SubStance* (Madison, WI), nos. 76–77 (1995): 132.

23. Jean-Marie Domenach, *Le crépuscule de la culture française?* (Paris: Plon, 1995), 200.

24. See Clarisse Fabre, "Budget culture: une hausse inattendue de 2.6% pour 2009," *Le Monde.fr*, 27 September 2008, http://www.lemonde.fr/.

25. Jean-Marie Bigard quoted in "Jean-Marie Bigard demande 'pardon' pour ses propos sur le 11-Septembre," *Le Monde.fr*, 8 September 2008, http://www.lemonde.fr/.

26. See, for example, Coline Serreau, "*L'école des femmes*: pièce subversive sur la fin d'un système," interview by Agnès Santi, *La Terrasse*, no. 176 (1 March 2006): 8.

27. Coline Serreau quoted in Marion Thébaud, "Coline Serreau et Molière le subversif," *Le Figaro*, 10 March 2006.

28. For example, Fabienne Pascaud, "L'Ecole des femmes," *Télérama*, no. 2932 (22 March 2006).

29. See Giovanni Macchia, "Un personnage non réalisé: conversation imaginaire avec la fille de Molière," chap. 3 of Giovanni Macchia, *Le silence de Molière*, trans. Jean-Paul Manganaro and Camille Dumoulié (Paris: Editions Desjonquères, 2004), 107–50; originally published as *Il silenzio di Molière* (Milan: Arnoldo Mondadori Editore, 1985).

30. Arthur Nauzyciel, conversation with the author, Saint-Brieuc, 14 February 2006.

31. Anne Delbée, "Propos recueillis par Jean-Pierre Jourdain, secrétaire général de la Comédie-Française, Février 2006," program notes for

her production of Paul Claudel's *Tête d'or*, Théâtre du Vieux-Colombier, 29 March–14 May 2006.

32. Bernard Thomas, "Tête d'or (Pompeux funèbre)," *Le Canard Enchaîné*, 12 April 2006.

33. Fabienne Darge, "Anne Delbée fait dériver Claudel jusqu'à la caricature," *Le Monde*, 7 April 2006.

34. Jean-Louis Pinte, "Claudel crucifié," *Le Figaroscope*, 12 April 2006.

35. Anne Delbée, conversation with the author, Paris, 31 July 2006.

36. Michel Corvin, "Cinquante ans de théâtre francophone mis en perspective dans l'avant et l'ailleurs du siècle," in vol. 3 of *Anthologie des auteurs dramatiques de langue française, de Godot à Zucco*, ed. Michel Azama (Paris: Editions Théâtrales, 2005), 300. Cocteau spoke of substituting a *"poésie* de *théâtre"* ("theatre poetry") for *"la poésie* au *théâtre"* ("poetry at the theatre") in his preface to *Les mariés de la tour Eiffel* (1921, my emphasis); see Corvin, "Cinquante ans," 294.

37. The only dissenters I identified were Fabienne Pascaud, "Pif gadgets," *Télérama*, no. 2944 (14 June 2006), and Armelle Héliot, "La tentation de l'opéra," *Le Figaro*, 8 June 2006.

38. Jean-Marie Apostolidès, *Cyrano, qui fut tout et qui ne fut rien* (Brussels: Les Impressions Nouvelles, 2006), 143.

39. Act 5, scene 5, line 2467; my translation from the French, *"Non, non, mon cher amour, je ne vous aimais pas!"*

Chapter 7. Boulevard, Experimental, and In-between

1. See Nathaniel Herzberg, "Le sacrifice des colonnes Morris," *Le Monde*, 19 January 2006.

2. Michel Corvin, "Boulevard (le théâtre de)," in Michel Corvin, ed., *Dictionnaire encyclopédique du théâtre à travers le monde*, 4th ed. (Paris: Bordas, 2008), 208.

3. Louise Doutreligne, public remarks at panel discussion, "Quels auteurs vivants pour quel(s) théâtre(s)?" Maison Jean Vilar, Avignon, 9 July 2010.

4. See table "Evolution de la fréquentation théâtrale à Paris," *La Lettre du Spectacle*, no. 253 (28 May 2010): 4.

5. *Moins 2* has been published in *L'Avant-Scène Théâtre*, no. 1188 (1 September 2005).

6. Laurent Baffie in H.C., "'Faire du théâtre pour les gens qui ont peur d'aller au théâtre,'" *Théâtral Magazine*, no. 10 (December 2006–January 2007): 41.

7. Odile Quirot, "La crise du théâtre est sans précédent: dramatique naufrage," *Le Nouvel Observateur*, no. 2112 (28 April 2005).

8. See "Paris: un label commun à certains théâtres privés," *La Lettre du Spectacle* (5 March 2010).

9. See Agence France-Presse, "Fréquentation stable dans les théâtres privés," *Le Monde*, 12 January 2007.

10. Odile Quirot, interview by François Varlin, *Théâtral Magazine*, no. 15 (March–April 2008): 46–47.

11. See Philippe Delaroche, "Les 100 livres préférés des Français," *Lire*, October 2004.

12. Eric-Emmanuel Schmitt, *Ma vie avec Mozart: roman* (Paris: Albin Michel, 2005); the book includes a CD of sixteen musical excerpts keyed to the text.

13. Jean-Marie Besset, conversation with the author, Paris, 11 May 2006.

14. Ibid.

15. Jean-Marie Besset, *Rue de Babylone, suivi de Les Grecs* (Paris: Grasset, 2004), 100, my translation.

16. Philippe Tesson, "Le mari, la femme, et les amants," *Le Figaro Magazine*, 13 May 2006. A major dissenting voice was Fabienne Pascaud in *Télérama*, no. 2732 (24 May 2006), who found the play to be drenched in "misogyny," "unintended xenophobia," and "an exasperating, paradox-loving *bel esprit.*"

17. Besset, conversation with the author, Paris, 11 May 2006.

18. See "Théâtre: les écrivains aux manettes," *La Lettre du Spectacle* (5 February 2010).

19. See Bruno Tackels, "De Malraux à Khadafi," *Mouvement*, no. 54 (January–March 2010): 16.

20. Jean-Marie Besset quoted in Nathaniel Herzberg, "La bataille privé-public divise la 'famille' du théâtre," *Le Monde*, 26 November 2009.

21. See David Ng, "The Americanization of Yasmina Reza," *American Theatre* (January 2007): 32.

22. Charles Isherwood, "Undercard of Jabbers Replaces Punchers," *New York Times*, 10 December 2009.

23. Yasmina Reza quoted in Adam Gopnik, "Fly on the Wall," *New Yorker* (19 May 2008).

24. Yasmina Reza, interview with *Le Nouvel Observateur*, quoted in Elaine Sciolino, "Portrait of a President, Craving Power, Enthralls France," *New York Times*, 24 August 2007.

25. Ben Brantley, review of Yasmina Reza's *The Unexpected Man*, *New York Times*, 25 October 2000.

26. Denis Guénoun, *Avez-vous lu Reza? une invitation philosophique* (Paris: Albin Michel, 2005), 256.

27. Philippe Minyana quoted in Manuel Piolat Soleymat, "L'ordinaire des jours," *La Terrasse*, no. 156 (March 2008): 9.

28. Philippe Minyana, *Chambres; Inventaires; André* (Paris: Editions Théâtrales, 1998). Philippa Wehle's English-language translation of *Inventaires* appears in Philippa Wehle, ed., *Act French: Contemporary Plays from France* (New York: PAJ Publications, 2007): 127–48.

29. Michel Corvin, preface to Michel Corvin, ed., *Philippe Minyana ou la parole visible* (Paris: Editions Théâtrales, 2000), 5.

30. See Philippe Minyana, *La maison des morts: version scénique* (Paris: Editions Théâtrales, 2006); this revised version resulted, Minyana specifies, "from the rehearsal work" for the Vieux-Colombier production (13).

31. Philippe Minyana, "La Maison des morts," *Le Journal des Trois Théâtres*, no. 18 (January 2006): 16.

32. Minyana, *La maison des morts: version scénique*, 13.

33. Minyana, "La Maison des morts," 17.

34. Ibid.

35. See Julie Sermon, "Noelle Renaude," in Corvin, *Dictionnaire encyclopédique*, 1155.

36. Mary Noonan, "*L'art de l'écrit s'incarnant*: The Theater of Noëlle Renaude," *Yale French Studies*, no. 112 (2007): 125, 122.

37. Noëlle Renaude, *Par les routes* (Paris: Théâtre Ouvert/Enjeux, 2005); this edition includes a series of essays by current and former creative collaborators on issues of space specific to Renaude's works.

38. Ibid., 60.

39. Ibid., 101.

40. Joël Pommerat quoted in Gwénola David, "A l'intensité des seuils," *Mouvement*, no. 40 (July–September 2006): 84.

41. Ibid.

42. Fabienne Arvers, "Cet enfant," *Les Inrockuptibles*, no. 544 (2 May 2006).

43. Brigitte Salino, "'Cet enfant' invente une parole aux cités," *Le Monde*, 28 April 2006.

44. See Jean-Marc Adolphe, "Gisèle Vienne, différence et répétition," *Mouvement*, no. 41 (October–December 2006): 86.

45. Günter Berghaus, *Avant-Garde Performance: Live Events and Electronic Technologies* (New York: Palgrave Macmillan, 2005), 261.

46. Gisèle Vienne, conversation with the author, Avignon, 10 July 2010.

47. Ibid.

48. Armelle Héliot, "Egarements collectifs: *L'homme de février* de Gildas Milin à la Colline," *Le Figaro*, 5 May 2006.

49. Gildas Milin, essay dated February 2006 in press packet for *L'homme de*

février, 6; see http://www.theatre-contemporain.net/spectacles/LHomme-de-fevrier/ensavoirplus/.

50. Gildas Milin, *L'homme de février* (Arles: Actes Sud-Papiers, 2006), 58.

51. Berghaus, *Avant-Garde Performance*, 264.

52. As part of ACT FRENCH's Carte Blanche: French-American Theatre Dialogue Series, Sobel and Foreman, on 25 October 2005 at the Martin E. Segal Theatre, CUNY/Graduate Center, New York, reflected on their quarter century of collaboration and assessed the current state of alternative theatre in their respective countries.

53. See, for example, François Regnault, "Le Théâtre de Gennevilliers va-t-il perdre son fondateur?" *Le Monde*, 18 February 2006.

54. See David Bobée, Kate Moran, Gilles Groppo, Antonin Ménard, Alexandre Meyer, Grégory Guilbert, and Virginie Vaillant (members of Pascal Rambert's troupe), "Aux hurleurs d'Avignon," *mrmr*, no. 7 (2006): 143.

55. Ibid., 144. Laurent Goumarre, in "DégueuLASS," *mrmr*, no. 7 (2006): 150, identifies the actress in question as "Hervée Delafont [a misspelling of Hervée de Lafond], codirector of the Théâtre de l'Unité" (Audincourt).

56. Bobée et al., "Aux hurleurs," 144.

57. Fabienne Darge, "Des vidéos réussies, un spectacle raté," *Le Monde*, 19 July 2005.

58. Pascal Rambert quoted in Clyde Chabot, "Ecrire des mots, écrire sur un plateau," *Théâtre/Public*, no. 184 (2007): 27–28.

59. The other pieces were Jan Decorte's *Dieu et les esprits vivants*, Jacques Delcuvellerie's *Anathème*, Wim Vandekeybus's *Puur*, and Marina Abramovic's *The Biography Remix*; see Patrice Pavis, "Staging Calamity: Mise-en-Scène and Performance at Avignon 2005," *Theater* (New Haven, CT) 36, no. 3 (2006): 5–27.

60. Ibid., 24, 25, 26.

61. In French, *'deux'* (two) is a near homonym of *'de'* (of).

62. See, for example, Pascal Rambert, "Pascal Rambert, directeur du CDN de Gennevilliers," interview by Hélène Chevrier, *Théâtral Magazine*, no. 11 (March–April 2007): 40.

Chapter 8. Three Prodigious Artists

1. Valère Novarina, *L'espace furieux* (Paris: P.O.L., 2006), 167.

2. Valère Novarina, conversation with the author, Avignon, 19 July 2006.

3. Valère Novarina, *L'avant-dernier des hommes* (Paris: P.O.L., 1997), 13. Translations from this play are mine.

4. Ibid., 25.

5. Ibid., 51–52.

6. Novarina, conversation with the author, Avignon, 19 July 2006.

7. Valère Novarina, "L'homme hors de lui," interview by Jean-Marie Thomasseau, *Europe: Revue Littéraire Mensuelle*, nos. 880–81 (August–September 2002): 163.

8. See, for example, Allen S. Weiss, "In Praise of Solecism," introduction to Valère Novarina, *The Theater of the Ears*, ed. and trans. Allen S. Weiss (Los Angeles: Sun & Moon, 1996), 36–37.

9. See Fabienne Arvers, "Le théâtre à mains nues: Valère Novarina," *Les Inrockuptibles*, no. 530 (25–31 January 2006): 8.

10. Novarina, conversation with the author, Avignon, 19 July 2006.

11. Valère Novarina, public remarks at the Lavoir Moderne Parisien, 15 February 2006.

12. For a full listing, see http://www.novarina.com. The main American/English translations are by Guy Bennett, *Adramelech's Monologue* (Los Angeles: Seeing Eye Books, 2004), reprinted in *Act French: Contemporary Plays from France*, ed. Philippa Wehle (New York: PAJ Publications, 2007): 93–104; and by Allen S. Weiss, in Novarina, *Theater of the Ears*; translations of Novarina by Weiss that have appeared in journals include *During Matter* in *Art and Text* (Melbourne), no. 41 (January 1992): 74–77; *The Drama of Life: Prolog* in *TDR: The Drama Review*, no. 138 (Summer 1993): 105–18; and *The Debate with Space* in *TDR: The Drama Review*, no. 169 (Spring 2001): 118–27.

13. See Weiss, translator's note to Novarina's *The Debate with Space*, 118.

14. Tom Sellar, "Body Language," *Theater* (New Haven, CT) 28, no. 1 (1998): 118.

15. See, for example, Jean-Pierre Thibaudat, "Novarina, la Comédie-Française lui sourit," *Libération*, 28 January 2006.

16. Sellar, "Body Language," 119.

17. Novarina, *Je suis* (Paris: P.O.L., 1991).

18. Novarina, *L'espace furieux* (Paris: P.O.L., 2006), 15–16, 18. An earlier version of *L'espace furieux*, mounted in 1991 at the Théâtre de la Bastille, was published by P.O.L. in 1997. Translations here and elsewhere are mine.

19. Ibid., 18.

20. Ibid., 19–20, 24, 45, 95.

21. Ibid., 30–31.

22. Ibid., 31, 48.

23. Ibid., 140, 143, 146, 147.

24. Ibid., 186.

25. René Solis, "Christine Fersen, une reine sort de scène," *Libération*, 28 May 2008.

26. Novarina, "Work for the Uncertain; Go to Sea; Step on a Board," in *Theater of the Ears*, 128.

27. The Grande Parade de Py productions are available in a boxed set of

eight DVDs, *Olivier Py*, Collection COPAT (Paris: Sopat, 2007); the set also includes a documentary, *La grande parade d'Olivier Py*, by Gilles Ivan and Vitold Krysinsky.

28. David Rohde, "The Betrayal of the Dead Weighs upon the Living," *New York Times*, 10 November 2000.

29. See, for example, Bruno Bayen, "Une décision sectaire," *Le Monde*, 5 May 2006.

30. Olivier Py, "A plus tard, Peter Handke," *Le Monde*, 11 May 2006. See also Jean-Louis Fournel and Emmanuel Wallon, "Peter Handke, un témoin sans histoire?" *Le Monde*, 19 May 2006.

31. Olivier Py quoted in Hervé Charton, "Politique culturelle: le climat, fin février," *nonfiction.fr*, 28 February 2008, http://www.nonfiction.fr/article-738-politique_culturelle_le_climat_fin_fevrier.htm.

32. Olivier Py, "'Le théâtre est une révolte contre le virtuel,'" interview by Fabienne Pascaud, *Télérama*, no. 2936 (19 April 2006): 16.

33. Olivier Py quoted in Sylvie Martin-Lahmani, "Un théâtre salutaire pour soi," *Alternatives Théâtrales*, nos. 85–86 (2005): 17.

34. Py, "'Le théâtre est une révolte,'" 14.

35. Olivier Py, "Avignon, le théâtre des questions," in *Le cas Avignon: regards critiques*, ed. Georges Banu and Bruno Tackels (Vic-la-Gardiole: L'Entretemps, 2005), 265.

36. Ibid.

37. Olivier Py quoted in Bruno Tackels, "Le travestissement, comble du théâtre," *Alternatives Théâtrales*, no. 92 (2007): 10.

38. Olivier Py quoted in Jean-Louis Perrier and Bruno Tackels, "La tentation de l'absolu," *Mouvement*, no. 39 (April–June 2006): 132.

39. Olivier Py, *Epître aux jeunes acteurs pour que soit rendue la Parole à la parole* (Arles: Actes Sud-Papiers, 2000), 20. Here and elsewhere I use David Edney's translation, *Epistle to Young Actors*, in *Olivier Py: Four Plays*, ed. and trans. David Edney (Lanham, MD: University Press of America, 2005). All references are to the French edition.

40. Ibid., 31.

41. Ibid., 14.

42. Ibid., 35.

43. Olivier Py quoted in René Solis, "Olivier Py, directeur de l'Odéon, se défend des accusations de prosélytisme," *Libération*, 12 May 2007.

44. Olivier Py, "Le sacré foulé aux pieds," *Mouvement*, no. 47 (April–June 2008): 61.

45. Valère Novarina, *L'origine rouge* (Paris: P.O.L., 2000), 34.

46. See Novarina, *Pour Louis de Funès*, in *Le théâtre des paroles* (Paris: P.O.L., 1989), 143–44.

47. Jean-Sébastien Trudel, "Dieu est la chose: une écriture théo-tauto-logique," in *La bouche théâtrale: études de l'oeuvre de Valère Novarina*, ed. Nicolas Tremblay (Montreal: XYZ Editeur, 2005), 106.

48. Olivier Py, "Deux contes," program note for productions of his *La jeune fille, le diable et le moulin* and *L'eau de la vie*, Théâtre du Rond-Point, 25 April–26 May 2006.

49. See Emmanuel Wallon, "Le spectacle vivant en chiffres (2010)," in *Politiques et pratiques culturelles*, collection "Les notices," ed. Philippe Poirrier (Paris: La Documentation Française, 2010), 128.

50. Dominique Bérody in interview by Chantal Boiron, *Ubu*, nos. 46–47 (2010): 17.

51. Marie Bernanoce in interview by Maïa Bouteillet, *Ubu*, nos. 46–47 (2010): 82.

52. Olivier Py, *Les vainqueurs* (Arles: Acte Sud-Papiers, 2005), 212.

53. Olivier Py, *Illusions comiques* (Arles: Actes Sud-Papiers, 2006), 77, 84.

54. Olivier Py, "Mettre en scène, c'est interroger la matière," *Théâtre Aujourd'hui*, no. 10 (2005): 223.

55. Py, *Illusions comiques*, 42–43.

56. Review of *Illusions comiques* in *Télérama: Guide Critique*, no. 2941 (24 May 2006).

57. Marie-Mai Corbel, "Du théâtre à l'air: à propos des *Illusions comiques*," *mrmr*, no. 8 (2006): 155, 156.

58. Py quoted in Perrier and Tackels, "La tentation," 132, 135.

59. Jean-Pierre Siméon, *Quel théâtre pour aujourd'hui? petite contribution au débat sur les travers du théâtre contemporain* (Besançon: Les Solitaires Intempestifs, 2007), 40.

60. Ibid., 42.

61. Olivier Py quoted in Catherine Robert, "Le théâtre comme amour du réel," *La Terrasse*, no. 150 (September 2007): 8.

62. Michel Vinaver, conversation with the author, Paris, 9 June 2006.

63. Ibid.

64. See Michel Vinaver, *Le compte rendu d'Avignon: des mille maux dont souffre l'édition théâtrale et des trente-sept remèdes pour l'en soulager* (Arles: Actes Sud, 1987).

65. See Vinaver, "La mise en trop," in Michel Vinaver, *Ecrits sur le théâtre*, vol. 2 (Paris: L'Arche, 1998), 137–46.

66. Michel Vinaver, *A la renverse*, in *Théâtre complet*, vol. 4 (Paris: L'Arche, 2002).

67. Vinaver, conversation with the author, Paris, 9 June 2006.

68. See Michel Vinaver, *La terre vague*, in *Po&sie* (Paris), no. 31 (1984): 4–19.

69. Michel Vinaver, public remarks on the occasion of a reading of ex-

cerpts from his plays and a panel discussion, Martin E. Segal Theatre, CUNY/ Graduate Center, New York, 26 April 2007.

70. Armelle Talbot, *Théâtres du pouvoir, théâtres du quotidien: retour sur les dramaturges des années 1970*, a special issue of *Etudes Théâtrales*, no. 43 (2008): 12–13.

71. Michel Vinaver, *L'ordinaire, suivi de Les voisins* (Arles: Actes Sud, 2002). Gideon Y. Schein's title for his English translation of *L'ordinaire* is *High Places*, in Michel Vinaver, *Plays:2*, ed. David Bradby (London: Methuen, 1997): 1–98.

72. Michel Vinaver, "A Reflection on My Works," *Theater* (New Haven, CT) 28, no. 1 (1998): 77.

73. Ibid.

74. Vinaver, conversation with the author, Paris, 9 June 2006.

75. Vinaver, "Parler du 11 septembre?" interview by Olivier Celik, *L'Avant-Scène Théâtre*, no. 1202 (1 May 2006): 84.

76. Michel Vinaver, "Theatre and Politics," interview by Joëlle Gayot, *Ubu*, no. 42 (May 2008): 32.

77. Michel Vinaver, foreword to *11 septembre 2001/11 September 2001* (Paris: L'Arche, 2002): 8.

78. Vinaver, conversation with the author, Paris, 9 June 2006.

79. Vinaver, *11 septembre 2001*, 22–26.

80. See Vinaver, "Parler du 11 Septembre?" 83.

81. Vinaver, *11 septembre 2001*, 60, 64–70.

82. Armelle Héliot, "Exercises sans style," *Le Figaro*, 10 June 2006.

83. Fabienne Darge, "Le 11 septembre polyphonique de Michel Vinaver," *Le Monde*, 11 June 2006.

84. Antoine de Baecque, "Les Twin Towers vues par Vinaver," *Libération*, 12 June 2006.

85. Kevin Doyle, the playwright and artistic director of the Brooklyn-based troupe Sponsored by Nobody, saw the Cantarella/CalArts production in Los Angeles as well as in Paris; he also directed his own production of *11 September 2001* in New York City in October 2003. Doyle reports that the Los Angeles performances were superior to those in Paris. In conversation with me on 10 June 2006 in Paris, he said: "Between the second and third rounds, the cast [in Los Angeles] attempted to speak their parts but were unable to do more than move to their assigned positions. In Paris, this mute interlude was rushed through so swiftly that it had no impact; in LA, it lent a solemn sense of ceremony to the third round that was truly cathartic."

86. Vinaver, conversation with the author, Paris, 9 June 2006.

87. See Don Shirley, "French Express Concern over Play about Sept. 11," *Los Angeles Times* online, 21 April 2005, http://articles.latimes.com/2005/apr/11/ entertainment/et-frenchplay11.

88. Travis Preston in e-mail to the author, 6 August 2008.

89. Ibid.

90. Vinaver, "Theatre and Politics," 32, 34. For the last sentence I have, for clarity, slightly modified the published English-language version.

91. Roland Barthes, "La fête du cordonnier," *Les Cahiers de Prospero*, no. 8 (July 1996): 59; originally published in *Théâtre Populaire*, no. 34 (1959).

92. Edwy Plenel, "Michel Vinaver, notre historien," *La Gazette Jaune: Scène Nationale Evreux Louviers*, no. 10 (March 2008): 20.

Chapter 9. Cultural Diversity (I)

1. Valérie Baran, "De la colonisation positive . . . ," preface to brochure on the Tarmac de la Villette's 2006 offerings, 1.

2. Maïmouna Gueye, "'J'ai fait un rejet total des non-dits, des désirs enfouis,'" interview by Brigitte Salino, *Le Monde*, 30 March 2006.

3. Quoted in Gérard Courtois, "Les blessures de la colonisation," *Le Monde*, 21 January 2006.

4. "Clefs," sidebar to Laetitia Van Eeckhout, "Lycéens, petits-enfants de l'empire," *Le Monde*, 21 January 2006.

5. See "Majority of France's Blacks Suffer Bias," *Daily Herald* (Saint Maarten), 1 February 2007; for a fuller description of the survey results, see "56% des Noirs disent subir des discriminations," *NouvelObs.com*, 23 June 2008, http://tempsreel.nouvelobs.com/actualite/societe/20070131.OBS9720/56-des-noirs-disent-subir-des-discriminations.html.

6. Jamel Debbouze quoted in Alan Riding, "Wartime Heroism with an Arab Face," *New York Times*, 10 September 2006.

7. Ibid.

8. Fabrice Eboué quoted in Florence Broizat, "La griffe Jamel," *Télérama*, no. 2974 (10 January 2007).

9. See Macha Séry, "Sur scène comme à l'écran, le rire est d'or," *Le Monde*, 18 April 2006; the report was issued by the Centre national de la chanson, des variétés et du jazz.

10. Kader Aoun quoted in Broizat, "La griffe Jamel."

11. See Brigitte Salino, "L'est parisien, nouvel eldorado théâtral," *Le Monde*, 20 March 2006.

12. Booder, "Clown format poche," interview by Macha Séry, *Le Monde*, 17 February 2006.

13. Fellag, "Mécano du rire," interview by Fabienne Darge, *Le Monde.fr*, 28 January 2010, http://www.lemonde.fr/.

14. Fellag's books include *Rue des petites daurades* (Paris: JC Lattès, 2001), *C'est à Alger* (Paris: JC Lattès, 2002), and *L'allumeur de rêves berbères* (Paris: JC Lattès, 2007).

15. Fellag quoted in Mary Blume, "For Comic, Despair Is Cloaked in Humor," *International Herald Tribune*, 18 February 2006.

16. Ibid.

17. Souria Adèle, online interview by Hervé Mbouguen, *Grioo.com*, 17 May 2005, http://www.grioo.com/info4724.html.

18. Dieudonné quoted in Jean-Michel Vernochet and Rodéric Mounir, "Dieudonné, candidat rebelle," *Le Courrier* (Geneva), 25 February 2006.

19. For full accounts, see Tom Reiss, "Laugh Riots: The French Star Who Became a Demagogue," *New Yorker* (19 November 2007), 47 ff.; and "La nouvelle affaire Dieudonné: l'humoriste français dérape à Alger," *Afrik.com*, 21 February 2005, http://www.afrik.com/article8139.html.

20. See Agence France-Presse, "Dieudonné reconnu coupable d'injure raciale' par la Cour de cassation," *Le Monde.fr*, 16 February 2007, http://www .lemonde.fr/old-societe/article/2007/02/16/dieudonne-reconnu-coupable-d-injure-raciale-par-la-cour-de-cassation_868461_3226.html.

21. See Olivier Mongin, *De quoi rions-nous? notre société et ses comiques* (Paris: Plon, 2006), 110.

22. For a detailed though far from dispassionate account of Dieudonné's treatment by the media, see Olivier Mukuna, *Egalité zéro, enquête sur le procès médiatique de Dieudonné* (Paris: Editions Blanche, 2005).

23. See Agence France-Presse and Reuters, "Des propos de l'humoriste Dieudonné sur la Shoah soulèvent l'indignation," *Le Monde.fr*, 18 February 2005, http://www.lemonde.fr/.

24. See Ariane Chemin, "L'historienne israélienne Idith Zertal dément avoir parlé de 'pornographie mémorielle' pour la Shoah," *Le Monde*, 26 February 2005.

25. Bernard-Henri Lévy, "Dieudonné, fils de Le Pen," *Le Point* (3 February 2005). On 28 January 2008, at the end of a Dieudonné show attended by Jean-Marie Le Pen and members of his family, the comedian invited the notorious Holocaust denier Robert Faurisson to join him on stage and receive from a technician dressed as a deported World War II Jew a trophy honoring Faurisson's "insolence"; see Mathieu Deslandes and Marie-Christine Tabet, *Journal du dimanche*, 23 December 2008. The Faurisson incident led to a lawsuit brought by eight civil rights associations and then a guilty verdict issued by the Tribunal correctional de Paris on 27 October 2009 for the charge of *"injure publique"* (roughly, public insult/defamation); see "Dieudonné condamné à 10 000 euros d'amende pour 'injures antisémites,'" Agence France-Presse and *Le Monde.fr*, 27 October 2009, http://www.lemonde.fr/.

26. Anne-Sophie Mercier, *La vérité sur Dieudonné* (Paris: Plon, 2005), 174.

27. See Matthew Kaminski, "Barbarians inside the Gate," *Wall Street Journal*, 27 February 2006, European edition.

28. See editorial, "Racisme banalisé," *Le Monde*, 21 March 2006.

29. Ibid.

30. Julien Dray, "'Quand on est un humoriste de talent, on a aussi une responsabilité,'" interview by Marie Vilain, *Libération.fr*, 13 May 2008, http://www.liberation.fr/politiques/010124647-julien-dray-quand-on-est-un-humo riste-de-talent-on-a-aussi-une-responsabilite/.

31. Dieudonné quoted in Tom Reiss, "Laugh Riots," 49.

32. See "Diffamation: poursuivi par Dieudonné, Julien Dray est relaxé," *TF1.fr*, 16 August 2008, http://lci.tf1.fr/france/justice/2008-06/poursuivi-par-dieudonne-julien-dray-est-relaxe-4866636.html.

33. Jamel Debbouze, "'Ouvrir la brèche pour les autres, c'est le kif du kif!'" interview by Fabienne Pascaud, *Télérama*, no. 2949 (19 July 2006).

34. Agence France-Presse, "Dieudonné reconnu coupable."

Chapter 10. Cultural Diversity (II)

1. See Emmanuel Wallon, "Le spectacle vivant en chiffres (2010)," in *Politiques et pratiques culturelles*, collection "Les notices," ed. Philippe Poirrier (Paris: La Documentation Française, 2010), 137.

2. Gérard Mortier quoted in Fernanda Eberstadt, "Storming the Bastille: How Gérard Mortier Is Rocketing the Paris Opera—and All Opera—into the 21st Century," *New York Times Magazine*, 5 December 2004, 66.

3. Gérard Mortier, "L'opéra mis en selle," interview by Jean-Marc Adolphe and David Sanson, *Mouvement* no. 45 (October–December 2007): 28.

4. See Y.P., "Mortier fier de son bilan," *La Lettre du Spectacle*, no. 256 (10 July 2009): 5.

5. Anthony Tommasini, "A 'Figaro' That's Fixed on Its Marriage License," *New York Times*, 22 April 2008.

6. See, for example, Patrick Sourd, "Don Giovanni," *Les Inrockuptibles*, no. 741 (8 February 2006): 77, and Christian Merlin, "Une vision forte et cohérente," *Le Figaro*, 30 January 2006.

7. See Dominique de Villepin, "Voeux du premier ministre à la presse," 10 January 2006, http://www.archives.premier-ministre.gouv.fr/villepin/ac teurs/interventions_premier_ministre_9/discours_498/voeux_premier_ministre_presse_55037.html.

8. Alexandre Adler, "Mozart, antidote au nihilisme," *Le Figaro*, 16 February 2006.

9. Kaija Saariaho quoted in Steve Smith, "Intimidated by Mozart's Ghost? Not Anymore," *New York Times*, 10 August 2008.

10. The full French-language libretto appears in the program booklet of the original production (Paris: Opéra Bastille, 2006), 73–85; it was published separately as Amin Maalouf, *Adriana Mater* (Paris: Grasset, 2006).

11. Amin Maalouf, in program booklet for the Opéra Bastille premiere production of Kaija Saariaho's *Adriana Mater,* "Les portes de l'enfer doivent se refermer," 58.

12. Ibid., 57.

13. Anthony Tommasini, "Brutal and All Too Timely, with a Hint of Melody," *New York Times,* 16 December 2006.

14. Alex Ross, "Birth," *New Yorker,* 24 April 2006, 178.

15. Ibid.

16. See Rosita Boisseau, "Le cirque contemporain appelle à l'aide," *Le Monde,* 16 June 2006, and Wallon, "Le spectacle vivant," 135.

17. See Marie Ballé, "La piste aux poètes," *Festiv'all,* May 2006, 43.

18. Ibid.

19. Ibid.

20. See Sylvestre Barré, "Le 'nouveau cirque traditionnel,'" in *Avant-garde, cirque!* ed. Jean-Michel Guy (Paris: Editions Autrement, 2001), 37–45.

21. Wallon, "Le spectacle vivant," 131.

22. See Julie Bordenave, book reviews of Marc Moreigne's *Les arts sauts* (Arles: Actes Sud/Cnac, 2009) and Gwénola David's *Cirque Plume* (Arles: Actes Sud/Cnac, 2009) in *Stradda* (Paris), no. 15 (January 2010): 59.

23. See Philippe Genty, interview by Gilles Costaz, *Théâtral Magazine,* no. 24 (May–June 2010): 13. Genty announces in this interview that his forthcoming book, tentatively titled *Carnet de fuites* (Notes on Evasions), will describe from a psychoanalytic point of view "my paranoia and fears" (13).

24. My observations, here and following, on the social profile of the Espace Chapiteaux audience are consistent with a study conducted by the Parc de la Villette between 1996 and 2001: see Florence Lévy, "A nouveaux cirques, nouveaux publics?" in Guy, *Avant-garde, cirque!* 183–200. See also Emmanuel Wallon, ed., *Le cirque au risque de l'art* (Arles: Actes Sud-Papiers, 2002), passim.

25. Collectif AOC, program note for their production *Question de directions,* Espace Chapiteaux, Parc de la Villette, 24 February–9 April 2006, 3.

26. The Collectif AOC's most recent piece, *Autochtone* (2010), is an even more deliberate effort to respond to the increased frustration of citizens vis-à-vis the economic and political forces ruling their lives. The company asserts: "In a society that manipulates them, individuals must confront what is being imposed upon them. They will sometimes feel helpless, sometimes rebellious. Their bodies will therefore behave in different ways within whatever space remains theirs, provided that such space still exists. They will fight, contest, and protect themselves by whatever means possible, sometimes with poetry, sometimes with humor"; see Gwénola David, "Gros plan/cirque: 'Autochtone,'" *La Terrasse,* no. 177 (April 2010). David, too, perceived

the show as being replete with "concrete metaphors of a totalitarian threat to human life."

Chapter 11. A Festival Turns Sixty

1. See Michel Henry, "La ville derrière son duo de directeurs," *Libération*, 24 July 2010.

2. See Emmanuel Ethis, Damien Malinas, and Olivier Zerbib, "Petite socio-morphologie des festivaliers ordinaires (I)," in *Avignon, le public réinventé: le festival sous le regard des sciences sociales*, ed. Emmanuel Ethis (Paris: La Documentation Française, 2002), 215.

3. See Emmanuel Pedler and Olivier Zerbib, "Le dessous des cartes: le festival comme révélateur d'un territoire culturel," in Ethis, *Avignon, le public réinventé*, 195.

4. Ibid., 197.

5. Ibid., 199.

6. Figures on non-French nationals come from Pedler and Zerbib, "Le dessous des cartes," 199, 210. Remarks on Asian, Eastern European, and U.S. attendees result largely from my experience of the festival over the past six years.

7. See René Solis, "La crise, quelle crise?" *Libération*, 28 July 2009.

8. Alain Brunsvick quoted in Dominique Buisine and Christophe Roque, eds., *Le festival d'Avignon: une école du spectateur* (Marseilles: CRDP/Académie d'Aix-Marseille, 2006), 51.

9. See Clarisse Fabre, "Le 'in' et le 'off' en quelques chiffres," *Le Monde*, 20 July 2010.

10. Hortense Archambault, "Le point sur le festival," interview by Chantal Boiron, *Théâtral Magazine*, no. 25 (July–August 2010): 49.

11. See Brigitte Salino, "André Benedetto," *Le Monde*, 16 July 2009.

12. André Benedetto quoted in Violeta Assier, "Hommage à André Benedetto, le président d'Avignon Festival et Compagnies s'est éteint hier," *Vaucluse Matin*, 14 July 2009.

13. Greg Germain, quoted in Muriel Steinmetz, "Greg Germain donne le *la* du off," *L'Humanité*, 9 July 2009. Vice president of Avignon Festival & Compagnies, Germain became its president following Benedetto's death.

14. Frédéric Mitterrand, "C'était une révolte féconde, une grand voix . . . ," *La Provence*, 14 July 2009.

15. See "Index by Type of Audience," *Off: Avignon 2009* (Avignon: Avignon Festival & Compagnies, 2009), 337.

16. For July 2006, rental fees for two-hour slots ranged from three thousand to seventeen thousand euros; see Fabien Vonnieux, "Le festival du fric?

Combien ça coûte aux compagnies," *Vaucluse-Hebdo*, no. 3231 (14 July 2006). The rule of thumb for 2009 was "one hundred euros per seat" according to Grégoire Biseau, "Je vous dis ça en off," *Libération*, 28 July 2009.

17. See Fabre, "Le 'in' et le 'off.'"

18. See Armelle Héliot, "Avignon: le in s'étiole, le off s'affirme," *Le Figaro*, 27 July 2007.

19. See Henry, "La ville derrière son duo."

20. Bernard Faivre d'Arcier, *Avignon, vue du pont: 60 ans de festival* (Arles: Actes Sud, 2007), 198.

21. "Plus d'un million d'entrées dans le Off?" *La Lettre du Spectacle*, no. 251 (30 April 2010).

22. René Solis, "Avignon sans coup de théâtre," *Libération*, 29 July 2006, 21; see also Jean-Pierre Léonardini, "Portrait de Vilar en Py," *L'Humanité*, 29 July 2006, 18.

23. Press remarks quoted in Emmanuelle Loyer and Antoine de Baecque, *Histoire du festival d'Avignon* (Paris: Gallimard, 2007), 557.

24. Clémence Coconnier, "Nadj ou l'indisciplinarité des corps de cirque," *Revue d'Etudes Théâtrales: Registres*, no. 13 (2008): 74–75.

25. Josef Nadj quoted in Tibor Várszegi, "Josef Nadj, humilité incarnée," *Alternatives Théâtrales*, no. 89 (July 2006): 27.

26. See Miquel Barceló and Josef Nadj, *Paso doble*, dir. Bruno Delbonnel, Les Poissons Volants (2006).

27. Hortense Archambault, conversation with the author, Avignon, 27 July 2006.

28. Frédéric Martel, "Les solitudes de Koltès," *Magazine Littéraire*, no. 395 (February 2001): 33.

29. D. J. R. Bruckner quoted in letter to the editor, "Listening for Koltès," by Lenora Champagne, Michaël Attias, et al., *American Theatre* 24, no. 7 (September 2007): 6.

30. See *Bernard-Marie Koltès: Plays 1*, ed. David Bradby, trans. David Bradby, Maria Delgado, and Martin Crimp (London: Methuen, 1997), and *Bernard-Marie Koltès: Plays 2*, ed. David Bradby and Maria Delgado, trans. David Fancy, Alex Johnston, and Joseph Long (London: Methuen, 2004).

31. Travis Preston, paraphrased in Maria Delgado and David Fancy, "The Theatre of Bernard-Marie Koltès and the 'Other Spaces' of Translation," *New Theatre Quarterly* 17, no. 66 (May 2001): 148.

32. See Stéphane Patrice, *Koltès subversif* (Paris: Descartes & Cie, 2008), 163 ff.

33. Bernard-Marie Koltès, *Combat de nègre et de chiens* (Paris: Editions de Minuit, 1989), 7.

34. Arthur Nauzyciel quoted in Alexandre Le Quéré, "Regards de metteurs en scène: vers le sud," *Les Nouveaux Cahiers de la Comédie Française*, no. 1 (March 2007): 80.

35. Arthur Nauzyciel, public remarks made at "Staging French Playwrights in North America/Working With American Actors," a session of ACT FRENCH's Carte Blanche: French-American Theatre Dialogue Series, Martin E. Segal Theatre, CUNY/Graduate Center, New York, 12 December 2005.

36. See "Regard sur Arthur Nauzyciel: retour à Atlanta," *Les Inrockuptibles*, special Avignon issue (July 2006): 26.

37. See, for example, Jean-Pierre Leonardini, "Bernard-Marie Koltès au pays de Scarlett O'Hara," *L'Humanité*, 11 July 2006.

38. Bernard-Marie Koltès, *Une part de ma vie: entretiens (1983–1989)* (Paris: Editions de Minuit, 1999), 21.

39. Ibid., 90.

40. See David Bradby and Maria M. Delgado, eds., *The Paris Jigsaw: Internationalism and the City's Stages* (Manchester, UK: Manchester University Press, 2002), 5.

41. Jacques Derrida, *Writing and Difference*, trans. Alan Bass (London: Routledge, 1978), 236; originally published as *L'écriture et la différence* (Paris: Editions du Seuil, 1967).

42. Marcial Di Fonzo Bo, "Copi et moi," umbrella program notes for his productions of *La tour de la défense*, *Les poulets n'ont pas de chaises*, and *Loretta Strong*, 2006 Avignon Festival, 5.

43. Beata Pilch, "Over the Ocean," interview by Valerie Jean Johnson, *Chicago New City*, 27 December 2007.

44. Joël Pommerat, "A l'intensité des seuils," interview by Gwénola David, *Mouvement*, no. 40 (July–September 2006): 84.

45. Joël Pommerat, public remarks at Calvet Museum, Avignon, 19 July 2006, published as Joël Pommerat, *Théâtres en présence* (Arles: Actes Sud-Papiers, 2007), 17.

46. Ibid., 15, 23.

47. Ibid., 9, 26, 13.

48. Pommerat, "A l'intensité," 84.

49. Joël Pommerat quoted in Claudine Galéa, "Joël Pommerat: vers l'autre langue," *Théâtre/Public*, no. 184 (2007): 19.

50. Joël Pommerat, *Les marchands* (Arles: Actes Sud, 2006), 7. I quote from excerpts translated by Garry White in *Ubu*, nos. 37–38 (April 2006): 103–13.

51. Joël Pommerat, *Au monde* (Arles: Actes Sud, 2004), 35. Pommerat specifies the Basque origin of The Hired Woman's dialogue in a note on page 8.

52. Ibid., 57.

53. Claire Moulène, "Portrait Stefan Kaegi: la vie des autres," *Les Inrockuptibles*, special Avignon issue (July 2006): 35.

54. Marie-José Sirach, "Gare à la Suisse!" *L'Humanité*, 15 July 2006.

55. Stefan Kaegi quoted in Sarah Brady, "*Cargo Sofia*: A Bulgarian Truck Ride through Dublin," *TDR: The Drama Review* 51, no. 4 (Winter 2007): 164.

56. See Hans-Thies Lehmann, *Postdramatic Theatre*, trans. Karen Jürs-Munby (London: Routledge, 2006), 154.

Chapter 12. Recap and Coda

1. Stefan Kaegi in Brigitte Salino, "Stefan Kaegi, spécialiste suisse," *Le Monde*, 6 July 2006.

2. I quote from David Bradby and Maria Delgado's translation, *Black Battles with Dogs*, in *Bernard-Marie Koltès: Plays 1*, ed. David Bradby, trans. David Bradby, Maria Delgado, and Martin Crimp (London: Methuen, 1997), 37–38.

3. Nicolas Sarkozy quoted in Jean-Marie Adolphe, editorial, "Travailler le jour, rêver la nuit?" *Mouvement*, no. 51 (April–June 2009): 7.

4. See Clarisse Fabre, "La feuille de route de l'Elysée à Christine Albanel inquiète les professionnels de la culture," *Le Monde*, 12 September 2007.

5. Sarkozy quoted in Adolphe, "Travailler le jour."

6. In fall 2009, Marin Karmitz announced the council's intent to launch ten broad projects that would be financed by a multiplicity of ministries; see Michel Guerrin and Nathaniel Herzberg, "Les dix travaux de Marin Karmitz pour la culture," *Le Monde*, 10 September 2009.

7. Dominique Hervieu, "'Impulser les idées pour l'art que je sers,'" interview by Philippe Verrièle, *La Lettre du Spectacle*, no. 236 (1 May 2009): 2.

8. Pascal Rogard quoted in Cyrille Planson, "Il faut faire plus de place aux créateurs," *La Scène*, no. 53 (Summer 2009): 11.

9. Olivier Py, "La culture, projet d'avenir," *Le Monde*, 15 February 2009.

10. Antoine de Baecque, *Crises dans la culture française* (Paris: Bayard, 2008), 236.

11. "Pendant le festival, les syndicats discutent," *Le Monde*, 16 July 2009, 19.

12. Berger (a pseudonym, taken from André Malraux's code name during the Resistance, for "several high-ranking officials of cultural institutions"), "Bon anniversaire Monsieur André Malraux," *La Scène*, no. 53 (Summer 2009): 30.

13. Bernard Stiegler, "Offensive Transversal Actions," excerpted in French and in English in *Ubu*, nos. 43–44 (2008): 28–29.

14. Ibid., 28.

15. Ibid., 28.

16. Ibid., 28–29.

17. Emmanuel Wallon, "The Indispensable Imponderable," excerpted in French and in English in *Ubu*, nos. 43–44 (2008): 29.

18. Ibid.

19. Ibid.

20. Ibid.

21. Robert Lepage, "Théâtre des métamorphoses," interview by Jean-Louis Perrier, *Mouvement*, no. 45 (October–December 2007): 121.

For Further Reading

This select annotated bibliography is intended primarily as a tool for general readers seeking additional matter on topics treated in *French Theatre Today*. I mainly list titles published since 2000 that, in addition to those cited in the notes, were particularly useful for my own investigation of the field.

Reference books and anthologies

Azama, Michel, ed. *Anthologie des auteurs dramatiques de langue française 1950–2000*. Vol. 1, *Continuité et renouvellements*. Vol. 2, *Récits de vie, le moi et l'intime*. Vol. 3, *Le bruit du monde*. Paris: Editions Théâtrales, 2003–2004. Two hundred textual excerpts are each preceded by brief critical and biographical remarks; each volume also includes several overview essays.

Biet, Christian, and Christophe Triau. *Qu'est-ce que le théâtre?* Paris: Gallimard, 2006. Offering deep historical perspective, this work provides a magisterial treatment of the ways in which the theatrical experience has evolved in recent decades.

Bossan, Sabine, ed. *Entr'actes* (Paris), http://entractes.sacd.fr. Formerly a dual-language (French and English) print periodical published by the Société des auteurs et compositeurs dramatiques (SACD), *Entr'actes* is now a SACD website designed to promote the works of living French-language playwrights around the world. Geared especially to agents, festivals, theatre personnel, and translators, it offers a newsletter, play excerpts, interviews with authors, and publication and translation information.

Confortès, Claude. *Répertoire du théâtre contemporain de langue française*. Paris: Nathan, 2000. Each entry in this inventory of 420 playwrights who have written in French between 1945 and 2000 gives bio- and bibliographic information and a short excerpt from one published play with brief introductory commentary. The volume is unique for its coverage of thirty-six countries in addition to France.

Corvin, Michel, ed. *Dictionnaire encyclopédique du théâtre à travers le monde*. 4th ed. Paris: Bordas, 2008. A thoroughly revised, updated, and expanded version of the original (1991), this work offers over 2,600 entries written by more than 300 specialists, covering individuals and troupes, forms and genres, critical and theoretical concepts, and institutional, political, and economic issues.

Ministère de la Culture et de la Communication. *Chiffres clés: statistiques de la culture*. Paris: La Documentation Française, appears annually; also available at http://www.culture.gouv.fr/deps. This presentation of economic and financial data on the arts and media in France includes figures on the ministry's funding for theatres and for writers for the stage, attendance at state-supported theatres, and box-office receipts for Parisian *théâtres privés*.

Wehle, Philippa, ed. *Act French: Contemporary Plays from France*. New York: PAJ Publications, 2007. This anthology provides English-language translations of complete plays by José Pliya, Olivier Cadiot, Michel Vinaver, Valère Novarina, Michèle Sigal, Philippe Minyana, and Emmanuelle Marie.

Journals

Alternatives Théâtrales (Brussels). Each issue is devoted to a specific subject. Nos. 85–86 (2006), *Jan Fabre, une oeuvre en marche*, edited by Georges Banu, focus on the 2005 edition of the Avignon Festival, with attention paid to Jan Fabre, Olivier Py, Josef Nadj, Gisèle Vienne, and Pascal Rambert, among others.

Etudes Théâtrales (Louvain-la-Neuve, Belgium). This journal of the Center for Theatre Studies at the Catholic University of Louvain and the Institute for Theatre Studies at the University of Paris-III produces three issues per year, each on a single theme. Especially pertinent are no. 13 (1998), *Théâtre en pièces: le texte en éclats*, edited by Emmanuel Wallon, on the fragmentation of traditional stage forms and language; no. 19 (2000), *Bernard-Marie Koltès au carrefour des écritures contemporaines*, edited by Sieghild Bogumil and Patricia Duquenet-Krämer, on the famed playwright's continuing influence; no. 22 (2001), *Poétique du drame moderne et contemporain: lexique d'une recherche*, edited by Jean-Pierre Sarrazac, an in-depth glossary of critical concepts that are key to discussions of "modern drama in crisis" (revised and expanded in book format as *Lexique du drame moderne et contemporain* [Belval: Editions Circé, 2005]); nos. 24–25 (2002), *Ecritures dramatiques contemporaines (1980–2000): l'avenir d'une crise*, edited by Joseph Danan and Jean-Pierre Ryngaert, the proceedings of a conference held in December 2001, under the auspices of the Research Group on the Poetics of Modern and Contemporary Drama of the Institute for Theatre Studies (University of

Paris-III) and La Colline–théâtre national, on the putative "return" of the text-based dramatic author; and nos. 38–39 (2007), *La réinvention du drame (sous l'influence de la scène)*, edited by Jean-Pierre Sarrazac and Catherine Naugrette, an attempt, in part, to bring historically grounded circumspection to Hans-Thies Lehmann's notion of the "postdramatic."

mrmr: La Revue Murmure (Saint-Martin de Fontenay, Normandy). This irregularly published journal focuses on nonmainstream performing arts and cultural politics.

Tadorne, le blog du spectacle vivant, http://www.festivalier.net. Begun in 1995 by Pascal Bély as an alternative to top-down professional media coverage of the performing arts, this blog mainly covers festivals (theatre, dance, performance, music, and photography). The number of reviewers other than Bély grows steadily, and the content is archived, with reader responses welcome.

Théâtre Aujourd'hui (Paris). Published intermittently since 1992 by the National Center for Pedagogic Documentation in collaboration with the Ministries of National Education and of Culture and Communication and edited by Claude Lallias, Jean-Jacques Arnault, and Michel Fournier, this journal treats a specific problem or theme in each issue, with contributions by academics, critics, and creative artists. Especially relevant is no. 10 (2005), *L'ère de la mise en scène*, on the tensions between texts and their staged realizations; figures dealt with include Bernard Sobel, Ariane Mnouchkine, Claude Régy, Robert Cantarella, and Olivier Py.

Théâtre/Public (Paris). This quarterly, formerly published by the Théâtre de Gennevilliers, is now run independently. No. 184 (2007), *Théâtre contemporain: écriture textuelle, écriture technique*, edited by Clyde Chabot, is devoted to current experimentation, with special attention paid to Valère Novarina, Joël Pommerat, Pascal Rambert, and Philippe Quesne, among others.

Les Trois Coups, http://www.lestroiscoups.com. This daily online review journal by independent journalists, critics, and authors features critiques of current offerings—subsidized and commercial, Parisian and regional. Archived and illustrated, the journal invites reader responses.

Ubu: Scènes d'Europe/European Stages (Paris). This valuable dual-language (French and English) quarterly focuses on nontraditional theatre.

History, theory, and criticism (general)

Bradby, David, and Maria M. Delgado, eds. *The Paris Jigsaw: Internationalism and the City's Stages*. Manchester, UK: Manchester University Press,

2002. Essays by scholars and creative artists address the history of international influences in Paris and their impact upon current debates about redefining boundaries and identities within contemporary Europe and beyond.

Bradby, David, and Annie Sparks. *Mise en Scène: French Theatre Now.* London: Methuen, 1997. This historical survey of drama and theatre in France from 1968 to the late 1990s was prompted by the three-month French Theatre Season presented in London and Stratford-upon-Avon in autumn 1997. It also contains transcripts of interviews with six figures, including Eric-Emmanuel Schmitt and Philippe Minyana, and a section titled "Practical Information for Theatre Professionals."

Brunet, Brigitte. *Le théâtre de boulevard.* Paris: Nathan, 2004. This work provides an overview of the history, dramaturgy, and key registers ("serious" and "comic") of this mainstream theatre tradition.

Garbagnati, Lucile, and Pierre Morelli, eds. *Thé@tre et nouvelles technologies.* Dijon: Editions Universitaires de Dijon, 2006. Contributors to this volume explore such issues as media hybridity, digital sound design, and "techno-poetics."

Lachaud, Jean-Marc, and Olivier Lussac, eds. *Arts et nouvelles technologies.* Paris: L'Harmattan, 2007. This work includes contributions by Bruno Tackels on scenographic *écriture*, Patrice Pavis on "intermediality," and Martine Maleval on New Circus.

Mounsef, Donia, and Josette Féral, eds. *The Transparency of the Text: Contemporary Writing for the Stage.* Issue no. 112 of *Yale French Studies* (New Haven, CT). Essays are presented under three main rubrics: "Avant and Après Garde," "(Under)writing the Stage," and "Disputed Textualities"; significant attention is directed to Michel Vinaver, Valère Novarina, Noëlle Renaude, and Koffi Kwahulé.

Pavis, Patrice. *Le théâtre contemporain: analyse des textes de Sarraute à Vinaver.* Paris: Nathan, 2002. This college-level guide to the textual analysis of theatrical works addresses plays by Michel Vinaver, Bernard-Marie Koltès, Philippe Minyana, Valère Novarina, and Yasmina Reza, among others.

Ryngaert, Jean-Pierre. *Lire le théâtre contemporain.* Paris: Nathan, 2003. This handbook for analyzing and contextualizing innovative theatre from Ionesco to Novarina ends with an anthology of artistic statements by numerous writers and directors.

Ryngaert, Jean-Pierre, and Julie Sermon. *Le personnage théâtral contemporain: décomposition, recomposition.* Montreuil-sous-Bois: Editions Théâtrales, 2006. This work offers a well-balanced historical

and theoretical analysis of the changing nature of character and
characterization in current French theatre.

Specific figures, forms, and organizations

THE AVIGNON FESTIVAL

Faivre d'Arcier, Bernard. *Avignon, vue du pont: 60 ans de festival.* Arles: Actes
Sud, 2007. A personal account of the festival's history is given by the man
who oversaw the festival from 1980 to 1984 and from 1993 to 2003.

Loyer, Emmanuelle, and Antoine de Baecque. *Histoire du festival d'Avignon.*
Paris: Gallimard, 2007. Meticulously researched and handsomely
illustrated, this history offers an in-depth chronicle from the festival's
beginnings to 2006.

Ribes, Jean-Michel, ed. *Une magnifique désolation.* Paris: Editions de
l'Amandier/Théâtre, 2003. This volume collects the responses—in
declarative prose, theatrical dialogue, poetic verse, and epistolary
format—of fifty French-language dramatists following the cancellation
of the 2003 Avignon "In" Festival (provoked by the crisis over state-
regulated benefits for the entertainment industry's *intermittents*, or
freelancers).

Tackels, Bruno. *Les voix d'Avignon.* Paris: Seuil/France Culture, 2007. This
annotated assemblage of archival documents and celebrity interviews
offers a multiperspective survey of many of the festival's high points.
It includes a CD of *Le feuilleton d'Avignon*, the seven-hour radio series
produced by France Culture and broadcast in July 2006, with testimony
from Ariane Mnouchkine, Olivier Py, Valère Novarina, Peter Brook,
Jeanne Moreau, and Claude Régy as well as from historical figures such
as Jean Vilar, Antoine Vitez, Roland Barthes, and Maria Casarès.

Viotte, Michel (film director). *Avignon: cour d'honneur et champs de bataille.*
DVD. Coproduced by ARTE France, the Institut national de l'audiovisuel,
and La Compagnie des Indes, 2007; distributed by La Compagnie des
Indes (Issy-les-Moulineaux). This 74-minute documentary, written by
Michel Viotte and Bernard Faivre d'Arcier, highlights adventuresome
festival productions by such figures as Maurice Béjart, Pina Bausch,
Antoine Vitez, and Jan Fabre. Commentary by Hortense Archambault,
Vincent Baudriller, Romeo Castellucci, Jan Fabre, Josef Nadj, Olivier Py,
and others is included.

OLIVIER CADIOT AND LUDOVIC LAGARDE

March, Florence. *Ludovic Lagarde: un théâtre pour quoi faire.* Besançon:
Les Solitaires Intempestifs, 2010. A book-length interview with Cadiot's

closest collaborator, director Ludovic Lagarde, is followed by March's essay on the "stakes and strategies" at play in adapting Cadiot's texts to the stage.

PATRICE CHÉREAU

Chéreau, Patrice. *J'y arriverai un jour*. Arles: Actes Sud, 2009. The artist is portrayed via a lengthy interview conducted by Georges Banu and testimonials from the director's colleagues. Banu's meditation on the force of Chéreau's staged readings of authors like Dostoyevsky and Hervé Guibert is outstanding.

Godard, Colette. *Patrice Chéreau: un trajet*. Paris: Rocher, 2007. This overview of Chéreau's career includes extensive, often dissenting, running commentary on Godard's text by Chéreau himself.

CIRCUS AND NEW CIRCUS

Circus and Street Arts: Contemporary Creation in Europe. Special issue (November 2009) of *Stradda*. This issue offers an English-language collection of selected articles from the French-language quarterly published since October 2006 by HorsLesMurs (Paris), the national resource center for street and circus arts.

Guy, Jean-Michel, ed. *Avant-garde, cirque! les arts de la piste en révolution*. Paris: Editions Autrement, 2001. This collection captures the vitality of contemporary circus and addresses the difficulties of categorizing its many types.

Mollard, Claude, ed. *Le cirque contemporain: la piste et la scène*. Issue no. 7 (2001) of *Théâtre Aujourd'hui*. This overview pays special attention to such companies as Archaos, Cirque Baroque, Que-Cir-Que, Les Nouveaux-Nez, and the Théâtre Equestre Zingaro.

Wallon, Emmanuel, ed. *Le cirque au risque de l'art*. Arles: Actes Sud-Papiers, 2002. The essays in this volume originated in a scholarly conference organized in 2001 to celebrate the Year of Circus Arts in France. The work is notable for its treatment of circus's connections, both historical and contemporary, with other performing arts.

BERNARD-MARIE KOLTÈS

Bident, Christophe, Régis Salado, and Christophe Triau, eds. *Voix de Koltès*. Paris: Séguier, 2004. This volume collects essays by academics, critics, translators, directors, and actors.

Muhleisen, Laurent. *Bernard-Marie Koltès*. Issue no. 1 (2007) of *Les Nouveaux Cahiers de la Comédie-Française* (Paris). This collection of short pieces, published to coincide with the Comédie-Française's 2007 production of Koltès's *Le retour au désert*, contains Cyril Desclés's survey of the dramatist's reception by producers worldwide.

Patrice, Stéphane. *Koltès subversif.* Paris: Descartes & Cie, 2008. This fresh interpretation of the major plays sharply critiques previous monographs and links Koltès's project to writings by Michel Foucault, Gilles Deleuze, and Jacques Derrida.

Salino, Brigitte. *Bernard-Marie Koltès.* Paris: Stock, 2009. The first full-scale biography of the writer, by the theatre critic of *Le Monde*, makes good use of Koltès's newly published correspondence, *Lettres* (Paris: Editions de Minuit, 2009), and recognizes the risks of overstating the delicate, elusive rapport between the life and the creative output.

PHILIPPE MINYANA

Corvin, Michel, ed. *Philippe Minyana ou la parole visible.* Paris: Editions Théâtrales, 2000. The collection's writers include dramatists, directors, and actors as well as scholars.

ARIANE MNOUCHKINE

Cramesnil, Joël. *La Cartoucherie: une aventure théâtrale.* Paris: L'Amandier, 2004. While Mnouchkine's Théâtre du Soleil receives ample treatment, this book's originality lies in tracing the history of the many theatres and companies that have occupied the Bois de Vincennes campus from 1936 to the end of the twentieth century.

Dusigne, Jean-François. *Le Théâtre du Soleil: des traditions orientales à la modernité occidentale.* Paris: Centre national de documentation pédagogique, 2003. This illustrated handbook is intended to help students prepare for the *baccalauréat* essay question on Western and Eastern influences in Mnouchkine's theatre.

Miller, Judith G. *Ariane Mnouchkine.* London: Routledge, 2007. This volume in the Routledge Performance Practitioners series, aimed at a high-level student readership, offers an overview of Mnouchkine's life, work, influences, and aspects of her creative process along with in-depth analyses of *1789*, *Richard II*, *L'Indiade*, and *Tambours sur la digue*.

JOSEF NADJ

Bloedé, Myriam. *Les tombeaux de Josef Nadj.* Paris: L'Oeil d'or, 2006. This work offers a study of the motifs and figures that animate, orient, and give scenic and pictorial coherence to the choreographer's art.

ARTHUR NAUZYCIEL

Godard, Colette. *Emmanuel Demarcy-Mota, Arthur Nauzyciel, James Thiérrée: un théâtre apatride.* Paris: L'Arche, 2009. This work presents biographical profiles of three younger showmen who in varying ways epitomize for Godard the twenty-first-century current of theatrical creation that exists independent of national borders. Her section on Nauzyciel is perhaps the richest of the three and supports most fully her understated hypothesis.

MARIE NDIAYE

Lindon, Mathieu. *Je vous écris: récits critiques.* Paris: P.O.L., 2004. Lindon's chapter on NDiaye addresses her novels, not her plays, but it is crucial for its insights into representations of race and skin color in her early oeuvre.

VALÈRE NOVARINA

Dieuzayde, Louis, ed. *Le théâtre de Valère Novarina: une scène de délivrance.* Aix-en-Provence: Publications de l'Université de Provence, 2004. The offshoot of an interdisciplinary colloquium held in May 2002, this volume includes essays on the challenges of translating Novarina's texts into other languages and on philosophical issues raised by his dramaturgy.

Dubouclez, Olivier. *Valère Novarina: la physique du drame.* Dijon: Les Presses du Réel, 2005. This work presents a philosopher's account of how structures of representation, linguistic operations, and a reconception of the actor contribute to a new theatrical "physics" that operates throughout Novarina's oeuvre.

Thomasseau, Jean-Marie, ed. Issue nos. 880–881 (August–September 2002) of *Europe: Revue Littéraire Mensuelle* (Paris). This collection offers scholarly essays on Novarina's works and interviews with his artistic collaborators, including Claude Merlin, Claude Buchvald, and Roséliane Goldstein.

JOËL POMMERAT

Pommerat, Joël. *Théâtres en présence.* Arles: Actes Sud-Papiers, 2007. This short but dense collection of pieces by Pommerat illuminates his artistic convictions. Some previously published, all of the works were publicly delivered by Pommerat at the Calvet Museum during the 2006 Avignon Festival and aired on national radio (France Culture).

Pommerat, Joël, and Joëlle Gayot. *Joël Pommerat, troubles.* Arles: Actes-Sud,

2009. Superbly illustrated, this volume presents a fluid assemblage of Pommerat's reflections on his plays and his art as related over a yearlong period to Gayot, who functions here as invisible interviewer, book editor, and occasional commentator.

PASCAL RAMBERT

Rambert, Pascal. *GENNEVILLIERSroman: 0708*. Besançon: Les Solitaires Intempestifs, 2007. Rambert offers a first-person account of his inaugural year as artistic director of the Théâtre2Gennevilliers.

STANDUP COMEDY

Mongin, Olivier. *De quoi rions-nous? notre société et ses comiques*. Paris: Plon, 2006. Mongin analyzes a range of sexual and ethnic humor and includes commentary on Jean-Marie Bigard, Fellag, Jamel Debbouze, and Dieudonné.

MICHEL VINAVER

Lallias, Jean-Claude, ed. *Michel Vinaver*. Issue no. 8 (2000) of *Théâtre Aujourd'hui*. An overview of Vinaver's oeuvre is followed by interviews with scenographers, actors, and directors, including Jacques Lassalle, Christian Schiaretti, and Alain Françon.

Thomasseau, Jean-Marie, ed. Issue no. 924 (April 2006) of *Europe: Revue Littéraire Mensuelle*. This issue includes essays on Vinaver by scholars and directors, plus several texts by the playwright, including one on the artists that nourish him.

ROBERT WILSON

Otto-Bernstein, Katharina. *Absolute Wilson: The Biography*. Munich: Prestel, 2006. This lavishly illustrated, detailed overview of Wilson's career is a companion to the author's 2006 documentary film of the same title.

Shevtsova, Maria. *Robert Wilson*. London: Routledge, 2007. This volume in the Routledge Performance Practitioners series, aimed at a high-level student readership, approaches Wilson as a precursor of globalization in the arts and pays special attention to *Einstein on the Beach*.

Index

Page references in italics refer to illustrations

national identity, French, xxvi-xxix, 38, 129, 228; multiplicity of, xxix; unity in, xxviii-xxix

Nauzyciel, Arthur: *Le malade imaginaire ou le silence de Molière*, 121, 122, 123; production of Koltès, 277, 279-80, 282

Nauzyciel, Emile, 123

NDiaye, Marie, xxiv, 39, 46-50; and French political climate, 49-50; otherness in work of, 46-50; place in French culture, 50; racial themes of, 48. Works: *Hilda*, 46-48, 315n25; *Papa doit manger*, 48-49; *Trois femmes puissantes*, 49

Ndiaye, Pap, 49

Neuenfels, Hans, 231

Next Wave Festival (New York), 29

Nicodemus the Hagiorite, *Pneumatika gymnasmata*, 180

Nième Compagnie (Vaulx-en-Velin), 58

Noonan, Mary, 153-54

North Africans, French, 38, 39, 223-24, 226-29

Nouno, Pierre, 246

nouveau cirque, 96, 97, 99, 238, 248-52, *253*, 254-55; characteristics of, 248; cultural democratization in, 255. *See also* circus, French

Novarina, Valère, xxiv, 64, 153, 176-83, 190-91; early life of, 177; influences on, 181-82; modernism of, 180, 196; on role of actors, 180. Works: *L'acte inconnu*, 181, 190; *Adramelech's Monologue*, 73, *74*, 75, 181; *L'avant-dernier des hommes*, 178-79; *Le discours aux animaux*, 181; *L'opérette imagi-*

naire, 179-80; *L'origine rouge*, 196; *Theater of the Ears*, 182; *Le théâtre des paroles*, 61. *See also L'espace furieux*

Observatoire national des zones urbaines sensibles (ONZUS), 60

Office national de diffusion artistique (ONDA), 106

opera, in Paris, xxv, 238-46

Opéra Bastille, 244

Opéra national de Paris, 239

Ostrovsky, Alexander: *Don, mécènes et adorateurs*, 167

otherness: African, 41; in *Le dernier caravansérail*, 297; in NDiaye's work, 46-50

Ouvroir de Littérature Potentielle (OuLiPo group), 180-81

Paccoud, Christian, 179, *184*

Paradis (unfolding time) (Rambert), *91*, 148, 168; multimedia in, 92; nudity in, 96; postdramatic aspects of, 90; text in, 92-93, 95; and theatre of *la parole*, 90, 92; Western science in, 93, 95

Paré, Zaven, 182

Pareti, Marc, 252

Palais Garnier (theatre), 239-40

Pasca, Daniele Finzi, 250

Pascaud, Fabienne, 326n16

Patrice, Stéphane, 279

Pavis, Patrice, 171

Perec, Georges, 79, 181

Performance Space 122 (New York), 78

Pétain, Philippe, 126

Peyronnet, Cécile, 280

Pilch, Beata, 287

Rattazzi, Steven, 72, 319n26
Redden, Nigel, 3, 14
refugees (to France), xxviii, 3, 4, 13;
Mnouchkine's work with, 5–6
Régy, Claude, 31, 33, 35–36, 89, 278;
influence on authors, 69, 156; on
supertitles, 30
La Reine Margot (film), 28
Renaude, Noëlle, 149; *Par les routes*,
153–54; and theatre of *la parole*,
153
Renoir, Jean: *La règle du jeu*, 213
Reza, Yasmina, 141, 146–48; post-
modernism of, 147–48. Works:
"Art," ix, 146; *Conversations après
un enterrement*, 147; *Dawn Dusk
or Night*, 146–47
Ribes, Jean-Michel, 51, 53, 191
Rimbaud, Arthur: *Illuminations*,
127
Robbe-Grillet, Alain, 158
Robbe-Grillet, Catherine, 157, 158
Rogard, Pascal, 301
Ronayette, Isabelle, 53
Ross, Alex, 246
Rostand, Edmond, 104. *See also
Cyrano de Bergerac*
Röttgerkamp, Anja, 157–58, *159*
Rozié, Fabrice: *Liaison transatlan-
tique*, 22–26
Rubinelli-Giordano, Marlène, 252
Ruf, Eric, 129, *131*
Ruf, Jean-Yves, 198
Ruhl, Sarah, 277
Rundle, Erika, 46, 48, 315n26
Ryngaert, Jean-Pierre, 63–64, 317n1

Saariaho, Kaija: *Adriana Mater*, 244–
46; *L'amour de loin*, 244–45; *La
Passion de Simone*, 245

Saavedra, Hilario, 73, *74*, 75
Sachs, Alain, 117
Salino, Brigitte, 156
Salonen, Esa-Pekka, 246
Salviat, Catherine, *184*
Sangaré, Bakary, 49
Sankai Juku (dance troupe), 276
Sarkozy, Nicolas, xxvi, 49, 228; cul-
tural policy of, 115–16, 145, 300–
302; immigration policies of, 5,
13, 71
Sartre, Jean-Paul, 25, 260; *Huis clos*,
223
Scheck, Frank, 35
Scheib, Jay, 277
Schmitt, Eric-Emmanuel: *Ma vie
avec Mozart*, 141–42, 242
Schoevaert, Marion, 279; *A.W.O.L.*,
71–73
Searle, John R., 67
Sellar, Tom, 182
Sellars, Peter, 244, 246
Semoun, Elie, 233–34
September 11 attacks, 71, 117, 245.
See also 11 September 2001
(Vinaver)
Sermon, Julie, 317n1
Serreau, Coline, 119–20, 246
7 Stages (theatre group), 277, 280,
282; U.S. Koltès Project, 283
Shakespeare, William, 18, 282, 283;
children's comprehension of,
75–76; *Richard II*, 260
Shaw, Helen, 73
Silverman, Adam, 72
Simenc, Jaka, 87
Siméon, Jean-Pierre: *Quel théâtre
pour aujourd'hui?*, 203–4
Sirach, Marie-José, 292
Sirjacq, Quentin, 222

STUDIES IN THEATRE HISTORY AND CULTURE